EXCAVATIONS AT KNOWTH 1

To the memory of P. J. Hartnett from whom I first learned the technique of passage tomb excavation.

ROYAL IRISH ACADEMY MONOGRAPHS IN ARCHAEOLOGY I

EXCAVATIONS AT KNOWTH 1

Smaller passage tombs, Neolithic occupation and Beaker activity

GEORGE EOGAN

Professor of Celtic Archaeology
University College, Dublin

Royal Irish Academy

DUBLIN

Published by the Royal Irish Academy, 19 Dawson Street, Dublin 2

© Royal Irish Academy 1984

Excavations at Knowth 1   ISBN 0 901714 34 8

Royal Irish Academy Monographs in Archaeology   ISSN 0790–1895

It is proposed to publish two further volumes on the Knowth excavations in this series, one dealing with the Iron Age–Early Christian and the Norman settlements, the other with the large passage tomb (Site 1).

Printed in Ireland by
Dublin University Press

CONTENTS

FOREWORD

It gives me great pleasure as President of the Royal Irish Academy to introduce this first volume of the Academy's projected new series of monographs in archaeology. The Academy's tradition of publication in archaeology dates from its inception in 1785 – first in the *Transactions* and subsequently in the *Proceedings of the Royal Irish Academy*.

For some time, however, we have felt the need for a new format in which to publish more extensive accounts of scholarly investigations in archaeology, of which Professor Eogan's work is an outstanding example. We were particularly fortunate that the Office of Public Works, which had funded the excavations over many years, found itself able to make a grant towards the cost of this publication and we express our gratitude to them. We are also indebted to the UNESCO Participation Programme which made a further grant towards the cost of this work on the advice of the Irish National Commission for UNESCO, whose support we are pleased to acknowledge.

It is particularly fitting that this new initiative in publication by the Academy should take place on the eve of our bicentenary. We look forward to further publications in this series. We believe it represents an important development in archaeological research in Ireland.

W. A. WATTS
President, Royal Irish Academy

December 1983.

ACKNOWLEDGEMENTS

It is my pleasure to record my gratitude to the many individuals and institutions who have helped to make this long programme of excavations a success. The work has been financed by state grants made available on the recommendation of the National Committee for Archaeology of the Royal Irish Academy and administered through the National Parks and Monuments Branch, Office of Public Works. University College, Dublin, also made generous contributions to the cost of different aspects of the research and in addition provided research facilities. During the initial years, the Inspector and Assistant Inspector of National Monuments, Office of Public Works, Mr W. P. Le Clerc and Marcus Uasal Ó h-Eochaidhe provided much valued assistance. Successive Directors of the National Parks and Monuments Branch, Mr P. Cearney, Séan Uasal Mac Cárthaigh, Mr J. O'Halloran and Mr P. Scanlon, the Chief Archaeologist, Mr Peter Danaher, the Inspector of National Monuments, Mr David Johnson, the Clerk of Works, the late Laurence Gaynor, and the officials of that Branch in general were exceedingly helpful throughout. The Branch's photographer, Mr James Banbury, supplied photographs of a number of features. The Board also loaned equipment and made money available for post-excavation work. Knowth is a National Monument in state care and I wish further to thank the Commissioners of Public Works for permission to excavate. Before the acquisition by the Commissioners of the land surrounding the large mound the owner, the late Mr Thomas Robinson, readily gave permission to excavate on his lands. We are further indebted to Mr and Mrs Robinson and their family for facilities and hospitality over the years.

Professor G. F. Mitchell, Trinity College, Dublin, has been a constant source of help and advice. All geological identifications of the megaliths are by him and he has also contributed a section on the landscape in this report. A study of the composition of the pottery was carried out by Professor J. C. Brindley, Department of Geology, University College, Dublin. Charcoal samples were identified by Ms Maura Scannell, National Botanic Gardens. Soil investigations were carried out by Dr Willy Groenman-van Waateringe, Instituut voor Prae- en Protohistorie, University of Amsterdam. Anatomical reports on the human remains were prepared by Dr Blanche Weekes, School of Anatomy, Trinity College, Dublin. Carbon 14 determinations were undertaken in the Palaeoecology Laboratory, Queen's University, Belfast, in the Research Laboratory, The British Museum, London, and in the Biologisch–Archaeologisch Instituut, Groningen. I am grateful to Professor Alan Smith and Drs Gordon Pearson, Jon Pilcher and Quentin Dresser in Belfast and to Dr Richard Burleigh, Dr Ian Longworth and Mr Gale Sieveking in London. Mr Leo Swan has assisted throughout with aerial photography. Ms Anna Brindley did much to bring order into the Beaker section. For generous discussions on Neolithic problems I am indebted to the late Professor Ruaidhri de Valera, to Professor

Michael Herity, Department of Archaeology, University College, Dublin, and to Dr Seán Ó Nualláin, Ordnance Survey. Dr Ó Nualláin also read the manuscript and gave most useful comments.

I am particularly grateful to the many volunteers, too numerous to list individually, who willingly assisted with the excavations. Their work contributed greatly to the success of the excavations. Mr Eoin Grogan and Mr John Bradley have given tremendous help both in the field and in the preparation of this report; in its final stages it owes much to Mr Grogan's commitment. For directing, surveying and recording, I am very grateful to Barra Boydell, Martin Cotter and Kevin Mooney. The assistance of Catherine Daly, Francesca Jay, Mary Lynch, Maeve Maher and Fionnghuala Williams in preparing illustrations of the finds is much valued and appreciated.

I am indebted to Ms Veronica Meenan of the Department of Archaeology, University College, Dublin, who undertook the laborious task of checking and typing the manuscript, and the Chief Technician, Mr Albert Glaholm, who sorted out various photographic problems. Ms Finola O'Carroll rendered considerable assistance with the proof-correcting.

Finally, I especially want to express my thanks to Barbara Young and Siobhán Parkinson in the Editorial Office of the Royal Irish Academy for all their help in seeing the manuscript through the press.

Unless otherwise stated the scales in the photographs are marked off at 30cm intervals.

SUMMARY

This report is divided into three parts.

Part I is an account of the excavation of seventeen passage tombs which, together with the large mound, constitute a cemetery. Because of damage it was not possible to get any information about the tomb plan of two sites (5 and 11), five had a cruciform chamber (2, 6, 9, 17 and 18), and in the remaining ten the chamber plan was undifferentiated but segmentation by sills was common. The roundish mounds were delineated by kerbstones. To the south-east of the area under excavation were some megalithic stones, which may be the remains of a tomb or tombs that were totally destroyed. Cremation was the burial rite and there is evidence for single, multiple and successive burials. Grave goods were few, mainly pins, beads and pendants. 'Carrowkeel' pottery turned up, mainly in the mounds. Art was a feature of both kerb and tomb stones. Two sites (13 and 16) predate the large mound.

Part II deals with an area of Neolithic settlement on the western edge of the large mound. This consists of a subrectangular structure, *c.* 13m long, possibly a house. Immediately to the south are a trench and some postholes which may represent another structure. Two concentric palisade trenches delineate an elongated area 65m by 12m. The structure and palisades predate the large mound and five smaller sites (6, 8, 9, 10 and 11). The eastern trench post-dates the structure. Within the palisades are pits, fireplaces and evidence for flint-knapping. To the west of the 'enclosure' is an area of pebbling 15m by 8m. The finds from the settlement in general consist of round-bottomed shouldered bowls, flint thumbscrapers and a stone axehead.

Part III describes the four areas (A, B, C and D) of Beaker activity that have been revealed. It appears that these represent domestic activity. No house sites have been found but pits and fireplaces have come to light. The main evidence at all four concentrations consists of a dark layer which produces sherds of pottery and flint artifacts. The average size is 130 square metres. At Concentrations B, C and D the pottery consists predominantly of fine ware but at A the majority of the sherds are of coarse ware. An undecorated beaker of fine ware accompanied a cremation in a secondary position in one of the smaller passage tombs, Site 15.

ACHOIMRE

Tá trí roinn sa tuarascáil seo.

I gCuid I tá cuntas ar thochailt a rinneadh ar sheacht gcinn déag de thuamaí pasáiste a áirítear in éineacht leis an tulach mhór mar reilig. De dheasca díobhála, níorbh fhéidir aon eolas a chruinniú faoin bplean tuama ag dhá cheann díobh (5 agus 11); bhí seomra crosdealbhach ag cúig cinn (2, 6, 9, 17 agus 18); agus sna deich gcinn eile ní léir aon phlean seomraí, ach ba choitianta iad a roinnt le leaca móra. Bhí leaca curtha ar chiumhais na dtulach cuartha. Ar an taobh thoirtheas de láthair na tochailte bhí roinnt clocha meigiliteacha. Is féidir gur iarsmaí iad seo de thuama nó de thuamaí a scriosadh go hiomlán. Ba é an gnás adhlactha ná dó corp agus tá fianaise ann ar adhlacadh aonair, ioladhlacadh agus adhlacthaí as a chéile. Ba ghann iad na hearraí sna huaigheanna: bioráin, coirníní agus siogairlíní. Fuarthas potaireacht 'Carrowkeel' sna tulaí go mórmhór. Bhí greanadh ealaíonta ar na leaca ciumhaise agus ar leaca na dtuamaí. Is sine dhá láthair (13 agus 16) ná an tulach mhór.

I gCuid II tugtar cursíos ar áitreabh neoiliteach suite ar an dtaobh thiar den tulach mhór. Structúr fo-dhronuilleanach c. 13m ar fhaid atá anseo; b'fhéidir gur teach é. Go díreach ó dheas tá clais agus roinnt poill cuaillí a sheasann do structúr eile, b'fhéidir. Tá láthair fadaithe 65m faoi 12m a aithnítear de réir dhá chlais phailise atá comhlárnach. Is sine an structúr agus na pailisí ná an tulach mhór agus cúig láthair eile (6, 8, 9, 10 agus 11). Is sine an chlais thoir ná an structúr. Taobh istigh de na pailisí tá poill sa talamh, teallaigh agus fianaise gur saothraíodh breochloch ann. Ar an dtaobh thiar den limistéar 'fálta' tá réimse púrógach 15m faoi 8m. I gcoitinne is iad na fionnachtana ón áitreabh ná babhlaí cruinntónacha le guaillí, scríobáin ordóige de bhreochloch agus ceann tua cloiche.

I gCuid III déantar cursíos ar cheithre láthair d'imeachtaí lucht na mBíocar, A, B, C agus D. Cuireann siad sin imeachtaí teaghlaigh in iúil de réir dealraimh. Ní bhfuarthas aon láithreacha tithe ach fritheadh poill sa talamh agus teallaigh. Is í an phríomhfhianaise ag gach ceann de na láithreacha ná sraith dorcha a bhfaightear sligí potaireachta agus earraí breochloiche inti. Gréithe míne atá sa photaireacht ag láithreacha B, C agus D ach is gréithe garbha iad formhór na sligí ag láthair A. Fuarthas bíocar mín i dteannta dó coirp in áit athúsáidthe i gceann de na tuamaí pasáiste is lú, uimhir 15.

INTRODUCTION

To-day Knowth (in Irish *Cnogba*) is a townland adjoining the River Boyne in County Meath. The highest part of the townland is only slightly over 200 feet (61m) above sea level. This is a ridge about 800m long by about 340m maximum width (Frontispiece, Fig. 1). It was the western part of this ridge that was extensively used by man on various occasions from the Neolithic period onwards. The main archaeological feature at Knowth is a large mound whose existence had been noted for some time in archaeological publications (Molyneux 1726, 200; Wakeman 1848, 108; Wilde 1849, 164–5; Borlase 1897, 370–1; Coffey 1892, 68; Coffey 1912, 60–1 and Ó Ríordáin and Daniel 1964, 72–7). This mound was taken into state ownership in 1939 (Nat. Mon. No. 409). In 1967 an area of four acres surrounding it was acquired (Nat. Mon. No. 409) and further lands were acquired in 1980. The first archaeological excavations were conducted by Professor R. A. S. Macalister in July 1941. He exposed the outer faces of a number of kerbstones of the large mound, mainly along the southern side. He also investigated the chamber of Site 14 and a souterrain on top of Site 1 (Macalister 1943).

Before excavation the land surrounding the large mound was generally flat and used for grazing purposes. On the north-east side was a rectangular depression which excavation showed was of no archaeological significance. On the western side in particular were the remains of ridge and furrow cultivation. In general, underneath the sod was a layer of soft dark earth, of Early Christian-Norman derivation, directly overlying the prehistoric remains.

When Neolithic man arrived in the Knowth area the countryside would have had forests of oak and elm on high ground with hazel, birch and alder in the river valley. Large clearances were made in this woodland and at least by the time passage tombs 1, 3, 14 and 15 were built the landscape was well opened up and the forest was largely confined to the valley.

While it is not certain that the passage tomb builders were the first people to have utilised the hill of Knowth, they certainly left the most enduring monuments.

The Knowth passage tomb[1] cemetery is part of the wider cemetery of Brugh na Bóinne (Coffey 1912; Ó Ríordáin and Daniel 1964; C. O'Kelly 1978, 45–64). In addition to the Knowth group there are the two other large passage tombs, Newgrange and Dowth, and fourteen other sites that are either proven or potential passage tombs (Fig. 2). In recent years excavations have been carried out at the principal

---

[1]In the process of standardising the terminology of the megalithic tombs of Ireland de Valera and Ó Nualláin (1972, xiii) have introduced the term 'passage tomb'. This standardisation has been amplified by the late Professor de Valera in Ó Ríordáin (1979, 102). De Valera has argued that since the word *tomb* is basic and as it can be used for all classes (court tomb and portal tomb, passage, wedge tomb) its use simplifies the terminology. Accordingly the term 'passage tomb' is being used in this report.

To Drogheda →

← Slane

R.L. 69.74 m.

79   79

78

79
78
77
76
75
73
72
71
70

69

68

67

66

65

64

63

62

61

60

59

58

7

| 25 | 0 | 25 | 50 Yards |

| 25 | 0 | 25 | 50 m. |

© G. Eogan 1979

2

mound at Newgrange and three adjacent passage tombs (cf. C. O'Kelly 1978; O'Kelly, Lynch and O'Kelly 1978) and also at the outlying site of Townleyhall (Eogan 1963, 37–81).

The problem

Excavation at Knowth commenced in 1962 and has continued each summer since then, some seasons being over four months in duration. The original purpose of the excavations was to follow up some problems, mainly typological, which excavations at a nearby site at Townleyhall had raised. That site was an undifferentiated passage tomb.[2] It overlay a Neolithic occupation site which has a C14 determination of 2730 ± 150 b.c. (B.M. 1768). The absence of a natural sod layer between the occupation and the passage tomb indicates that the tomb was built shortly after the desertion of the occupation site (Eogan 1963). The tomb plan of Townleyhall showed at least a superficial resemblance to tombs of the Scilly-Tramore Group, which were considered late, even well into the Bronze Age (Piggott 1954, 266–7). In view of its relationship to the occupation the Townleyhall tomb could be dated to the Neolithic. This raised such questions as: was there any relationship between the Townleyhall passage tomb and the tombs of the Scilly-Tramore group and could passage tombs of the simple variety be contemporary with the more elaborate cruciform types? In order to try and answer these questions it was felt appropriate to excavate one or two of the small sites within the Brugh na Bóinne cemetery. Professor G. F. Mitchell and I examined a number of sites before selecting Knowth. Macalister's excavation of a small chamber on the north side of the large mound (Macalister 1943, 132–4) and the presence of four large stones to the north-west of the large mound suggested the existence of small, independent tombs close by. Work commenced, therefore, on a small mound on 18 June 1962. Not only did this site prove to be a passage tomb mound, but it had an undifferentiated chamber surrounded by a low core of stones (Site 12). When this site was being excavated a hint of another site to the south-west of it emerged. This was excavated in 1963 (Site 11). In 1964 the chamber excavated by Macalister (Site 14) was investigated and part of another site (13) as well as the portion of the kerb of the large mound came to light. By now it was clear that Knowth was a rich passage-tomb centre and it was decided to plan the excavations as a comprehensive long-term project.

Lay-out of excavation   (Fig. 3; Pl. 1)

The excavation lay-out varied in accordance with the problems being tackled. The sites excavated initially (7, 11 and 12, 13 and 14 together with a small portion of Site 1) were dug on the basis of a grid of three-metre squares. The large mound was dug by a combination of large cuttings and four-metre squares, set out in relation to four baselines placed along the flat ground at the base of the large mound and measuring 116m by 104m. The cuttings were the simplest method of examining the steep slope of the large mound. In other

---

[2] Although it is not strictly speaking correct (a number of sites have sillstones), the term 'undifferentiated' is being retained as it has gained general currency. By this term is meant a tomb the ground plan of which is formed by a gradual widening out of each side; side chambers are lacking.

Fig. 1—Contour plan of large mound and adjoining area at Knowth (contours at 1 m intervals). Arrow at top indicates displaced kerbstone (p. 159).

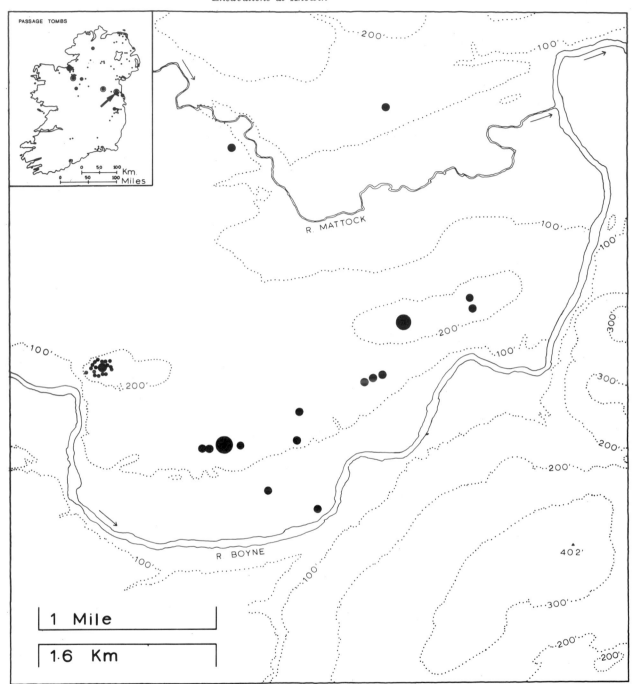

Fig. 2–Brugh na Bóinne showing distribution of passage tombs or possible passage tombs (contours at 100 ft.). Knowth group is concentration on left. Inset: distribution of passage tombs in Ireland.

areas four-metre squares were found to be more appropriate. Diagonal cuttings were opened occasionally to examine features or sectors.

Summary of results to date

Excavations have shown that this low hill-top was first used during the Neolithic period but that it was attractive for settlement and other uses during many subsequent periods. Four main phases of activity occur.

Phase I: Neolithic. (a) Occupation. An elongated area 65m long and averaging 12m wide was delimited, at least on either side, by a palisade. Internally there are pits, fireplaces and evidence for flint knapping, while a short distance away on the west side is an area of pebbling. The palisade 'enclosure' is predated by a squarish structure, *c.*13m across, possibly a house. The finds from the occupation area in general include round-bottomed shouldered bowls, flint thumb scrapers and a stone axehead (p. 211).

(b) Burial. A cemetery of passage tombs, consisting of the large mound and at least seventeen smaller sites, has been uncovered. The main site, which tends to be circular, measures approximately 90m (N–S) by 80m (E–W) and is about 11m in maximum height. It was methodically constructed by laying down layers of different material (sod, boulder, clay, shale and stones) in an ordered fashion. The mound is bounded by a series of impressive kerbstones, the majority of which are decorated. It covers two huge tombs which are placed back-to-back. One, 34.2m long, has its entrance on the west and a

Fig. 3–Layout of excavation.

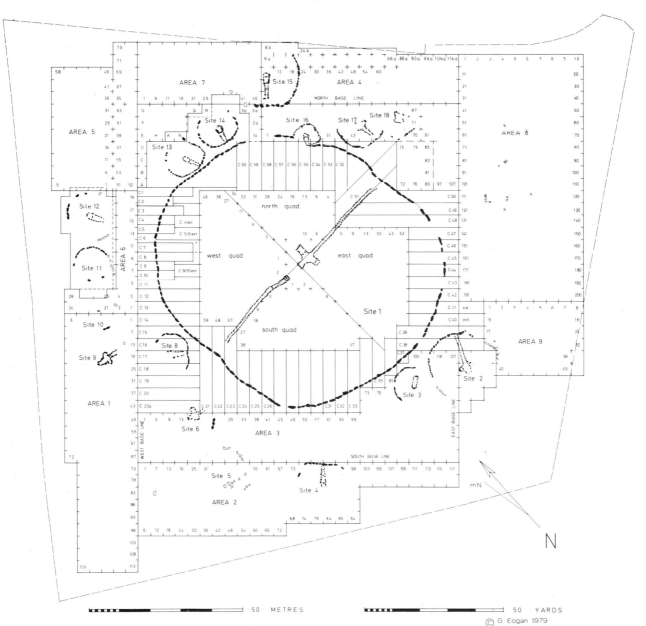

50 METRES   50 YARDS

© G. Eogan 1979

parallel-sided but bent passage leads into a simple chamber, squarish in plan. The other tomb, 40m long, also has a parallel-sided passage. Its chamber is cruciform in plan and the magnificent corbelled roof rises to a height of about 6m. Excavation is now in progress in the cruciform tomb. A large number of the structural stones of both tombs and also the kerb are decorated, some very elaborately, with megalithic art.

The smaller and independent tombs are close to the large mound. Because of damage it has not been possible to uncover the tomb plan in two sites. In the remaining fifteen, ten have tombs of undifferentiated plan and five have tombs with cruciform chambers. The burial rite was cremation, and grave goods, in the main typical of finds from other Irish passage tombs, included Carrowkeel pottery, stone pendants and bone pins. Like the main mound some of the structural stones bear megalithic art. At least two of the small sites (13, 16) predate the large mound.

Pl. 1–Knowth:
air view from west, 1974
(Photo: D. L. Swan)

Phase II: Beaker. Four areas of Beaker activity have been uncovered. It appears that these represent domestic activity. There is no evidence for houses but pits and fireplaces have come to light. The main evidence at all four areas consists of a dark layer that produced sherds of pottery and flint artifacts. The average size is 130 square metres. An unornamented beaker of fine ware accompanied a cremation in a secondary position in one of the small passage tombs. (Site 15)

Phase III: Iron Age—Early Christian. Probably early in the first millennium A.D. the large mound was transformed into a well-protected settlement site by the digging of two concentric penannular ditches, one at the base, the other around the top edge. The entrance causeway was on the south-east side. It is assumed that houses stood on the summit but as the top has been damaged no evidence for these survived. However, there are some inhumation burials.

In about the eighth to ninth centuries A.D. a considerable expansion in the area of occupation took place. The almost completely filled-up ditches provided hollowed areas for habitation. To date there is evidence for ten houses, ten souterrains, numerous fireplaces, areas of paving, etc. There were also industrial areas, in one of which iron was smelted and in another bronze and enamel-making took place. Ample evidence for corn-growing and the keeping of domestic animals also came to light. During the latter stage of the Early Christian period Knowth was an important settlement and historical sources indicate that it was the royal residence of the Kings of Northern Brega.

Phase IV: Norman. Early Christian settlement appears to have continued down to the twelfth century, near the end of which the site was taken over by the Normans. Their activity is represented by the construction of a large rectangular stone building on the summit. Glazed pottery was abundant and other artifacts of the period were also recovered. Norman occupation continued down to the late thirteenth/early fourteenth century.

THE LANDSCAPE

G. F. Mitchell

The River Boyne, as it flows eastwards below Slane, suddenly makes a right-angle turn to the south, probably following a fault in the underlying rock structure. The rock wall, against which the river turns, is the western end of a ridge of Carboniferous shales at about 200 ft O.D., which runs eastwards for three miles and carries the megalithic tombs of Knowth, Newgrange and Dowth, and a great circular earthwork (Site Q, C. O'Kelly 1978). The river next swings east, to flow parallel with the ridge, and then turns abruptly northwards following a gorge cut through the ridge by glacial meltwaters, thus completing the *Bend of the Boyne*. It now enters the east-west valley of the Devlin (and its tributary the Mattock) and turns eastwards once more to Drogheda and the sea (Fig. 4).

Apart from this remarkable bend, the Boyne in its lower reaches trends generally slightly north of east and flows across rocks of Carboniferous age, chiefly limestones, often deeply buried by glacial deposits. Just to the north of the river the contact between the Carboniferous rocks and the older slaty Lower Palaeozoic rocks follows a similar trend. North of the contact the ground level rises, glacial deposits thin out, and the brown podzolic soils are relatively well-drained. South-east of Duleek we see a similar contact, and again the ground level rises onto older rocks and thinner soils.

Around Knowth itself much of the country lies at a general level of about 150 ft O.D. and is deeply mantled by glacial deposits. Two parent materials contribute to the glacial deposits, an eastern component from the Irish Sea, rich in clay and with a high content of calcium carbonate, and a western component, less rich in clay and calcium carbonate. To-day the dominant soil is a fertile if rather poorly drained grey-brown podzolic, chiefly given over to grassland, like most of County Meath. It is not easy to say what its nature was when it was first cleared of woodland by the Neolithic farmers, but it may well have been looser in texture and still richer in basic nutrients. It would have yielded rich crops to hand cultivation, particularly when we remember that this is one of the drier parts of Ireland.

Knobs of rock, often rising to over 200 ft O.D., protrude through this glacial cover. These are generally of limestone, often with low crags and hollows, and indeed one area north of Duleek resembles Lough Gur in County Limerick on a small scale. But between McGruder's Cross Roads, Donore and Kentstown there is a triangular area of black shales which are stratigraphically above the limestone. As we have seen, the ridge north of the Bend of the Boyne is built up of these shales and these rise into the elongated knolls at 200 ft or over on which the great tombs are situated, each tomb resting directly on rock.

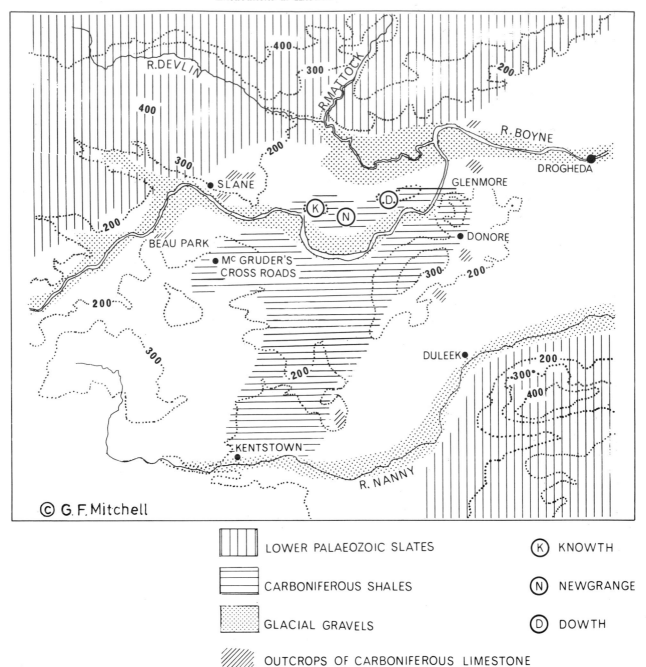

LOWER PALAEOZOIC SLATES   (K) KNOWTH

CARBONIFEROUS SHALES   (N) NEWGRANGE

GLACIAL GRAVELS   (D) DOWTH

OUTCROPS OF CARBONIFEROUS LIMESTONE

Fig. 4–Geology of Knowth region (contours at 100 ft.).

The Boyne has entrenched itself into the glacial plain. This entrenchment probably took place when the ice was retreating to the north-west and the trench is largely floored by glacial outwash gravels, rich in limestone. In places, as on the opposite bank of the river at Knowth, the gravels have a more morainic character, and often largely choke or constrict the trench, rather than merely flooring it. The Mattock valley is similarly incised and similarly choked with gravels. On the gravels soil development is weaker and we have skeletal grey-brown podzolics or brown earths. Though fertile and easy to work, these soils are liable to drought-damage.

It must have been the dramatic geomorphological 'island' lying in the Bend of the Boyne, often called *Brugh na Bóinne,* that drew the megalith builders to this particular site. South-west of Donore we have a still higher rockridge, also built of shale, and had the monuments been placed there, we would have had a still more conspicuous siting, recalling to us *Sliabh na Caillighe* to the north-west, or the Fourknocks Hills to the south-east.

The local limestone hills were also avoided. Feltrim Hill, in north County Dublin, though it did not have a passage tomb, showed rich evidence of Neolithic occupation, and also had a small Iron Age fort. Near Donore a limestone rise showed a similar Iron Age fort, but there was no evidence of Neolithic settlement. It is indeed very curious that the limestone outcrops of the *Brugh na Bóinne* area should be so deficient in evidence of Neolithic occupation, when we recall the passage tombs on limestone in County Sligo and the richness of the Neolithic occupation on the limestone hills around Lough Gur.

The megalithic farmers, when they stood on top of the great mound at Knowth, would have looked down on an expanse of good agricultural land. Part of it was heavy clayey soil, part was light gravelly soil, part was light slaty soil, all was fertile. The variety of soil in the neighbourhood meant that neither excessive rainfall nor excessive drought could destroy all the crops of the area.

If they looked to the south-east, the ground rose and the Fourknocks Hills with their megalithic tombs could be seen. On a clear day, further to the south the outline of the Wicklow Hills, where there were also megalithic tombs, would be visible. Such farmers, controlling extensive areas of good land, could well have been wealthy and so able to afford the luxury of three great monuments and numerous ancillary smaller structures, all crowded together in *Brugh na Bóinne*. For successive generations, prehistoric, Anglo-Norman and modern, the fertile soils of the Boyne valley have remained a continuing source of profit.

Part one

The smaller passage tombs

This is an account of the excavation of seventeen passage tombs together with a description of some isolated features which may be the only remains of similar tombs. Although comparatively smaller than the large mound, many of the tombs are substantial structures. Together with the large mound, the smaller sites form a closely-knit cemetery. Apart from one example (No. 7), which is 145m away, all the tombs are within 20m of the large mound (Site 1). Site 1 abuts on two (Nos 13 and 16). In six sites (2, 3, 8, 14, 17 and 18) the nearest point is not more than 10m away from Site 1. The average distance from Site 1 of the remaining sites (4, 5, 6, 9, 10, 11, 12 and 15) is 15m (Fig. 5). The large mound is termed Site 1 and the smaller sites are numbered from the south, clockwise, from 2 to 18. Twelve of the sites have been published already. Following the progression of the excavation these had previously been numbered from 2 to 13 (Eogan 1968, 305–36, Sites 1–6; 1974, 17–66, Sites 7–13). These sites have now been re-numbered as follows:

New number	Old number	Date of excavation	*PRIA* ref. 1968/1974	New number	Old number	Date of excavation	*PRIA* ref. 1968/1974
2	13	1968-1970	1974	11	5	1963	1968
3	12	1968/1969	1974	12	4	1962	1968
4	11	1967-1968	1974	13	3	1964	1968
5	10	1967	1974	14	2	1964	1968
6	9	1967	1974	15	—	1973-1975	—
7	6	1967	1968	16	—	1973-1975	—
8	8	1966	1974	17	—	1968-1969	—
9	—	1978	—	18	—	1968/69 1973	—
10	7	1972 & 1977	1974				

For this report the descriptions of tombs previously published have been streamlined, but all essential information has been retained.

All the smaller tombs had been damaged, often with a ruthless thoroughness. In some sites (e.g. No. 9) virtually the entire tomb had been removed as had all the kerbstones. In Nos 5 and 11 no evidence for either passage or chamber survived. The best preserved example was No. 16. Tombs were entirely absent from an area to the east of Site 1, perhaps because of the large scale disturbance that occurred in the area on a number of occasions, particularly in the last century. However, this area did produce a number of large stones which appear to have been kerbstones, and large flakes that seem to have been derived from orthostats or kerbstones (Fig. 5).

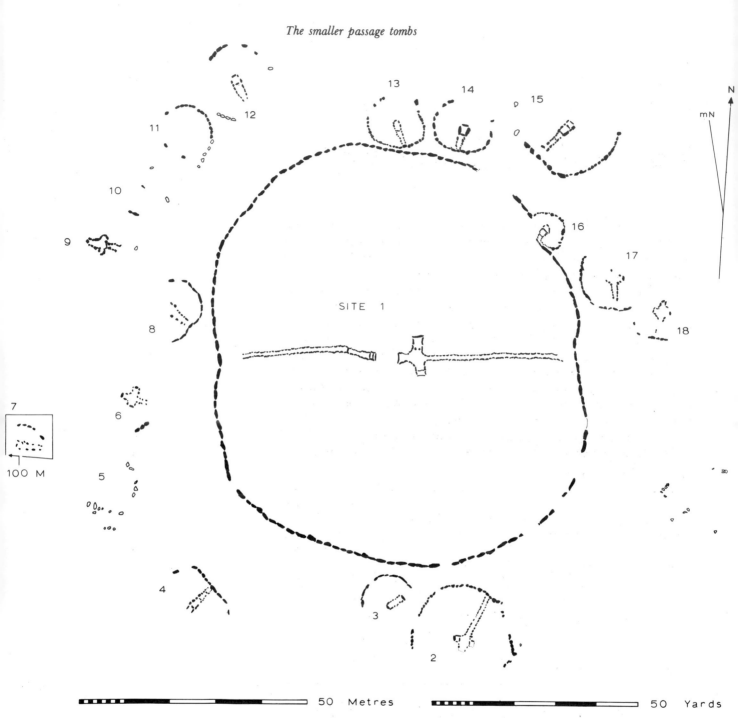

Fig. 5—The passage tomb cemetery at Knowth.

Evidence for destruction goes back to the Neolithic period, when Sites 13, 16 and 18 were altered. Considerable destruction took place during the Early Christian period when many stones from the tombs, including some decorated examples, were used to build souterrains.

A natural sod layer covering the area underneath the mound was present at only six sites, 2, 12, 15, 16, 17 and 18. A fair amount of natural sod was present at Site 9, but at the other sites it appears that the natural sod was stripped away before the tomb was built. The stripping away of the natural sod also occurred outside the main mound at Newgrange (O'Kelly, Lynch and O'Kelly 1978, 343).

In the plans and sections accompanying the descriptions of the tombs the following conventions are used.

PLANS   SECTIONS

☐ – – –	Disturbance (Ditches, Drains, Pits)
☐ – · –	Extent of Surviving Mound
☐ ·.·.·	Overhang
☐ – – –	Lean
☒	Displaced Orthostat
☐ ////	Packing Stones
☐ ⊞	Cremated Bone
☐ ////	Displaced (or probable kerbstone)
☐ ////	Replaced Kerbstone.
■	Kerbstone or Orthostat in situ
S =	Socket
K =	Kerbstone

☐ ⊓⊓⊓	Humus
☐ ·.·.·	Soft Dark Earth
☐ ////	Boulder Clay
☒	Shale
☐	Other
☐ ⊔⊔⊔	Natural Sod
☐ ∿	Charcoal
☐ ·.·.·	Ditch Fill
☐ //////	Till
☒	Yellow Earth
☐ ////	Brown Clay Silt
☐ + + +	Grey Clay Silt
☐ °°°	Ashy Material
☐ ▬ ▬ ▬	Iron Pan

Boulder Clay, Shale, Other } MOUND

SITE 2 (Fig. 6; Pl. 2a)

Before excavation the extreme tips of orthostats 14 and 26 protruded over the surface. These provided the only hint that further structures might be concealed below. At its nearest point this site is less than 5m away from the large mound.

The tomb (Fig. 7)

This cruciform tomb[1] was extensively damaged. It was about 13m long internally and was aligned north-east/south-west with the entrance at the north-eastern end.

The *passage* had thirty orthostats, fourteen on the eastern and sixteen on the western side. Only ten survived, four at the entrance (1, 2, 43, 44) and six at the chamber end (12–14, 30–32); 30–32 were damaged and had fallen in against 12–14. The tops were broken off 12, 30 and 32. The orthostats were in sockets and were well secured in position by packing stones. The sockets of 12–14 were merged into a trench. The stump of an orthostat survived in sockets 7, 10, 34, 35, 37. Otherwise the middle portion was defined by sockets only. The stump in socket 10 was across the socket. Apparently it was moved and this may also have happened to the stumps in sockets 34 and 35.

[1] In this and the following descriptions the term 'tomb' is applied to that part of the monument which was directly associated with burial i.e. *both* passage and chamber.

The smaller passage tombs

The sockets averaged 25cm in depth but No. 34 was 40cm deep. This latter depth may have been due to disturbance at the time of the removal of the orthostat. Socket 6 was longer than average. Nos 38–39 were very shallow but subsequent disturbance may have removed the upper portion. The passage is about 9.50m long. From 50cm at the entrance it gradually widens to 75cm between sockets 14 and 29. The surviving orthostats stood to a fairly uniform height of about 1m above the old ground level.

The *chamber* had three recesses. There are two sockets at the junction between the passage and chamber (15, 28) and No. 28 has the stump of an orthostat. The digging of a pit, 1.30m in diameter at

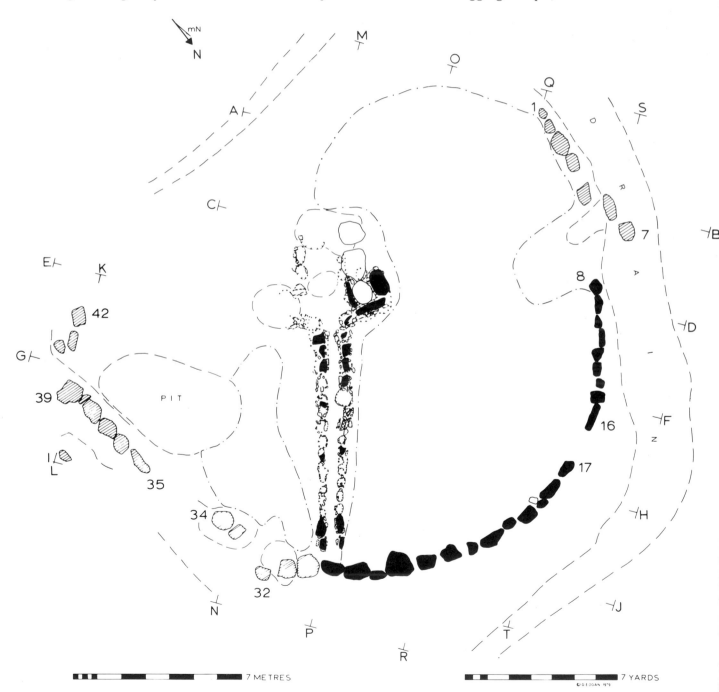

Fig. 6–Site 2: ground plan.

7 METRES

7 YARDS

© GEOGAN 1979

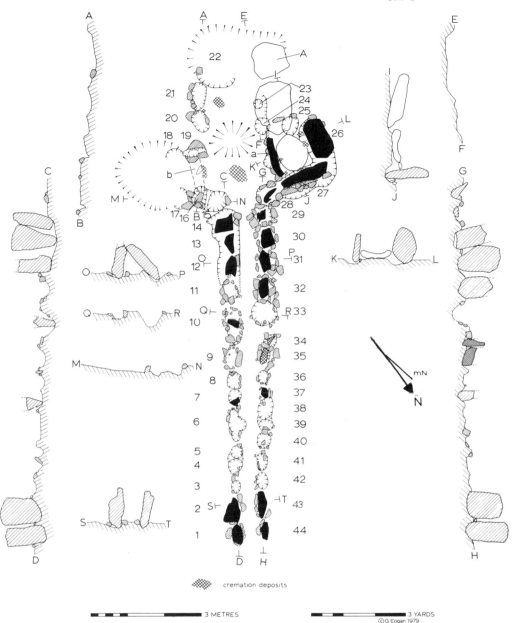

cremation deposits

3 METRES   3 YARDS
©G Eogan 1979

the mouth and 83cm deep, destroyed part of the interior of the chamber.

The right-hand recess was reasonably well preserved. It was formed from a backstone, a stone on each side and a sillstone (**a**). All were secured by propping stones at their bases but one (25) had fallen outwards and its base lay over the socket. Nos 26–28 were in a trench and orthostat 27 was skilfully erected. It was almost rectangular in elevation but longer at the western end than at the eastern. In order to provide stability the eastern end was propped up by first placing a small flag in the partly filled-up socket. Above this, and immediately under the corner of the orthostat, two smaller stones were inserted.

The recess measures 95cm by 105cm internally. Most of it is occupied by a *sandstone basin* (Pl. 3a) which measures 1m by 80cm externally and 23cm in maximum thickness. The hollow is about

Fig. 7–Site 2: ground plan and elevation of tomb.

25cm in maximum depth and around its edge there is a pocked line. The under surface is rougher than the top. The basin was sitting on the old surface (soil) and was stabilised by placing smaller, angular stones under the edge.

Pl. 2a–Site 2: tomb from south-west after excavation.

No structural stones of the left-hand recess survive; indeed, the digging of a pit destroyed most of the evidence here. However, there are the remains of two sockets on each side and these have packing stones (16–17 and 18–19); 16 was at a slight angle; 16 and 19 have flakes of green grit in the base, apparently the last remains of orthostats. There was a prostrate flag 80cm long across the entrance to the recess (**b**) which, despite the absence of a socket, may have been a sillstone. The recess would have been about 1m in internal width.

Most of the end recess was also destroyed by the digging of another pit. This recess appears to have been formed with five orthostats, two on each side and one at the back. The two eastern sockets (20,21) have survived. Only the inner edge of the back socket (22) remains. Two shallow depressions may be the vestigial remains of the western sockets (23–24). A prostrate stone (A) in the pit may have been a side stone.

Because of destruction it is possible only to estimate the dimensions of the chamber, which is about 4m by 4m internally. No evidence for the chamber roof emerged, but it was probably corbelled like the roofs of other cruciform tombs in Ireland. During removal of a nearby fence in 1967 a flagstone of green grit, *c.*1.10m long was found. This could have served as an orthostat or captstone.

MATERIALS AND DIMENSIONS OF PASSAGE AND CHAMBER STONES

No.	Type of Rock	Maximum dimensions (cm)		
		Length	Width	Height
1	Green grit = Greywacke	50	28	112
2	Limestone	68	40	106
7	Limestone	48	28	43
10	Siltstone	98	30	56
12	Green grit	56	36	86
13	Green grit	62	34	120
14	Green grit	52	46	112
16	Green grit	—	—	—
19	Green grit	—	—	—
25	Siltstone	104	36	144
26	Agglomerate (?)	112	64	110
27	Siltstone	154	25	114
28	Green grit	62	14	48
29	Fine sandstone	59	44	14
30	Green grit	53	38	90
31	Micaceous sandstone	60	28	130
32	Siltstone	62	22	84
34	Coarse sandstone	36	36	61
35	Sandstone	42	36	28
37	Limestone	37	25	47
43	Dolomitic limestone	74	24	102
44	Micaceous sandstone	58	20	122
Sillstone **a**	Sandstone	100	22	80
Sillstone **b**	Sandstone	80	30	**60**

Pl. 2b–Site 2: kerbstones 35–42 from south.

Burials

Cremated and uncremated bones were scattered over most of the chamber area. They were unprotected and it is doubtful if any are in their original position.

120.[2] In the right-hand recess fragments of cremated bone were found outside the basin, between it and the side stones. Other fragments had percolated downwards and were found amongst the prop stones. There was no deposit beneath the basin. Most were too small to identify. Dr Weekes recognised a human talus, parts of a human skull, part of the head of a humerus of a two- to three-year-old child and three human teeth from a young person. The deposit weighed 900g (1 lb. 15 oz.).

118a. From the left-hand recess Dr Weekes identified a human clavicle of the right side and parts of the vault of a skull, part of what may have been the head of a humerus and part of a rib. There were also some unidentifiable pieces of bone and some animal bone. Cremated bone formed the bulk of the material.

This deposit was at the entrance to the recess. From the sillstone it extended towards orthostat 14. Nowhere was the deposit very thick and it was mixed with dark grey silt-like material similar to the pit fill in the recess. The top of the cremation was about 10cm above the level of the passage floor. This deposit was, therefore, not in its original position. It could have been thrown in from the left-hand recess at the time of the disturbance. It weighed 807g (1 lb. 12 oz.).

Pl. 3a—Site 2: right-hand recess from south showing basin and orthostat 27 with concentric circle decoration.

[2] The finds have been deposited by the Commissioners of Public Works in the National Museum of Ireland. Their registration numbers start at E70:1 and continue. In the descriptions and on the illustrations the prefix E 70 is omitted and only the consecutive numbers are given.

Three fragments of pottery (122, not illustrated) of uncertain type were found amongst the cremation. There are small grits in the ware. One surface is smooth and buff in colour.

A few scraps of cremation probably derived from the deposit, turned up in socket 16 (118b) and a handful in socket 19 (118c).

119. The end recess had many fragments of cremated bone, some of which may be human. The deposit weighed 556g (1 lb. 3 oz.).

117. In the centre of the chamber were many fragments of bone, mostly unidentifiable but including both animal and human. Dr Weekes identified a human cuboid bone and a thumb metacarpal (both unburnt). There were also several other pieces of human bones some of which were cremated. Two molar teeth and two incisors of a child and some adult teeth were also present. The deposit weighed 1.330kg (2 lb. 15 oz.).

121a and b. There was a small collection of cremated bone in the fill of socket 27 both on the inside and on the outside. Fragments also turned up in the fill of the socket of sillstone **a** (121c).

The presence of bone in three sockets shows that bone was on the site during the construction of at least the right-hand recess.

The mound (Figs 8 and 9)

Remains of the mound survived on the western side between the kerb and the chamber and also over a small area to the east of the passage. The larger segment remained to a maximum height of 80cm; the smaller to a height of 30cm. Over most of the site the original natural sod layer was well defined. In the chamber area a layer of stones sloped upwards and inwards from the old sod level (sections C–D, E–F). This layer is absent from the neighbourhood of the passage but as only the basal few centimetres of the mound

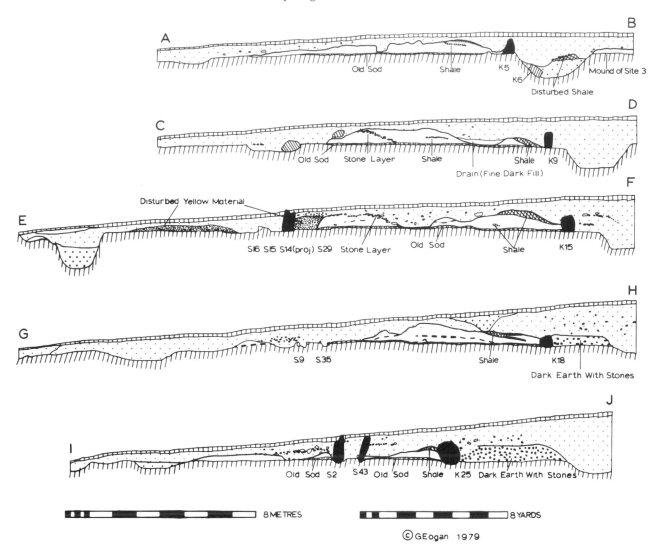

Fig. 8–Site 2: sections (A–B to I–J).

survived in that area it could have been destroyed. The material above and below the layer of stones is similar re-deposited boulder clay; nevertheless the layer of stones may have been the capping of a core that surrounded the chamber. In general the composition of the mound appears to have been a mixture of boulder clay and sods. In some parts this is interleaved with shale (sections A–B, E–F, Q–R, S–T) and layers of iron pan also occur in the mound. At a point 1m to the west of socket 31 there was a small charcoal spread within the mound. This produced a C14 determination of 4158 ± 126 B.P. (*c.*2208 b.c.; B.M. 785).

The kerb (Fig. 6; Pl. 2b)

Forty-two kerbstones survived. These were on the northern half of the site but not all were in their original position. The best-preserved section was an arc of twenty-two stones (8–29); a stone is missing between 16 and 17; 19–22 were in shallow pits, the remainder were on the old ground surface and some were secured by packing stones at the base. Nos 1–5 may not be in their original position. They tend to form a straight line and may have been adjusted to form an edging to the lip of a later ditch. Two probable kerbstones (6–7) lie at the bottom of this ditch. Kerbstones 30–34 have also been disturbed and they are lying in shallow pits. Nos 35–39 are in a straight line, set in a shallow drain 2m wide at the mouth and probably of fairly recent date. Nos 40–41 are sitting on the boulder clay, 42 is inserted into the boulder clay and may be in its original position, 40 and 42 are poorly preserved. The external diameter of the kerb was about 22m.

MATERIALS AND DIMENSIONS OF KERBSTONES

No.	Type of Rock	Maximum dimensions (cm)		
		Length	Width	Height
1	Volcanic ash	42	26	78
2	Fine agglomerate or coarse sandstone	53	42	58
3	Coarse dolerite	102	64	62
4	Dolomitic limestone	80	60	54
5	Limestone	70	42	62
6	Agglomerate	108	32	51
7	Fine agglomerate (?)	84	45	45
8	Dolerite	61	51	66
9	Limestone	78	28	58
10	Dolerite	48	50	66
11	Dolerite	82	39	57
12	Dolerite	53	56	70
13	Sandstone	65	32	67
14	Ashy agglomerate	45	43	63
15	Dolomitic limestone	66	61	67
16	Crinoidal limestone	120	28	66
17	Fine agglomerate	86	46	64
18	Dolerite	97	47	56
19	Dolerite	57	41	66
20	Dolerite	94	56	80
21	Agglomerate	61	47	90
22	Dolomitic limestone	118	72	77
23	Dolerite	55	60	73
24	Dolerite	102	85	75
25	Fine agglomerate	103	71	82
26	Grit	126	105	87
27	Fine-banded agglomerate	70	49	64
28	Ashy agglomerate (?)	112	91	66
29	Dolomitic limestone	94	74	57
30	Agglomerate	101	93	65
31	Sandstone	80	81	78
32	Agglomerate	65	43	56
33	Dolerite	42	44	72
34	Ashy agglomerate (?)	96	41	84
35	Limestone	127	43	36
36	Agglomerate	83	62	38
37	Agglomerate	89	67	27
38	Sandstone	105	70	45
39	Sandstone	118	99	42
40	Weathered coarse-grained igneous with felspar (plagioclase)	61	44	15
41	Fine-grained green sandstone or grit	84	40	36
42	Limestone	88	56	15

Isolated finds (Fig. 11)

123. *Sherd* of 'Carrowkeel' ware, 20mm thick, with large grits. The outer surface has three lines, not well executed, of stab-and-drag decoration. The sherd was in the corner of the right-hand recess

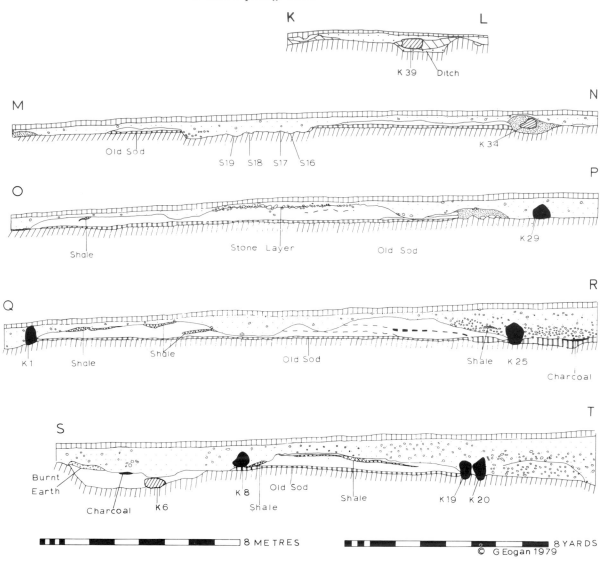

Fig. 9–Site 2: sections (K–L to S–T).

outside the basin and between orthostats 24 and 25. Therefore it may have been from a vessel deposited with burials in that recess.

124.   Curved piece of *bone*, 22mm long, tapering from one end to the other, with extreme point broken off. It was found in the stone basin. It may either be the tip of a pin or it may be natural, the root of a pig's tooth, for instance. As the soft dark earth fill in the stone basin was not primary the bone may be an intrusion.

125.   *Chalk ball* 16mm in diameter (Fig. 11). No. 126 is part of a chalk ball of about the same size as 125 (Fig. 11). The balls were found beside each other in top soil above kerbstone 18.

127.   *Lump of chalk* (Fig. 11). An uneven featureless piece, not an artifact. Found in the fill of the pit in the end recess.

128–43.   *Hoard of flints* (Fig. 10), consisting of sixteen well-struck flakes or parts of flakes. When found they were tightly packed together and partly upright under the slightly overhanging corner of kerbstone 26 opposite kerbstone 25. None are finished artifacts. The large size of the flakes suggests that they were struck from a block that was derived from a natural deposit of flint and not from drift flint.

Nos 128–138 are rough-outs for hollow scrapers and 139 is part of a similar flake. There is evidence of slight working on all examples,

Fig. 10–Hoard of flints from Site 2.

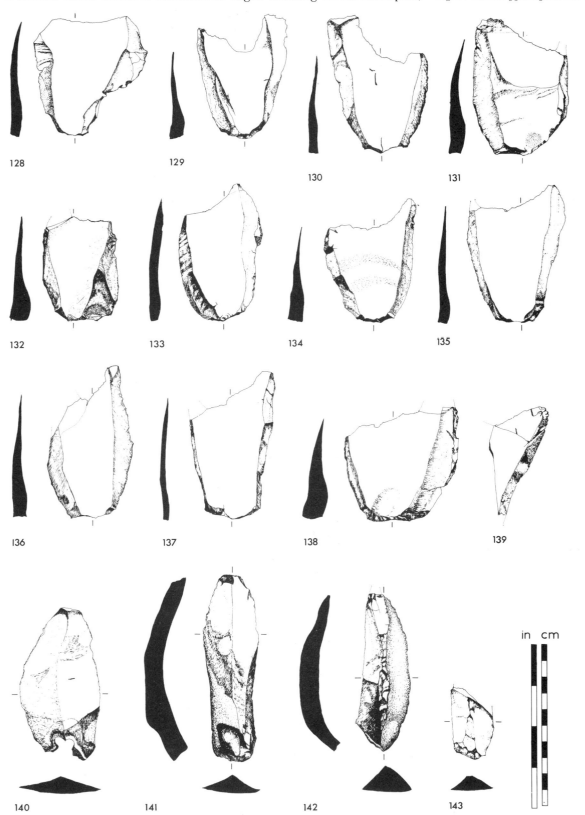

either along the concave edge or on the side. In 128 and 138 the outer edge of the bulb has been trimmed. No. 140 is a leaf-shaped flake with a medial line. It has a small bulb of percussion and the opposite end is jagged because of a fault in the flint. The edges are serrated. Nos 141–142 are outer core flakes with some cortex surviving. Each is curved when viewed from the side. There are slight serrations along the edges. No. 143 is part of a flake of triangular cross-section.

Hoards of flint objects dating to the Neolithic period are known from other parts of the country (Flanagan 1966; Woodman 1967) and the deposit from outside the large mound at nearby Newgrange may also be contemporary (Hartnett 1954).

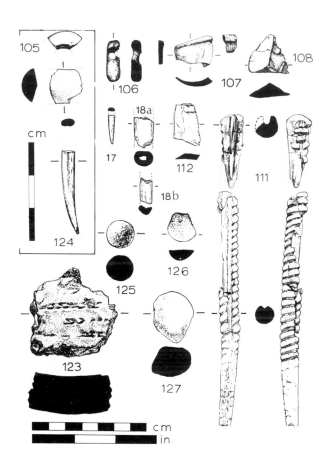

Fig. 11–Grave goods (17, 18a, 18b, 105–108 and 111–112) and disturbed finds (123–127) from Sites 2, 3, 6 and 12.

Megalithic art

Pocked designs have been found on three orthostats, one kerbstone and the stone basin.

Orthostat 14 (Fig. 61:1; Pl. 40b). The principal motif is a multiple circle of three members but the outer two are not placed concentrically to the inner one. At one point between the outer and middle circle there is an arc. For a short part of its circumference the middle circle is incised but it is not certain that this is an original feature. There are also four single circles and four arcs or stems.

Orthostat 27 (Fig. 61:3; Pl. 3a). The single motif consists of a lightly pocked circle with an arc extending out of its upper side. The motif is in the form of an inverted Q.

Orthostat 30 (Fig. 61:2; Pls 41a and b). The upper part has been broken off. The inner face has four irregular lozenges that touch at the apex. The edge adjoining orthostat 31 has three horizontal rows of broad chevrons.

Kerbstone 28 (Fig. 61:4; Pl. 42a) has a single circle on the outer face.

Basin. This has a pocked line around the inner edge (Pl. 3a).

SITE 3 (Fig. 12; Pl. 3b)

There were no surface indications when excavations commenced.

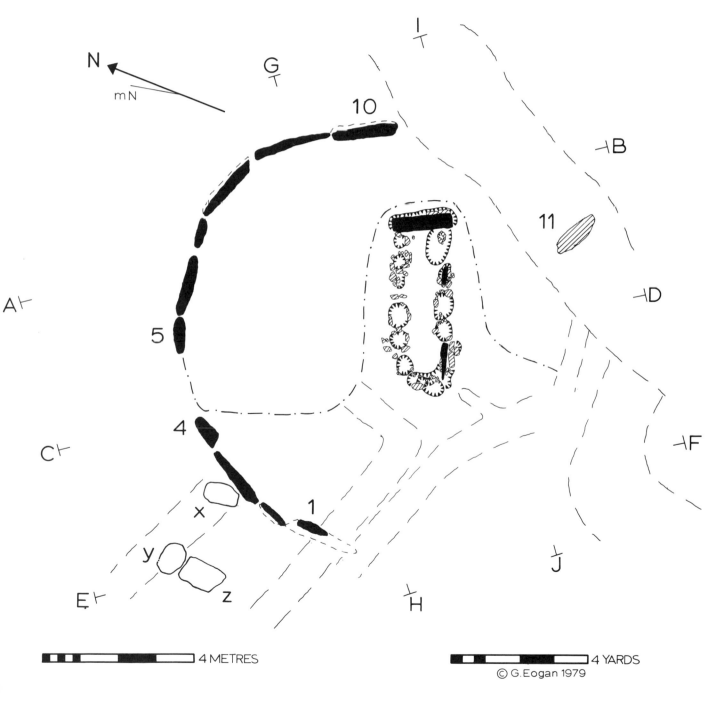

Fig. 12–Site 3: ground plan.

4 METRES

4 YARDS

© G. Eogan 1979

The tomb (Fig. 13; Pl. 4a)

This was an unusual tomb with no evidence for a passage. If such existed it would have been at the south-west end as the mound continued across the north-east end. The south-west end was interfered with, especially by the digging of drains, but despite this some evidence for sockets might have been expected had a passage existed. However it should be noted that orthostats 1, 2 and 21 of Site 15 were standing on the old ground surface.

The chamber, more or less centrally placed within the mound, was aligned north-east/south-west and measured 3.50m by 90cm. There was a socket across each end (Nos 1 and 7). Although only 43cm high the orthostat in socket 1 appears to be complete. It has packing stones around the base and one end projects slightly over socket 2. No other orthostats remain although stumps survive in sockets 3 and 6. The southern side of the chamber had five sockets (2–6) and the northern side six (8–13), all with packing stones. The sockets varied in size and No. 2 was at a slight angle to the other sockets on the southern side.

Fig. 13–Site 3: ground plan and elevation of tomb.

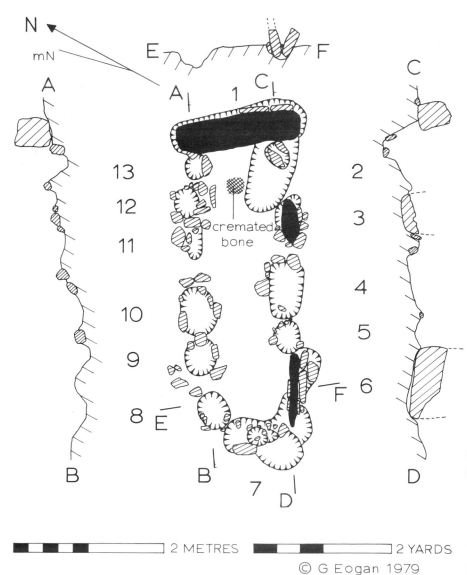

2 METRES   2 YARDS

© G Eogan 1979

Pl. 4a–Site 3: tomb from north-east after excavation.

MATERIALS AND DIMENSIONS OF ORTHOSTATS
(OR THE PORTIONS THAT SURVIVE)

No.	Type of Rock	Maximum dimensions (cm)		
		Length	Width	Height
1	Limestone	170	42	43
3	Sandstone	55	30	18
6	Current-bedded sandstone	91	15	40

Burials and grave goods

There was a deposit of cremated bone (110) near the eastern end of the chamber about 50cm in from the inner edge of socket 1. This was on the floor of the chamber and the material above it was disturbed. The bones were fairly well burnt, only a few pieces being over 4cm long. Dr Weekes considered that the bones represented part of one skeleton. The smallness of the bones, the thinness of the skull bones and the depth of the suture lines between bones of the skull indicated that the remains were those of a young person aged between fifteen and twenty years. The teeth, though small, are the second dentition. The deposit weighed 1223.5g (2 lb. 11 oz.).

Two objects were found amongst the bones.

111. *Antler or bone object* (Fig. 11). The object is warped and broken which is perhaps due to heat: it may have been in the cremation pyre. The tip is missing but the object was around or slightly over 20cm long when complete. The domed head is 16mm across. From there it

tapers to the broken end. The upper part is decorated with grooves, U-shaped in cross-section, which are placed at an angle and give a helical effect. A vertical channel on one side narrowing from top to bottom interrupts the continuity of the grooves.

This object can be compared to the stone object from Knowth (p. 163). Both pieces have parallels in Iberia, in the 'idols' which Almagro Gorbea calls betals with engraved decoration, an exclusive Portugese type that is found mainly in the Lisbon area (Almagro Gorbea 1973a, 78–90, cf. Fig. 15; Leisner 1965, Taf. 150).

112. *Chip of flint* (Fig. 11). Lop-sided with one flat and one scarred surface. There is faint working along the shorter edge. Length 28mm.

The mound (Fig. 14)

Disturbance, especially ditch-digging along the eastern side and drains on the southern half, destroyed a large portion of the mound. The surviving portion reached a maximum height of only 40cm. It covered an area of 11m–12m in diameter. There was evidence for layering. The basal layer of sods was covered by boulder clay and over a small area inside kerb 9 the boulder clay was overlain by shale (section G–H).

The kerb (Fig. 12; Pl. 3b)

The kerb was probably about 11.25m in external diameter. Because of the damage already mentioned no kerbstones survived around the southern and eastern edges. One kerbstone (11) was found at the base of the ditch on the eastern side. On the northern side there was a fairly complete arc of ten kerbstones (1–10) placed on the old ground surface. Some were supported with packing stones. 1–3 and 8 are leaning outwards. Most of the kerbstones were fairly regular in shape.

MATERIALS AND DIMENSIONS OF KERB

No.	Type of Rock	Maximum dimensions (cm)		
		Length	Width	Height
1	Green grit	205	22	47
2	Siltstone	85	22	46
3	Green siltstone	178	26	45
4	Limestone	89	38	62
5	Current-bedded sandstone	102	21	48
6	Green siltstone	172	30	53
7	Dolomitic limestone	90	28	58
8	Green siltstone	189	35	61
9	Green micaceous siltstone	208	34	40
10	Green grit	180	42	46
11	Green grit	137	33	53

Three stones (X, Y, Z) outside the kerb to the west are more irregular in shape than the kerbstones and so unlikely to be disturbed kerbstones.

Isolated finds

The following objects were found in disturbed soil close to the chamber.

113a. *Pottery sherd* of 'Carrowkeel' ware (Fig. 49), 15mm thick. The inner surface varies from brown to dark and the core is dark.

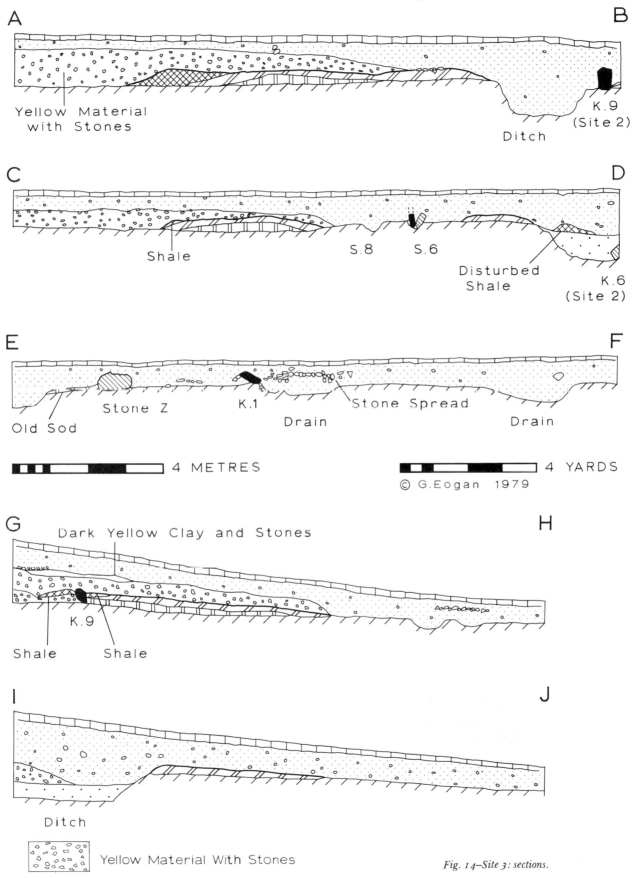

A

B

Yellow Material
with Stones

Ditch

K.9
(Site 2)

C

D

Shale

S.8   S.6

Disturbed
Shale

K.6
(Site 2)

E

F

Old Sod

Stone Z

K.1

Drain

Stone Spread

Drain

4 METRES

4 YARDS

© G.Eogan 1979

G

H

Dark Yellow Clay and Stones

K.9

Shale   Shale

I

J

Ditch

Yellow Material With Stones

Fig. 14–Site 3: sections.

The outer surface is worn but the remains of two rows of stab-and-drag decoration survive. Found about 60cm to the east of the southern end of socket 1, and 65cm below the surface. May be the only surviving fragment of a vessel that could have formed part of the grave goods of the chamber.

113b.   Sherd of similar ware to 113a, 18mm thick. The dark ware has a buff outer crust. It contains large angular sandstone grits, some of which protrude through the outer surface. The outer face has the remains of three parallel rows of somewhat elongated stab impressions. The single remaining stab of the third row has an impression, probably made by small bone, in the base (Fig. 49). Found in a dump of material taken from the vicinity of Site 3.

114–116.   Irregular *lumps of chalk* (?) (Fig. 49), found fairly close to each other just outside the northern end of the chamber. Chalk balls are known from Irish passage tombs but these are featureless pieces and their association with this tomb cannot be proven.

Megalithic art

Kerbstone 10 (Fig. 63:1; Pl. 42b) bears three spirals and a circle. The weathered spiral on the left-hand side and the central spiral are single. The one on the right begins as a double spiral but after one and a half turns the second member discontinues. There are also some areas of light pocking.

SITE 4 (Fig. 15; Pl. 4b)

There were no surface indications for the presence of a tomb before the excavations commenced.

The tomb (Fig. 16; Pl. 5)

The tomb is aligned north-east/south-west with the entrance on the north-eastern side. Apart from a stump in socket 11, no orthostats survive but the presence of twenty sockets shows that it is

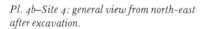

Pl. 4b–Site 4: general view from north-east after excavation.

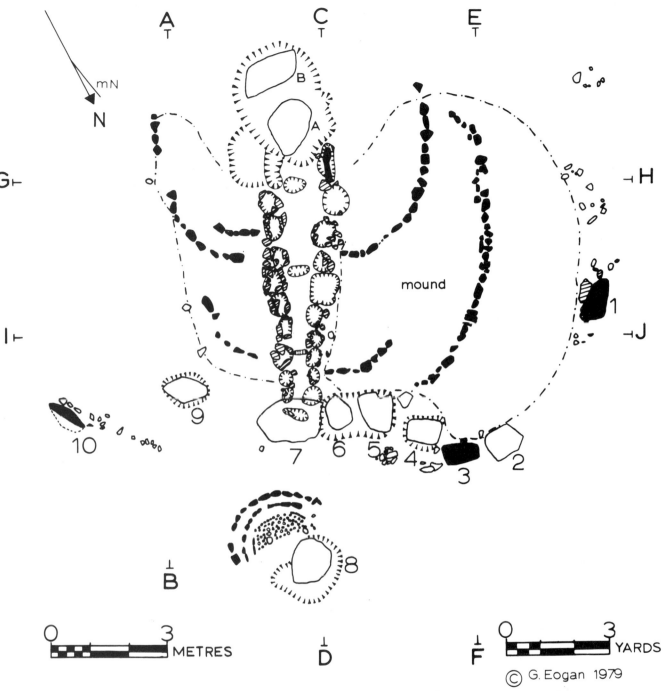

Fig. 15—Site 4: ground plan.

mound

© G. Eogan 1979

an undifferentiated passage tomb. The tomb is 28cm in internal width at the entrance. From there each side diverges outwards to sockets 9 and 12 where the tomb is 1.20m wide internally. Sockets 10 and 11 are parallel to each other and their inner edges are 1m apart. Socket 11 is 105cm long, 35cm wide and 15cm deep. The inner end of socket 10 has been destroyed but it appears that it had the same dimensions as No. 11. Amongst the remaining sockets sixteen average 50cm by 45cm by 20cm deep; 12 and 15 are slightly larger while 1 and 2 are slightly smaller. The passage has three transverse sockets (b, c and d) which probably held sillstones, and another socket (a) across the entrance to the passage. The inner part of the

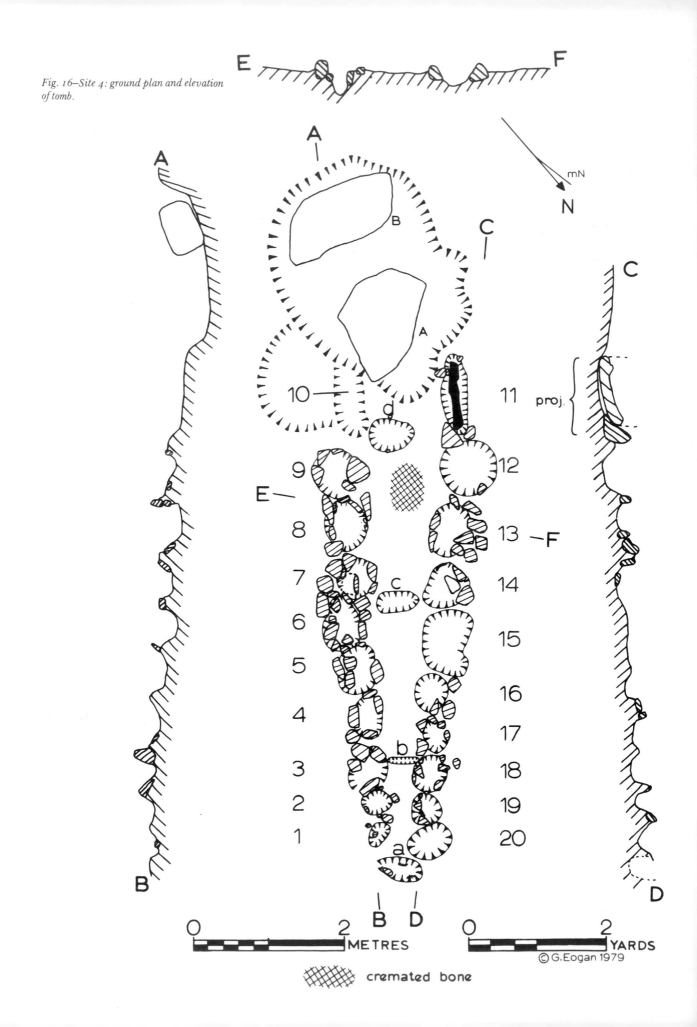

Fig. 16—Site 4: ground plan and elevation of tomb.

E   F

A

A

B

C

mN

N

10

d

11   proj.

9

E

12

8

13 — F

7

c

14

6

15

5

16

4

17

3

b

18

2

19

1

20

a

B   D

0   2 METRES   0   2 YARDS

© G.Eogan 1979

cremated bone

tomb and an area beyond it were destroyed by the digging of a large pit, probably dug to receive two large stones which lay in it (A and B). The shape of B suggests that it is a rolled-in kerbstone. Stone A is V-shaped and is decorated on the top and on both of the broad faces. It is assumed that the narrow end stood in the socket since it is undecorated. This stone might have served as a back-stone but it should be noted that its pointed end was close to a transverse socket (d). Perhaps it served as a sillstone, delimiting the outer edge of a squarish inner segment of the tomb. If so it would have been much higher than any of the sillstones known in other tombs at Knowth, or indeed elsewhere in Ireland. But high sillstones at the inner end of the tomb are known abroad, for instance at the bent passage grave of Goërem at Gâvres in Brittany (L'Helgouach 1970).

MATERIALS AND DIMENSIONS OF STONES

No.	Type of Rock	Maximum dimensions (cm)		
		Length	Width	Height
11	Dolomitic limestone (?)	92	20	15
A	Green ash (?)	148	35	149
B	Dolomitic limestone	155	53	81

Burials

There was a small deposit of cremated bone (109) on the floor of the tomb between sockets c and d. Dr Weekes was unable to identify any of the pieces. There were also three unburnt animal teeth.

Pl. 5a–Site 4: Tomb from north-east after excavation—
(foreground) portion of circular setting before entrance damaged by digging of pit in which kerbstone 8 is lying,
(background) stone settings on either side of tomb.

Pl. 5b–Site 4: general view from south-west after excavation.

The mound and stone settings (Figs 15 and 17; Pl. 5a–b)

The mound was originally about 16m in diameter but a large part has been removed. Surviving portions to the north-east of the passage and on the western side of the passage had a maximum height of 40cm. An iron pan layer separated the mound from the natural base but a definite old sod layer could not be detected. The mound was layered. The yellowish basal layer seems to have been boulder clay and was overlain in some places by a layer of shale (sections E–F, G–H, I–J). There is a series of six curved stone settings on the old ground level. None of the stones was longer than 40cm and some were much shorter. The width varied between 30cm and 10cm and the average height was 20cm. Five settings extended out from the tomb and another was further out on the western side. Four of the settings were entirely covered by the mound and their full extent is known but, as the ends of the other two coincide with the present edge of the mound, they may have been more extensive. However, there is no evidence in the stratification that they formed an edging to a core. If an outer arc existed on the eastern side matching that at the west, this could have been destroyed when the mound was removed.

The kerb (Fig. 15; Pl. 4b)

Externally the kerb was about 17m in diameter. As already remarked stone B from the pit in the inner end of the tomb was probably a kerbstone. There were ten other stones which can definitely be considered kerbstones but only three of these (1, 3 and 10) were in their original position. No. 2 had fallen outwards, 4–6 and 8–9 were buried in pits, 8 being a few metres away from the line of the kerb, 7 was lying on the ground surface. Kerbstone 3 was in a slight socket (section E–F), but elsewhere the stones had been placed on the surface and secured with packing stones at the base. These stones mark the positions of kerbstones 2, 4 and 5. Further stones to the south-west of kerbstone 1 and north-west of kerbstone 10 possibly indicate the positions of further kerbstones. The precise position of the kerbstones before the entrance cannot be determined but the kerb may have flattened out along that sector.

Fig. 17–Site 4: sections.

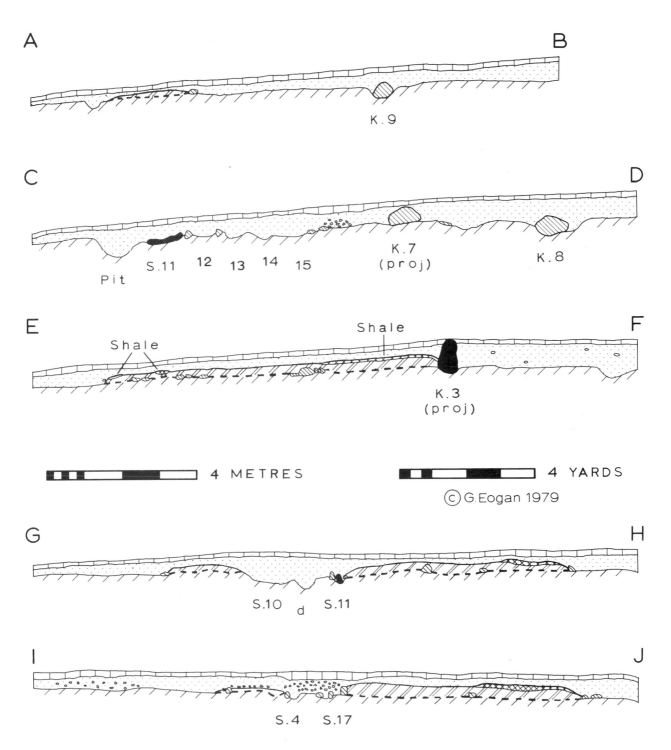

© G. Eogan 1979

MATERIALS AND DIMENSIONS OF KERBSTONES

		Maximum dimensions (cm)		
No.	Type of Rock	Length	Width	Height
1	Ashy agglomerate	120	64	53
2	Dolomitic limestone	92	25	81
3	Dolomitic limestone	86	50	74
4	Red sandstone	93	46	72
5	Ash (?)	92	50	112
6	Agglomerate	70	60	95
7	Sandstone	164	44	107
8	Agglomerate	70	56	100
9	Lamprophyre	118	42	68
10	Crinoidal limestone	112	20	64

Two stones, found a few metres outside the southern periphery of the site, may have been displaced kerbstones.

Other primary features (Fig. 15; Pl. 4a)

Two metres directly in front of the entrance to the passage were the remains of a circular area paved with quartz and enclosed by two closely-set concentric circles of stones averaging 20cm in length. The overall diameter of this feature had been about 2.25m but the digging of the pit in which kerbstone 8 lies destroyed the northern half.

Megalithic art (Fig. 62; Pl. 43a–b)

There is art on both faces, on the top and on the side of a single stone, A. The upper face as found is being called face 1. The decoration was damaged by plough-scores, but it appears to have consisted of concentric arcs which tend to follow the outline of the top of the stone. Some lines join up at the ends. Pocking was used.

On face 2 (the lower one as found), which is highly decorated, both incision and pocking were used. Three main motifs were formed by incision: zig-zags, lozenges and a subrectangular motif. Zig-zags occur at various places on the upper part of the stone. The subrectangular motif, also on the upper part, consists of at least seven concentric members. Part of it was destroyed when one of the lozenges was pocked. There are remains of other incised lines, especially around the centre of the stone, where some of the lines are vertical and others form a lozenge. They may even have been guide-lines for the pocked lozenges. Certainly, at some points the pocking cuts across them.

The main *pocked* design is a series of thirteen lozenge-shaped motifs in three horizontal rows, each one touching one or more of its immediate neighbours. The right-hand lozenge of the upper row is incomplete and some pocking on the outside of it may indicate a further incomplete lozenge. In an unpocked lozenge-shaped area, between the first and second lozenges from the left of the top and middle rows, there is a pocked triangle with an unpocked triangular area in the centre. Running parallel to most of the curved top of the stone is a pocked line, which can be compared to the lines on face 1. Just below it, at about mid-point, there is a short vertical zig-zag. Some natural lines and depressions across the left centre of this face have been accentuated by pocking, as has a depression towards the right-hand side. The top has two pocked lozenges and five roughly parallel pocked lines of varied length. There is also some slight random pocking. The side has three areas of incised decoration. One consists of eight concentric lines. Above and below there are clusters of roughly parallel lines.

SITE 5 (Fig. 18; Pl. 6a)

There were no surface indications at the commencement of excavations. A number of largish stones were revealed. It cannot be conclusively established that a passage tomb stood here but the presence of portion of a mound together with a decorated stone

Fig. 18–Site 5: ground plan.

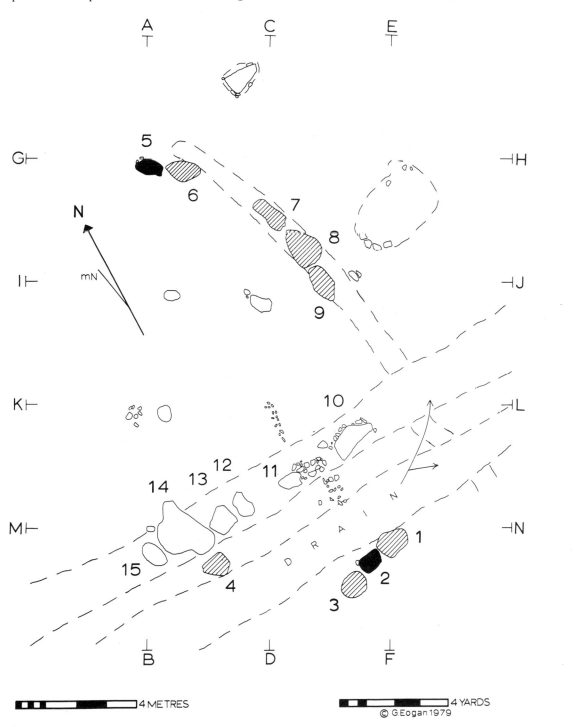

4 METRES

4 YARDS

© G.Eogan 1979

make it very likely. The area had been extensively interfered with. Two drains run across the site in an east-west direction and there is another drain at right angles to these.

Pl. 6a–Site 5: General view from south after excavation.

There is a pit, 30cm in maximum depth, about 1.20m to the east of stone 8. Flat stones were set along the south-western edge. Between 80cm and 2m to the east of stone 7 there are four holes that may have held posts. These do not form a pattern. Around the outermost hole was a small area of burnt earth. No dating evidence for the pit and holes came to light.

The tomb area

No evidence for a structure survived but some of the flat stones (10–15), now lying in a drain, may have been capstones.

The mound (Fig. 19)

To the south-west of stones 5–7 was a small area of re-deposited boulder clay. This material was overlaid by a wedge of shale on the inside of stone 5 (section A–B). This could well represent the remains of a layered mound.

The kerb (Fig. 18)

Nine of the stones could have served as kerbstones. 1–3 occur in a line on the southern side, 4 is between two drains and 5–9 are along the north-eastern side of the site. Of these stones only 2 and 5 seem to be *in situ*.

MATERIALS AND DIMENSIONS OF STONES DESCRIBED

No.	Type of Rock	Maximum dimensions (cm)		
		Length	Width	Height
1	Dolomitic limestone	108	78	61
2	Dolomitic limestone	75	56	56
3	Ashy agglomerate	91	75	35
4	Dolomitic limestone	89	75	39
5	Fine-grained limestone	92	55	48
6	Agglomerate	111	66	55
7	Limestone	130	60	53
8	Green grit	136	90	88
9	Fine-grained limestone	130	64	73
10	Dolerite	140	67	46
11	Dolomitic limestone	82	45	32
12	Coarse grit with band of pebbles	71	53	45
13	Gabbro	86	81	36
14	Gabbro	211	141	34
15	Sandstone	58	52	30

Less than 3m to the north-east of stone 6 is a stone, 84cm long, lying in a shallow pit. It is not known if this stone had any connection with the site.

Finds

No artifacts were recovered nor was there any evidence of burial.

Megalithic art (Fig. 63:2; Pl. 44a)

One stone, 8, has art. This stone was damaged and it is not in its original position. The centre of one face has a small circle with a slight projection at the bottom right and another at the top left. A short distance away to the right, and at a slightly lower level, there is an irregularly shaped motif. It has two short projections at the top. The main area of decoration is towards the right end, where there is a poorly formed zig-zag with pocked lines immediately beneath it. A short distance above this motif there is an irregular zig-zag with a small area of pocking to the left.

SITE 6 (Fig. 20; Pl. 7a)

Only the extreme tips of kerbstones 2 and 3 were visible before excavation commenced.

The tomb (Fig. 21; Pl. 6b)

The entrance to this cruciform tomb is on the south-eastern side. Originally it was probably about 8m long but the outer portion of the passage has been obliterated. In this area are two small holes, A in line with the southern side of the passage, B at an angle. There are two tiny depressions (C and D) to the north of B. A may be the remains of a socket. There is evidence for twenty-one definite sockets, the majority of which have packing stones along the edges. Eight held passage orthostats (1–4 and 18–21), 4 and 18 at the junction with the chamber are the largest, averaging 70cm long by 30cm deep, and the others vary in shape, size and depth. Nos 1 and 21 are very shallow, only about 4cm deep, but they may have been damaged by the shifting of stone X. The parallel-sided passage was around 50cm wide and appears to have been about 5m long.

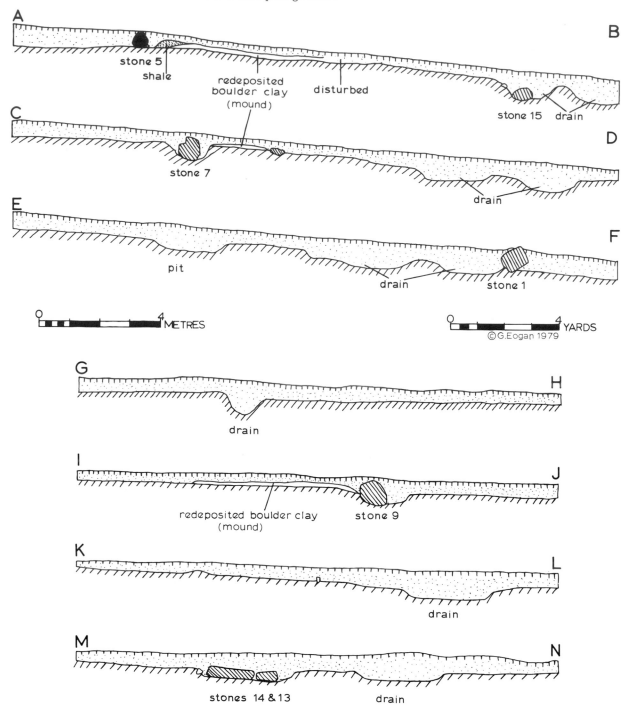

A ——— B

stone 5
shale
redeposited
boulder clay
(mound)
disturbed
stone 15   drain

C ——— D

redeposited
boulder clay
(mound)
stone 7
drain

E ——— F

pit
drain   stone 1

0 ————————— 4 METRES   0 ——————— 4 YARDS
© G.Eogan 1979

G ——— H

drain

I ——— J

redeposited boulder clay
(mound)
stone 9

K ——— L

drain

M ——— N

stones 14 & 13   drain

Fig. 19–Site 5: sections.

The central area of the chamber measures about 1.80m by 1.40m
internally. Three sockets (9–11), one at the end and one on each side,
form the end recess which is almost 1m long and 60cm wide. The left-
hand recess appears to have been of similar size and construction,
but the digging of a pit has damaged the end. Between sockets 7 and
9 is a hole 25cm in diameter (No. 8). Although it is small it appears to
have held an orthostat. It also occupies a position similar to 12. The
right-hand recess is almost 2m long. It is 1m wide at the inner end,
and slightly wider between sockets 12 and 18. In addition there is a

back socket and two sockets (13–17) on each of the long sides. This is the largest of the three recesses, a feature which also exists at other passage graves. The back sockets in each of the three recesses are the largest in the chamber, that in the end recess being 1m long. The other chamber sockets average 60cm long by 20cm deep.

Pl. 6b–Site 6: tomb from east after excavation.

Burials and grave goods

There was a deposit of cremated bone (104) in the right-hand recess. Dr Weekes reports that it represents the remains of several individuals. Some were adults but the remains of at least one child, about three years of age, are represented. The upper part of the deposit was disturbed. The remains of two skeletons overlay it but these are probably of much later date (Eogan 1974, 29, 71, burials 7 and 8, renumbered 14 and 13). The deposit weighed 1125g (2 lb. 8 oz.) Around the edge of the deposit were sherds of coarse Beaker pottery (p. 312). There was a small deposit of cremated bone (104a), too fragmentary for identification, in the left-hand recess. Some pieces had trickled into sockets 5 and 7 probably at the time of the removal of the orthostats.

The following objects were amongst the large deposit of cremated bone (104) in the right-hand recess.

105. *Bead* (Fig. 11). Only about a quarter survives. It has an hourglass perforation and the outside is convex. The material is pottery fired from micaceous clay (information from Professor Mitchell).

106. *Pendant* (Fig. 11). Bone, 25mm by 9.5mm with sub-rectangular cross-section. Near one end is an oblique perforation and along one side the wall is missing. Apparently the object was subjected to heat.

107. Piece of *bone* (Fig. 11), part of a larger object of uncertain shape. Curved, with a slight outward expanding 'rim'. The surfaces, especially the outer ones, are smooth. On the circumference the piece widens from a thin, artificially-shaped edge, to 5mm at the other end. Dr Brenda Healy reports that the piece resembles the jugal area (lower edge of the orbit) of an unidentified animal, the 'bone is not natural and must have been fashioned'.

108. Piece of *flint* (Fig. 11), triangular in shape and in cross-section with slight secondary working along one edge. Perhaps the tip of a blade.

The mound (Fig. 22; Pl. 7a)

Only a small portion of the mound survives. This is on the inside of kerbstones 1–3, and is 40cm in maximum height. The material is boulder clay. The mound may have had a diameter of about 14m.

Fig. 20—Site 6: ground plan.

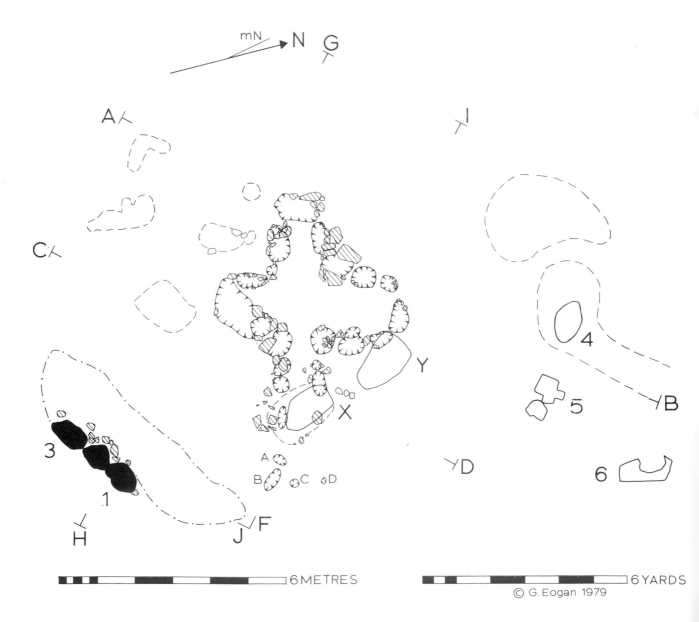

© G. Eogan 1979

The kerb (Fig. 20; Pl. 7a)

Only three kerbstones (1–3), on the south-eastern side, remained *in situ.* They were on the old ground surface and were, in part, supported by packing stones. Three largish stones (4–6) on the northern periphery of the site may be displaced kerbstones. No. 4 is in a pit, a later feature than the tomb; 5 is leaning and it is not in its original position; 6 lies on the old ground surface. Two largish displaced stones (X and Y) in the area of the chamber, may have been kerbstones, while a flag lying in a depression 20m to the west could have been a capstone (Z) (Area 2: square 9).

Pl. 7a–Site 6: general view from east after excavation. stones X and Y have been shifted from find position (see Fig. 20).

MATERIALS AND DIMENSIONS OF KERBSTONES AND POSSIBLE KERBSTONES

		Maximum dimensions (cm)		
No.	Type of Rock	Length	Width	Height
1	Fine-grained limestone	112	77	67
2	Sandstone	71	63	68
3	Dolomitic limestone	110	69	59
4	Limestone	99	62	89
5	Limestone	111	78	40
6	Limestone	201	59	73
X	Conglomerate	129	77	61
Y	Green grit	158	91	63
Z	Green grit	155	95	19

SITE 7 (Fig. 23; Pl. 7b)

This tomb is the furthest away from the hill-top, 120m to the west of Site 1. It is 23m back from the top edge of the steep terrace that forms the left bank of the River Boyne. Before excavation the tips of kerbstones 1–3 and very slight traces of a mound were visible.

The tomb (Fig. 23; Pl. 7b)

Because of damage and the difficult nature of the subsoil, a thin layer of boulder clay over shale, the complete plan of the tomb was

Fig. 21–Site 6: ground plan and elevation of tomb.

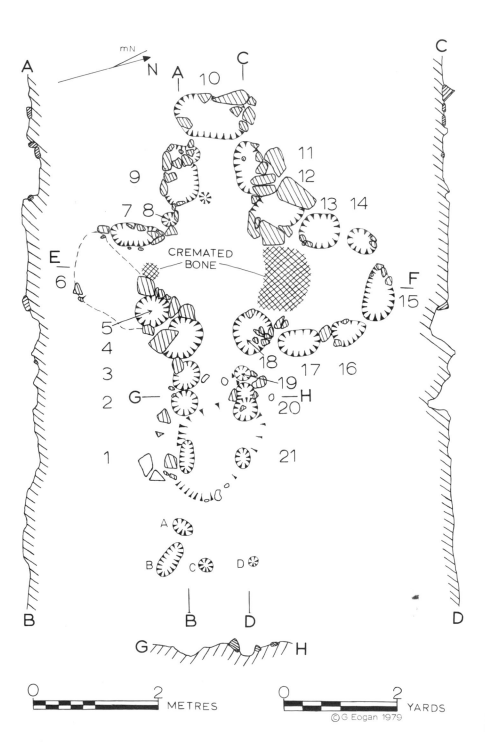

CREMATED BONE

© G Eogan 1979

0   2 METRES

0   2 YARDS

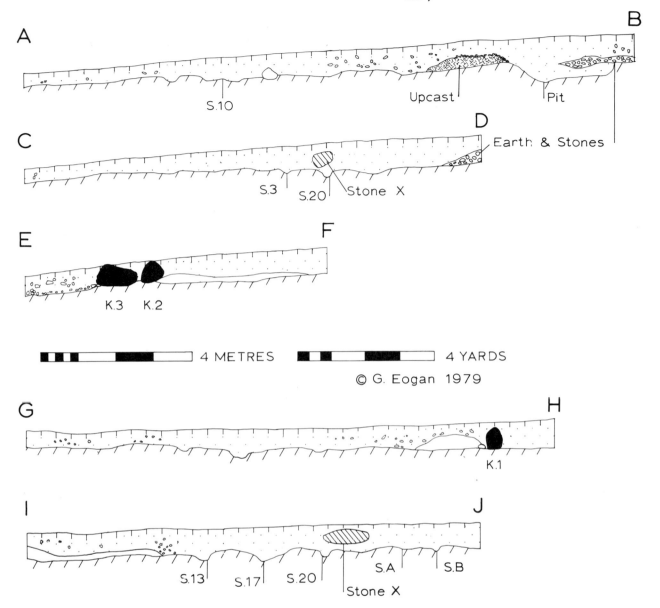

A

S.10   Upcast   Pit

B

C   D   Earth & Stones

S.3   S.20   Stone X

E   F

K.3   K.2

████ ███ ████████ 4 METRES   ████ ██ ████████ 4 YARDS

© G. Eogan 1979

G   H

K.1

I   J

S.13   S.17   S.20   S.A   S.B

Stone X

not discovered. There were four definite sockets (1, 10, 11, 12). These averaged 12cm in depth and all had prop stones. Some of the eight other holes could represent sockets but this was not definitely established. The evidence is somewhat inadequate, but it appears that the tomb was undifferentiated, about 5.40m long internally, aligned roughly east-west, with the entrance on the east. At the entrance the internal width was about 60cm and at the back about 1.20m. There was no evidence for burial.

Fig. 22–Site 6: sections.

The mound (Fig. 24; Pl. 7b)

The surviving portion of the mound was of dark shale-like material and about 20cm in maximum height. The mound, which had been completely removed on the western side, would originally have been approximately 10m in diameter. The fact that the mound material extended over the area of the tomb can be attributed to infiltration after the removal of the structural stones.

Pl. 7b–Site 7: general view from east after excavation.

The kerb (Fig. 23; Pl. 7b)

The five surviving kerbstones are on the northern side. 2–4 are set close together.

MATERIALS AND DIMENSIONS OF KERBSTONES

No.	Type of Rock	Maximum dimensions (cm)		
		Length	Width	Height
1	Limestone	77	22	38
2	Limestone	95	50	60
3	Decalcified calcareous sandstone	84	50	53
4	Fine-grained grit	91	58	73
5	Fine-grained dark lava	117	52	60

Finds (Fig. 54)

47. The only find, a flint double hollow scraper, was discovered in the mound. One hollow, on the end opposite the bulb of percussion, is deep and crescentic. The other hollow is shallow and on one side. On the opposite side there is slight evidence of utilisation.

SITE 8 (Fig. 25; Pl. 8b)

No features were visible when excavation commenced.

The tomb (Fig. 26; Pl. 8a)

Only limited evidence for the tomb remains. None of the orthostats was in position. The digging of a fairly extensive pit destroyed the inner portion of the tomb and another portion was destroyed by the digging of a drain across the passage. Two large stones in the pit appear to have been derived from the tomb. Stone A, standing upright along part of the northern edge of the pit, may be a displaced orthostat. Stone B, apparently a rolled-in kerbstone, was lying across the middle of the pit.

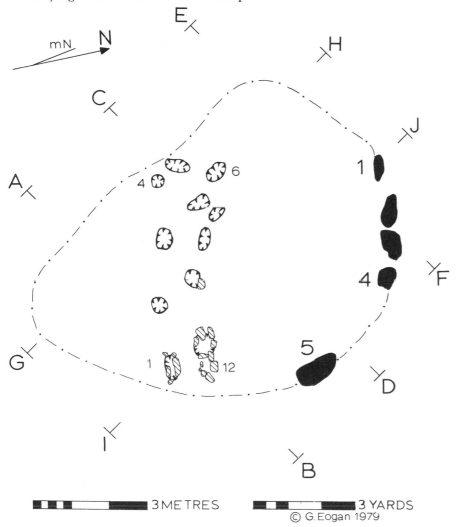

3 METRES   3 YARDS

© G. Eogan 1979

Fig. 23—Site 7: ground plan.

MATERIALS AND DIMENSIONS OF STONES

No.	Type of Rock	Maximum dimensions (cm)		
		Length	Width	Height
A	Green grit	112	35	156
B	Coarse crinoidal limestone, with chert	161	82	48

Immediately to the west of stone A was another, lower, upright stone, while in the western end of the pit were some small stones. Three holes (X, Y, Z) outside the northern edge of the pit correspond in size to sockets but their location, at an angle to the main line of the chamber, appears to exclude them from this function. Furthermore, hole X impinges on socket 5. However, evidence exists for six complete sockets (1, 2, 6, 7, 10, 11) and the remains of five (3, 4, 5, 8, 9). Mainly oval in shape, they vary in length from 25cm to 80cm. The tomb widens from the entrance inwards indicating an undifferentiated passage tomb. It was at least 6m long, and aligned north-west/south-east with the entrance on the south-eastern side.

Pl. 8a–Site 8: tomb from east after excavation.

The mound (Fig. 27)

The remains of the mound covered an area 12m–13m in diameter. Only the basal portion survived, to a maximum height of 50cm, but along the western side and in the area of the tomb and drain the mound was completely removed. The material is boulder clay but on the inside of kerbstone 8 (section C–D) this layer was overlain by shale. The mound may, therefore, have been of layer construction.

The kerb (Fig. 25; Pl. 8b)

Only about half of the original kerbstones remain, twelve *in situ* (1–12), and a possibly moved example (B) has already been referred to. Those in position are along the eastern arc of the site and 2–12 were more or less contiguous. Most are subrectangular. On the south-eastern side the kerb curves inwards to form a shallow recess before the entrance. The entrance stone is flat-topped. None of the stones is in a socket. Nos 2–7 and 9–11 overlay Neolithic domestic features (p. 211) and 1, 8 and 12 were placed on the old ground surface.

MATERIALS AND DIMENSIONS OF KERBSTONES

No.	Type of Rock	Maximum dimensions (cm)		
		Length	Width	Height
1	Coarse crinoidal limestone with chert	153	33	56
2	Coarse crinoidal limestone	141	72	74
3	Coarse crinoidal limestone with chert	142	50	60
4	Brown sandstone	133	15	85
5	Green grit	241	24	79
6	Pale sandstone	192	20	89
7	Brown sandstone	154	15	87
8	Limestone	179	28	33
9	Limestone	133	52	49
10	Green grit	132	22	101
11	Brown sandstone	162	19	49
12	Dolomitic limestone	153	17	75

Finds

No finds that could be associated with the building and primary use of the tomb were made.

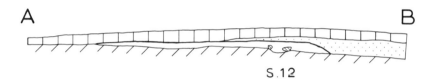

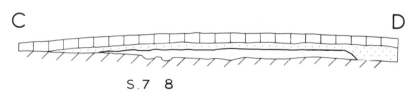

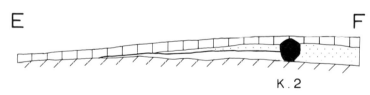

Fig. 24—Site 7: sections.

© G.Eogan 1979

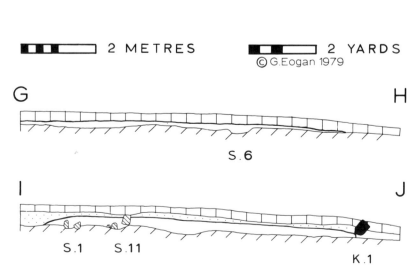

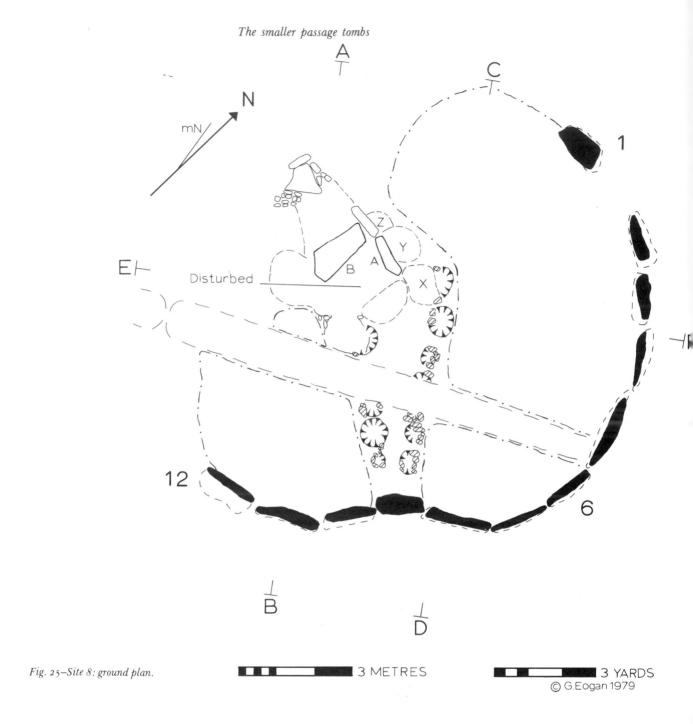

Fig. 25—Site 8: ground plan.

3 METRES

3 YARDS

© G. Eogan 1979

Megalithic art

There is art on two kerbstones.

Kerbstone 5 (Fig. 63:3; Pl. 44b) has two pocked motifs on the outer face. One motif, almost circular, has a projection at the bottom right with an irregular unpocked interior. The other is a short zig-zag.

Kerbstone 11 (Fig. 63:4; Pl. 45a) has decoration on the base; it is pocked but the motifs are vague. Somewhat heart-shaped area near one end has a dot in the centre. There is a pocked area of irregular shape in the centre and near the other end a curved line and transverse stem.

SITE 9 (Fig. 28; Pl. 9b)

There were no surface indications of this rather unusual cruciform tomb before work commenced. The site had been badly damaged. With one possible exception all the kerbstones had been removed. Only the stump of one orthostat (8), was preserved. The digging of a ditch (Ditch No. 2, Eogan 1968, 355) destroyed the outer part of the passage. Another ditch had been dug across the northern side of the mound. The tomb had also been interfered with. An inhumation burial (16), probably of the Iron Age or later, had been inserted across the right-hand recess.

The tomb (Fig. 29; Pl. 9a)

Evidence for the tomb is provided by twenty-eight sockets, dug into the boulder clay for an average depth of 25cm. They are generally well preserved, especially in the chamber area where many of the packing stones remain *in situ*. Positive evidence for only one orthostat remained, in socket 8. This is a stump of green grit 25cm high.

The tomb, consisting of a passage leading into a cruciform chamber, is aligned east-west with the entrance at the eastern side facing Site 1. From the inner edge of socket 14 to the edge of the ditch the surviving part of the tomb is 6.80m in length.

Only ten sockets (1–4, 23–28) of the passage remain. The old ground surface had been removed from around at least sockets 1–2 and 26–28, so their original edges do not survive. The damage may have been done when the ditch (No. 2 Eogan 1968, 355) was dug.

Pl. 8b–Site 8: general view from east after excavation.
Portion of kerb of Site 1 is in foreground, upright stones between it and Site 8 are part of a stone alignment.
Scatter of stones outside entrance to Site 8 is superficial material not excavated when photograph was taken.

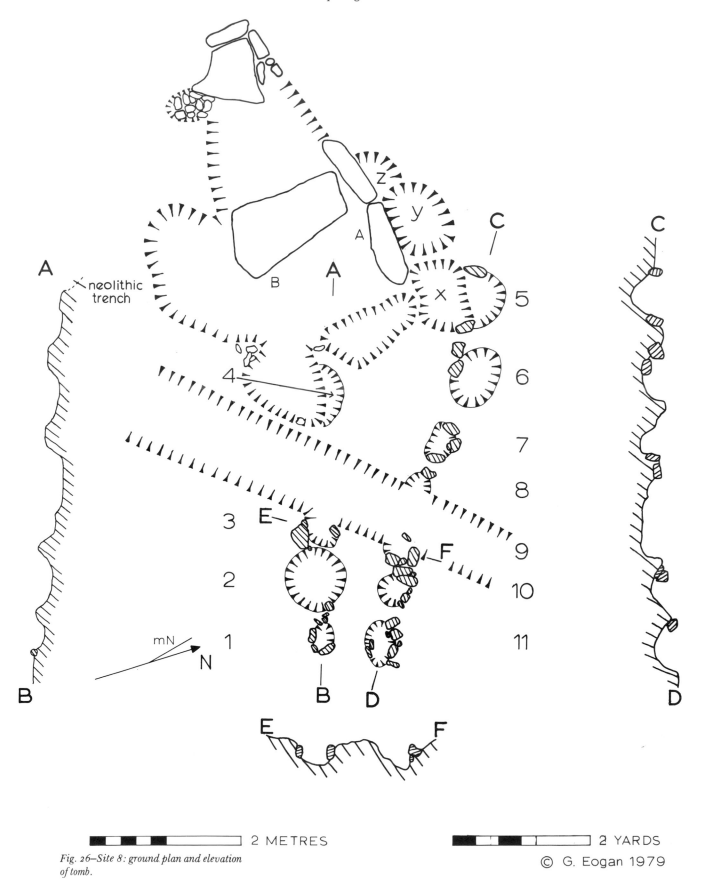

Fig. 26—Site 8: ground plan and elevation of tomb.

2 METRES

2 YARDS

© G. Eogan 1979

Some packing stones remained in Nos 3–4 and 23–25. The angle between the sides of the passage suggests that it widened towards the entrance.

There had been at least one sillstone (a). This stood at the junction between the passage and the chamber. The socket extends for the full width of the passage 85cm at this point, between sockets 4 and 22.

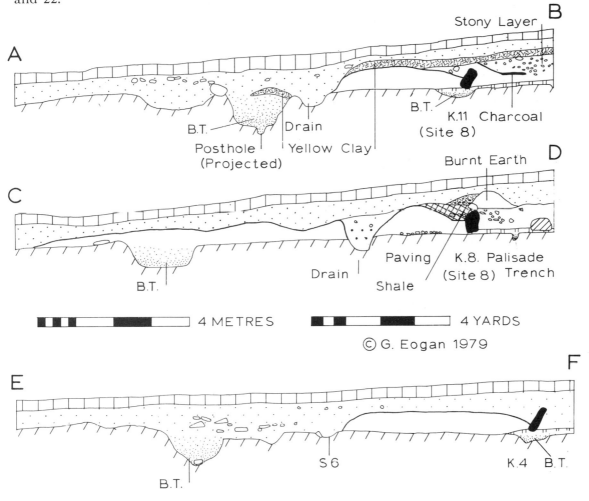

B.T. = Bedding Trench of Structure (see p. 211)

Fig. 27–Site 8: sections.

The approximate internal dimensions of the chamber are 4.00m by 3.80m. The right-hand recess measures 1.10m by 90cm internally and consists of five sockets (18–22). The inner edges of sockets 19–21 were damaged when the inhumation burial (16) was inserted into the recess. Socket 20 would have contained the backstone. The left-hand recess is slightly smaller, 1.10m by 70cm. It also consists of five sockets (5–9). As indicated above, socket 8 contains the only remaining orthostat. The end recess is delimited by eight sockets (10–17), and is 2.80m long, narrowing from 1.40m at the entrance to 78cm at the end socket.

The floor of the chamber consists of natural sod. The inner edges of the chamber sockets were dug through this level before penetrating the old ground surface (see section C–D, Fig. 30).

Some small and generally flattish, corbel-like stones were found in the immediate vicinity, especially overlying the central area of the chamber. Chips and flakes of green grits, probably fragments of broken orthostats, were also found. This tumble contained an inhumation burial (15) (publication pending).

The fill in the sockets was of dark clay with some flecks of charcoal and boulder clay. Socket 10 had a higher charcoal content than the others. 19–21 contained considerably more boulder clay owing to the disturbance caused by a later inhumation burial (16).

Pl. 9a–Site 9: general view from south after excavation showing ditch (on right) cutting across passage.

Burials

Two burial deposits were found (Fig. 29) in the end recess. The rite was cremation. No. 3806 lay on the floor between sockets 13, 14 and 15. It covered an oval area 38cm by 22cm and was 2cm deep. It appeared to be in its original position. Dr Weekes reports: 'These are mostly the bones of a child, and there is not more than one child here. There are also at least two pieces of bone which are probably from an adult.' The second deposit (3807) occurred in the eastern portion of the end recess. Part had been removed in more recent times when an inhumation burial (15) was inserted over the central area of the tomb. Some scattered pieces were found mixed in with the inhumation burial and in the sockets (9–11 and 17). It covers a discontinuous area 1.60m by 1.20m. Dr Weekes reports that this represented the remains of at least two individuals, an adult and a child. The adult bones include a permanent lateral incisor, showing little wear, which could be from an individual of about twenty years. There is also a small part of an adult femoral head. The child remains include two deciduous teeth, one a molar. Some charcoal associated with this deposit was examined by Ms Scannell who identified small fragments of *Pteridophyte rhizome* (fern stem), probably *Pteridium* (bracken).

The mound (Fig. 30)

The surviving mound has approximate dimensions of 11.90m north-south and 10.80m east-west. The maximum surviving height is

40cm, while the average is only 15cm. The mound consists of boulder clay. 5.20m south of the end recess is a band of shale which lies partially on the old ground surface and rises up over the basal layer of the mound itself (see section E–F). Lying on this shale is a line of eight flattish boulders with average dimensions of 37cm by 32cm by 15cm. Neither the shale nor the boulder clay extends beyond these stones, perhaps because of destruction, and it is likely that the stones formed part of a setting in the mound within the kerb.

There is little evidence of mound immediately around the chamber, probably because of disturbance when the tomb was destroyed.

The kerb

There is one possible kerbstone (1) which is now in a disturbed position on the eastern edge of Ditch 2 (Eogan 1968, 355). As it is closer to this site than to any other it may have been part of its kerb.

Isolated finds (Fig. 116)

Five sherds of *Beaker pottery* (3745–6) were recovered from disturbed material in the sockets. These sherds are described under *Isolated finds of Beaker pottery* (p. 307; Fig. 116).

Fifteen pieces of *flint* were found. Six of these (3808–13) came from the disturbed fill of the sockets and cannot be considered primary. Of the other pieces, two unworked chips (3814–15) were found with the primary cremation deposit but these may have intruded when the tomb was destroyed. The others (3816–22) were found in the disturbed material which directly overlay the old ground surface where the floor of the tomb had been removed.

Pl. 9b–Site 9: general view from east. Possible kerbstone (right foreground) incorporated in a later ditch revetment.

Fireplace (**Fig. 28**). This underlies the mound 2.20m to the west of the end recess and overlies an area of pebbling which is associated with a wider area of Neolithic activity predating the use of the tomb (see p. 242). A thin layer of brown earth, *c*.3cm deep separates the reddened base of the fireplace from the pebbling. In a central core of charcoal measuring 74cm by 62cm by 4cm deep, two sherds of 'Carrowkeel' ware were found (Fig. 54).

No. 3823 Rimsherd, light in colour throughout, with a pointed rim. Decorated with closely-set oblique lines and below the rim with a row of herring-bone, both formed by stab-and-drag.

No. 3824 Bodysherd, light in colour throughout with traces of what may be a herring-bone pattern executed in stab-and-drag.

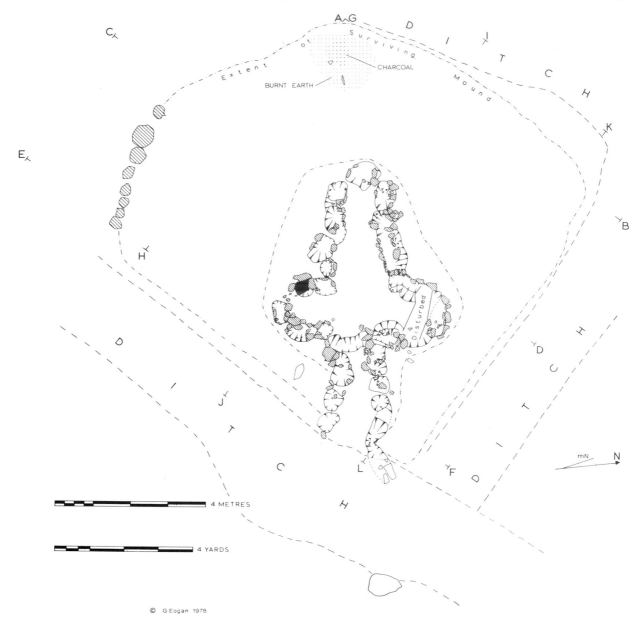

Fig. 28–Site 9: ground plan.

The fireplace also produced two **unworked** chips of burnt flint (Nos 3825–26). The presence of the layer of brown earth between the fireplace and the pebbling, the fact that the mound directly overlies it and the occurrence of 'Carrowkeel' ware in the charcoal suggest that the fireplace was associated with the construction of the tomb rather than the wider area of Neolithic domestic activity. Charcoal from the fireplace was examined by Ms Scannell but because of its fragmentary condition only two pieces, of *Crataegus* (hawthorn), could be identified.

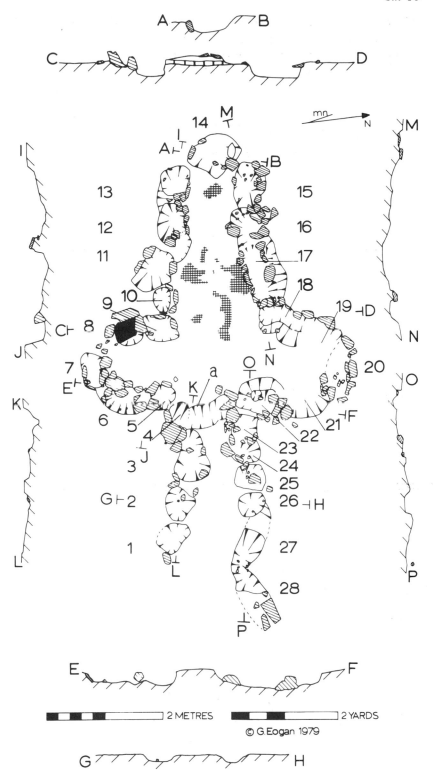

Fig. 29—Site 9: ground plan and elevation of tomb.

SITE 10 (Figs 31 and 32; Pls 10a–b, 11a)

This site came to light during excavations in 1972. It had been very badly damaged. After construction a ditch was dug along the south-eastern side, a continuation of the ditch already noted (Eogan 1968,

355–6, Ditch 2). From the edge of this ditch a drain runs north-westwards across the site. The covering mound was completely removed. The only definite passage-tomb features that survived were two kerbstones and the remains of the chamber.

Fig. 30–Site 9: sections.

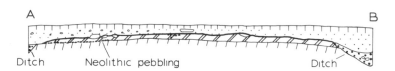

A   B

Ditch   Neolithic pebbling   Ditch

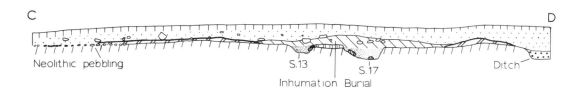

C   D

Neolithic pebbling   S.13   S.17   Ditch

Inhumation Burial

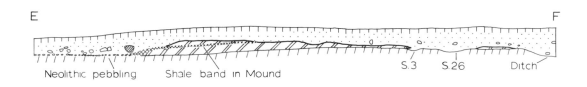

E   F

Neolithic pebbling   Shale band in Mound   S.3   S.26   Ditch

4 METRES   4 YARDS

© G. Eogan 1979

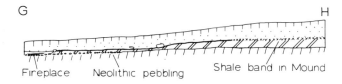

G   H

Fireplace   Neolithic pebbling   Shale band in Mound

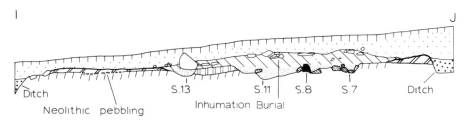

I   J

Ditch   S.13   S.11   S.8   S.7   Ditch

Neolithic pebbling   Inhumation Burial

K   L

Ditch   S.27 S.28   Ditch

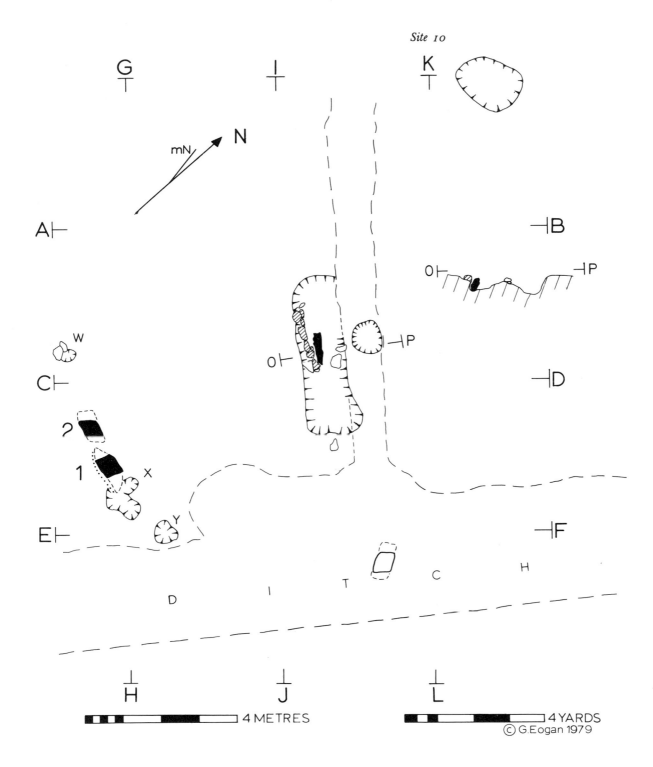

Fig. 31–Site 10: ground plan.

The tomb (Pl. 10b)

A pit and a shallow hole in the base of the drain are being taken as representing the remains of the chamber. The pit, to a large extent, appears to be due to disturbance, possibly when orthostats were being removed. However, the stump of a sandstone orthostat survives and in the pit immediately around it were several chips of sandstone. It seems likely that the orthostat was broken up and that these chips were not removed. To the south of the orthostat stump the pit has a setting of stones along the edge. These appear to be original prop stones. The pit is slightly over 4m long and is deepest at the south-eastern end. A few unidentifiable fragments of cremated bone, probably the remains of the burial deposit, turned up in the fill. The digging of the drain could have destroyed all evidence for the other side of the chamber except for the shallow hole which may be the remains of an orthostat socket. The evidence is too meagre to indicate precisely the type of chamber; in fact the absence of sockets (or even a continuation of the pit) between its south-eastern end and the edge of the drain presents a puzzle. However, it is possible that the tomb was undifferentiated and aligned north-west/south-east with the entrance at the latter side.

Pl. 10a–Site 10: passage sockets from east during excavation and (right) modern drain, (top left) western 'palisade trench' (p. 219).

The kerb (Fig. 31; Pl. 11a)

As already mentioned, no evidence for the mound survives. The two remaining kerbstones occur side by side on the southern part of the site and are set on the old ground surface. No. 1, a volcanic agglomerate, tends to be triangular. The narrow end rests on the old ground surface. The stone has its maximum length, 140cm, close to the top. It is 40cm in maximum width and 90cm high. Despite a packing stone under the eastern corner the top-heavy nature of the stone caused it to lean outwards. No. 2, a limestone, has a much wider base and so is more firmly set. It is 93cm by 45cm and 73cm high.

*Pl. 10b—Site 10: passage sockets from east
showing shattered stump of orthostat.
30 cm scale (right) is in depression that may
be base of socket.*

Another stone lying in the upper fill of the ditch may originally
have been a kerbstone. There are three holes (W, X, Y) on what
appears to be the curve of the kerb but their purpose or date has not
been established. A further stone (V) was found between this site and
Site 11. It was not in its original position but was probably a
kerbstone of one of these sites.

SITE 11 (Figs 33 and 34; Pl. 11b)

Before excavation the area was quite flat and only the extreme tips
of four kerbstones were visible.

The kerb (Fig. 33)

The remains consist of an arc of stones that averaged 95cm long by
65cm high. Twenty-one stones remain, sixteen in their original
position. A stone is missing between 7 and 8; otherwise there is a
complete stretch between 3 and 15. Five stones have been displaced:
three (16–18) were moved only slightly, 19 was lying on the inner lip
of Ditch 2, while 20 was in its fill. None was in a socket but most had
propstones at the bases. There was a small amount of deposited earth
under No. 1. No. 21 overlay portion of the eastern palisade trench (p.
219 below), in the fill of which a foundation of small stones was
placed. Groups of small stones to the south-east of No. 1, between 1
and 2 and close to the west end of 3 may also have been propstones.

MATERIAL AND DIMENSIONS OF STONES

No.	Type of Rock	Maximum dimensions (cm)		
		Length	Width	Height
1	Dolerite	90	47	45
2	Dolerite	94	72	67
3	Conglomerate	80	30	60
4	Dolerite	100	72	64
5	Dolerite	74	38	54
6	Fossiliferous limestone	77	40	53
7	Fossiliferous limestone	95	50	52
8	Dolomitic limestone	76	56	51
9	Fossiliferous limestone	82	60	50
10	Fossiliferous limestone	76	55	60
11	Fossiliferous limestone	94	57	74
12	Fossiliferous limestone	75	40	60
13	Agglomerate (?) striated	115	90	78
14	Fossiliferous limestone	95	65	63
15	Fossiliferous limestone	110	82	57
16	Fossiliferous limestone	115	70	78
17	Fossiliferous limestone	86	65	54
18	Finegrained limestone	100	68	82
19	Sandstone	92	50	75
20	Fossiliferous limestone	100	45	58
21	Finegrained limestone	75	42	66

Fig. 32—Site 10: sections.

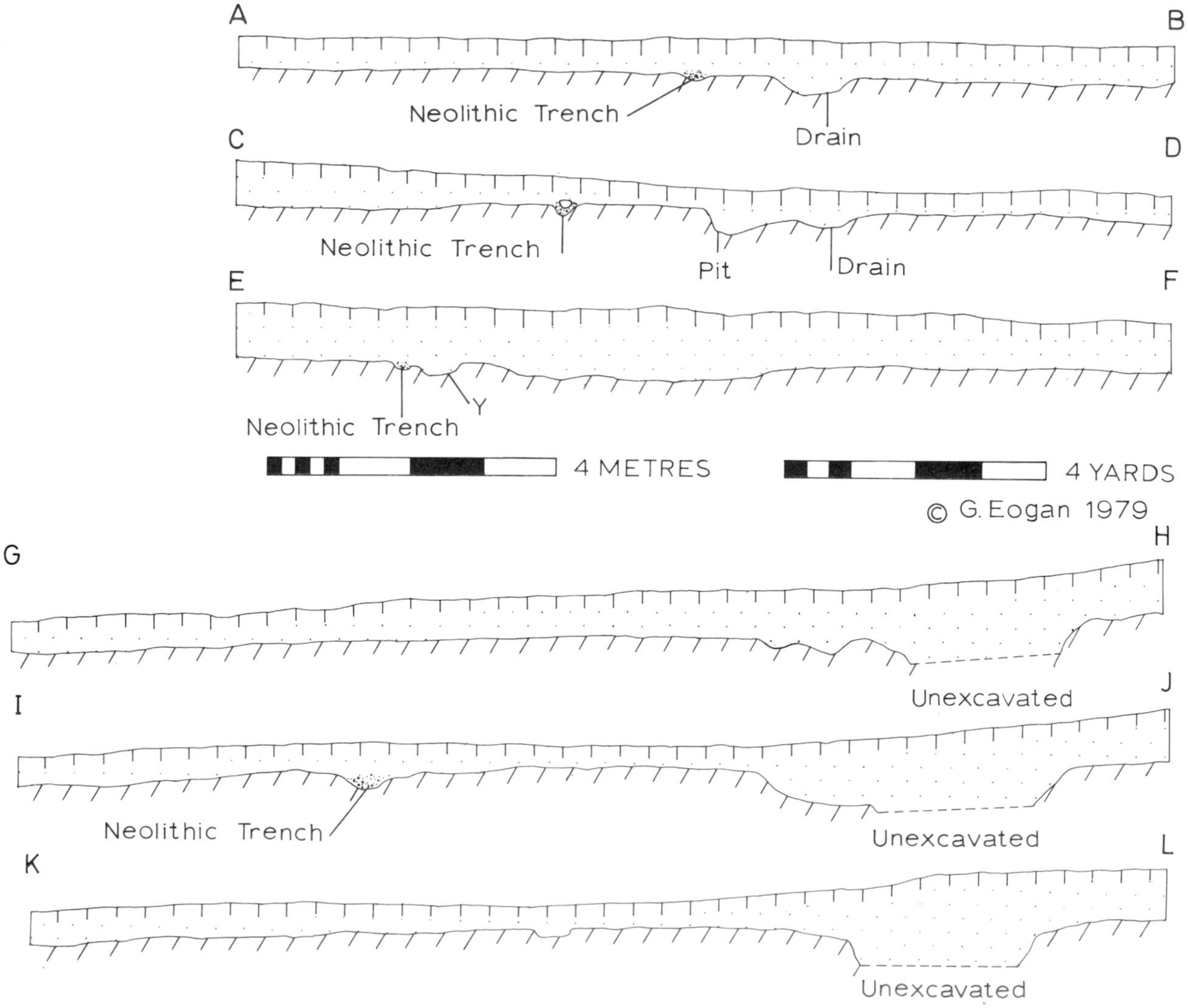

A — B
Neolithic Trench
Drain

C — D
Neolithic Trench
Pit
Drain

E — F
Neolithic Trench
Y

4 METRES   4 YARDS

© G. Eogan 1979

G — H
Unexcavated

I — J
Neolithic Trench
Unexcavated

K — L
Unexcavated

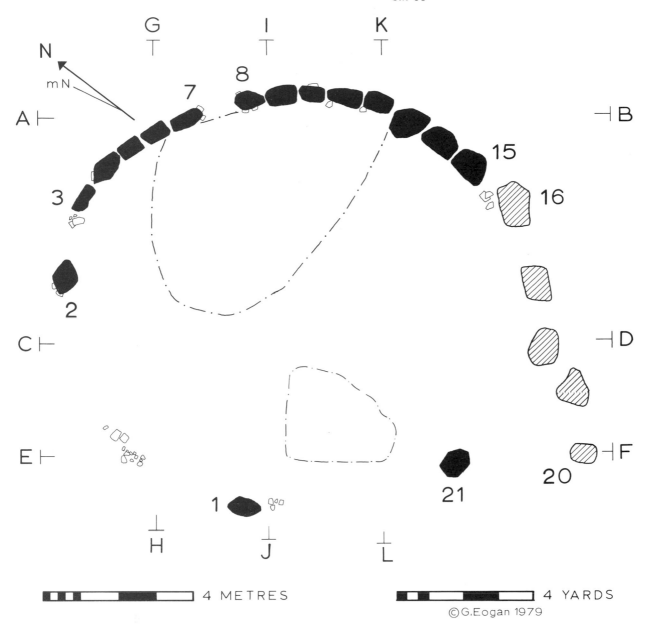

Fig. 33—Site 11: ground plan.

The stones indicated a circular area *c.* 11.50m in diameter. The only internal feature was a pit, 186cm by 92cm and 40cm deep. There were animal bones in the fill of dark earth. At least ox and horse were represented but it appears that these were of fairly recent date, as suggested by lack of bleaching, for instance (Eogan 1968, 363, Pit No. 3). There was no positive evidence for a mound. Underlying the humus, the enclosed area had a fill of soft dark earth over the natural subsoil which was boulder clay with shale protruding through it in places. However, in some places, especially in the northern half, brown soil occurred over the subsoil. This averaged 30cm thick. On the inside of stones 12 and 13 a wedge-shaped layer of shale extended inwards for 1.00m to 1.30m.

Despite the lack of evidence for a tomb, the stones, the layering (if only in a limited area) and the site's presence within a passage tomb complex indicate that these remains are part of a passage tomb.

Finds

Eighteen flints were found (45, 46a-q). Only one burnt piece (45) has definite evidence of working along the concave edge. Found on the surface of the subsoil. The other pieces were in the dark earth. One is a poor specimen of a blade (46a); the remainder are waste pieces (46b-q). None is illustrated.

Pl. 11a—Site 10: kerbstones from north-east after excavation.

SITE 12 (Fig. 35; Pl. 12b)

Before excavation kerbstones 1–4 and part of kerb 5 were visible. The tips of 6 and 7 and orthostat 4 protruded. Because of the presence of the kerbstones, traces of the mound remained along the northern side.

The tomb (Fig. 36; Pl. 12a)

This undifferentiated passage tomb was aligned north-south, with the entrance on the southern side. At least fifteen orthostats formed the tomb, seven on each side and one at the back, but only the backstone, two sidestones and part of a sillstone survived. Of these, only one (4), a micaceous grit, was intact and in its original position. It is 1.14m in maximum height; the inner face is flat but widens outwards at the back and is 55cm in maximum thickness at midpoint. The other sidestone (5), also a micaceous grit, was pushed inwards to the northern end of its socket and its upper portion broken off. The backstone (8) was lying flat in the tomb. It is sandstone, 1.27m in maximum height, at the broad end 1m wide and 36cm thick. Although the broad end was furthest from the socket its size indicates that it was the base. In the attempt to remove it from the site it must have been turned around. The uppermost face as discovered is slightly concave and most of its surface is pocked over. A band 20cm wide and parallel to the broad end remains unpocked, probably because the dressing took place after the erection of the stone while its base was in the socket and obscured by fill.

The sockets average 15cm in depth but some sockets, notably 4 and 10, were so shallow that the orthostats must have been held in position mainly by packing stones. Except No. 8, which may have been damaged when its orthostat was being removed, all the other sockets had packing stones. The tomb tends to be trapezoidal. Only part of the sillstone that cuts off the inner end of the tomb survived.

Fig. 34–Site 11: sections.

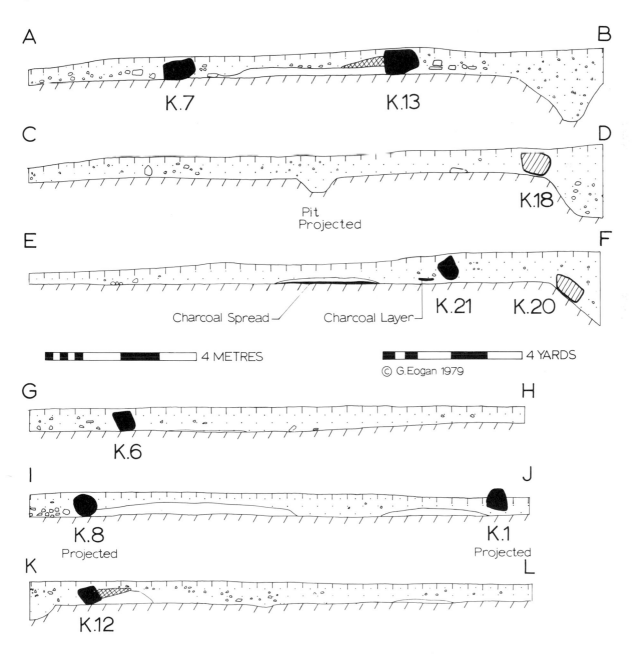

A — B
K.7   K.13

C — D
Pit Projected   K.18

E — F
Charcoal Spread   Charcoal Layer   K.21   K.20

4 METRES   4 YARDS

© G.Eogan 1979

G — H
K.6

I — J
K.8 Projected   K.1 Projected

K — L
K.12

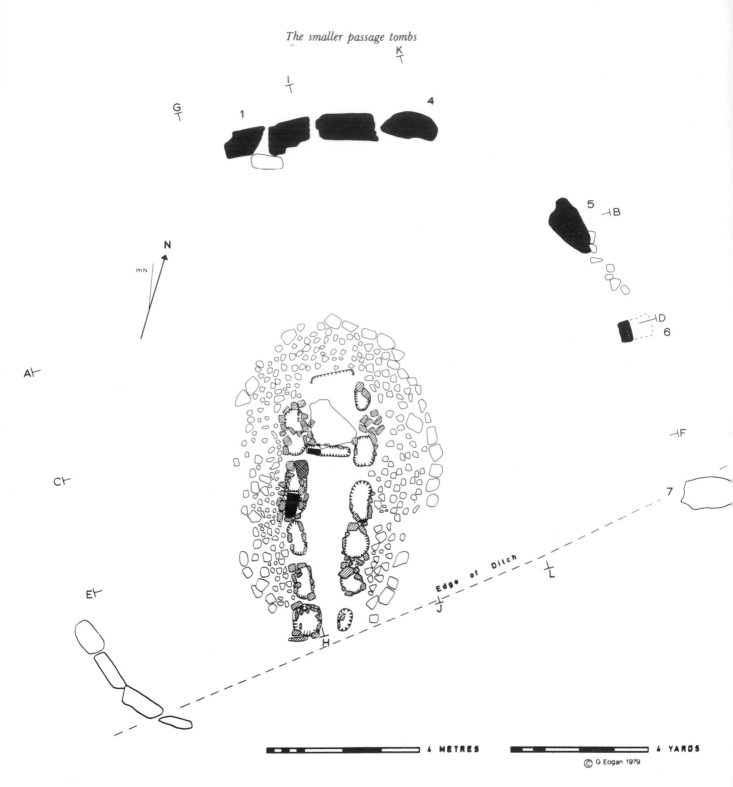

Fig. 35–Site 12: ground plan.

It is 45cm high and sunk into the socket to a depth of 25cm. The socket is 1.14m long. The tomb is 6.75m long internally but this may not be its total length as there is a ditch along the southern side. However, the narrowing of the tomb would have made it impossible to enter if it extended further northwards.

The tomb was enclosed with a low, oval-shaped *core* of stones. On the western side the edge is irregular but on the northern and eastern sides stones larger than those in the cairn were regularly placed along the edge. The insertion of a hearth, of much later date, damaged a portion of the eastern side.

Burials and grave goods

Some cremated bone was found in the 'chamber' (the part inward from the sillstone). Owing to their fragmented condition it was not possible for Dr Weekes to identify many pieces. The identifiable pieces consist of a fragment of the supraorbital margin of a skull, another skull fragment from the region of the suture, a tibia of an infant under one year, probably parts of the ribs of an infant, and an adult tooth, probably a right lower second molar of the second dentition which shows some caries but no attrition (16).

Associated with the bones were pieces of polished bone pins (Fig. 11). No. 17 is a tip 17.5mm long. It has a D-shaped cross-section and is 4mm wide at the fracture. 18a is part of a stem that tends to be oval in cross-section but with a flat surface on one side. It is 19mm long and 12.5mm in maximum width. This is a more substantial piece than No. 17. The third piece (18b), also from a shaft, is smaller in diameter and may be part of another pin.

The mound (Fig. 37)

The mound survived over a fairly large area but only to a maximum height of 75cm. Very little remained over the core; at other points hearths and a pit were dug into it. In the main the mound was composed of dark shaly material but at some points, especially on the west side the basal 20cm or so was sticky and greyish. This is probably due to mixing sods with shale. The original sod layer remained and over most of its surface there was iron pan about 1cm thick.

Pl. 11b—Site 11: View from east after excavation.

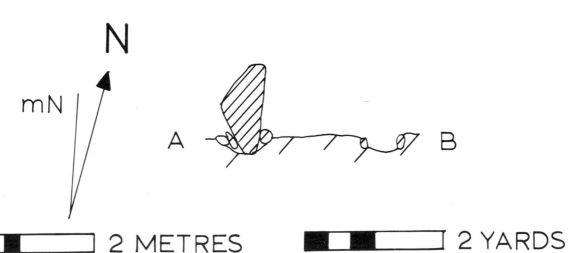

8
7
6
5
4
3
2
1

9
10
11
12
13
14
15

$\overline{A}$
$\overline{A}$

$\overline{B}$
$\overline{B}$

N

mN

A   B

■□■□▭ 2 METRES

■□■▭ 2 YARDS

Fig. 36—Site 12: ground plan and elevation of tomb.

© G Eogan 1979

Finds (Fig. 54)

Six flints (21–26) were found in the mound. None is an artifact but all have limited evidence of working. 21–22 have been burnt.

The kerb (Fig. 35; Pl. 13a)

Eleven stones are considered to be from the kerb. Six are in their original positions (1–6) but No. 6 had tilted outwards. 1–4 are contiguous. The disturbed stones (7–11) were moved outwards but precisely where they stood originally has not been established. Between kerbs 5 and 6 are some small stones that may have been props. There is no evidence for sockets. The kerb appears to have been about 14.7m in external diameter.

Pl. 12a–Site 12: Tomb and surrounding cairn during excavation. View from southeast.

MATERIALS AND DIMENSIONS OF KERBSTONES

| No. | Type of Rock | Maximum dimensions (cm) | | |
		Length	Width	Height
1	Agglomerate	114	70	84
2	Limestone	116	78	87
3	Dolomitic limestone	157	64	88
4	Dolerite	150	70	85
5	Dolomitic limestone	150	77	75
6	Sandstone	55	35	71
7	Agglomerate	145	79	75
8	Green grit	128	57	*c.*80
9	Volcanic agglomerate	128	42	*c.*80
10	Limestone	107	45	*c.*80
11	Volcanic ash	*c.*60	40	*c.*80

Megalithic art (Fig. 64:1; Pl. 46a)

There is art, consisting of two groups of pocked circles, on one kerbstone (6). The smaller group has a depression in the centre, surrounded by three circles. Part of the outer arc is missing as a flake has become detached. A groove running out from the depression is hardly original. The large group has four circles, but the outer one is irregular, and between the two groups there is some pocking.

Almost the entire inner surface of the backstone of the tomb (8) is pocked (Pl. 45b).

Pl. 12b–Site 12: tomb from south-east after excavation.

SITE 13 (Fig. 38; Pl. 13b)

No features were visible before excavation began.

The tomb (Fig. 39; Pl. 14a-b)

The tomb is aligned north-north-west/south-south-east with the entrance on the south-south-east side. It is 5.60m in internal length and tends to be bottle-shaped. About half-way in is a sillstone, 90cm long and 50cm high. The portion of the tomb between the sillstone and the entrance is parallel-sided, 3m long, and has six sockets on the western side and five on the eastern. There is evidence for eight orthostats. Five stones (1–2 and 18–20) are intact, but the upper portions of 3–5 have been broken off. There are three capstones at the outer part of the passage. Two are over orthostats 1, 2, 19, 20. The third was in an almost vertical position between kerbstone 16 and orthostats 1 and 20 (Pl. 14a).

The portion of the tomb from the sill inwards is 2.50m in internal length. There are four sockets on each side and one at the back. The orthostats or capstones have not survived. All sockets, including that for the sillstones, have packing stones. The stone in the northern part of socket 13 is much larger than normal but does not appear to be the remains of an orthostat. Extending towards socket 9 from between sockets 13 and 14 is a row of four small stones. These are angular and therefore were not paving stones. Neither do they appear to have supported another sillstone.

MATERIALS AND DIMENSIONS OF ORTHOSTATS

No.	Type of Rock	Maximum dimensions (cm)		
		Length	Width	Height
1	Slate	46	20	93
2	Dolomitic limestone	50	22	129
3	Green grit	54	23	—
4	Calcareous sandstone	35	31	—
5	Calcareous sandstone	46	44	—
18	Cleaved grit	60	22	124
19	Limestone	48	34	128
20	Fine-grained grit	53	36	110
Sill	Limestone	8	10	53

Burials

There was a scatter of cremated bone over the floor of the inner part of the tomb beyond the sill. As they were in a very fragmentary state it was not possible for Dr Weekes to identify any pieces (10).

Fig. 37–Site 12: sections.

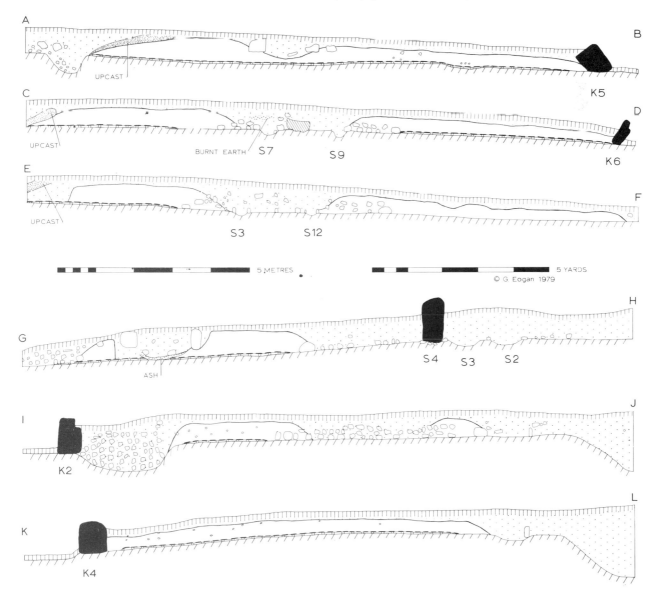

© G. Eogan 1979

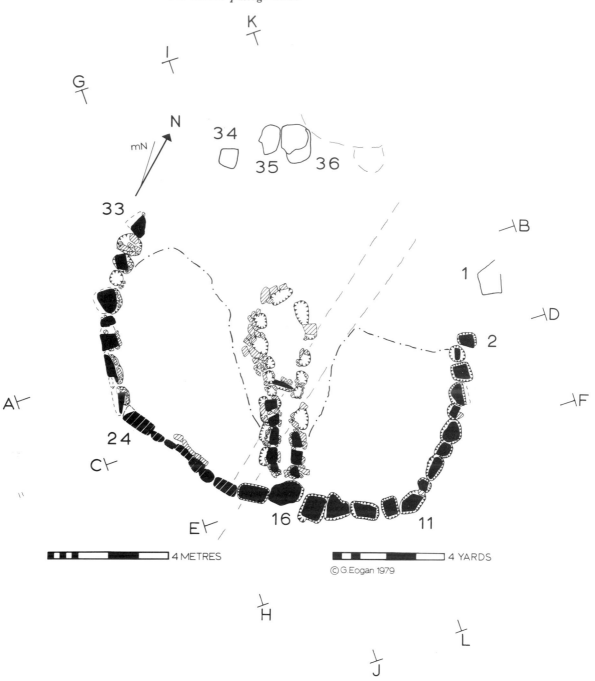

Fig. 38–Site 13: ground plan.

The mound (Fig. 40)

Only portions of the mound to the east and west of the chamber survive and these reach a maximum height of 80cm. Sod was the material used. The diameter seems to have been about 12m.

The kerb (Fig. 38; Pl. 13b)

The northern portion is missing and part of the perimeter at the south-west was altered in antiquity (see below p. 79). With the exception of two stones (30 and 32) the kerb is complete from 2 to 33. Nos 1 and 34–36 may be displaced kerbstones. Except **18–24** the stones were standing in shallow sockets and some were further secured with packing stones at the base. 18–23 are much smaller than the other kerbstones. Their tops are at the same height as the others but to achieve this they were placed on top of a fill of small stones (sections C–D, G–H, Fig. 40; Pl. 15a).

MATERIALS AND DIMENSIONS OF KERBSTONES

No.	Type of Rock	Maximum dimensions (cm)		
		Length	Width	Height
1	Limestone	105	71	35
2	Slate	47	35	100
3	Limestone	40	18	53
4	Dolerite	55	60	80
5	Agglomerate	68	60	115
6	Limestone	60	30	60
7	Dolomitic limestone	64	60	90
8	Dolomitic limestone	62	35	105
9	Agglomerate	85	53	89
10	Dolomitic limestone	49	42	116
11	Limestone	76	60	91
12	Dolomitic limestone	70	53	132
13	Limestone	88	25	112
14	Limestone	90	77	106
15	Micaceous grit	65	68	121
16	Coarse limestone	131	75	98
17	Green grit	82	45	111
18	Dolerite	90	50	46
19	Dolerite	45	29	33
20	Dolerite	50	35	55
21	Calcareous sandstone	57	28	71
22	Dolerite	48	37	35
23	Dolomitic limestone	50	26	41
24	Calcareous sandstone	101	45	43
25	Limestone	98	21	130
26	Dolomitic limestone	124	18	112
27	Coarse grit	70	52	112
28	Fine green grit	30	34	96
29	Dolerite	90	69	105
30	—	—	—	—
31	Agglomerate	59	53	103
32	—	—	—	—
33	Limestone	67	25	88
34	Limestone	67	52	45
35	Calcareous sandstone	97	57	43
36	Agglomerate	This stone has been split in the middle		

Finds (Fig. 54)

Two flint artifacts, a slug knife and a thumb scraper were the only finds. The *slug-shaped flint knife* (13) had a worked convex surface; the other side is flat. Found in the mound to the east of the tomb.

The *thumb-shaped scraper* (11) was found in disturbed material in the chamber so it cannot definitely be associated with the tomb. It is made from a flake that thickens from the bulbar end to the scraping edge, which has been damaged slightly, and there are scars on one surface.

Megalithic art

There was art on one of the passage orthostats, four kerbstones and a further possible kerbstone.

Pl. 13a–Site 12: kerbstones 1–4 (right to left).

Pl. 13b–Site 13: general view from south after excavation.

Orthostat 3 (Fig. 64:2) had a number of finely incised lines and a small area of pocking on the inner surface.

Stone 15 (Fig. 64:3; Pl. 46b) has a spiral of three turns on the top. On the outer face, to the left, is a small gapped circle surrounded by

Fig. 39—Site 13: ground plan and elevation of tomb.

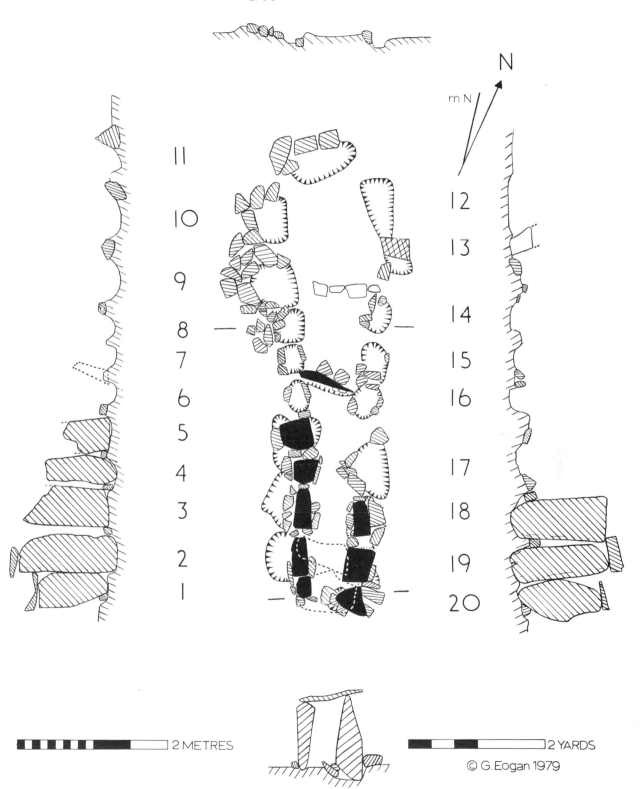

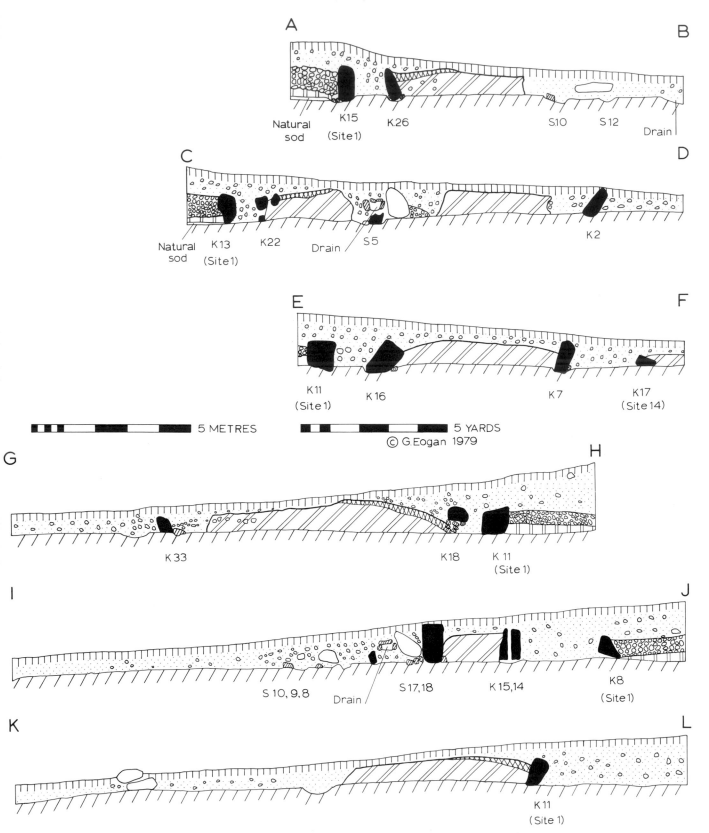

Fig. 40—Site 13: sections.

an oval with another gapped circle on the outside. Three concentric gapped circles form the other design.

Stone 16 (Fig. 64:4; Pl. 47a). The design on this stone is damaged by weathering but it may have been a spiral within a spiral. There are the remains of another motif, perhaps three concentric gapped circles, to the left.

Stone 17 (Fig. 64:5; Pl. 47b) has two short areas of pocking near the top right-hand corner.

Stone 24 (Fig. 64:6; Pl. 48a) has a single motif on the upper face consisting of a zig-zag with rounded curves and a horizontal extension at one end.

Another *stone* (Fig. 64:7; Pl. 48b) formed portion of the side of a late drain on the eastern side of the tomb. Originally it might have been a kerbstone. One motif is a multiple concentric circle, the other appears to be a spiral.

Remarks

Like Site 16, this site was altered when Site 1 was built. The kerb of Site 1 was curved inwards to avoid Site 13 as far as possible, and part of the kerb and mound of Site 13 was removed so that the kerb of Site 1 would not have to curve so far inwards to avoid it. Along the newly created edge of Site 13 a new kerb, symbolic rather than functional, consisting of seven smallish stones (18–24) propped up on rubble, was erected. This alteration is responsible for the irregular shape of the kerb: originally it would have had a flattish façade.

Pl. 14a–Site 13: tomb from south after excavation.

Pl. 14b–Site 13: tomb from north after excavation.

SITE 14 (Fig. 41; Pl. 15b)

The protruding tips of some of the tomb stones over ground led Coffey (1892, 68; 1912, 61) to believe that these represented a passage leading into the large mound (Site 1). Following this suggestion of Coffey's, Macalister excavated the interior of the tomb (Macalister 1943, 132–4).

The tomb (Fig. 42; Pl. 15b)

The tomb is aligned north-north-east/south-south-west with the entrance on the south-south-west side. Internally the tomb is 5.40m long. Although termed 'undifferentiated' the tomb is divided into a passage and chamber. This is clear not only from the prominent sillstone 70cm high but also because the chamber has two massive side-stones, whereas the side-stones of the passage are much smaller. The passage is 3.40m long. It was formed by eleven orthostats, six on the eastern side and five on the western, one of which (5) has been removed. Orthostats 1 and 10 were sitting on the old ground surface and were held in place by packing stones at the base. 11 and 14 were in shallow sockets and the remainder stood in sockets that averaged from 10cm to 20cm in depth. These orthostats also had packing stones at their bases. On the inside of orthostats 11 and 12 were seven flat stones on the old ground surface, forming a sort of paving. A pit containing dark earth and charcoal occurred at the entrance. Its association with the tomb or date in general has not been established.

The chamber is 1.67m long internally by 1.60m in average width. Neither the backstone, which had fallen outwards, nor the sillstone was in a socket. The side-stones, however, were well secured. The socket of No. 6 was 46cm in maximum depth and that of No. 8 was 22cm in maximum depth. Added security was provided by packing stones. The only evidence for a roof was a capstone found in a displaced position on the outside of orthostat 9 (section C–D, Fig. 43).

MATERIAL AND DIMENSIONS OF ORTHOSTA

No.	Type of Rock	Maximum dimensions (cm)		
		Length	Width	Height
1	Green slate	44	20	135
2	Green slate	30	30	135
3	Green cleaved grit	50	19	134
4	Green cleaved grit	80	22	140
5	——	—	—	—
6	Green slate	295	67	178
7	Green cleaved grit	173	35	90
8	Green cleaved grit	238	82	164
9	Green cleaved grit	58	30	140
10	Micaceous sandstone	65	36	125
11	Green cleaved grit	78	26	135
12	Green cleaved grit	34	12	125
13	Green cleaved grit	28	13	136
14	Green cleaved grit	43	32	130
Sill	Green slate	120	38	64

Pl. 15a–Site 13: kerbstones 18–24 and rubble support from north.

Burials (6)

The few fragments of cremated bone found on the old ground surface under the southern end of orthostat 6 were too fragmented for Dr Weekes to say if they were human. Macalister, who cleaned out the tomb, did not record any burials. However, Professor Estyn Evans, who was present for a time while the tomb was being excavated, made notes and sketches. These show that there was a scatter of cremated bone over the old ground surface in the inner segment (chamber) (Fig. 44).

The mound (Fig. 43)

This covered a circular area *c*. 12.50m in diameter. It survived to a maximum height of only 60cm. Boulder clay was the material used.

The kerb (Fig. 41: Pls 15b and 16a)

This measured 13.22m in external **diameter**. Twenty stones survive but a fairly large portion is missing on the northern side. No. 1 had slid into a drain, the remainder are in their original position and the

Fig. 41—Site 14: ground plan.

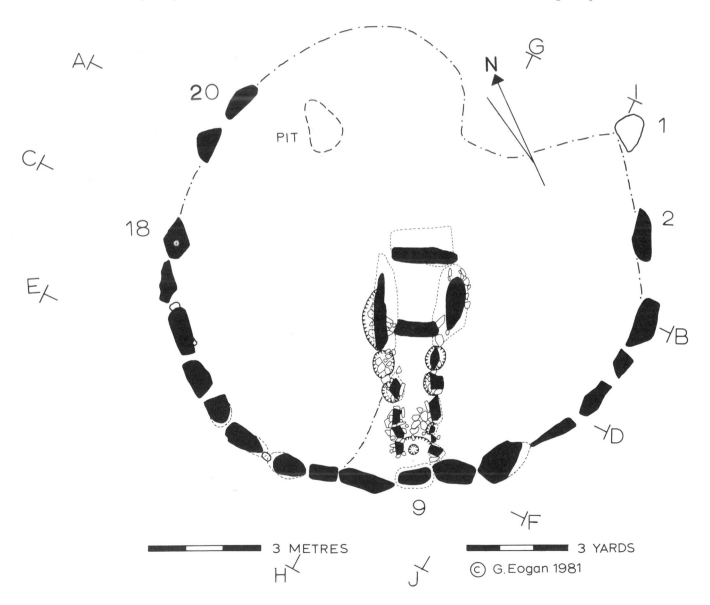

arc from **3** to **18** is complete. All the stones were placed on the old ground surface, some have packing stones at the base.

Pl. 15b–Site 14: general view from south after excavation.

MATERIALS AND DIMENSIONS OF KERBSTONES

No.	Type of Rock	Maximum dimensions (cm)		
		Length	Width	Height
1	Dolomitic limestone	88	65	62
2	Dolerite	140	75	65
3	Agglomerate	150	75	95
4	Green slate	145	50	96
5	Dolomitic limestone	100	60	105
6	Green grit	145	60	120
7	Micaceous (biotite) igneous rock	180	80	90
8	Limestone	110	70	90
9	Dolerite	100	60	75
10	Limestone	110	45	98
11	Conglomerate	95	60	75
12	Coarse sandstone	134	65	90
13	Limestone	115	60	70
14	Dolomitic limestone	105	70	85
15	Agglomerate	115	50	90
16	Agglomerate	135	55	80
17	Dolomitic limestone	115	25	70
18	Dolomitic limestone	100	55	60
19	Limestone	90	60	63
20	Crinoidal limestone	110	48	40

On the eastern side of the passage a *fire* had been lit on the old ground surface. Ms Scannell identified the following woods from the

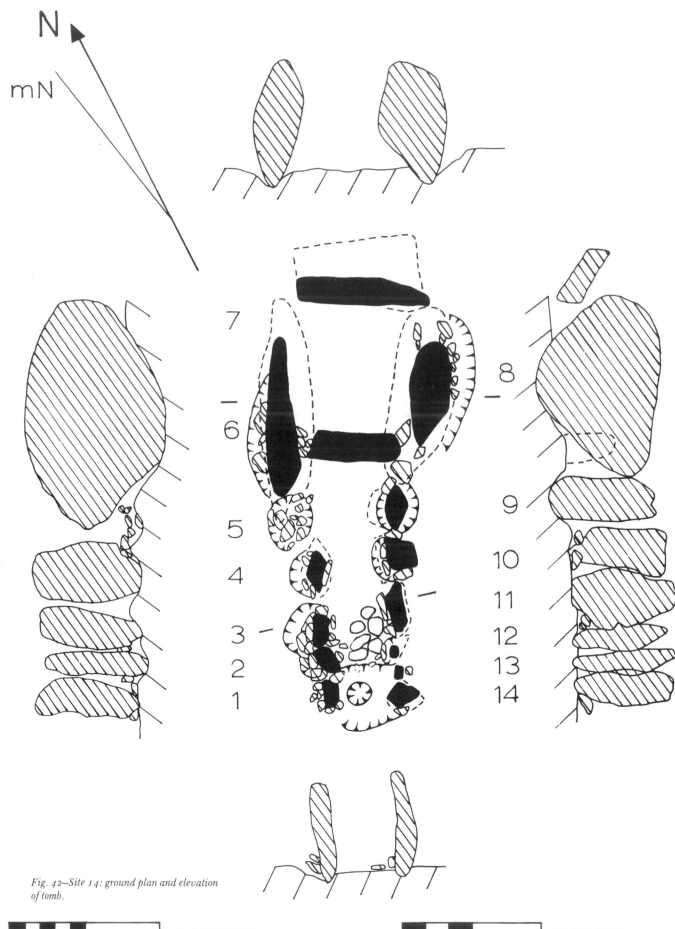

N

mN

7

6

5

4

3

2

1

8

9

10

11

12

13

14

Fig. 42—Site 14: ground plan and elevation
of tomb.

2 METRES

2 YARDS

charcoal: *corylus* (hazel), *quercus* (oak), *ilex* (holly), *salix-populus* (willow poplar), *ulmus* (elm) and *fraxinus* (ash). To the north of the tomb was a pit 48cm deep. The fill consisted of dark earth and charcoal. Amongst the fifty identifiable pieces of charcoal only one was *fraxinus* (ash) and the remaining forty-nine pieces were of *quercus* (oak).

Isolated finds (Fig. 54)

Two flint scrapers were the only finds. One is a *thumb-scraper* (7) that widens from the bulbar end to the steep edge. From the original surface north-east of Pit 1. The other *scraper* (8) is irregular in shape. At one point there is a patch of cortex. Secondary working runs around most of the edge. Found just west of the chamber on top of the mound, but it could not be established whether it was originally deposited in the mound (Eogan 1968, 308, Fig. 20;7).

Megalithic art

Five tomb orthostats and three kerbstones have ornament.

Orthostat 4 (Fig. 65:1; Pl. 49a) has pocked spiral of four and two-thirds turns. To the left is a lobe, and below a pocked area. On the lower right of the spiral is an area of finely incised lines, part of which forms a 'net' pattern. Lower down the stone, to each side, are two designs like a cup and circle. Between them is a poorly formed design resembling a spiral with a single turn.

Orthostat 7 (Fig. 65:2). The designs are faint but one can distinguish two single gapped circles, an arc and other areas of pocking. Macalister (1943, 134, Fig. 3:3) considered that the stone was more highly decorated.

Orthostat 8. There is decoration on the inner and outer faces. Apart from a few incised motifs it is all applied by pocking.

Most of *the inner face* (Fig. 66; Pl. 49b) has ornament. The principal motifs are as follows:

1.   Spiral with lateral motif (Pl. 50b) in the top right-hand central area, consisting of a large spiral of at least six turns. Two parallel lines extend from near the centre to beyond the edge of the motif.

Fig. 43–Site 14: sections.

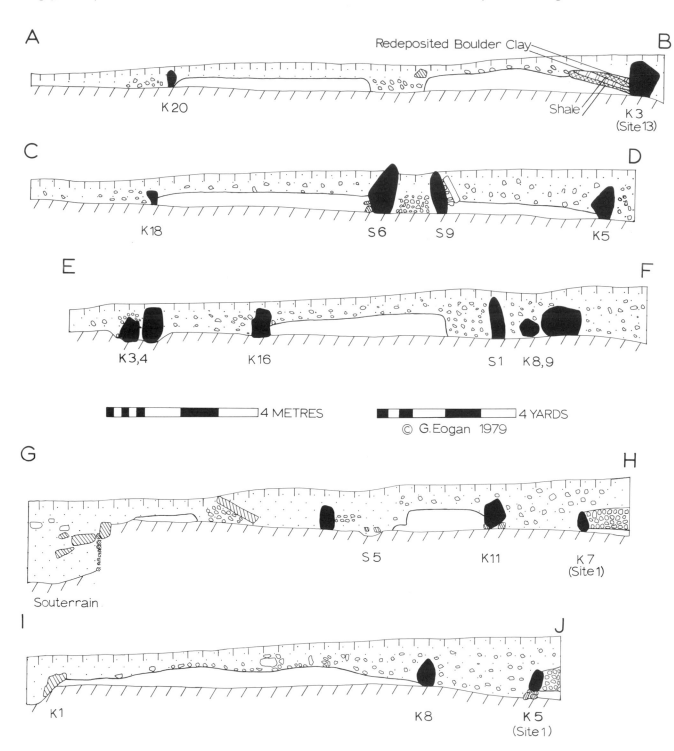

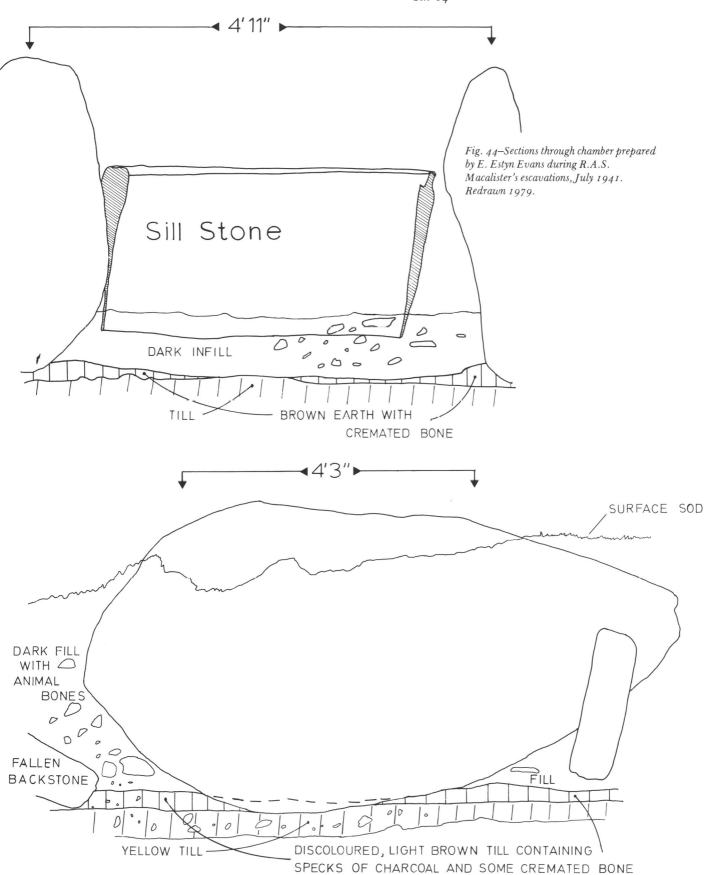

4' 11"

Sill Stone

DARK INFILL

TILL — BROWN EARTH WITH CREMATED BONE

Fig. 44—Sections through chamber prepared by E. Estyn Evans during R.A.S. Macalister's escavations, July 1941. Redrawn 1979.

4'3"

SURFACE SOD

DARK FILL WITH ANIMAL BONES

FALLEN BACKSTONE

FILL

YELLOW TILL — DISCOLOURED, LIGHT BROWN TILL CONTAINING SPECKS OF CHARCOAL AND SOME CREMATED BONE

Attached to the outer turn of the spiral are what appear to be three concentric lozenges.

2. Circles: (a) single circles, (b) multiple circles, (c) gapped or incomplete circles. One design (at the bottom left) consists of a cup mark flanked on one side by six semi-circles.

3. Hurdle-patterns: (a) vertebrates, (b) comb-shaped.

4. Chevrons or zig-zags.

5. Serpentiforms.

6. Triangles, with pocked interiors.

7. Cup marks.

There are also pocked areas, which do not form a design.

The outer face (Fig. 66; Pl. 50a) has the following principal designs:

1. Circles: (a) single circles, (b) multiple circles, (c) multiple circle with lateral motif attached.

2. Dot with external arc of eight rays and four rows of dots on the outside (Pl. 51a).

3. Single spirals.

4. Multiple arcs.

5. Fir-tree or herringbone pattern.

6. Chevrons or zig-zags.

7. Serpentiforms.

Some examples of the last two designs terminate in swellings.

8. Triangles of solid pocked areas.

9. Lozenges: (a) single outline, (b) double outline, (c) solid pocked areas.

Pl. 16b—Sites 1 and 13: kerbs from west at their nearest point.

One design consists of a parallelogram with two-line border, divided by diagonals forming four triangles. Two of these, opposed to each other, are pocked and two are blank.

10. Cup marks.

In addition there are other areas of pocking where specific motifs cannot be identified. Not all the art was applied at the same time. The spiral at the top left-hand corner is superimposed on part of the 'fir-tree' pattern and on a triangle.

Pl. 17a–Site 15: tomb from north during excavation.

Orthostat 10. About the centre there is a pocked circle *c.* 11cm in diameter.

Orthostat 13 (Fig. 65: 3) has an incised vertical **zigzag** of at least four points, *c.* 22cm long, towards the top right side of the inner face.

Stone 4 (Fig. 65:4; Pl. 51b). On the southern end is a zig-zag with rounded curves and one bulbous end. To the lower left there is a small pocked area.

Stone 5 has an arc or gapped circle 6.5cm by 4cm on the back. This may be a natural feature.

Stone 6 (Fig. 65:5; Pl. 52a) has two spirals. That on the left has two and a half turns with an arc attached to it laterally. The other spiral has four turns but it may be unfinished. Between the spirals is some pocking.

Pl. 17b–Site 15: tomb from south during excavation.
Kerbstones 21–23 (bottom).

SITE 15 (Fig. 45; Pls 17–22)

The site had been damaged. The upper part of the mound was lowered and on the western and northern sides portions of it were entirely removed. The kerbstones too had been removed on these sides. The tomb had also been interfered with. During Beaker times a cremation burial accompanied by a Bell beaker was inserted in the tomb (see Fig. 48, S–T; Eogan 1976, 262–64). In the Early Christian period a souterrain was built across part of the site.

The tomb (Figs 46 and 47; Pls 17–20)

This tomb is aligned north-east/south-west. The entrance is on the south-western side and it faces Site 1. The distance from the inner face of kerbstone 22 to the inner face of the socket of the backstone (12) is 9.20m. The tomb was constructed with at least twenty-one orthostats, nineteen of which have survived. Sockets were found for numbers 11 and 12. In these the fill in the central part of the socket differed from that along the edges. The soft stoneless central fill appeared to indicate the actual position of the orthostat.

The position of orthostat 1, at right angles to the line of the passage and leaning slightly towards the kerb, is unusual. It matches orthostat 21 on the opposite side of the passage in length, the face towards the passage is decorated (pp 107–8) and the top of the edge and the outer face have been dressed to give a smoother corner. If the orthostat was set in a straight line the decorated face would be hidden. The orthostat may have been moved around to form part of the small recess immediately inside kerbstone 22, which was created when the entrance area was interfered with by the souterrain builders. If orthostat 1 was originally set lengthwise the western side of the passage would have been longer than the eastern side. Thus it is possible that at least an orthostat is missing from the eastern side, but it does appear that there was a gap between the orthostats and the kerb. Orthostats 16–19 leaned heavily inwards and 20 had fallen outwards. On the outside of 20 was an elongated pit, extending back into the mound which may have been dug as part of an attempt to remove the orthostat. Orthostat 2 may have shifted slightly: its upper end now leans onto No. 1. Orthostats 11 and 12 were missing. In that area a large pit was dug into the mound and at the centre it slightly penetrated the subsoil.

Fig. 45–Site 15: ground plan.

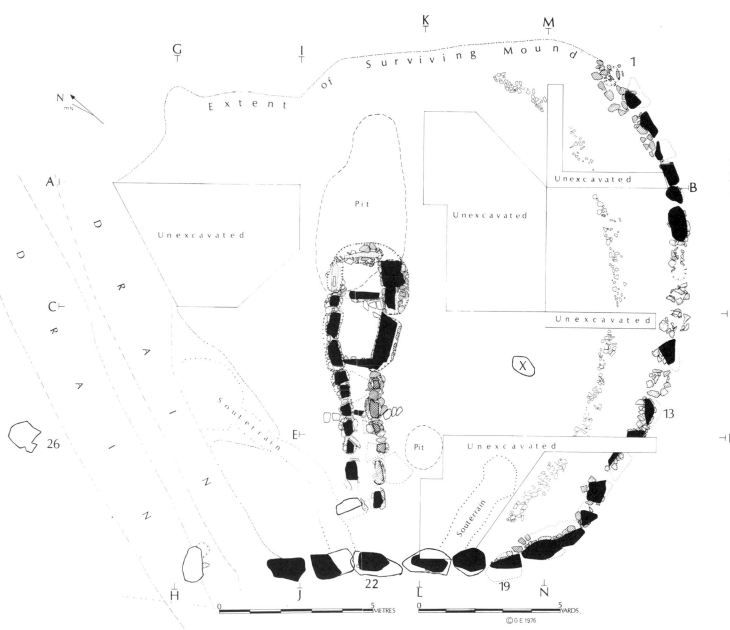

Orthostats 1, 2 and 21 were erected on the old ground surface. The remaining orthostats were in sockets which in most cases were less than 10cm deep. From 8 to 14 the sockets tended to merge into one another. This was especially noticeable with 13 and 14 where there was a pit. Each orthostat was secured by packing or prop stones or by a combination of both. There was a tendency to use a large number of such stones, as at socket 16. The fill of the sockets consisted of earth and packing stones. To give added stability, especially to those stones that were sitting on the old ground surface, prop stones were placed along the edge or ends. Usually these were either partially or wholly under the overhang of the orthostat. Prop stones were placed under the overhanging ends of orthostat 2 and under the ends of the orthostats that stood in sockets 10, 15 and 17–20. In some of the gaps between the orthostats were small stones, which appear to have been placed there deliberately, but not skilfully, and while possibly serving the same function the fillings could not be described as dry-stone walling (Pl. 19).

The orthostats varied in size and shape. The majority have fairly broad tops and the narrow ends, pointed in some cases, are placed downwards (especially 5, 6, 14, 16, 19, 20, 21; two of these, 16 and 19, have pointed ends). There is a tendency for the orthostats to increase in size from the entrance inwards. There are discrepancies in height. It is, therefore, likely that smaller stones were used on top of some orthostats to bring the tops to a uniform height. Some flat flag-like stones which could have served such a purpose were found in the fill of the tomb. All the orthostats appear to be glacial erratics.

Pl. 18a–Site 15: tomb from north after excavation.

Pl. 18b—Site 15: tomb from south after excavation. Part of damaged passage of souterrain 7 (at left).

MATERIALS AND DIMENSIONS OF ORTHOSTATS

No.	Type of Rock	Maximum dimensions (cm)		
		Length	Width	Height
1	Sandy dolomite	96	45	96
2	Sandy dolomite	120	39	120
3	Fine-grained agglomerate	61	32	132
4	Limestone with fossils	64	33	80
5	Sandy dolomite	54	27	104
6	Limestone	53	28	102
7	Sandy dolomite	39	38	120
8	Green grey whacke	100	43	130
9	Sandy dolomite	96	40	116
10	Sandy dolomite	45	37	140
13	Brown sandstone	84	65	149
14	Sandy dolomite	96	41	152
15	Dolomitised limestone	182	59	106
16	Dolomitised limestone	102	35	120
17	Dolomitised limestone	71	30	97
18	Limestone	60	26	105
19	Sandy dolomite	59	33	114
20	Sandy dolomite	100	39	125
21	Limestone	58	24	114

No capstones survived.

In the chamber and inner segment of the passage the lowermost portion of the fill was a grey-brown silt (Fig. 48, layer 1). In the rest of

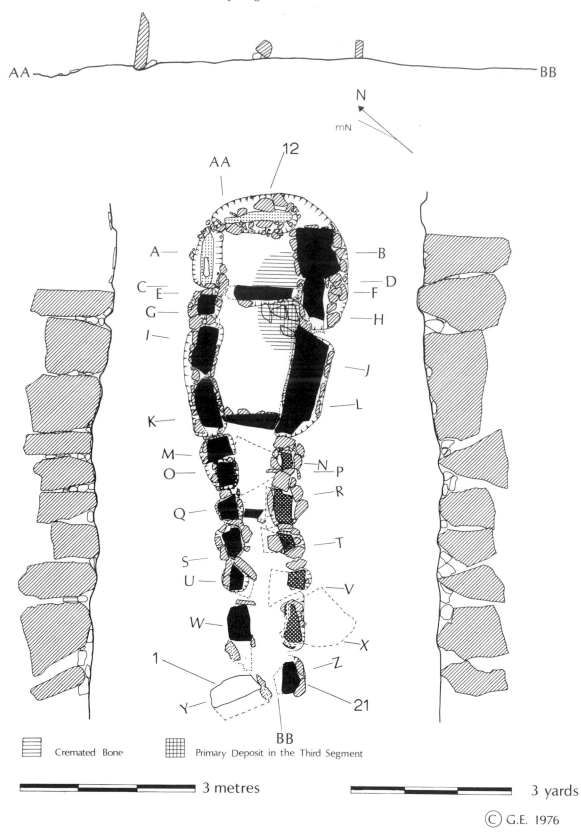

Cremated Bone　　Primary Deposit in the Third Segment

3 metres

3 yards

© G.E. 1976

Fig. 46—Site 15: ground plan and elevation of tomb.

the tomb the lower portion of the fill was soft, silt-like, yellow-brown material (Fig. 48, layer 2). This may have filtered in when the capstones were in position. The upper part of the fill consisted of a mixture of earth and stones (Fig. 48, layer 3). The proportions varied from one part to another. Apparently this material accumulated after the removal of the capstones. In the inner segment (chamber) the pit fill consisted of soft dark earth and stones (Fig. 48, A–B, layer 3).

Pl. 19a–Site 15: view of tomb from west. Chamber of souterrain 7 (foreground).

There were three sillstones, all of green grit. The outermost example (**a**) is 4.40m in from the back of kerbstone 22 and sits on the old ground surface wedged between orthostats 5 and 17. The ends overhang. The second sill (**b**) is 1.40m from the last. It is also sitting on the old ground surface but is well secured on the inner side and gripped between orthostats 8 and 15. Sillstones **a** and **b** are about the same height but the inner sill (**c**) is twice as high and unless the height of the passage was raised by at least 30cm (by placing corbels on the orthostats) it would not be possible to enter the inner segment (chamber).. This inner sill is placed directly against the edge of its socket on the inside, and on the outer side are packing stones.

The tomb tends to be bottled-shaped and consists of four segments. The first pair of orthostats (1 and 21) is about 1.50m from the kerb; they are 40cm apart internally. It is likely that this gap, or part of it, is due to subsequent alteration. From there up to sillstone **a** the passage widens only slightly, to 60cm. After this point the passage splay continues to the inner ends of orthostats 8 and 15 where both sides straighten out and reach a maximum internal width of 1.50m. The inner segment, the chamber, is rectangular, 1.40m by 1.00m internally. Segment 3 is 1.90m long and 1.50m in maximum width. Segment 2 is 1.40m long and it widens inwards from 60cm to 90cm.

Pl. 19b–Site 15: view of tomb from east. Inside the kerb (foreground) is part of setting of small stones delimiting the core. Stone X (centre foreground) has been moved slightly to north of original find position.

Burials

Burial deposits were found in the third and fourth segments. The rite was cremation.

Segment 4 (chamber). The burial occurred in the southern area of the segment (No. 595). It was in the corner and was bounded on one side by orthostat 14 and on another by sillstone c (Fig. 46; Pl. 20a). It covered a sub-triangular area that extended 36cm northwards from the sillstone and 75cm from orthostat 14 towards socket 11. The deposit was mainly a thin scatter of cremated bone mixed with dark earth near the edges. This was probably due to disturbance when this part of the tomb was damaged. The deposit may have been more extensive originally and part of it may have been removed at the time of destruction. However, what survives, or most of it, is in its original position. The deposit was placed on the old ground surface but there is no evidence to indicate whether it was a single deposit or successive deposits. An unburnt human clavicle was found at the top of the cremation and seems to be intrusive. It may be remarked that there were three post-passage-tomb inhumation burials (28–30) in the adjoined segment (3). The clavicle might have been derived from that source. Dr Weekes reports that the cremation deposit is 'a collection of small fragments of bone, the majority so small that it is impossible to identify them. Some at least, including the two largest pieces, are animal bones. There would appear to be two individuals here — a child and a young adult. There are many small pieces which appear to be parts of the limb bones of a child, but none are identifiable.

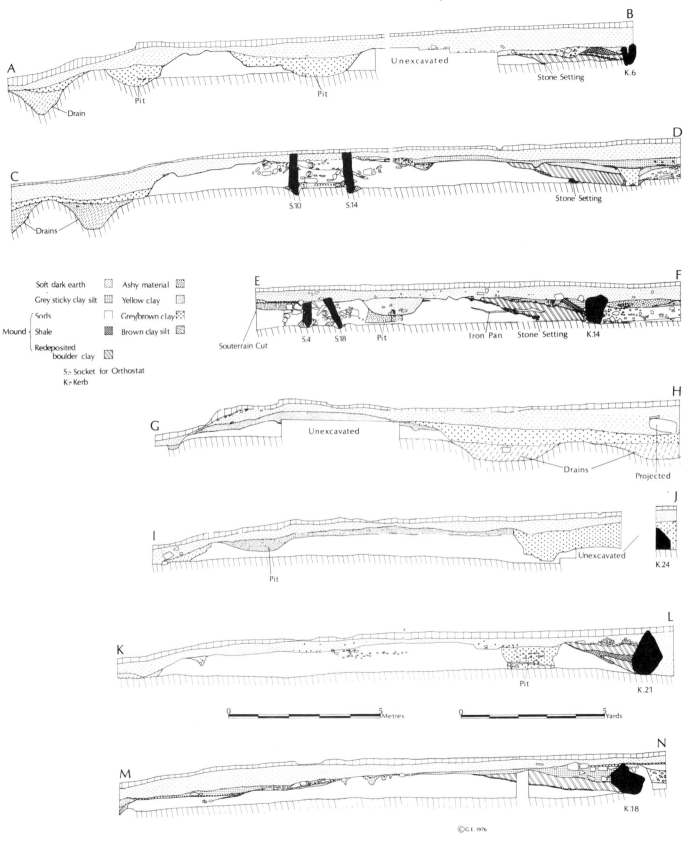

Soft dark earth
Grey sticky clay silt

Mound
{ Sods
  Shale
  Redeposited
  boulder clay }

Ashy material
Yellow clay
Grey/brown clay
Brown clay silt

S.= Socket for Orthostat
K = Kerb

Fig. 47—Site 15: sections.

©G.E. 1976

Pl. 20a–Site 15: chamber from north-west showing cremation deposit (E70:595).
Socket 11 is at bottom of photograph opposite base of orthostat 13
North face of sillstone 3 is at right.
Scale is near centre of burial deposit.

There are some bones that are definitely adult — the left hand of the mandible, part of the left clavicle, part of the axillary border of a scapula, parts of ribs, part of the metacarpal of the right index finger, a right medial cruciform bone, part of the lower end of the right tibia, the spine of a thoracic vertebra, and a molar tooth. There are also many small pieces of skull, the distal phalanx of the big toe, and the distal part of the proximal phalanx of the thumb.'

The deposit weighed 1477.5g (3lb. 4oz). Two flints were associated with the bones (Fig. 49: 596–7), one of which (596) is part of a blade. This was well struck and is pointed. The side that was next the body of the core is flat and smooth, and the other face has flake scars. The other piece (597) is a featureless scrap.

Segment 3 (Fig. 46; Pl. 20b). There was a sequence of burial in this segment but it has not been possible to gauge the time-lag between the deposits. In the north-east corner was a small deposit (598) weighing 294.5g (10 oz) on the ground surface. This was covered by four flat stones. Dr Weekes reports: 'These are cremated bone fragments, and appear to be the bones of a child. There is a terminal phalanx of the finger, portion of triquetral and part of a deciduous molar. The size of these and the thickness of the fragments of vault of the skull seem to indicate a child of perhaps over six years.'

This deposit and its covering stones were overlain by a much larger deposit (599) that also extended beyond the area of the first deposit. It covered a somewhat sub-triangular area that extended 50cm southwards from sill **c** and 60cm westwards from orthostats 14–15. Outside the main deposit a scatter of cremated bone extended for 1m towards sillstone **b** and isolated fragments occurred as far as the sillstone. There were also a few fragments of cremated bone mixed through inhumation burials 28–30 (post-passage-tomb in date, to be published later) and indeed these burials may have slightly interfered with the deposit. Otherwise this deposit seems to be intact but it has not been established whether it represents a single or successive deposits. The remains of at least one child and two adults are present. Dr Weekes reports:'This is a collection of fragmented charred human bones. There are also the bones of probably one animal, not burned. There are fragments of human skulls, fragments which may be parts of cervical vertebrae, and fragments of adult phalanges of fingers. There are parts of limb bones of one or perhaps more children and an odontoid process of the axis, and coronoid process of mandible, probably young. There are a number of deciduous teeth — about five molars and about seven canines or incisors. There are two heads of mandible, both from the right side, indicating two individuals, both adult; there is also one piece of temporal bone with the articular socket. There are two pieces of patella, one at least from an adult. There is a fragment of occipital bone with very well marked superior nuchal line, suggesting a male.' The deposit weighed 4785g (10lb. 9oz).

Two bone beads were associated with the deposit (Fig. 49: 600–1). About a third of one bead (600) is missing. This bead, which has been burnt, is flat, averages 4mm in thickness, and tends to be circular. It would have been approximately 11mm across and the central circular hole is 4.5mm in diameter. The outer surface, which may be

Pl. 20b–Site 15: segment 3 from north-west during excavation with most of secondary burial deposit (E70:590) and two of the four flat stones that overlay the primary deposit removed.
Stone at bottom centre was a sidestone of post-passage-grave inhumation burials 28–30.

Fig. 48—Site 15: sections across tomb.

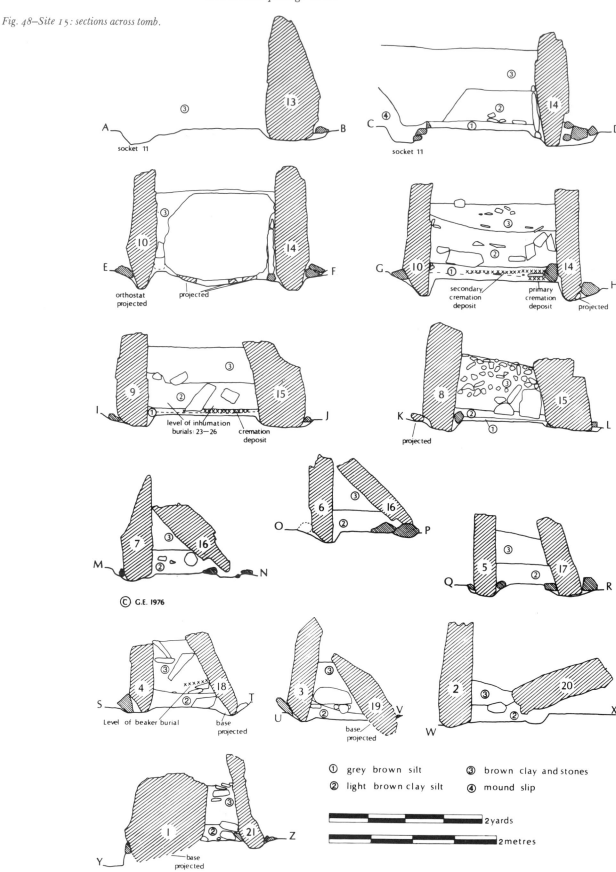

© G.E. 1976

① grey brown silt   ③ brown clay and stones
② light brown clay silt   ④ mound slip

2 yards
2 metres

Fig. 49—Sites 15 and 3: finds. Site 15 — grave goods (596, 597, 600, 601), finds from the old ground surface (603) and from the mound (604–635). Site 3 — passage-tomb type finds from disturbed context (113–116).

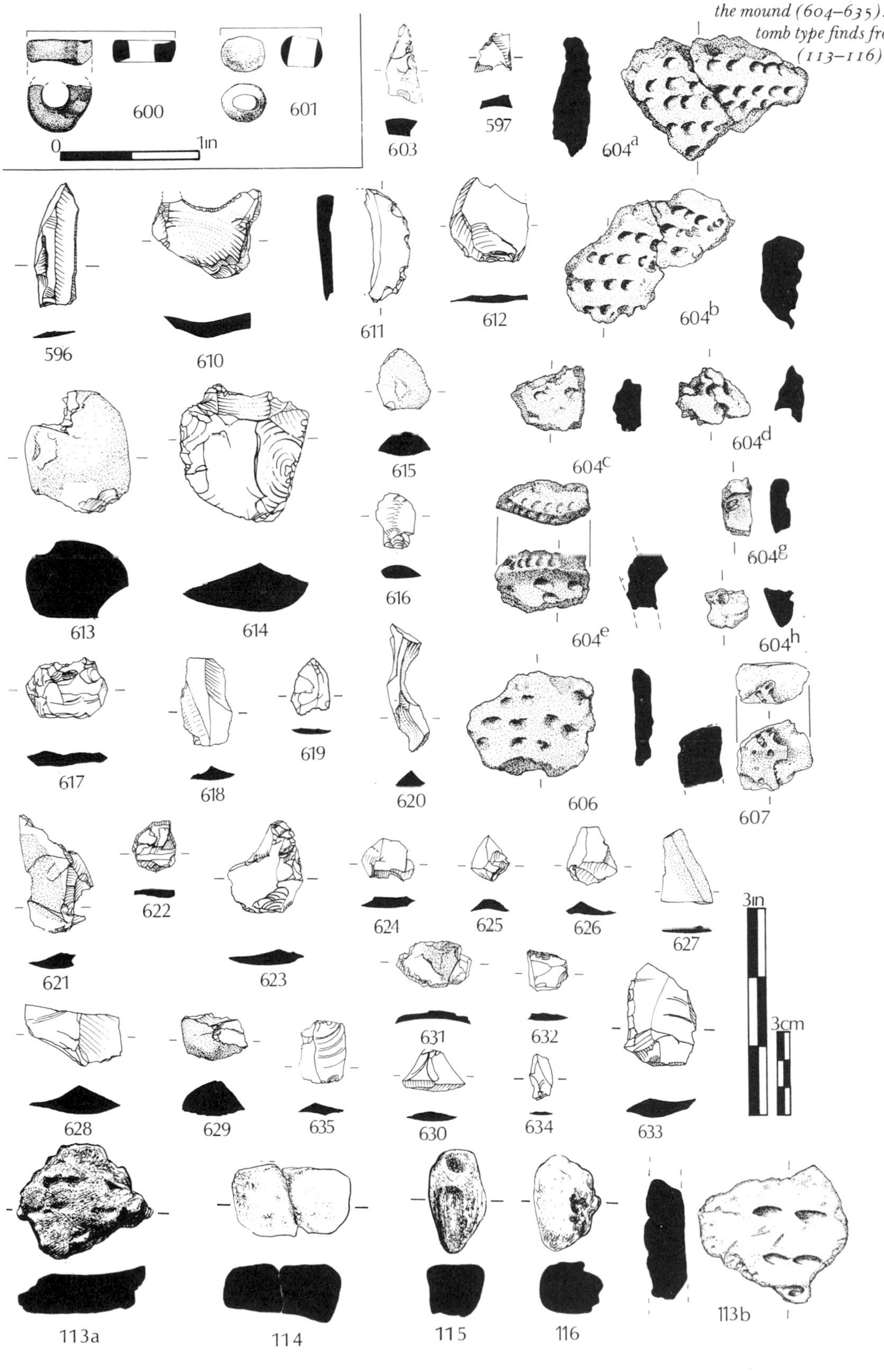

600   601

0   1in

603   597   604ᵃ

596   610   611   612   604ᵇ

615   604ᶜ   604ᵈ

613   614   616   604ᵉ   604ᵍ   604ʰ

617   618   619   620   606   607

622   624   625   626   627

621   623   631   632

628   629   635   630   634   633

3in

3cm

113a   114   115   116   113b

natural, and the edge of the central hole are smooth. The other bead (601) has an outer convex surface but the sides of the central perforation are straight. It has been broken and a small piece is missing. The external diameter is 8mm and the internal 4.5mm. It is 7mm high.

The mound (Figs 45 and 47; Pls 21, 22a)

The upper portion has been removed but a spread of yellowish earth extending eastwards from the site may have been derived from it. Originally the mound covered an almost circular area 20m in diameter. On the western side it has been completely removed, apparently by the digging of drains, and on the northern side another drain caused similar damage. Over the remainder of the site the mound survived to a maximum height of 90cm. The surface of the surviving portion was penetrated by pits and souterrain passages.

Pl. 21a–Site 15: north face of section C–D just outside orthostat 9.

When the mound was built there was a natural sod layer, now 10cm thick, over the surface which was not removed. There were at least two constructional phases in the mound but there is no evidence for a hiatus: one phase seems to have followed the other directly. Firstly a large *core*, consisting of sods with a small amount of boulder clay, was built around the tomb. The material was mixed and there was no deliberate layering. In some places iron pan horizons and grey humic layers characteristic of sods were very distinct. The iron pans occurred at intervals of 3cm to 8cm above each other. Some stones

Pl. 21b–Site 15: south face of section C–D beside orthostats 8 and 9.

were incorporated in the mound material, close to the orthostats on the eastern side. It is impossible to determine the exact shape of the core because of the destruction of the mound on the northern and western sides. The evidence on the southern and eastern sides indicated that it backed onto kerbstones 20 and 21, then curved, and was delimited by a setting of small, angular, fine-grained, iron-bedded sandstones along the eastern side. This setting was on the old ground surface and averaged 40cm in width. From the curvature on the eastern side a width of about 16m can be suggested for the core. A band of shale 5cm thick starts at the setting and extends over the core. The core, band of shale and stone setting were covered by the outer portion of the mound. The absence of slip from the band suggests that the outer part of the mound was laid down soon after the deposition of the shale. The main material in the outer portion of the mound was boulder clay. There is a further band of shale which starts at the back of the kerbstones about 30cm up from the old ground level and slopes upwards. For most of the circumference very little of this band survives. On the southern side, especially inwards from kerbstone 21 (Fig. 47, section K–L) the layer is 20cm thick behind the kerbstones. Its inner end merges into the shale layer that covers the outer part of the core.

Starting a short distance to the west of kerbstone 1 and extending inwards for about 1m there is a somewhat D-shaped scatter of stones, almost 1.3m in maximum length. Along the outer edge this is overlain by the band of shale.

On the old ground surface, outside the passage on either side, opposite sillstone **a**, was a short straight setting of smooth stones.

These abutted onto the orthostats. The setting extending out from orthostat 5 consisted of two stones. In the other setting, directly opposite, were three stones.

Pl. 22a–Site 15: north face of section across mound F–E.
Note band of shale on right of setting of small stones delimiting the core. This band immediately overlies the core and separates it from outer layer of redeposited boulder clay.

The kerb (Figs 45 and 47)

A considerable portion of the kerb on the western and northern sides is missing. Twenty-six stones survive and of these nineteen are in their original position. These, together with five positions indicated by packing stones (1, 8–10, 12) provide a complete arc on the southern and eastern sides (1–24). No. 25 has fallen; 26 seems to be a displaced kerbstone. Overlying the surviving portion of the mound in square 11 a stone was found (X on Fig. 45). This might have been a small kerbstone that was disturbed. There is a slight depression alongside 24 but it is extremely doubtful if this is the remains of a socket. Kerbstones 1–8 were in sockets dug into the subsoil. The other stones were sitting on the old ground surface. The stones in the sockets were further secured by packing stones, and prop stones were placed around the base of the other kerbstones. The kerbstones in front of the tomb are large and angular and average 1.40m in length but they gradually decrease in bulk from the entrance area outwards and some of the smaller ones are rounded and smooth. Smallish angular fine-grained iron-bedded sandstones occur between a number of the kerbstones. These appear to have been placed in position deliberately, presumably to prevent soil creep. Outside the kerb, on the eastern side, is a scatter of similarly shaped stones (Pl. 22b). These are lying on the old ground surface and were either deposited in that position or slipped from the mound. If slip, their stratigraphical position indicates that they must have come down immediately after the building of the mound. All the kerbstones appear to be glacial erratics.

MATERIALS AND DIMENSIONS OF KERBSTONES

No.	Type of Rock	Maximum dimensions (cm)		
		Length	Width	Height
2	Coarse andesite	80	47	102
3	Carboniferous limestone	97	66	80
4	Carboniferous limestone	62	35	80
5	Agglomerate	84	46	60
6	Lava ?	65	56	90
7	Coarse andesite	118	64	78
11	Dolomite	90	90	130
13	Partially dolomitised limestone	101	63	105
14	Coarse limestone with crinoid stems	57	70	102
15	Brown sandstone	127	66	96
16	Crudely bedded sandstone	95	84	101
17	Crudely bedded sandstone	76	67	132
18	Crudely bedded sandstone	210	99	86
19	Crudely bedded sandstone	128	88	95
20	Coarse sandstone	106	95	132
21	Fine-grained agglomerate or coarse sandstone	148	95	148
22	Dolomite	203	85	128
23	Bedded sandstone	135	77	114
24	Sandy dolomite	139	66	97
25	Coarse limestone, some chert, and crinoids	119	42	73
26	Sandy dolomite	129	86	104

Pl. 22b–Site 15: scatter of stones outside kerbstones 11–13.

Finds (other than burials)

Unless otherwise stated, all the artifacts in the descriptions are illustrated (Fig. 49). Two finds were made on the old ground surface underneath the mound. One is a sherd of pottery (602 not illustrated) probably from the body of a vessel. One face is fairly smooth, the other is missing. The ware is unusual but can be compared to some sherds from the mound, i.e. 609. The other find is a featureless piece of flint (603). All other finds are from the mound.

Pottery. All the sherds recovered (604–09) appear to be Carrowkeel ware and apart from 609 all have grits of quartzite and granite.

604a–i. All except one are body sherds that average 14mm in thickness and have dark inner surfaces. The outer surfaces are buff-coloured and decorated with stab designs in rows. The other sherd (604e), part of a lug, is of a similar colour. The outer face and one other surface of the lug are decorated with shallow stabs. It is likely that these sherds were part of the same vessel. (Sherds f and i are not illustrated.)

Pl. 23a–Site 16: general view from northwest. Kerbstone 127 on the west of Site 1 (foreground) penetrates the mound of Site 16.
Symbolic kerb of the small site occurs to the right of it. The patch of paving on south edge of mound (right) is of Iron Age or Early Christian date.
Kerbstones of Site 17 are visible (top). The heap of quartz outside the small tomb is a collection of individual pieces, all of which were found in disturbed material around the site.

605. A featureless sherd, 19mm thick (not illustrated). No. 606 is also decorated with stabs but these are not as smooth or definite as the stabs on 604. They also appear to have been placed in a more haphazard manner. This piece appears to have flaked off a thicker sherd. It is 18mm thick.

607. Appears to be part of a rim with an outward bevel. The outer surface is applied and there are small depressions in it. The ware is

dark throughout and is more compact than that of the preceding sherds.

608 and 609. Featureless fragments of coarse ware like, for instance, 605. The outer surface of 609 (not illustrated) is absent.

Pl. 23b—Site 16: general view from east.

Flints (Fig. 49). Twenty-six flints came from the mound but only three show evidence of use. One is a definite artifact, a hollow scraper (610) made from a flake. The edge is finely worked but only from one face and the sides have been slightly trimmed. The tip of one of the wings has broken off and is missing, 611 appears to be part of a round scraper and 612 is part of a blade. There is slight nibbling along the convex edge.

The remaining pieces (613–35) are scrap: 613 is a pebble from which some pieces have been knocked off, 614 is a piece detached from a large pebble, and 615 and 616 were also detached from pebbles.

636. A fragment tending to be triangular was an isolated find. It may have been a piece of a blade. From socket of orthostat 12 of tomb. Beaker material has been found in this area and this flint could have been derived from that source. (Not illustrated.)

Megalithic art

Art was found on three of the tomb orthostats and on two kerbstones. Unless otherwise stated the technique used is pocking.

Orthostat 1 (Fig. 67:1; Pl. 52b). The art is confined to the inner narrow face. The large elongated pit near the top is natural. The lowermost

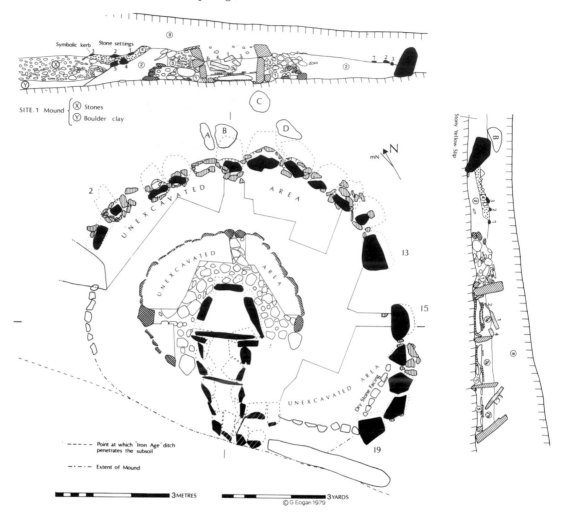

Fig. 50—Site 16: ground plan and sections.

motif consists of a cup-mark 108mm in maximum diameter and
82mm in maximum depth and is surrounded by a gapped circle of
irregular width. Above this are three irregularly shaped motifs close
to each other. One seems to be a crude pock-mark with a 'loop'
above it. Another is a sort of figure-of-eight motif and above this is
an irregular 'circle'. One corner of the stone near the top is pocked
and there is some vague pocking on the top edge.

Orthostat 14. The *inner face,* the face towards the passage (Fig. 67:2; Pls
53b and 54a) has two motifs. They are close to each other around the
centre of the stone. One is a spiral of two and a half turns, and the
other is circular but, because of wear, its form is uncertain. It may be
one of two concentric circles. On the *outer face* (Fig. 67:2; Pl. 54b) the
sole motif consists of a small cup-mark surrounded by a circle. At
one point on the circumference, and slightly impinging on the
circle, is another small cup-mark.

Sillstone c. The *outer face,* the face towards the entrance (Fig. 67:3; Pl.
53a) has both pocked and incised motifs. On the upper part of the
stone is a lozenge-shaped design. To the right of it is a larger,
somewhat U-shaped design placed partially sideways. This may have
a connecting line across the top but owing to wear or the faintness of
the pocking one cannot be certain. A short distance below and

slightly to one side of the lozenge design is an inverted U-shaped motif. There are also outer areas of miscellaneous pocking. The main incised design, to the right of the U-shaped design, is a three-pointed chevron. There are various other incised lines that do not form a design. On the *inner face,* the face towards the chamber (Fig. 67:3, on left), there is a short, slightly curved line, poorly executed by pocking. There are also two small areas of miscellaneous pocking.

Kerbstone 22 has two small conjoined circles on the inner face.

Kerbstone 6 (Fig. 67:4; Pl. 55a). Decoration, confined to the outer face, consists of five parallel arcs which may be the remains of concentric circles that are now incomplete because of weathering. The basic technique used was pocking but subsequently some of the pocked areas were smoothed down. This is more noticeable in the second and fifth arcs from the centre. In some places, for instance in the first arc from the centre, the design is barely perceptible. There are two natural grooves running across the outer face from the lower left corner to the upper right corner. There are also a number of small pock-like depressions over this surface which appear to be natural.

SITE 16 (Fig. 50; Pls 24 and 25)

The evidence indicates that this site predates Site 1. When Site 1 was being constructed it impinged on this passage tomb. As a result Site 16 was modified to facilitate its continued existence as an independent tomb. In order to do this a gap was left in the kerb of Site 1. On the eastern side of the gap the last stones in the kerb curve inwards, and on the western side the regular curve is maintained, but the last kerbstone abuts onto the mound of Site 16. It is difficult to assess the precise damage that was caused to the site when Site 1 was being built. However, it can be shown that the kerb, mound and tomb were interfered with.

On the evidence from the other passage tombs at Knowth and from passage tombs elsewhere it can be reasonably assumed that the mound of Site 16 was originally surrounded by kerbstones, but no kerbstones now survive along the southern side: the digging of a fosse (ditch) around the base of Site 1 during the Iron Age could have destroyed some. In the area that was not disturbed, along the edge of the south-western arc of the mound between the ditch and the kerb of Site 1, no kerbstones or even traces of them survive either. It seems, therefore, that some of the kerbstones were removed when Site 1 was being built. As a result of this interference the surviving portion of the kerb at Site 16 is somewhat D-shaped. At least on the southern side the builders of Site 1 lowered the mound and subsequently a small portion of it was completely removed by the diggers of the Iron Age ditch. The tomb was also interfered with. Again on the evidence from other sites at Knowth its passage should have been straight and should have extended to the original edge of its mound. Continued access by way of the original entrance would obviously have been impossible due to the building of the large mound. Therefore, the outer part of the passage was removed. The portion of the passage that now leads in from the eastern side of the kerb edge, including the first sillstone, is secondary and was constructed in order to maintain access to the chamber. In the construction of the secondary passage the orthostats used may have been those removed from the primary passage.

Because of the Iron Age and Early Christian activity it is not possible to determine the extent to which Site 16 was covered by the mound of Site 1. At least along the south-western sides a basal layer of redeposited sod of Site 1, and a layer of clean stones (layers X and Y, Fig. 50) above it, extended over the surviving part of the mound of this passage grave. At one point there was a spread of boulder-clay-like material and above this was a layer of shale with some stones mixed through it (layer 4, Fig. 50). The stones were formally laid down and they may have been a sort of symbolic kerb somewhat like that on Site 13 (p. 79 above). The stratification described along the south-western side is standard layering for the mound of Site 1 (cf. Eogan 1968, Fig. 8) but the overlying shale layer is confusing. This shale band incorporates the stone settings 1 and 2 and it must, therefore, be a layer of the small site. But the outer portion of it overlies the layers that are assumed to be those of Site 1 (layers X, Y) and the 'symbolic kerb' is also sitting on it. This is conflicting evidence and the apparently homogeneous shale layer makes the unravelling of the sequence difficult. As this shale layer incorporates both stone settings 1 and 2 (which go with the mound of the small site) and the 'symbolic kerb' (apparently the work of the builders of Site 1) then, taken at its face value, the two mounds were built simultaneously. However, this seems unlikely and another interpretation can be put forward. The boulder clay of the mound of

Pl. 24a–Site 16: general view from north showing stone settings in mound. Drystone wall (bottom left) is part of souterrain 7.

Pl. 24b–Site 16: tomb from south. Stone chips along left (west) side of passage are part of fill of later 'destruction' trench.

the small site has an overlying layer of shale. On the south-western side this still survives out to about stone setting 2 but was removed from the outer side of the mound probably when the kerbstones were removed. Subsequently the mound of Site I was built, covering up part of the mound of the small site, and at a height coinciding with the surviving shale layer the builders of the Site I mound extended that layer outwards. There is no noticeable break in the layer but this could be because shale bonds together easily.

Further modifications may have taken place during the Iron Age – Early Christian period. On the sloping south-western side of the small site there was an area of paving (Pl. 23a) extending over a somewhat rectangular area 2.20m by 1.90m. There was a light scattering of shale between the paving and it overlay a fill of rubble-like material, which in turn overlay the stony layer (layer X) of the mound of Site I (Fig. 50). Part of a jet bracelet was found amongst the rubble (this will be published at a later stage). Thus it is unlikely that the rubble is earlier than the Iron Age. It may have been laid down about the same time that the basal Iron Age ditch around Site I was dug, in order to prevent slip into the ditch.

Apparently in more recent times — precisely when has not been established — other damage to the small site took place. This mainly involved the removal of the upper portion of the mound, the destruction of the roof of the passage and chamber, and the removal of some kerbstones. A trench was also dug along each side of the passage on the outside. On the western side it penetrated down to within 10cm above the old ground surface for most of its length, but on the eastern side it stopped about 15cm above the old ground surface. The purpose of this trench may have been to facilitate the removal of the orthostats. However, none of the orthostats was removed, but the backs of a number were damaged by sledging and flakes broken off as a result were lying in the fill (Pl. 24b). Orthostat 16 was split. On both sides the fill of the trenches was fairly constant, consisting of a mixture of stones and earth, but there was a concentration of stones in the basal 80cm (layer 3). A number of flat stones overlay the trench fill. (These are further discussed below where it is suggested that they are roofing stones from the passage. If this is so then the trenches were dug before the passage roofstones were removed.)

In the immediate vicinity of the tomb a couple of dozen pieces of quartz were found. All were in disturbed material.

The tomb: primary portion of the passage (Figs 50–53; Pls 23–29)

The passage had been altered by the builders of Site 1 and as a result it now consists of a primary and a secondary portion. The primary portion consisted of orthostats 5–9, 13–17 and sillstones **b**

Fig. 51–Site 16: ground plan and elevation of tomb.

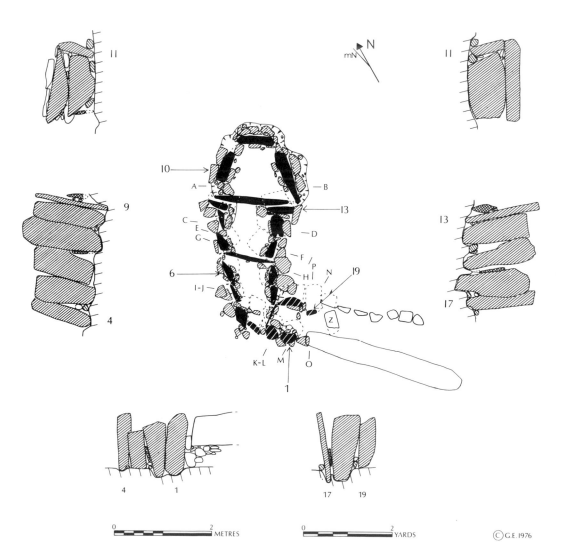

and **c**. It is also very likely that orthostat 4 is in its original position. The orthostats were placed longitudinally except 9 and 13 which were placed transversely just on the outer side of the ends of sillstone **c** (innermost) and gave the impression of jambstones. The surviving portion of the primary passage is 3.60m long and it widens from about 60cm to about 1.10m. It is divided by two sillstones, **b** and **c**, into two segments, the inner one of which is 1.50m long. If sillstone **a** (outermost) is a re-set original then the passage was divided into at least three segments. Throughout the passage there was fairly consistent stratification. The upper fill of the segments was similar and uniform, a layer of stones and earth (9). Underneath this again in both segments was a layer of brownish earth and stones (7a and b). In the inner segment earth was more consistent (7a) whereas in the outer segment there was a slight shale mixture (7b). This layer overlay, in both segments, a level of small flat flags which formed a 'paving.' The basal layer, overlying the old ground surface, is sticky grey earth, possibly silt, which averaged 10cm thick (5).

There were no roof stones in position, but a number of stones in the immediate area may have been derived from the roof (Fig. 52; Pl. 25a). In layers 9 and 7b of the outer segment there was a flag (east corbel 1, abbreviated to EC 1 etc. in text and illustrations) 70cm long, lying at an angle. On the western side were two stones (west corbel WC 1 and 2) which may also have served as roof stones. On the eastern side were six stones (2–7; Pl. 25a) that could have formed part of the roof. 4 and possibly 2 and 6 may have been capstones, while 3 and 7 may have been corbels from the chamber. EC 7, a large stone, much thicker at one end than the other, is of uncertain use but in shape it can be compared to the corbel over orthostat 12, and it may have been another corbel sitting on top of the surviving one.

The orthostats had a fairly uniform height of 1.15m above the old ground surface. Only one (7) was clearly taller than any of the others. All were in individual sockets. No. 6 is about 3cm in maximum depth; 16 is over 20cm in maximum depth and the depths of the other sockets range between these extremes. No. 8 almost filled the entire socket, 4 and 7 occupied the centre of the sockets, 5 and 6 were placed alongside the inner edge of the sockets and 14–17 were placed alongside the outer edge of the socket. The transverse orthostats or jambstones (9 and 13) occupied the centre of the socket. Packing stones were used in all instances. These were placed on top of the fill in 4, 5, 7, 8 and 15–17. On the outside of the orthostat in socket 6 packing stones and earth were in the fill; on the inside the fill consisted of earth with packing stones placed on top of it. In some cases, especially where the orthostat was placed along the edge of the socket the old sod was removed to provide a foundation for the packing stones.

It seems that it was when a trench was dug along the outer faces of the orthostats that they were damaged; 16 was split and pieces were sledged off the backs of others. This damage may also have caused a number of orthostats to lean. Nos 4, 7 and 14–16 lean into the passage. The remaining orthostats (5, 6, 8, 9 and 17) are upright and 4–8 and 13–15 lean very slightly towards the chamber.

The inner segment of the passage was used for burial (see below). The widening passage merges into the *chamber*. This is especially noticeable on the western side where, taken together, the sides of

Pl. 25a–Site 16: possible roofstones on eastern side of primary passage.

passage and chamber form a curve. Nevertheless there is a distinction between the passage and the inner end of the tomb which is self-contained. This is emphasised by sillstone **c**, by the transverse positioning of the two orthostats on the outside of it to form jambs (9 and 13) and by the distinctive trapezoidal shape of the inner element itself, which may be referred to as the chamber. It is delimited on the outer and wider side by sillstone **c**. Each of the other sides is formed by a single orthostat (10–12) in a very shallow socket. The sockets were mainly formed by the removal of the old sod. Packing and wedge stones were skilfully used around the bases. The side stones had a smooth inner surface and stood upright. The back stone was leaning outwards slightly. There was a largish stone, almost rectangular when viewed from the chamber, on top of orthostat 12 and another largish stone on orthostat 10. This tended to be boatshaped in long section and it was supported at each end by smallish stones. Overlying it were three flat stones which projected inwards slightly. There were six largish flat stones in the fill of the chamber (Pl. 25b) whose shape suggests that they were collapsed roof stones. One of them was upright and partly parallel to the sillstone in the south-east corner. The others were around the centre of the chamber and the lowermost was just above the tertiary cremation. The sloping position of stones 3 and 6 suggests that they fell from the western side of the chamber.

Burials and grave goods occurred both in the chamber and in the inner segment of the passage. There were five separate deposits and at least sixteen individuals were identified.

There were three stratified deposits in the chamber. The rite was cremation (Fig. 53; Pls 26, 27). The *primary deposit* (637) lay on the old ground surface. It extended over most of the chamber area and was covered by a flag which rested on small flat stones around the edge of the chamber. These stones were also post-deposit and it would appear that they were placed in position to provide a level surface for the flag. Other small stones filled the spaces along the edge. Because of the size of this flag, it would have been extremely difficult, if not impossible, to get it into the tomb after its completion. Therefore the primary burial was probably in place and was covered by the flag before the chamber was roofed. As the flag was neatly sitting on the small flat stones it seems that it was lowered into the tomb by means of a shear-legs or a similar hoisting apparatus. The burial contained the remains of a number of individuals. The remains of at least two adults and three children were positively identified.

Pl. 25b–Site 16: roofstones in chamber from north.

Dr Weekes reports: 'There seem to be here parts of the skeletons of several individuals. One would appear to be a child about the time of birth as shown by the presence of part of a mandible, parts of cervical vertebrae and parts of two femora and two tibiae, appropriate to this age. There appear to be two older children, not the same age. There are parts of orbit, phalanges and head of mandible which could be from the skeleton of a child several years younger.

'There are also parts of the bones of the skeleton of an adult – parts of condyles of femur, two bits of head of radius, parts of navicular and talus and of thoracic vertebra, pieces of skull and many pieces of long bones. It may be that there are here parts of skeletons

Fig. 52—Site 16: sections across tomb.

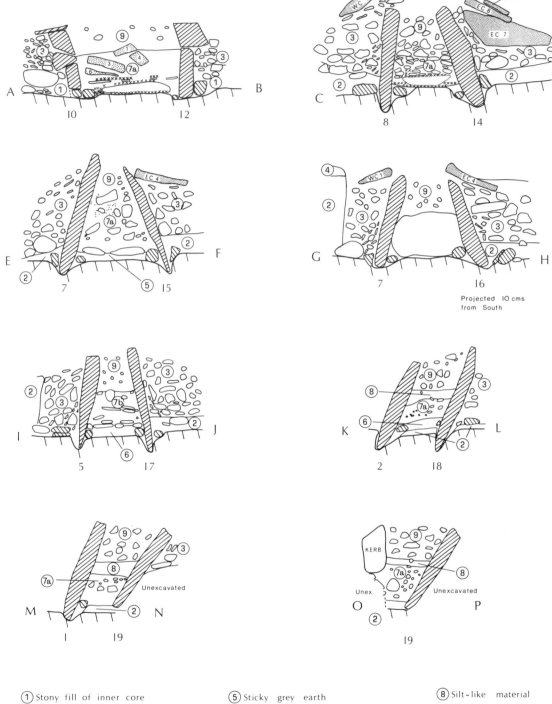

① Stony fill of inner core	⑤ Sticky grey earth	⑧ Silt-like material
② Redeposited boulder clay	⑥ Brown gritty earth	⑨ Earth and stones
③ Stony fill of trench	⑦ₐ Brownish earth with stones	
④ Shale	⑦♭ Brown clay with shale	x x x Cremated burial deposits

0   2 METRES

0   2 YARDS

ⓒ G.E. 1976

of two individuals as there is the medial part of the head of first right metatarsal bone of a small adult, and a finer proximal phalanx which appears to be from a fairly large adult. There is part of a vertebra showing lipping which suggests that one of these adults was advanced in years. There is also a piece of pelvis from the iliopubic region which gives the impression of a wide sciatic notch, and therefore may be female.' The deposit weighed 2131g (4 lb. 11 oz.)

Portion of the stem of a pin (638, Fig. 54), 52mm long, was found amongst the deposit. This had a rounded cross-section and at one of the fractured ends was 4mm in diameter. From there it tapered to 3mm. Ms Colette Dowling reports that the pin was made from 'the tarsal bone from the leg of a small bird (possibly a wading bird)'.

The *secondary deposit* (639) was lying on the flag that covered the primary deposit and extended over the surface of the flag. The deposit was covered by a paving of smallish flat stones. It contained the remains of at least a baby, two young children and an adult and weighed 4297g (9 lb. 8 oz.)

Dr Weekes reports: 'This is a collection of fragments of bone, a mixture of human and animal. There appear to be a baby at about full term (as shown by the presence of an ilium and a tibia appropriate to this age), and two young persons and an adult. The two young persons would be about six years of age; there are parts of condyloid processes of two mandibles, one odontoid process, a small finger phalanx, and a thoracic spine, which would be appropriate for persons of this age. There is a condyloid process of a mandible and a coronoid process, about ten phalanges, parts of mandible with tooth sockets, part of a clavicle, and a somewhat worn tooth. All these come from the skeleton of an adult. There are many bones of skull, vault and base, and roots of teeth.'

An incomplete object (640, Fig. 54) of bone and with a very smooth surface was associated with the deposit. The two ends are missing. At the narrow end the body has a circular cross-section and it is 7mm in diameter. At the other end the object tends to be sub-rectangular in cross-section. It was perforated at this end but the outer portion has been broken off. The perforating was not skilfully carried out. Holes were worked from both sides but were not started opposite each other. This object may have been part of a pin or more likely a pendant. Ms Dowling reports that 'it was most possibly from the leg bone of a small mammal'.

The *tertiary deposit* (641) was the final burial deposit to be placed in the chamber. It was deposited over the paving of stones that overlay the secondary deposit. There was no upper protection from the base of the chamber fill already described, so the deposit had a considerable amount of clay and small stones mixed through it. It contains the remains of at least a child and an adult and weighed 2396g (5lb. 5oz.)

Dr Weekes reports: 'Many of these bones are certainly animal but there are many human cremated bones. Most of these appear to be from an adult, as judged by the thickness of the skull, but some of these pieces of skull would indicate a child.'

There were two featureless fragments of white flint associated with this deposit (642, 643, Fig. 54).

The inner segment of the *passage* was used for burial. As in the chamber the rite was cremation and there were two stratified deposits (Fig. 53; Pl. 28). The *primary deposit* (644) occupied the inner half or so of segment 3. It was delimited by sillstone **c** on the chamber side, and orthostat 8 on the western side. It extended almost to orthostat 14 on the eastern side of the segment. On the outside was a transverse stone which acted as a limiting feature on that side and the deposit, covered by a flag with smaller stones around its edge, overlay most of it. The remains of at least four individuals were represented. The deposit weighed 1601g (3 lb. 8 oz.)

Pl. 26a–Site 16: old ground surface of chamber from south after removal of primary deposit. Smaller stones around the edge are supports for overlying flagstone (see Pl. 27a).

Dr Weekes reports: 'These fragments of bone contain many small pieces of skull and long bone. There are two well worn pre-molar teeth, three finger phalanges, a piece of head of mandible, the posterior part of the mandible in the mid-line, fragments of ribs and vertebrae, petrous temporal bone, a great toe, metatarsal head, and some very thick pieces of skull. There are pieces of orbital margin probably from three different skulls. In addition there is a piece of thin skull, indicating a young person, the coronoid process of a young mandible, and part of a young tooth.'

The *secondary deposit* (645) covered most of the segment. It overlay the flag and small stones that covered the primary deposit. In turn it was covered by a paving of smallish flat stones. The deposit weighed 2376g (5 lb. 4 oz.)

Dr Weekes reports: 'Some of these fragments of bone are certainly unburnt animal. The human bones which can be identified are part of petrous temporal, head of mandible, roots of adult teeth, some phalanges of fingers and toes, and some unusually thick pieces of skull, indicating an adult.'

The fill of the chamber above the paving that overlay the secondary deposit consisted of stones and some earth, similar to the layer in the outer segment.

There are similarities between the burials in chamber and passage. In both cases the burial rite was cremation. The primary deposit was placed on the old ground surface and a flag directly on top of it. The absence of natural fill underneath the flags indicates that these were put in position straight after the burial deposition. In each case a secondary deposit was placed on top of the flagstone. Overlying these secondary deposits was a stone 'paving' and the paving was also found in the outer segment of the primary passage. On top of this paving, but only in the chamber, was a tertiary cremation deposit.

Apart from the area occupied by the primary cremation and its covering flag in the passage the remainder of that segment, and also the outer segment, has a layer 10cm–15cm thick over the old ground surface. This appears to be natural silt-like material that percolated in through cavities between the roof stones (layer 5, Fig. 50). There is no positive evidence that the primary burial and its covering stone were inserted into a pit dug into the layer of 'silt'. As the secondary deposit overlies the 'silt' it appears that a period elapsed between the first deposit and the secondary deposit and this may also be so in the chamber.

Pl. 26b–Site 16: Chamber from south showing primary cremation deposit (E70:637).

Above the tertiary burial in the chamber is a layer of earth and stones, and a layer of similar material occurs above the paving in the two segments of the passage (7a). The collapsed roof stones are found partly embedded in this layer so it is probably material that infiltrated when the roof of the tomb was being destroyed.

The tomb: secondary portion of passage (Figs 50–53; Pl. 29b)

This was at right angles to the primary passage and it was constructed as part of the remodelling that took place consequent to the destruction of part of the site when the large mound was constructed. When the secondary passage was being constructed the mound was not removed down to the old surface: about 30cm of it survived. Thus, the base of the passage was undisturbed primary mound.

The *outer part* of the passage is formed on one side by a kerbstone of Site 1 and on the other side by drystone walling which is set against the mound. This wall has an inward batter due to settling of the material behind it. The kerbstone of Site 1 and the wall of Site 16 parallel to it are sitting on top of the remains of the primary mound of Site 16. The kerbstone is supported by small stones at the base (Fig. 52; section O–P). There is no evidence that this part of the passage was roofed. At the inner end is a transverse block of stone that may have acted as a sill or as a blocking to the entrance (Fig. 51, z; Pl. 29b). This tends to be V-shaped and its narrow end is sitting on the surface. From the outer face of that stone to the entrance, this section of the passage is 1.90m long and it averages 60cm in width at the base. The fill consisted of smallish stones averaging 20cm across.

The *inner part* of the passage was constructed from orthostats, three on the southern side (1–3) and two on the northern side (18–19). These orthostats may have been those that were removed from the destroyed portion of the primary passage. Nos 1 and 2 were set in well-formed sockets, 17cm and 20cm respectively in maximum depth, 3 was in a shallow socket, really only a scoop. All, especially 3, leaned inwards. Along the top, the horizontal line dropped from 1 to 3. No. 18 was also in a well-formed socket 30cm in maximum depth. It was taller than 19 which stood in a shallow scoop. A sillstone (a), almost in the line of the eastern side of the primary passage, is apparently a feature of the secondary passage, but, like the orthostats, may originally have had a primary function. From the outer face of sill **a** to the inner face of the large transverse stone this part of the passage is 1.17cm long and averages 47cm in width. The fill was stratified into four layers. The basal layer consisted of brown gritty earth (6). It reached its maximum height of 15cm along sillstone **a**, and tapered to 5cm along the inner face of the large transverse stone. Above this was a layer of stones mixed with earth similar to that above the paving in the chamber and primary passage (7a). Above this there was a layer of silt-like material (8) which thickens outward from the sill. There is no counterpart to this layer in the primary passage or chamber. The upper layer of earth and stones is similar to the uniform layer that forms the upper fill of the primary passage and chamber (9) (Figs 50, 52). There was no evidence for a roof.

The primary burials in both chamber and passage probably took place about the same time. It has previously been suggested that the

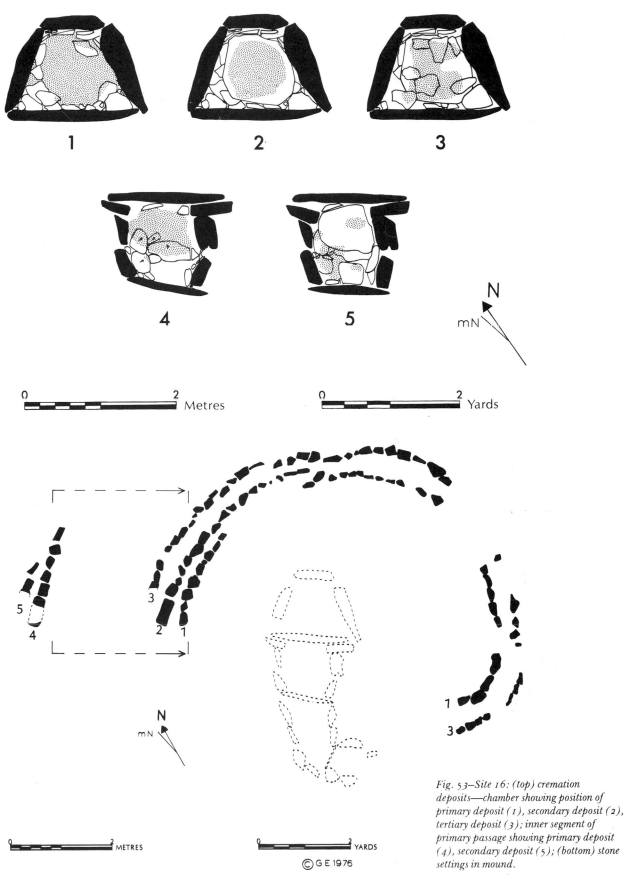

Fig. 53–Site 16: (top) cremation deposits—chamber showing position of primary deposit (1), secondary deposit (2), tertiary deposit (3); inner segment of primary passage showing primary deposit (4), secondary deposit (5); (bottom) stone settings in mound.

© G E. 1976

Fig. 54–Sites 7, 9, 12, 13, 14 and 16: finds.
Grave goods from Site 16 (638, 640, 642, 643);
from the mounds of Sites 7 (47), 9 (3823,
3824), 12 (21–26), 13 (11, 13), 14 (7) and 16 (661–671);
from the old ground surface Site 16
(646–657).

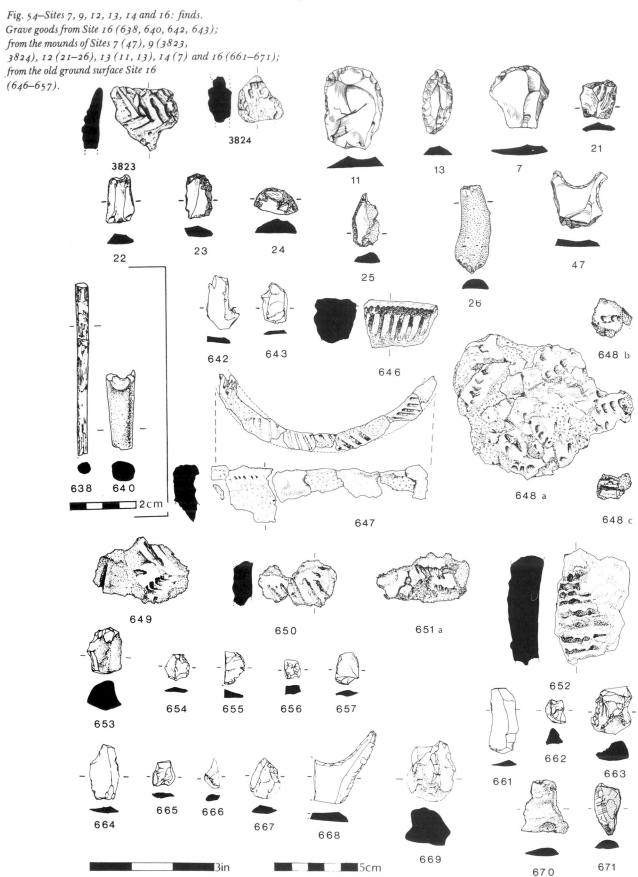

primary burial in the passage predates the silty layer (5), which resembles layer 6 of the secondary passage in both stratigraphical position and composition. If that is so the construction of the secondary passage would have taken place at an early stage in the history of this site. The paving and the overlying secondary burial in the primary passage would therefore have been laid down after the remodelling. As the paving overlying the tertiary burial in the chamber appears to be similar to that in the passage, the tertiary burial in the chamber should be approximately contemporary with the secondary burial in the passage. The layer of stones mixed with earth (7a and b) found in the primary and secondary passages would appear to date from the period of the removal of the capstones or just after. Some of the removed cap or corbel stones are incorporated in it.

Cleaved greywacke was used for all the orthostats and sills.

DIMENSIONS OF ORTHOSTATS

No.	Maximum dimensions (cm)		
	Length	Width	Height
1	43	28	142
2	47	21	122
3	42	20	104
4	37	33	129
5	56	22	126
6	56	25	134
7	65	20	165
8	39	30	151
9	65	17	155
10	128	33	54
11	89	23	80
12	136	30	78
13	46	18	154
14	51	31	140
15	58	21	150
16	59	20	157
17	36	13	163
18	57	19	141
19	34	18	123
Sillstone **a**	53	3	38
Sillstone **b**	106	11	70
Sillstone **c**	156	15	46

The mound

Parts of the mound had been removed. The surviving portion provided evidence of composite construction. Its main features consist of a core, a layer of re-deposited boulder clay and a layer of shale on top of this.

The *core* was built around the chamber and the inner part of the passage (Fig. 50; Pls 30, 31a). It is delimited by a formal edge consisting of a drystone facing, 50cm in average height, which has an inward batter and consists of three layers of stones. The stones of the basal layer are the largest, averaging 40cm in length. The core is approximately circular, 4.25m across, and the chamber is placed centrally within it. It consists of stones with a small amount of earth, which probably filtered in. At present the core tends to be flat-topped and 55cm in maximum height. Its outer edges are overlain by the redeposited boulder clay which indicates that the present shape of the core is original. The trench dug along the back of the orthostats (see p. 111) penetrated the core for a short distance on either side of the passage, but more so on the eastern side. This interference explains the absence of the boulder clay layer over the inner part of the core. The end stones of the core (Fig. 50, unhatched) are not in their original position, but they seem to be derived from the kerb of the core. When complete the core would have joined the passage at about sockets 7 and 15.

Pl. 27a–Site 16: flagstone overlying primary deposit in chamber. View from south after removal of secondary cremation deposit (E70:639).

The *redeposited boulder clay* forms the main layer. Outside the tomb it covers the entire site within the kerb except for the inner part of the core from which it was probably removed. Within this layer, on the eastern side, was a small scatter of stones at about 15cm above the old ground surface. No significance can be attached to this. On the inside of kerb 1 were a few largish stones which take the place of the boulder clay at this point. Behind kerbstones 17–19 a poor attempt was made at drystone facing, apparently when the mound was constructed.

The *shale layer* extends over the layer of boulder clay but owing to damage it is missing from the areas immediately around the tomb. This layer varied in thickness from 5cm to 40cm.

There was a series of *stone settings* within the mound (Fig. 53; Pls 23a, 30a). The stones averaged 22cm in length. Their surfaces were smooth and they may have been derived from glacial deposits, such as gravel. The settings were placed concentrically in relation to the kerb. There is evidence for five settings. Settings 4 and 5 are at a lower level than 1–3. They are sitting on the redeposited boulder clay, 4 largely underneath 2, and 5 at the same level but between 2 and 3. Both 4 and 5 occur only on the western side and they are short: 4 has six stones, 5 only three. Of the three upper settings the inner one has thirty stones but there are three gaps in it, 2 is a shortish arc of seventeen stones on the western side and the outer setting (3) is gapped and has forty-one stones. These three settings are sitting in the shale just under disturbed material and it is possible that some of them could have been removed. At the southern end the curve is more abrupt than at other points. Beyond this point disturbed material existed down to the level of the settings and some stones may have been removed. It is very likely that all five settings extended further on the western side and that the ends were removed when the site was remodelled and the large mound (Site 1) built.

A spread of charcoal sealed in the mound material gave a C14 determination of 4399 ± 67 B.P. (c.2449 b.c., B.M. 1078).

The kerb (Fig. 50)

Because part of the site was removed when the large mound was being constructed the original shape of the kerb and mound cannot be determined. The surviving kerb encloses a somewhat D-shaped area and is 8.60m in maximum external diameter. The surviving portion of the kerb consisted of sixteen stones and sockets for three others (3, 6, 14). There were four largish stones (A–D) lying at about

Pl. 27b—Site 16: paving in chamber from south. This paving overlay secondary cremation deposit (E70:639) and was in turn overlain by tertiary cremation deposit (E70:641).

Pl. 28a–Site 16: inner segment of primary passage after removal of primary burial deposit (E70:644). Smaller stones around the edge are supports for overlying flagstone (see Pl. 28b).

the height of the tops of the kerbs just outside kerbstones 7–9, some of which may have been displaced kerbs. Kerbstones 2, 5–9 and 11 were in sockets, averaging 5cm in depth. The others were sitting on the old ground surface. With the exception of 19 all were supported at the base by packing or wedge stones. All except 1 and 16–19 leaned outwards. It may also be noted that 9, 10 and 12 had the narrow pointed portion at the base. Above was a large overhang. These features may have been the greatest cause of their collapse.

MATERIALS AND DIMENSIONS OF KERBSTONES

No.	Type of Rock	Maximum dimensions (cm)		
		Length	Width	Height
1	Fine sandstone	107	49	80
2	Limestone	56	18	105
4	Limestone	68	35	106
5	Conglomerate	70	39	89
7	Limestone	73	44	113
8	Sandy dolomite	95	60	139
9	Fine conglomerate	112	48	87
10	Sandy dolomite	88	57	89
11	Agglomerate	62	33	105
12	Coarse bedded conglomerate and sandstone	83	33	87
13	Sandy dolomite	117	73	62
15	Dolerite	92	41	77
16	Dolerite	62	61	62
17	Dolerite	60	63	61
18	Fine grained conglomerate	94	49	94
19	Coarse conglomerate	93	69	74

Finds from the old ground surface

646–51 (Fig. 54). A scatter of fragmentary 'Carrowkeel' *pottery* sherds that were found in cutting 55, centred *c.* 0.60m from north, 1.80m from west. At least three, possibly four, vessels are represented.

646. Flat-topped rimsherd, the inner edge of the top and one of the sides of which are worn away. There are quartzite grits in the ware and decoration on the intact side. Immediately under the rim is a horizontal channel with shallow oblique stabs in it. Underneath this are closely set vertical grooves. The oblique stabs run into the vertical grooves indicating that the grooves were made before the stabs. The ware is brownish with a dark outer surface.

647. Part of a rim, thinner and less coarse than 646, dark in colour throughout. The rim is flat-topped and has a slight inward expansion. It is decorated with incised, closely set oblique lines. On the outer face immediately under the rim are the remains of a horizontal line which may have been formed by stab-and-drag.

648a. Bodysherd, one surface of which is decorated almost all over. Apart from a few short rows, the decoration is in a confused mass. It is applied by the stab-and-drag method but at least two forms of implement were used, or the same implement was used in different ways. In one sort of decoration the implement had a blunt U–shaped end, not entirely smooth, as there are faint ridges. In other cases the same type of implement may have been used but more at an angle. A third type has narrow stabs so the implement may have been

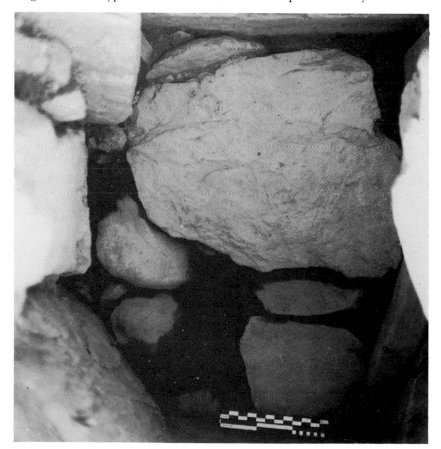

Pl. 28b–Site 16: inner segment of primary passage showing small stones and flagstones in position. Secondary cremation deposit (E70:645) overlay these stones.

used on its side. The confused nature of the ornament suggests that this sherd may have come from near the base of a vessel. It differs in texture and decoration from 647 and although like 646 is not quite similar in decoration and ware so it must have come from a different vessel. There are three other sherds (648b,c,d) that seem to be part of the same vessel. Sherd 648d is not illustrated as it is only a fragment.

649. Poorly preserved sherd, most likely from the body of a vessel, although it is not clear whether it belongs to the same vessel as any of the other sherds. At one point it is decorated with oblique stabs.

Pl. 29a–Site 16: paving in outer segment of primary pasage from north.

650. Bodysherd decorated with five parallel lines formed by stab-and-drag and with two stabs on another part of the sherd. This sherd has not been related to any of the other sherds. There are also fragmentary sherds (651a–k). 651a is decorated with a row of five oblique stabs (Fig. 54). The ware is similar to 649. 651b–k are not illustrated.

652 (Fig. 54). Bodysherd whose inner face is smooth. The other face is decorated with parallel rows of stab-and-drag ornament. The stab is deeper along one side than the other. Square 19, 2.38m from north, 1.55m from west.

Five pieces of *flint* were found. One of these (653) was part of a pebble from which some pieces were struck off. The other four pieces are small featureless scraps (654–7).

Pl. 29b—Site 16: secondary passage from east with some of stony fill of outer part in position.

Finds from the mound

Pottery sherds were found in the layer of redeposited boulder clay. None is illustrated.

658 and 659. Small featureless sherds of coarse ware; 658 is probably 'Carrowkeel' ware. Both inner and outer faces of 659 are worn off and it is not possible to determine the precise nature of the ware.

660. A small bodysherd of fine ware of indeterminate type with small grits of granite. Although this sherd was found in redeposited boulder clay it is not Neolithic pottery. There was an area of disturbance close by behind the kerbstones and it is likely that the sherd intruded subsequently.

Three pieces of *flint* were found amongst the stones of the core. One (661) is a rough blade with medial line on one side, triangular in cross-section and with slight secondary working along the edges. The other two pieces (662 and 663) are scraps (Fig. 54).

Forty-four flints came from the layer of redeposited boulder clay (664–707, Figs 54–55). Four were in a spread of charcoal that occurred on the western side of the primary passage of which one (664) is a poorly-formed blade with flake scars on one side and slight evidence of utilisation along the edges; 665–6 are waste chips; 667 is crude but tends to be thumb-shaped with secondary working

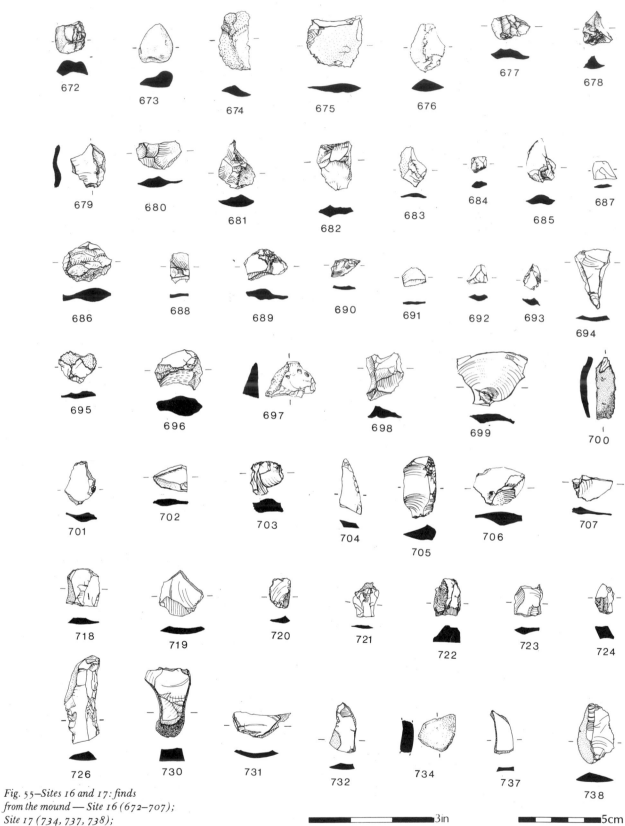

*Fig. 55—Sites 16 and 17: finds
from the mound — Site 16 (672–707);
Site 17 (734, 737, 738);
Site 17, from the dark layer (718–724) and
from a disturbed context in the passage
(730–732).*

3in

5cm

along one edge. The other flints were found in different parts of the mound. Only one (668) is an artifact and this is incomplete: it is about half of a hollow scraper. The scraping edge is worked from one side and there is working along the surviving long side.

Eight flints, all waste, were found in disturbed material (708–15). None is illustrated.

Two objects, a sherd of pottery and a tubular piece of bone, were found on the site but cannot definitely be associated with the passage tomb. The sherd found at the junction between the fill of the basal 'Iron Age' ditch of Site 1 and the mound of Site 16 may have come from the body of a vessel. It is 16mm thick and the brownish ware is compact with tiny quartz grits. It differs from 'Carrowkeel' and **Western Neolithic** wares (716) and its nature is uncertain. Not illustrated. Portion of the bone object is missing (717). Its cross-section tends to be D-shaped and it is 22mm wide. From the inner segment of the primary passage in layer 9. Not illustrated.

Megalithic art

Three orthostats (4, 9 and 13) and two corbels bear art. Unless otherwise stated the technique used was pocking and the art occurs on the inner faces.

Orthostat 4 (Fig. 68:1; Pl. 55b). The art is on the outer face and is confined to a small area near one edge and close to the mid-point. The technique used was incision. The two uppermost motifs are poorly formed arcs, placed one above the other. The opening on each is on the side and they face in opposite directions. The third motif also tends to be in the shape of an arc. There is an extension from one corner. Within this motif are two upright lines.

Orthostat 9 (Fig. 68:2; Pl. 56a). The art is confined to the southern face of the orthostat, the broad side facing orthostat 8. Near the top of the stone are four zig-zags, placed vertically and grouped in pairs. One is larger than the others and below this is a V-shaped design placed sideways. There are two small areas of pocking further down and near the base on the left-hand side is another zig-zag at the bottom of which is an arc placed sidewise.

Corbel directly over orthostat 10 (Fig. 68:5; Pl. 56b). Depressions in the surface appear to be natural but the upper edge of the stone is dressed. Three techniques were used; smoothing, pocking and incision. The only pocked motif is a zig-zag on the right-hand end. There are three main elements in the incised decoration: vertical lines parallel to each other, tending to concentrate around the centre where they are more regularly spaced and extend from the top to the bottom of the face; curving lines confined to a portion of the stone to the left of the centre, one of which is a single-line chevron that extends upwards from slightly to the left of centre to a point above the right-hand end of the multiple chevron; and four lozenges near the left-hand end only two of which are complete. All are defined by smoothing the surface of the stone and in places the edge is delimited by a single incised line. In places, mainly towards the edges, the smoothing technique has left striations. The lozenges are later than the vertical lines which were removed in the relevant areas. Some of the curved lines extend across the lozenges so are probably a later addition. Apart from the main elements there are miscellaneous lines, including some transverse lines.

Corbel directly over orthostat 12 (Fig. 68:4). Incision is the technique used. Near the middle is a series of lines among which are two poorly formed lozenges. A short distance to the left of these is an irregular motif and a short distance further along are three lozenges, two of which are conjoined. Near the right-hand end is a small rectangular area lightly pocked.

Pl. 30a–Site 16: view from east showing core, parts of internal stone settings and kerb.

Orthostat 13. The stone is decorated on three faces. Parts of the left-hand edge of the southern face (Fig. 68:3A; Pl. 57b) have been dressed. The art, which is incised, occurs near the right-hand edge. It consists of a three- to four-pointed zig-zag, three double-pointed zig-zags and other lines that do not form a definite pattern. The decoration on the eastern face (Fig. 68:3B) consists of a single incised motif, a three/four-pointed zig-zag. The single motif on the northern face (Fig. 68:3C; Pl. 57a) is on the top of the orthostat. It consists of a multiple chevron of at least five members, worn in places, possibly because of external exposure at some time in the past.

SITE 17

There were no surface indications of this cruciform passage tomb before work commenced. Most of the structural stones in the south-western half of the site survived but the remainder of the site was badly damaged.

Dark layer under the mound (Fig. 56; Pl. 32)

Evidence for a natural sod layer was found over most of the area covered by the mound. However, over square 56 and parts of squares 49, 50, 57, 60 and 63 the equivalent level consisted of a dark layer. This layer reached a maximum thickness of 12cm. In texture this layer appeared as soft dark earth. It is doubtful if it is entirely natural and it may be an old sod that was somewhat altered by such human activity as the incorporation of occupation material. In support of this view it should be noted that there was a small area within it that had a stone scatter (square 56, southern corner) while from other parts of the layer seven featureless chips of flint were found (718–24, Fig. 55). On top of the layer a chip of flint (732) with a slight curve and faint working along the edge turned up (square 56, 25cm from north, 1.70m from west).

Pl. 30b–Site 16: core around chamber from north.

A further flint was found on the surface of the dark layer during tidying up at the commencement of the 1973 season. It has not been established if it came from this layer. It consists of a blade of triangular cross-section with rude working along the edges (725).

Two C14 determinations came from charcoal in this layer. The first is 4875 ± 150 B.P. (*c.* 2925 b.c., U.B. 318) and the second is 4795 ± 185 B.P. (*c.* 2845 b.c., U.B. 319).

The tomb (Fig. 57; Pls 34, 35)

This was aligned north/south with the entrance at the southern end. The outermost stones of the passage stood about 1.60m in from the back of kerbstone 19. The area between these and the kerb was

Pl. 31a–Site 16: orthostats of primary passage from west showing fill of core (upper centre) and stone placed haphazardly in the mound (bottom centre).

not blocked off by the mound although some of it had slipped in from both sides, leaving a channel somewhat U-shaped in cross-section and with a fill of stones through the mound. The stones were larger at the bottom than at the top and the fill between orthostats 1 and 20 consisted of largish stones. It is not clear when this fill was laid down.

The passage consisted of thirteen orthostats; seven on the western side and six on the eastern. Orthostat 17 was missing. The remainder survived although some, especially 5, were damaged. The orthostats on the eastern side lean inwards, 15 had virtually fallen and its base was out of place, 16 was leaning against 6 and on the western side 7 had fallen forward. The remainder were leaning outwards. From the south inwards the orthostats increased in height. Packing stones were used in all sockets. In 6 a stone was placed under the corner next to orthostat 5. Except 15 and 16 the sockets on the eastern side are less well defined than those on the western.

On the western side there was a flag 94cm in maximum length lying on the outside of orthostat 6. Its shape suggests that it might have been a capstone. The material is fossiliferous limestone.

There were two layers of fill in the passage and these were consistent for its entire length. The bottom layer (2), which filled the lower two-thirds of the chamber, consisted of soft brownish material which was probably derived from the mound. Above this was soft dark earth similar to that under the humus all over the site (No. 3, Fig. 58).

The passage is 4m long at present, 70cm wide at the south and *c.* 1m at the junction with the chamber.

MATERIALS AND DIMENSIONS OF ORTHOSTATS

No.	Type of Rock	Maximum dimensions (cm)		
		Length	Width	Height
1	Limestone	41	26	88
2	Green cleaved grit	46	36	98
3	Limestone with chert	48	38	110
4	Leached sandy limestone	82	14	108
5	Green cleaved grit	53	50	141
6	Green cleaved grit	82	35	138
7	Green cleaved grit	73	34	168
13	Green cleaved grit	145	52	146
15	Green cleaved grit	62	33	112
16	Green cleaved grit	78	15	110
18	Weathered sandy limestone	75	17	105
19	Weathered sandy limestone	68	36	168
20	Green cleaved grit	55	32	154

The chamber area was badly damaged. Some sockets (8–14) survived but only one orthostat (13) remained. A great deal of the damage was caused by the digging of a drain across the inner end of the chamber and a pit in the centre. The pit, which was dug into the subsoil to a maximum depth of 40cm, was filled with a mixture of soft dark earth and smallish stones with a spread of charcoal over the base. The chamber was cruciform in plan and it measured internally 3.60m across and 3.20m in length. Only two sockets each of the western (8,9) and northern (10,11) recesses survived. The eastern recess was more complete. The sides are represented by single sockets. The back stone survives but leans heavily outwards. The

Pl. 31b–Site 17: general view from south showing tomb during excavation.

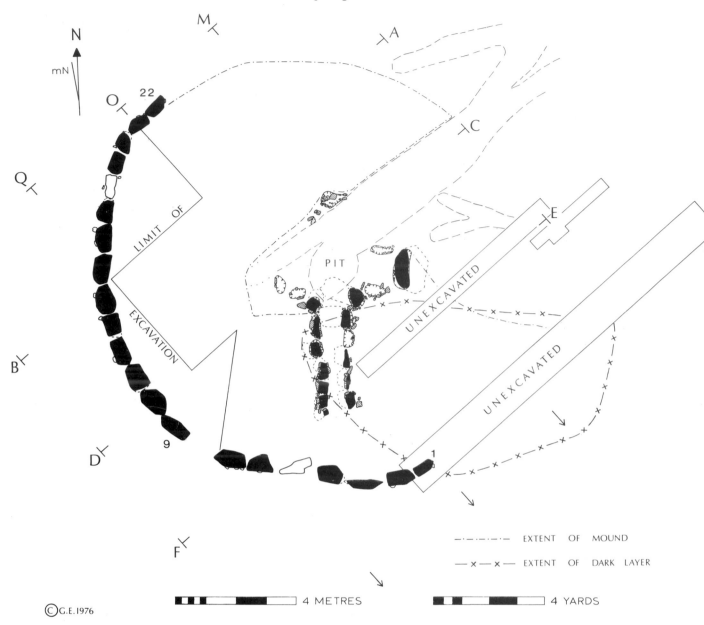

EXTENT OF MOUND
EXTENT OF DARK LAYER

4 METRES   4 YARDS

©G.E.1976

Fig. 56–Site 17: ground plan.

eastern recess was 1.20m long and 1m wide internally. The fill of sockets 12 and 13 consisted largely of chips of green cleaved grit; at other places in the chamber further chips of the same rock were found indicating that considerable sledging took place when the orthostats were being removed.

Burials

Cremated bone which must have been derived from burials was found at various places. High up in the fill of the passage between orthostats 2 and 19 was a scatter of cremated bone (726). This was not in a primary position. The only pieces that Dr Weekes could identify are two portions of the vault of a human skull. These are thin and may have belonged to a child. There are also fragments of long bones and some animal bones.

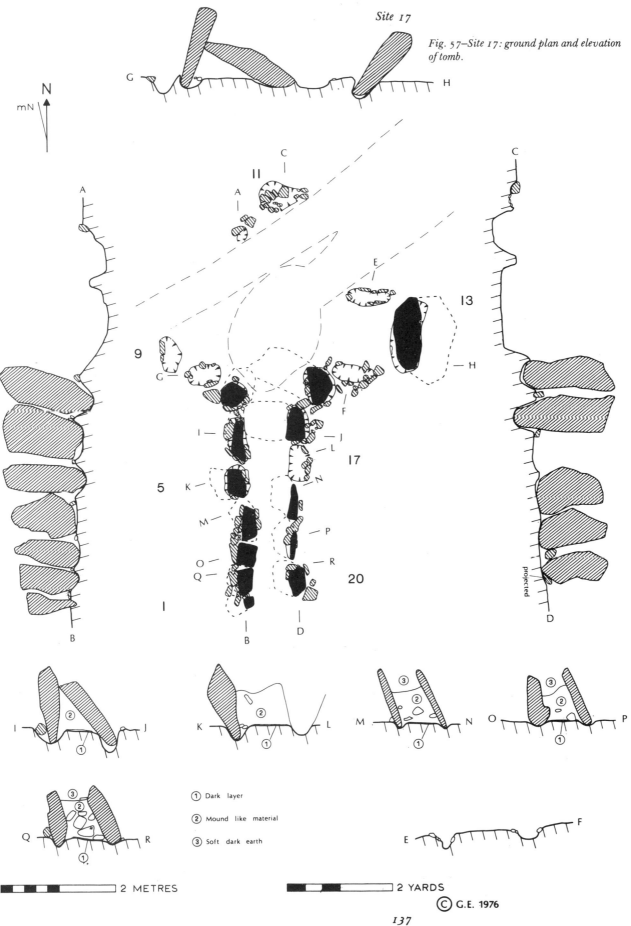

Site 17

Fig. 57—Site 17: ground plan and elevation of tomb.

mN N

G   H

C

11

A

A

E

13

9

G

H

F

I   J

L

17

5   K   N

M

P

O   R

Q   20

1

B   D

projected

D

I   J   K   L   M   N   O   P

Q   R

① Dark layer

② Mound like material

③ Soft dark earth

E   F

2 METRES   2 YARDS

© G.E. 1976

137

Another scatter (727) was in disturbed material in the inner end of the passage and extending over to socket 7. Amongst the fragments were some pieces of the vault of a skull probably from an adult and part of the shaft of the fibula which is small and may have belonged to a child. There were also fragments of long bones.

There was a small deposit along the inner side of socket 11. The identifiable fragments were pieces of the vault of a thin skull and the distal half of a phalanx of a small finger which may have belonged to a child. There are also fragments of long bones (728).

These two scatters (727 and 728) seem to have been part of a chamber deposit. The third scatter (726) may have been thrown out during the disturbance to the chamber. A few fragments of cremated bone (729) were found on later paving on the outside of orthostat 13. The pieces were 10cm out from the orthostat.

Pl. 32a–Site 17: general view from east showing tomb during excavation.

The mound

The remains of the mound survived over most of the site and it rose to a maximum height of 70cm along the south-western side. The material used was boulder clay and in places there appears to have been a mixture of sods, which gave the surviving mound a greyish colour. The material alongside the passage on the eastern side differed from the main part of the mound and was laid down afterwards (Fig. 58, E–F, O–P; Pls 32b, 33b). This is probably because the mound, or part of it, was being laid down before the construction of the tomb was completed. After the completion of the tomb, the area left open was filled in.

The kerb

Twenty-one kerbstones survive. They form an arc on the south-western side which apart from one missing stone was continuous. The stones are rough. At the northern part of the site were two stones (not on plan) which may be displaced kerbstones.

MATERIALS AND DIMENSIONS OF KERBSTONES

No.	Type of Rock	Maximum dimensions (cm)		
		Length	Width	Height
1	Fine-grained volcanic agglomerate	72	35	60
2	Dolerite	96	48	47
3	Leached sandy limestone	126	31	75
4	Volcanic tuff	103	65	63
5	Dolerite (shattered)	–	–	–
6	Limestone (carboniferous)	92	65	55
7	Limestone (carboniferous)	112	55	56
9	Limestone (carboniferous)	107	47	60
10	Limestone (carboniferous)	104	66	65
11	Fine-grained volcanic agglomerate	98	64	70
12	Dolomitic limestone	91	47	76
13	Volcanic tuff	76	63	57
14	Agglomerate (volcanic)	95	64	62
15	Pale brown sandstone	94	61	68
16	Green cleaved grit	94	61	65
17	Dolerite	82	58	59
18	Dolerite (shattered)	–	–	–
19	Limestone	74	52	52
20	Dolerite	72	48	59
21	Dolerite	79	43	58
22	Weathered sandstone	80	51	55

Pl. 32b–Site 17: general view from west showing stumps of orthostats and kerbstones of Site 18 (right of standing figure).

Finds (Fig. 55)

730 and 731. Two unworked pieces of flint found on the floor of the passage on the old ground surface between orthostats 2 and 20. One fragment (730) has a smooth cortex around its side. It has not been established that these flints were associated with the tomb; they could have been derived from the basal dark layer or they might even have been intrusive at a later date. The rest of the finds came from the mound.

Pl. 33a–Site 17: Tomb from east. Dark surface between two baulks in foreground is part of underlying dark layer.

733. Sherd of coarse pottery, possibly 'Carrowkeel' ware, 2cm thick. Both surfaces have been worn away (not illustrated).

734. Sherd of fine ware of indeterminate type but with some grits 6.5mm thick. The outer surface is brownish and the inner dark. It resembles Beaker ware.

735 and 736. Sherds of brownish fairly fine ware of indeterminate type. The outer surface is smooth but the inner has been worn away (not illustrated).

Only two small chips of flint (737–8) were found.

The following objects were found in a disturbed position and as it has not been established that these finds were associated with the passage grave they are listed but not illustrated. 739 is a small sherd of fine pottery from the top of the mound; 740 is a rounded scraper which had been burnt and 741 is a lop-sided flint scraper. Two rough pieces of flint (742 and 743) were also found.

744. Bone pin with tip missing, 5cm long with a circular cross-section along the stem. It expands towards the head where the cross-section is rectangular. There is a single perforation through the head. An area of paving (apparently of Early Christian date) was found near here, and the pin is probably best considered as linked with that feature.

Pl. 33b–Site 17: passage from west after excavation.

Megalithic art

The art is confined to five orthostats of the tomb. Unless otherwise stated, the technique used was pocking and the art occurs on the inner faces.

Orthostat 6 (Fig. 69:1; Pl. 58a) has a simple motif, a poorly executed double-pointed chevron, on the inner face.

Orthostat 7. Art occurs on two faces.

Face along-passage (Fig. 69:2). Art consisting of two short zig-zags closely set one above the other occurs about the middle of the stone.

Face along chamber (Fig. 69:2, on right; Pl. 58b). There are three small areas of pocking. One is in the shape of an inverted V, another tends to be angular. These are adjacent to each other. The third is irregular.

Orthostat 13 (Fig. 69:4; Pl. 59a). The art occurs on the inner face. The orthostat has been slightly damaged towards the top, but motifs may not have been destroyed as no trace of art is visible on the upper part of the stone. Three of the motifs are pocked. One tends to be

Fig. 58—Sites 17 and 18: sections.

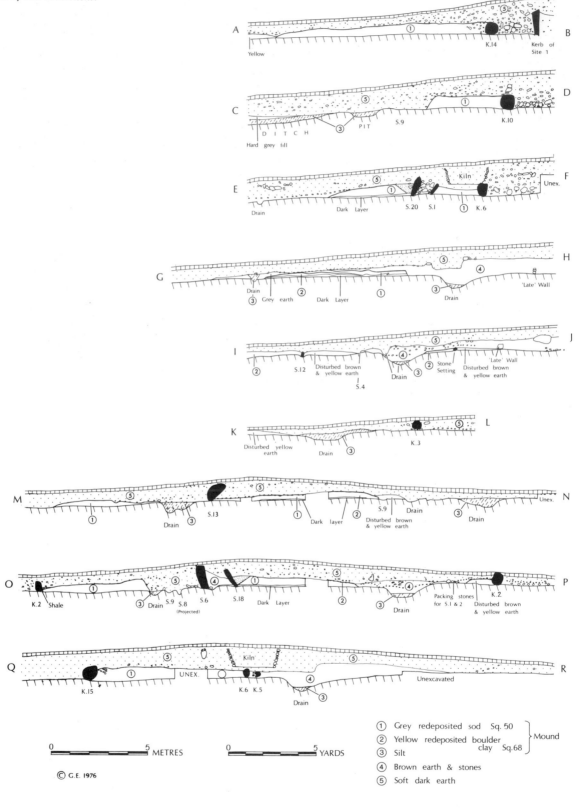

0   5 METRES

0   5 YARDS

Ⓒ G.E. 1976

① Grey redeposited sod   Sq. 50 ⎫
② Yellow redeposited boulder   ⎬ Mound
      clay Sq. 68 ⎭
③ Silt
④ Brown earth & stones
⑤ Soft dark earth

Pl. 34a—Site 17: tomb from south after excavation. Darker mound material beside\orthostats was laid down after main part.

Pl. 34b—Site 17: tomb from north showing damage to chamber area from subsequent digging of pit and drain.

Pl. 35a–Site 17: tomb from south showing fill at entrance.

square and an incised line runs parallel to the pocking on the inside. In the interior are poorly executed incised zig-zags. Another pocked motif is a spiral, part of which has been smoothed down. The third pocked motif is a short zig-zag. Around this same part of the stone is a considerable amount of incised decoration. This is a confused mass but zig-zags and horizontal and transverse lines are the main motifs. To the left of this area are some incised lines but these do not form definite motifs.

Orthostat 15 (Fig. 69:5; Pl. 59b). In the top right hand corner is a spiral part of which is missing. A short distance below are three, in places four, parallel rows of zig-zags. At the base of this are three lozenges, one double, and one partly incorporated into the band of zig-zags. Around the middle of the stone is another spiral and below it an unusual motif consisting of a somewhat circular area with four incised lines tending to fan out within it. There is also an area of pocking to the right of centre.

Orthostat 16 (Fig. 69:3; Pl. 60a). The single motif is irregular but it approaches a double lozenge in shape.

Sites 17–18: *Possible sequential relationships*

If Sites 17 and 18, like the other mounds at Knowth, had been circular or roughly circular mounds, then we could assume that one site predated the other. But the large-scale destruction that went on at these sites makes it impossible to solve this problem. It is being assumed that the earlier mound was circular and that the later mound (which could not be circular) impinged upon the earlier one. In the attempt to sort out the problem of which comes first, particular attention was paid to the area around where the junction between the two sites would have been. In this area the few basal centimetres of mound survived but there were no kerbstones or even traces of them. Therefore, some of the kerbstones of one of the sites must have been removed in antiquity. There was not much difference between the materials of the two mounds, although the mound of Site 18 was more boulder-clay-like and yellowish and the mound of Site 17 was more sod-like and greyish. Now, along the area of supposed contact the yellowish material underlies the greyish material. This is slender evidence but it suggests that Site 18 is the earlier of the two (Fig. 58, G–H). However, it should be emphasised that the layer of yellow material is very thin at the area of supposed junction between the sites. If this layer is part of the mound of Site 18 then that mound, at least along the north-western side, must have been lowered considerably and portion removed completely before the building of the mound of Site 17.

There is also the problem of the chronological relationship between Site 17 and Site 1. Extending outwards from Site 1 to the southern side of Site 17 is a spread of stones including granite boulders and quartz. It occurs over an area outside the entrance to Site 1 and appears to be associated with that site. At least one of the kerbstones (7) of Site 17 appears to post-date the spread. In any case it is sitting on stones that seem to be part of the spread (Pl. 35b)

Pl. 35b–Site 17: kerbstone 7 and spread of stones. It appears that this kerbstone partly overlies some stones of the spread. This spread of stones is found beside the entrance to the eastern tomb of Site 1 and may be slip derived from the Site 1 mound.

The sections between Sites 1 and 17 were also studied in detail but these did not provide any chronological evidence. There was no evidence for primary slip from either site and the material was an undifferentiated mixture of stones and earth (cf. Pl. 36a).

SITE 18

Before the commencement of excavations there were no surface indications of this cruciform tomb. The site has been badly damaged. Most of the kerbstones, nearly all of the mound and, except for a couple of stumps, all the orthostats and capstones had been removed. Two drains had been dug across the site and at other points shallow scoops or pits have penetrated the original surface.

The dark layer noted under the tomb in square 50 (p. 133) extends under portion of the mound of this site.

Pl. 36a–Site 17: east face of section between cutting 51 extension and cutting 52, with kerbs of Site 1 (left) and Site 17 (right).

The tomb (Figs 59, 60; Pls 36b–40a)

Evidence for the structure of the tomb is provided by fifteen sockets dug into the boulder clay to an average depth of 14cm. They vary in size. Four sockets (6, 7, 11, 12) have stumps of orthostats, 6, 7 and 12 are green cleaved grit and 11 is a green grit. In 6 and 12 only a small part survives, but in 7 and 12 the stumps are more substantial. In at least sockets 6 and 13–15 the old ground surface has been removed so the original edges of these sockets have also been removed.

The tomb consists of a passage leading into a cruciform chamber aligned north/south with the entrance at the southern end. From the inner edge of socket 10 to the inside of kerbstone 3, the tomb is 7.80m long.

Evidence for only five sockets (1–3, 14–15) of the passage survived. Packing stones occurred in 1, 2, 14 and 15. Nos 3 and 14–15 are set at an angle, so perhaps the passage widened at the inner end. Three of the orthostats of the chamber, 4, 8 and 12 (originally there must have been four), were obliquely placed in relation to the adjoining orthostats of the recesses. This arrangement increased the spatial area of the chamber. The eastern recess has been severely damaged and a drain dug across part of it. Socket 13 probably held an orthostat, but it is difficult to be certain. This socket may have been enlarged when the orthostat was removed. The northern end recess is well defined. It was formed with three orthostats but all that survives of these is the lower portion of No. 11. The northern end of this orthostat is in a shallow socket but the southern end is over ground level and is propped up with small stones. These three sockets are the largest in the tomb and they average 90cm by 45cm. The western recess was formed by an orthostat on each side. The sockets are large. No. 6 is 70cm by 28cm, 7 is 90cm by 55cm and both are approximately 20cm deep. Packing stones occur around the edges and orthostat 7 was further secured by a wedge stone under its western end. Outside the western end of orthostat 7 is a depression but this does not appear to be a socket. It may have been dug at the

Pl. 36b–Site 18: general view from south showing tomb during excavation.

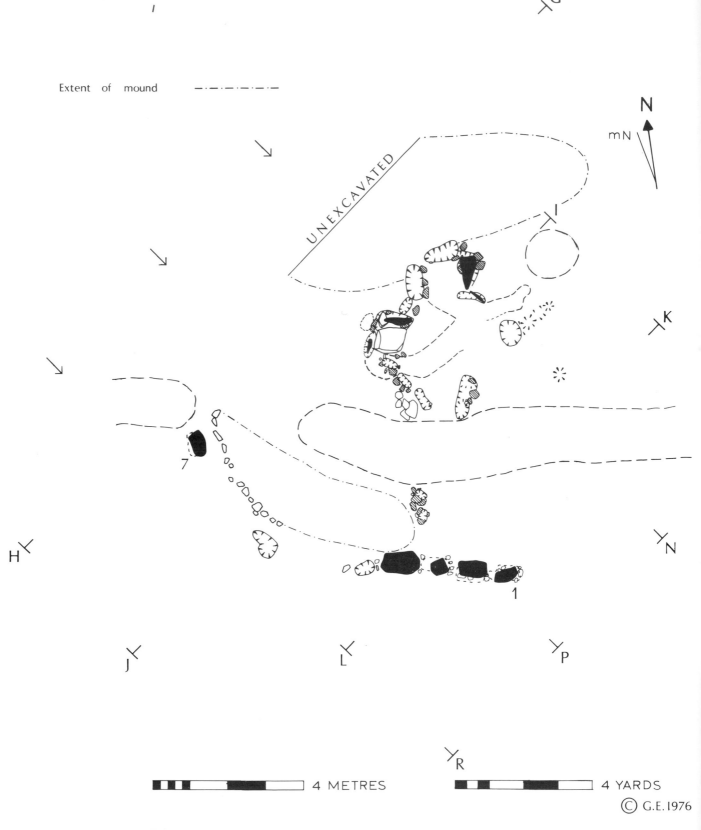

Fig. 59—Site 18: ground plan.

Pl. 37a–Site 18: general view of tomb from east.

Pl. 37b–Site 18: tomb from south after excavation.

time of destruction. Nearly all of this recess is occupied by a rectangular flag of green grit 80cm by 70cm. The flag extends over the inner edge of sockets 6 and 7. Internally the recess measures approximately 90cm by 90cm.

The approximate internal measurements of the chamber are 3.02m by 3.00m.

Pl. 38a–Site 18: tomb from north after excavation.

Burials

The chamber area was disturbed down to the old ground surface and in some places the old surface was penetrated. It was overlain by soft dark earth containing animal bones.

In the area of the eastern recess was a scatter of cremated bone (745) weighing 231.2g (8oz) on the old surface. This occurred between sockets 12 and 13, about 50cm north of the northern edge of socket 13. It extended over a narrow area 45cm long. It is doubtful if this scatter was in its precise original position, but the fact that it was in the area of the eastern recess suggests that it was a burial deposit, or part of one. Dr Weekes reports that the only recognisable pieces are part of the vault of a skull, and appear to be of adult thickness.

There was a small scatter of cremated bone (746), weighing 50.6g (2 oz.) in a disturbed context almost 2m west of socket 5. This was probably part of an original burial deposit from the chamber. Dr Weekes reports that 'the only recognisable pieces are two fragments of skull and some fragments of long bone'.

In the western recess was a sealed cremation deposit (747). This was a thin scatter and except for a small portion of the recess to the south-east it extended over the recess and the filling of sockets 6 and

7 on the inside. The deposit lay directly on the old ground surface of natural sod. Dr Weekes reports that 'the pieces which can definitely be identified are parts of human skull, probably that of an adult. There are also small pieces of human long bones.'

The flagstone was placed directly on top of the cremation deposit, perhaps immediately after deposition of the cremation, as there was an absence of silt or other natural covering. The central part of the upper surface of the flag is flat and small flakes have been trimmed off at some points along the edge. Indeed, it may be assumed that the flag served, or was intended to serve, the function of a basin. However, no cremated bone was found on it. Overlying it was a mixed deposit of charcoal, pottery sherds, flints, a fragment of a human skull and animal bones which appear to belong to a Beaker context (see p. 312). Five flints were found in the chamber area a short distance in from the front of the recess. They might have been derived from the deposit just described. Eight flints, including four thumb scrapers, were found in the tomb area but not in a context.

Pl. 38b–Site 18: chamber from east after excavation.

The chronological position and cultural status of the deposit overlying the flag and the isolated finds of flints are difficult to establish. If the objects over the flag form a deposit then perhaps they were part of a domestic assemblage of Beaker date. Accordingly they are being published with the Beaker material (p. 312). As the isolated flints lack a context they will be published in a subsequent volume.

Fig. 60—Site 18: ground plan and elevation of tomb.

CREMATED BONE

2 METRES

0

2 YARDS

© G.E. 1976

Pl. 39a—Site 18: kerbstones 1–4 (right to left) from south.

Pl. 39b—Site 18: west recess from west after excavation.

The mound (Figs 58, 59)

This was missing over the north-eastern part of the site. Where it survived it only did so to a maximum height of 30cm. Within the mound, *c*. 8cm over the original surface, and close to the western edge was a row of fifteen stones averaging 34cm by 28cm. The surviving portion of the mound was made from boulder clay and at the time of its construction an old sod covered the area.

Pl. 40a–Site 18: flagstone in west recess that lay directly on top of cremation deposit E70:747.

The kerb (Fig. 59; Pls 37b, 39a)

At least four (1–4) and possibly five (7) kerbstones survive. Nos 1–4 form a continuous line across the entrance, sitting on the original surface. To the west of 4 are two depressions (5–6) which may represent the positions of kerbstones. The kerb appears to have been straight across the entrance to the tomb. The surviving kerbstones are undressed blocks; 7 is badly shattered.

MATERIALS AND DIMENSIONS OF KERBSTONES

No.	Type of Rock	Maximum dimensions (cm)		
		Length	Width	Height
1	Current bedded sandstone ?Dolomite	89	53	66
2	Sandstone	93	57	66
3	Dolerite	98	47	60
4	Sandstone (bedded)	102	58	82
7	Limestone (carboniferous)	68	49	30

Megalithic art

Orthostat 11, the only decorated stone, was decorated on both the inner and outer faces and on the base but as only a stump of this stone survives most of the art is missing. The technique is pocking (Fig. 68:6; Pls 60b, 61b).

The inner face has a vertical line which extends from just below the fractured edge to the base. On either side of it at the base are two small areas of pocking. To one side of the line, at about mid-point, is an irregular spiral. In the inner part the pocking is distinctive but it becomes fainter towards the end (Fig. 68: 6 B; Pl. 61a).

The designs on the *outer face* are more deeply pocked. Along one end are four parallel vertical lines, the ends of the outer and inner of which extend for a short distance on to the base. From the bottom of the inner line a horizontal line runs parallel to the base for most of the stone. Near the other end is a circular pocked area. At one point a line extends up from it and there is further pocking at another point. These designs are 'cut off' from the remainder of the face by an oblique line which extends from the present top corner to the base at about mid-point. Extending from the base to about half way is another line parallel to this which curves around at the top. This

Pl. 40b—Site 2: orthostat 14, inner face.

design forms one side of a V-shaped area of light pocking (Fig. 68: 6A; Pl. 60b).

There are four distinct cup marks close to each other on the *base*. The central cup mark is 4mm deep; the others are 9mm deep. Beside this cluster is another cup mark, also 9mm deep, joined to a further cup mark about 8cm away by a well-pocked line. Near the broad end of the stone are other areas of pocking consisting of an irregular area and poorly formed curved lines (Fig. 68: 6C; Pl. 61b).

POSSIBLE EVIDENCE FOR OTHER TOMBS

In an area to the east and south-east of Site 1 and within 30m to 40m from its kerb, nineteen glacial erratic boulders came to light (Figs 3, 5). They look like kerbstones and may be from a tomb or tombs which have been destroyed.

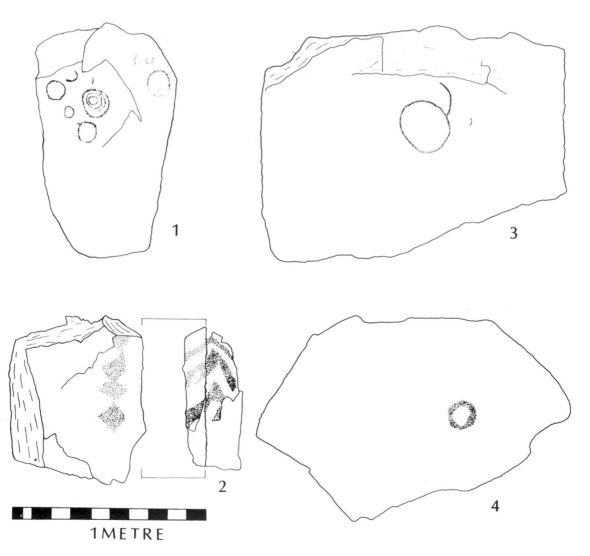

Fig. 61–Megalithic art, Site 2:
1, 2 and 3–orthostats 14, 30 and 27;
4–kerbstone 28.

Pl. 41a–Site 2: orthostat 28, inner face. Removed from socket for photographic purposes.

Pl. 41b–Site 2: orthostat 28, side face. Removed from socket for photographic purposes.

MATERIALS AND DIMENSIONS OF KERBSTONES

No.	Type of Rock	Maximum dimensions (cm)		
		Length	Width	Height
1	Sandstone	105	65	38
2	Green grit	68	28	17
3	Purple andesite	64	58	23
4	Purple andesite	80	34	35
5	Green grit	80	18	39
6	Purple andesite	64	22	19
7	Coarse dolerite with platy crystals Augite?	58	46	52
8	Dolerite	80	60	49
9	Coarse agglomerate	120	80	67
10	Calcareous sandstone	88	56	63
11	—	54	30	37
12	Fine-grained bedded grit	66	32	23
13	Coarse grit with mica	56	36	27
14	Weathered calcareous sandstone	80	60	26
15	Sandstone	108	52	18
16	Bedded calcareous sandstone	80	69	65
17	Dolerite	75	56	51
18	Green grit	90	75	80
19	Limestone	80	40	22

Pl. 42a–Site 2: kerbstone 28, outer face.

In addition about 300 broken and fragmented pieces of green grit, a type of rock frequently used for orthostats and kerbstones, also came to light. These varied in length from 10cm to 60cm. There was no trace of art on any of these fragments. Activity during medieval times and in particular during the last century probably obliterated all further evidence for tombs in this area.

There is another large boulder incorporated into a fence on the northern side of the public road (see Fig. 1 for position). Its shape and size suggest that it may have been a kerbstone. There are, however, no surface indications of a tomb in that area.

POSSIBLE PASSAGE TOMB AT KNOWTH HOUSE

Knowth House is on the eastern side of the public road, *c.*65m from the kerb of Site 1. Dr Herity has published an account of two large stones which appeared in the Ordnance Survey Namebook (1836). The description is as follows:

> In front of Miss Maguire's house are two upright stones about 6 feet high overgrown with ivy which may have been a Cromlech or a Tomb in the centre of a Cairn similar to those opened in Dowth parish. The plan of the stones is ⌐. They are so much covered in ivy that a passer-by would suppose the whole to be only an Ivy bush.

The present farmhouse was built about 1860–70 and as Herity has suggested the stones may have been cleared away then (Herity 1967, 141).

MEGALITHIC ART: ISOLATED FINDS

1. *Capstone* 7, souterrain 4 (Fig. 70: 1; Pl. 62a). This stone had at least five motifs, all pocked, two of which are incomplete because of damage to the stone. The three intact motifs are two spirals and an irregular 'circle'. One of the damaged motifs may have been a spiral. Of the fifth only portion of an arc survives.

2. *Capstone* 3, souterrain 9 (Fig. 70: 2; Pl. 62b). There are one D-shaped and six circular, or approximately circular, motifs. There is also a lightly pocked arc and some other short areas of pocking.

3. *Capstone* 1, entrance to souterrain complex, eastern tomb, Site 1 (Fig. 70: 3). There is one large motif, pocked. It has been subjected to weathering and as a result it is difficult to know whether the motif is the remains of a spiral or a multiple concentric circle. It consisted of twelve members. Towards the other end a portion of the surface has been smoothed down.

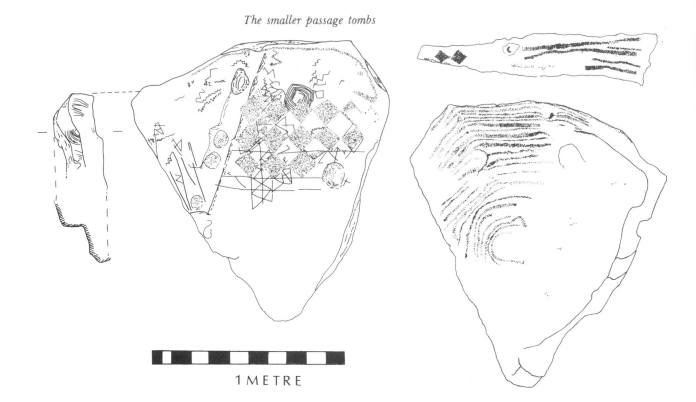

1 METRE

Fig. 62–Megalithic art, Site 4: stone A (face 1 at right).

4. *Capstone* 13, souterrain 1. This is a portion of a larger stone of green grit. The remaining decoration could have been part of a multiple concentric circle or spiral (Pl. 63a).

Pl. 43a–Site 4: stone A, face 2.

Pl. 43b–Site 4: stone A, face 1.

5 (Fig. 70: 5; Pl. 63b). Sandstone. The two motifs are spirals and both are pocked. The larger is near the centre and has seven turns but there are gaps in the three outer rings, which are probably due to weathering. At one point four of the outer members are crossed by a transverse line. The other spiral is of four and a half turns. This stone forms part of the entrance to an Early Christian house, House J (publication pending).

6 (Fig. 70: 6; 64a). Green grit. The three motifs are pocked. That in the centre is a concentric circle of three members. To its left is a gapped circle of two members and the motif on the right-hand side has been damaged but was either concentric circles or a spiral. As the members are close to each other along one portion it is more likely to have been a spiral. In the wall of the remains of a fairly modern house site in cutting 41.

7 (Fig. 70: 7; Pl. 64b). Green grit, 57cm by 39cm, with art over one surface. All the motifs are pocked and consist of complete circles, gapped circles, meanders and other designs.

8 (Fig. 70: 8; Pl. 65a). A flake 40cm by 20cm, having part of two roughly pocked arcs.

7 and 8 are both flakes from larger stones. They were found beside each other in a scatter of stones 9m to the west of kerbstone 49 of Site 1, about 40cm below the surface.

Pl. 44a–Site 5: stone 8.

9 (Fig. 70: 9; Pl. 65b). A sandstone flag with art on the narrow side, which measures 72cm by 17cm. There are three pocked lozenges and the remains of a fourth. It may have been a lintel, from Site 2. Found over the kerb of Site 1, 6m from Site 3 and 3.50m from Site 2. It was part of a setting of stones underneath the sod.

10. A sandstone fragment (Fig. 70: 10) with the remains of what appear to be two concentric circles. Found in a pit *c.* 1m out from kerbstone 60 of Site 1.

11 (Fig. 70: 11). Piece of green grit 54cm by 40cm. The decoration consists of the remains of a double concentric circle, an irregular, gapped subrectangular motif and the remains of what may have been a chevron. It may have been the top portion of an orthostat. Found in the humus over Site 1, cutting 51.

Pl. 44b–Site 8: kerbstone 5, outer face.

DECORATED STONE OBJECT (Fig. 71; Pl. 66)

3906. A sandstone object broken across about a third of the way up from the tip. It was found, unassociated, in a small depression outside but close to the entrance to the western tomb in the large mound (Site 1).

The object is 25.5cm long. From the unexpanded head, which is slightly bevelled along the outer edge, it tapers from 39mm to a blunt point. A channel, V-shaped in cross-section, narrowing and

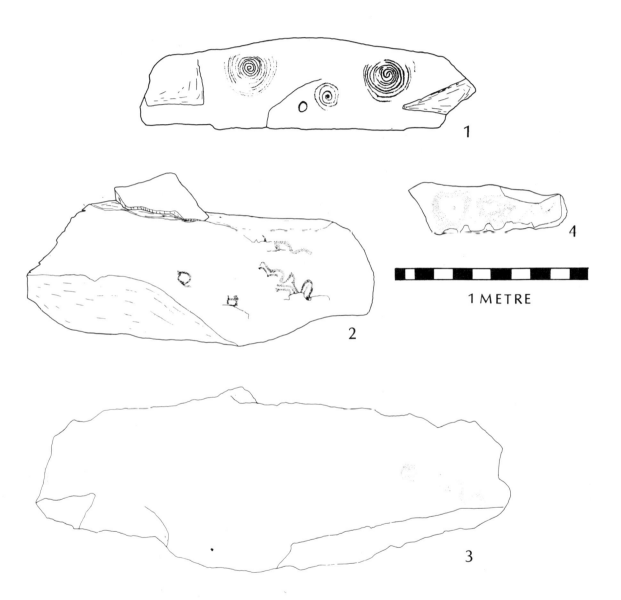

1 METRE

becoming shallower from the top to the bottom, runs down one side almost to the tip. It is funnelled at the top. The lower 7cm is undecorated but above this the body is ornamented with a series of arched grooves which terminate at the channel. Between the uppermost groove and the head are three arcs. It can be compared to the antler or bone object from Site 3 (p. 29–30).

Fig. 63—Megalithic art, Sites 3, 5 and 8:
1—Site 3, kerbstone 10;
2—Site 5, stone 8;
3 and 4—Site 8, kerbstones 5 and 11.

FASHIONED STONE (Fig. 72; Pl. 67)

This stone is 49.5cm long and 30cm in maximum width. The wider end is rounded at the top. The narrow end is blunt and rough. Except for the narrow end the surface is pocked. Most of one ridge between two grooves is polished. The body tends to have a rounded cross-section but there are somewhat flattened areas which give a sort of five-sided effect. Vertical decoration occurs on three of these. Two of the faces adjoin each other but between these and the other decorated face are blank areas.

The vertical decoration consists of twelve grooves formed by pocking which vary in length, width and depth. The longest groove is 37cm long, 6cm in maximum width and 5mm in maximum depth; the shortest is about 10cm long. These grooves were formed by pocking. Two adjoining faces have three grooves each, the third has six, but one, which is short, is an outlier. At the base is a horizontal line also formed by pocking. At the top is a similar line and for part of the circumference there is a second parallel line. Most of the surface of one ridge has been polished and patches of polishing also occur on another ridge.

Pl. 45a–Site 8: kerbstone 11, base.

In its technique of manufacture and, in part, its decorative scheme, this piece of sculpture resembles the stone basin in the eastern tomb of Site 1 (Eogan 1969, Pls 2 and 3) and to a lesser extent the stone object just described. The stone was found lying on its side, apparently in a disturbed position just below the base of the humus, a short distance to the east of the entrance to Site 12 (Area 5, square 51, 1.40m from north, 1.4m from west). Perhaps it may have stood slightly closer to that site like the nodules ('baetyls') that occur outside the entrance to the western tomb of Site 1 (publication pending).

STONE 'URN' (Pl. 68).

Writing in 1725 Molyneux (p. 200) describes the finding of a fashioned stone at Knowth as follows:

Another urn . . . was twelve years since [*c.* 1713] discovered in a mound at *Knowth,* a place in the county of *Meath,* within four miles of *Drogheda;* 'twas found inclosed in a square stone box, about five foot long and four foot broad, made of four rude large flag stones set together edgeways. The urn it self was one great heavy stone, of an oblong round figure, somewhat of the shape of the upper part of a man's scull, but five or six times as large; 'twas of a sandy greet like freestone, but much coarser and harder; its length about sixteen inches, about twelve in breadth, and eleven in height, its cavity but shallow, not above five inches deep, rudely hollowed by cutting out some part of the stone in which was found loose fragments of burnt bones: they seem to have taken pains in adorning the outside with rude lines and carving, yet the work shows more the labour than skill of the artist, who has graved five furrows one above the other, round the upper part of the urn; and in the middle of each side and at each end, rude figures expressing, as I take it, the great luminaries of the world, the sun and moon: and I'm the more inclined to favour this conjecture, because 'tis sure, those two caelestial bodies were very religiously adored by all the northern nations in time of paganism . .

This urn now in my possession, being a singular piece of *Danish* antiquity, and the only one of stone I have heard that has been found in this or in our neighbouring island; I thought it well deserved to be exprest by the two following figures.

Pl. 45b–Site 12: orthostat 8.

Fig. 64—Megalithic art, Sites 12 and 13:
1—Site 12, kerbstone 6;
2—Site 13, orthostat 3;
3, 4, 5 and 6—Site 13, kerbstones 15, 16,
17 and 24;
7—disturbed stone found near Site 13.

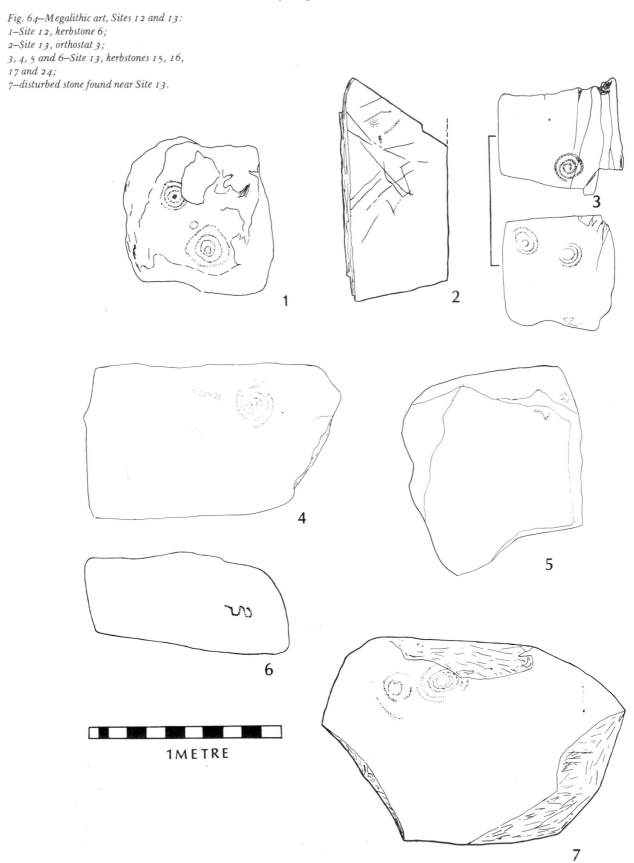

Pl. 46a–Site 12: kerbstone 6.

Pl. 46b–Site 13: kerbstone 15.

The smaller passage tombs

The whereabouts of this object is now unknown. It may have been lost in the eighteenth century, for although it is mentioned by Wilde, MacAdam, Wood-Martin and Borlase none of them appears to have had first hand knowledge of the piece (Wilde 1857, 134; Macadam 1861–2, 283; Wood-Martin 1895, 359; Borlase 1897, ii, 345). Wakeman, writing in 1848, confused it with a stone vessel (N.M.I. No. W-50) formerly in the collection of Dean Dawson, whose findplace is unknown (1894, 181). The shape of the piece and the circumstances of discovery suggest that it may have been a small stone basin. The layout of decoration resembles that on the basin stone in the eastern tomb of Site 1 (Eogan 1969, **Pls 2–3**).

Perhaps the 'square stone box' described by Molyneux was a recess of a cruciform passage tomb. From the description and illustration it is not possible to identify the exact nature of the piece but it may be best interpreted as a small basin.

Pl. 47a–Site 13: kerbstone 16.

DISCUSSION

Morphology, grave goods and art

The excavations have revealed a new cemetery of passage tombs and as a result the number of tombs in the Brugh na Bóinne cemetery has been doubled. Apart from the cemetery concentration the Knowth group has a number of typical Irish passage tomb features such as the hill-top siting, the round mounds with kerbs, the use of

Pl. 47b–Site 13: kerbstone 17.

megalithic stones, art, grave goods and burial rite.

Despite the widespread damage that the sites have suffered, a considerable amount of new information has come to light. It is clear that the *orientation* of the sites varied. Except Site 7 — incidentally the most outward example of the group — the entrances to the undifferentiated tombs opened onto the hill-top (Fig. 73B). This contrasts with the cruciform tombs and with Site 3, which produced no definite evidence for a passage. Only one cruciform tomb (Site 9) focused on the ridge but of course its line can be extended across to the eastern side. The others avoided the centre and their focal point was on the eastern side of the large mound (Fig. 73B). During excavations nothing unusual was found in that area but it was much disturbed and if a focal feature, such as a tomb, existed it seems to have been removed without trace. The orientation of the entrances to the smaller tombs all fall within an arc extending from the north-east to the south-west (Fig. 73A). Of course, the fact that no tombs have survived on the eastern side may mean that this is not a true picture.

The sites also varied considerably in *size*. Two sites, Nos 2 and 15, were exceptionally large, the external diameter of the kerbs being about 20m. The tomb of Site 2 was about 13m in internal length and that of Site 15 was 9.20m long. The smallest site was 16 which had an external diameter of 8.60m. The average external diameter of the other sites is *c.* 12m.

Pl. 48a–Site 13: kerbstone 24, top.

Evidence for the *methods of construction* also varied. In all surviving cases both tomb and kerb were of megalithic construction. The kerbstones were undressed and Professor Mitchell found no clear evidence that they were quarried. Their origin appears to have been local, some being definite glacial erractics. The tombstones were mainly green grit and were more regular in shape. Natural sod was missing from underneath some of the sites (3–8, 10–11, 13–14). This could be due to deliberate stripping before building but it could also be the result of cultivation in the period immediately before the building of the tombs. It can be suggested that the tomb orthostats were usually erected first, but at Site 17 it appears that an area immediately around the tomb was left clear, possibly in order to enable tomb and mound construction to go ahead simultaneously. Except at Site 15 where orthostats 1, 2 and 21 were sitting on the old ground surface, the orthostats were inserted into sockets at all the tombs where evidence was available. Evidence indicates that better quality stones were selected for the orthostats than for the kerbstones. The orthostats were of a more regular shape with flat surfaces and a number were green grit. Apart from Site 10, portions of the mound survive at all sites and boulder clay is the predominant material used. In some, small quantities of shale also occur, and where this is found the material was deposited in layers (Sites 2, 3, 4, 8, 9, 15 and 16). Apart from the cores in Sites 12 and 16 small stones were not used in mound construction. In general, the kerbstones were rough and boulder-like, but two tombs, Sites 3 and 8, had some sub-rectangular slabs. Unlike the orthostats, the kerbstones were usually placed on the old ground surface. Often they were supported by prop stones at the base and it was only on rare occasions that they were inserted into sockets. Evidence for sockets is mainly confined to Sites 13, 15 and 16. The surviving kerbstones indicate that they enclosed a more or less circular area. At least at Site 8 the kerb curved inwards before the entrance while at Site 15 there was a flattening of the kerb before the entrance. This may also have been so at Site 13 and possibly at Sites 4 and 18. The kerbs continued across the entrance to the passage and at least in Sites 2, 4, 8, 13 and 14 the passage stones articulated with the kerb. At present there is a gap between the outermost passage orthostats and the kerb in Sites 15, 17 and 18. If this is an original feature then it would appear that the outer part of the passage was unroofed and that its sides were formed of dry-stone walling or sods, or that the area may have been blocked off (cf. Lynch 1973, esp. pp 149 ff).

Pl. 48b–Site 13: displaced stone.

No evidence for a *tomb* survived at Sites 5 and 11. In the remaining fifteen sites, five (2, 6, 9, 17 and 18) had cruciform chambers and in the other ten the chambers were of undifferentiated plan. At Site 16 the remains of dry-stone work survived above the orthostats of the chamber. One site (13) provided evidence for a roof *in situ*: capstones covered the outer part of the passage. A displaced capstone survived at Site 14. At Site 16 there were a number of collapsed roofstones in

Pl. 49a–Site 14: orthostat 4.
(Photo: Commissioners of Public Works)

Pl. 49b–Site 14: orthostat 8, inner face.
(Photo: Commissioners of Public Works)

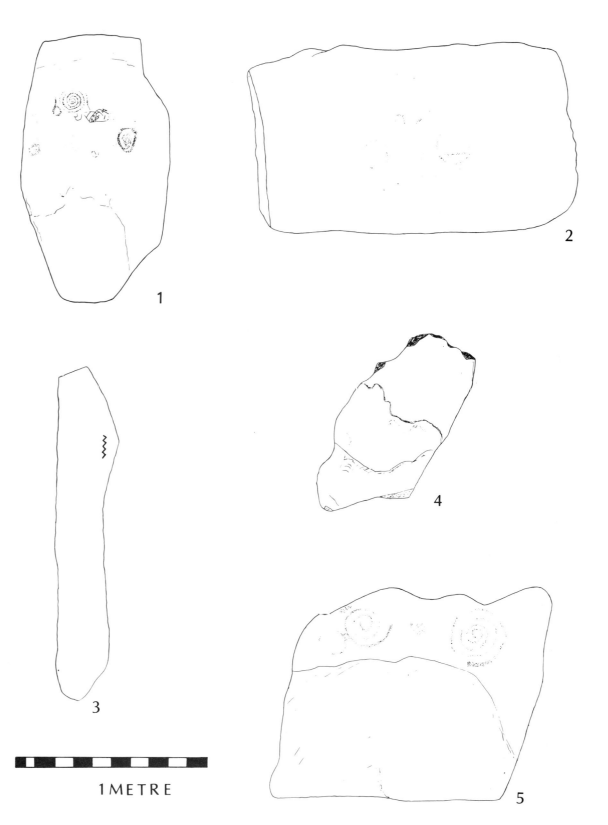

1METRE

Fig. 65—Megalithic art, Site 14:
1, 2 and 3—orthostats 4, 7 and 13;
4 and 5—kerbstones 4 and 6.

the chamber and in the passage. Some were apparently displaced corbels, but others could have been capstones.

Typological differences exist within the two divisions, cruciform and undifferentiated. In the cruciform type the passage tends to be parallel-sided but in Site 2 the passage widens slightly from the entrance inwards, and at Site 9 the passage narrows from the entrance to the chamber. In four of the five cruciform tombs, Sites 2, 6, 9 and 17, the right-hand recess (as one enters the chamber) was the largest. Only one cruciform site (9) produced evidence for a transverse sillstone and here the sill was placed at the inner end of the passage. In Site 2 there was a sillstone across the front of each side recess. The centre of the chamber was well defined in Sites 2 and 18 and possibly in Site 17 while in Sites 6 and 9 the side recesses opened more directly off the passage.

The general tendency amongst the undifferentiated tombs was for the passage sides to widen outwards from the entrance to the inner end. 13 and 15 tended to be bottle-shaped. Site 3 presents a problem as it has a long rectangular chamber but no evidence for a passage. Sillstones were common. In No. 4 there was a socket across the entrance and three further sillstones divided the tomb into four segments. Likewise, 15 and 16 were divided into four segments. 12, 13 and 14 had a single sillstone. In 13 this was about two-thirds of the way in. In 12 it was closer to the inner end. There was a much higher sillstone in 14 which together with the two massive sidestones created a squarish inner chamber. A somewhat similar chamber existed in 15 and possibly also in 4. The chamber of 16 tends to be trapezoidal. The stone dividing the chamber from the passage, together with the transverse orthostats flanking it at either end,

Pl. 50a—Site 14: orthostat 8, outer face.

Pl. 50b—Site 14: orthostat 8, detail of spiral on top right corner of inner face.

combine to form a jamb and sill arrangement. Sillstones varied in height. Site 4 may have had a virtually closed-off inner segment and the inner sillstones in Sites 14–16 were fairly high. One tomb had evidence of formal flooring. This was a small area of paving in the passage of Site 14.

A *core* of stones surrounded the tomb of Site 12 and the chamber of Site 16. A large core, sods mixed with boulder clay, enclosed the tomb of Site 15. The outer edge of this was delimited by a setting consisting of a number of small stones. A core may also have existed at Site 2. This is suggested by an inward sloping layer of stones within the mound. If such a core existed here it appears to have been confined to the chamber area.

On each side of the tomb of Site 4 on the old ground surface were arc-like *settings* of varied length, composed of stones averaging 20cm long. In Site 16 was a series of settings of similarly sized stones within the mound. What may also be part of an arc exists at Sites 9 and 15.

Outside the entrance to Site 4 were the remains of a circular area 2.25m in diameter, paved with quartz stones and surrounded by two concentric rings of stones of different material.

The *burial record* is limited because of destruction but there is evidence that deposits consisted simply of the remains of an individual (Sites 3, 4, 13, 18) or, more frequently, the remains of more than one individual collectively deposited. Successive burials also took place (e.g. Sites 15, 16 and 18). Cremation burial was found at twelve sites. Some pieces of unburnt human bone turned up in Site 2

Pl. 51a–Site 14: orthostat 8, detail of dot with external arc of rays on north-east end of orthostat.
(Photo: Commissioners of Public Works)

Pl. 51b–Site 14: end of kerbstone 4.

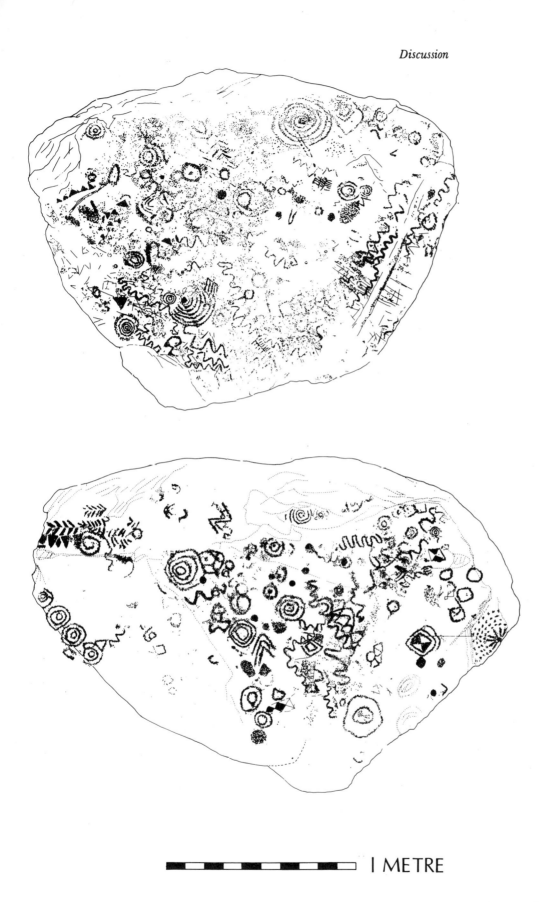

I METRE

Fig. 66—Megalithic art, Site *14*: orthostat 8
(inner face at top).

but where undisturbed burials were found these did not contain any unburnt bones. Cremation was therefore the predominant rite. No evidence of burial survived in Sites 5, 7, 8, 10 and 11. There was a scatter of cremation in Sites 4, 13 and 14 and a few fragments in Site 10. The cremation deposits in Sites 2 and 6 contained the remains of several individuals. At Site 2 there were the remains of at least two children and two adults, and the remains of an adult and a child were identified at Site 12. Site 3 had the remains of a youth aged between fifteen and twenty years, and at least four individuals were represented in Site 9, two adults and two children. One of the adults was aged about twenty. There were the remains of six individuals, three adults and three children, at Site 15, at Site 17 at least four individuals, three children and one adult, and at Site 18 at least a child and one adult. The cremation deposits in Site 16 contained the largest number of individuals, a minimum of sixteen and amongst these were five adults and seven children. However, it may be noted that this was the best preserved of the smaller tombs at Knowth. Taking the burial evidence from all the smaller passage tombs the number of individuals buried was at least thirty, and this number is fairly evenly divided between adults and children. But it must be emphasised that this figure is the minimum. The demolition of tombs must have destroyed burials, and because the burial rite was cremation exact calculation of the number of individuals is almost impossible. Nevertheless, it does appear that the number buried varied between tombs.

Pl. 52a–Site 14: kerbstone 6.

Pl. 52b—Site 15: orthostat 1, art.

Burials were deposited directly on the old ground surface in at least Sites 3, 4, 6, 9 and 12–18. Among the cruciform tombs there was a stone basin in the right-hand recess of Site 2. Outside it were human bones. At that site remains of burials also occur in the end and left-hand recesses and in the centre of the chamber. Owing to destruction it is difficult to prove if any were in their original position. In the left-hand recess of Site 18 was a flag which may have served as a repository for a burial deposit. It overlay an earlier deposit on the old ground surface. In Site 6 what appears to have been the main cremation deposit was in the right-hand recess and there was a smaller deposit in the left-hand recess. In Site 9 the deposits were in the end recess. There were three areas of cremated bone in Site 17. Two were certainly in a disturbed position but that in the inner part of the end recess, on the old ground surface, appears to have been *in situ* and was probably the remains of a larger deposit.

As for the undifferentiated tombs, burials took place in the inner part of Sites 12–16 and in Site 3. Burial also took place in the adjoining segment in Sites 15, 16 and the equivalent segment of Site 4 (the inner segment was largely destroyed). The deposit in Site 3 contained only the remains of one individual and this also may have been so in some other sites, such as 13. The deposit in other tombs consisted of the remains of more than one individual, for instance the initial primary deposit in the chamber of Site 16. It is evident that successive burial took place in at least two of the undifferentiated passage tombs. In 15 there were two successive burials in the third segment, separated from each other by four small flags. The best evidence is provided by Site 16. At that site there were three successive burials in the chamber and two in the inner segment of the passage. The second deposit in both the chamber and the inner segment of the passage was on flags.

Grave goods were present but not in great numbers. Amongst these were three pieces of bone pins, a well-decorated bone or antler object, a tapering piece of bone, a piece of worked bone, two bone beads, two bone pendants, six pieces of flint, three fragments of

Fig. 67—Megalithic art, Site 15:
1 and 2—orthostats 1 and 14;
3—sillstone C;
4—kerbstone 6.

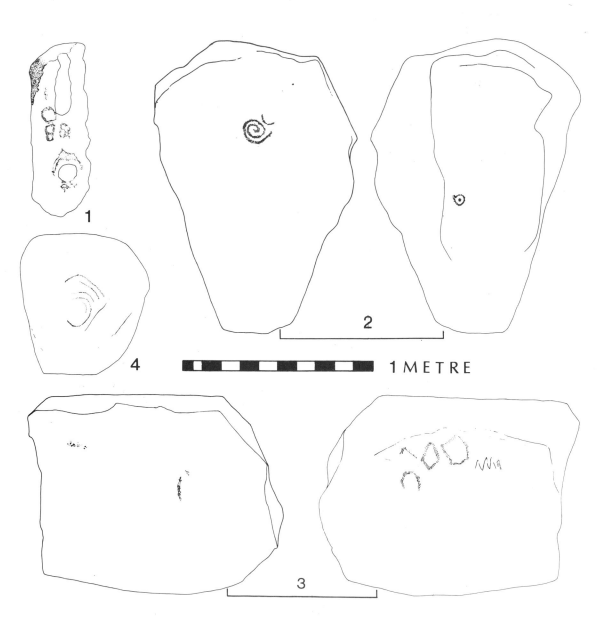

Pl. 53a–Site 15: sillstone C, outer face art.
(Photo: Commissioners of Public Works)

Pl. 53b–Site 15: orthostat 14, inner face
art.

pottery of indeterminate type (found together) and a sherd of Carrowkeel ware, which came from the right-hand recess of Site 2 and was not directly associated with burial but may have been originally.

Pl. 54a–Site 15: orthostat 14, inner face detail of art.
(Photo: Commissioners of Public Works)

There were other finds dating to the primary period from the mounds. These are sherds of Carrowkeel ware from Sites 15 and 16, single hollow scrapers from Sites 7 and 16, a round scraper from Site 14, a 'slug-knife' from Site 13, utilised flint from Sites 12 and 13 and flint scraps from Sites 12, 15, 16 and 17. Other primary finds discovered in disturbed material were a sherd of Carrowkeel ware from Site 3 and two chalk balls from Site 2. A hoard of struck flints was found under the corner of one of the kerbstones of Site 2.

Art occurs on two media, mobile objects and structural stones. Amongst mobile objects the pottery is well decorated, mainly by lines formed by stab-and-drag. The bone object (111) from Site 3 and the stone object (3906) have somewhat similar decoration. The baetyl stone (p. 164) has horizontal and vertical lines and a small, highly polished area but this piece, taken in conjunction with the stone basin in Site 2, must be considered a piece of sculpture.

Megalithic art has been found at thirteen sites both in the tomb and on the kerbstones, the exceptions being Sites 6, 7, 9, 10 and 11. In addition to forty decorated stones from the sites there are eleven other stones with art which must originally have been removed from the tombs. Among these fifty-one stones decoration is found on sixty-three faces. It occurs on two faces on six stones (Site 2: orthostat 8; Site 13: kerbstone 15; Site 14: orthostat 8; Site 15: orthostat 14 and sillstone C; Site 17: orthostat 7), on three faces on two stones (Sites 16: orthostat 13; Site 18: orthostat 11) and on four faces on one stone (stone [sill] A of Site 4).

In the ornamentation about sixteen motifs were used, most of which recur. Destruction must have diminished the number of decorated stones. For instance, there is evidence for the existence of about two hundred and seventy-two orthostats but only one hundred and five survive in a complete or near complete condition. Art principally occurs on green grits (about fifty per cent) or on similar types of rock such as green ash, green slate and grits (about twenty-five per cent). Among the softer stones, art has been found on seven sandstones and three limestones (together about twenty-five per cent of the total). There is no clear evidence for deliberate shaping of the stones before decorating. The inner surface of orthostat 8 of Site 12 has been pocked out but there is no decoration and small areas of pocking occur on two corbels in the chamber of Site 16. Both incised and pocked designs occur. The incised designs are fairly incoherent but

Pl. 54b—Site 15: orthostat 14, outer face art.

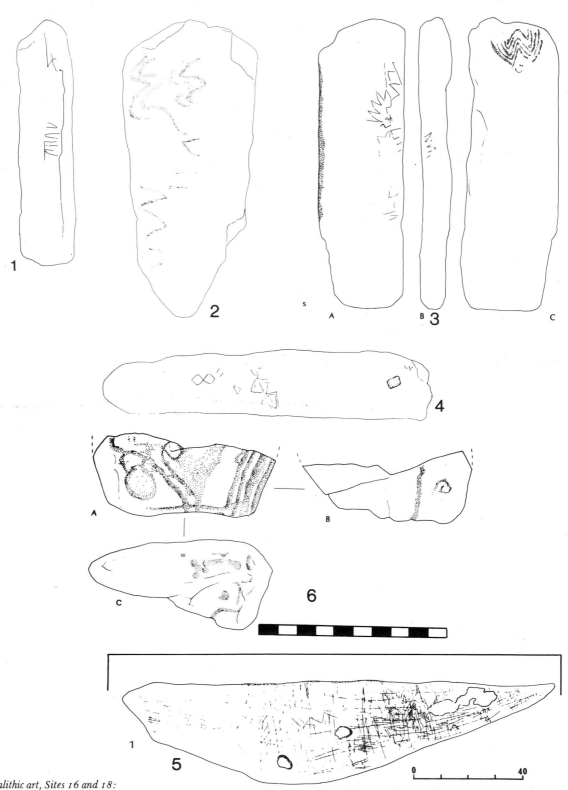

Fig. 68–Megalithic art, Sites 16 and 18:
1, 2 and 3–Site 16, orthostats 4, 9 and 13;
4 and 5–Site 16, corbels over orthostats 12
and 10;
6–Site 18, orthostat 11.

Pl. 55a–Site 15: kerbstone 6, art.
(Photo: Commissioners of Public Works)

Pl. 55b–Site 16: orthostat 4, art.
(Photo: Commissioners of Public Works)

on stone A of Site 4 they form a grid which gave guidance to the application of the design of pocked lozenges. An undressed area on the lower part of orthostat 8 of Site 12 indicates that the stone was in position before dressing. Art on the base of kerbstone 11 of Site 8, on the base and back of orthostat 11 of Site 18, on the backs of orthostats 8 of Site 14 and 14 of Site 15, and on the back of orthostat 4, Site 16 shows that these were decorated before erection. It is not possible to know whether the other stones were decorated before or after erection. On the smaller tombs at Knowth the art was intended to be seen. Hidden art occurs only on the five stones mentioned above.

Pl. 56a–Site 16: orthostat 9, art.
(Photo: Commissioners of Public Works)

The techniques of decoration can be paralleled at other passage tombs (Crawford 1955). Incised guide lines are known from Newgrange and Fourknocks 1 (Shee 1973, 168, Fig. 4; Hartnett 1957, 221, Stone 4) and incised motifs also occur at other sites (cf. Millin Bay, Co. Down, Collins and Waterman 1955, esp. pp 38–9). On one of the Site 16 corbels there is a concentration of incisions but otherwise incision is fairly limited and is more in the nature of doodling on the other 11 stones on which it occurs. Pocking was more commonly used but both the range of motifs and their numbers are limited. Apart from orthostat 11 of Site 18 and stone 7 of the miscellaneous group, the designs are fairly shallow. The lozenges on stone (sill) A of Site 4 provide good evidence of area pocking. Internal art is found in Sites 2 and 13–18. In the main, the designs occur on the broad inner faces of the orthostats but are also found on the base of orthostat 11, Site 18. Decoration occurs on both of the broad faces of that orthostat and also on No. 8 of Site 14, No. 14 of Site 15 and Nos 9 and 13 (the jambs) of Site 16. Art occurs on one of the narrow sides of orthostat 30 of Site 2 and 7 of Site 17. Two sills are decorated. On A of Site 4 the decoration occurs on both of the broader faces, on the top and on one side. The limited decoration on sill C of Site 15 is on the broad side facing towards the entrance. A corbel in Site 16 has all-over incision on one face.

Art has been found on the kerbstones of eight sites, 2 (No. 28), 3 (No. 10), 5 (No. 8), 8 (Nos 5 and 11), 12 (No. 6), 13 (Nos 15, 16, 17 and 24), 14 (Nos 4, 5 and 6) and 15 (No. 6). Except for the base of stone 11, Site 8, and the downward sloping face of 15, Site 13, art always occurs on the outer face. Of a total of 238 kerbstones only fifteen (6.3%) are decorated. At Sites 2, 3, 8, 11, 13–17 large portions of the kerb survive but in these nine sites out of 200 surviving kerbstones only fourteen are decorated. This limited evidence suggests that in the main decoration on the kerbstones was not a common feature. Much

Pl. 56b—Site 16: corbel over orthostat 10, art.
(Photo: Commissioners of Public Works)

greater emphasis on decoration is found within the tombs. Furthermore, boulder-like stones were mainly used for the kerbs and these are ill-suited to art. This contrasts with the kerb of Site 1 where better-formed stones were used and much more lavish art was applied.

Table A—The occurrence of art motifs at Knowth

Key: T = TOMB, K = KERB, O = OTHER; F1 = FRONT, F2 = BACK, S = SIDE, B = BASE.

Site No. / stones:
- Site 2: T14, T27 (F), T30 (S)
- Site 3: K28, K10
- Site 4: T(A) — F1, T, F2, S
- Site 5: K8
- Site 8: K5
- Site 12: K11
- Site 13: K6, T3 (B), K15, T16 (T), K17 (S), K24
- Site 14: T4, T7, T8 (F1), T13 (F2), ...
- Site 15: T4, K5, K6 (F1), T1 (F2), 'C' (F2)
- Site 16: K6 (F1), T4, T9 (F2), K10 (S)
- Site 17: T12 (F1), T13 (F2), T6
- Site 18: T7 (F1), T13 (F2), T15 (B), T16, T11
- Isolated Finds of Megalithic Art: 1–11

Motif	2	3	4	5	8	12	13	14	15	16	17	18	Isolated Finds
SPIRALS a) Plain Spiral		3					1, 1	1, 1, 4	1		1 2, 1		3, ? 2 2 1
b) Spiral with lateral motif								1	1				
CIRCLES, Full a) Single	3	1 1						7+, 3	3	?			1 2+, 2+
b) Double								5					1, ?
c) Multiple	1		?				1, 1	4+, 5		?			
d) With lateral motif	1 1		2 1				?	5 2			1		
CIRCLES, Gapped a) Single	1						1	? 1	1				
b) Double													1 1
c) Multiple							2 ?	1+					1
d) With lateral motif							?	1					
ARCS a) Single	3						1, ?	2 ? 2	1 1, 1	3 1			1
b) Multiple		1	1					1 1					1
CUP MARK							1 ?	2, 5 10	1		6		? 1
DOT or CUP AND CIRCLE							?	2, 2	1				
CUP MARK or DOT FLANKED BY SEMI-CIRCLE								1					
DOT AND EXTERNAL ARC OF RAYS								1					
SERPENTIFORM			1, 2 1				? 1	1, 19+ 3+, 1	4	1, 2	1	1	1
CHEVRONS (or ZIG-ZAGS) a) Single			20+					6+ 3 1		3, 1 1, 1 1, 1 6	1	1	
b) Multiple		3						2	1	3 1	1 1		1, 1
LOZENGES a) Single outline								6	1	5	2 2		
b) Single pocked	4		2 13					4					4
c) Double outline											1 1		
d) Multiple single outline								?					
TRIANGLES a) Outline			1										
b) Single solid pocked areas			3					9 4					
HURDLE PATTERN a) Vertebrates								2					
b) Comb-shaped								1					
NET PATTERN							?	? ?					
FIR TREE								? 4					
PARALLEL LINES			5 6 13				?	?		2			
MISCELLANEOUS			2					1					1, 1

Pl. 57a–Site 16: orthostat 13, north face art.
(Photo: Commissioners of Public Works)

Pl. 57b–Site 16: orthostat 13, south face art.
(Photo: Commissioners of Public Works)

There is, however, a major difference in the pattern of decoration that occurs on stones within the tombs and that on the kerbstones. There is a complete absence of rectilinear decoration on the kerbstones. On the internal stones about 45% of the decoration is rectilinear and 54% curvilinear.

Pl. 58a–Site 17:orthostat 6, art.

Comprehensive decoration is found on only two stones, orthostat 8 of Site 14 and sillstone A of Site 4. Together these stones have 60% of the total art with orthostat 8 having about 40%, including about 55% of the serpentiform designs. There are so many designs on both faces of that orthostat that an over-crowded, incoherent composition emerges. This comprehensive decoration can be compared to that on the backs of kerbstones 13 and 18 at Newgrange (C. O'Kelly 1978, 19–23, Figs 4 and 5). On sill A a more ordered and restrained layout is found and the decoration on the two faces differs. On the other stones a limited range of motifs occurs as Table A shows. These have counterparts in megalithic art from Brugh na Bóinne and Loughcrew (C. O'Kelly 1973; Frazer 1893). There are seventeen major motifs (spirals, full circles, gapped circles, etc.) and twenty-two subgroups represented. The most common major motifs are circles (*c.* 21%), chevrons or zig-zags (17.6%), lozenges and serpentiforms (14.28%) and cupmarks (9.30%). Of the subgroups single chevrons or zig-zags (14.28%), single pocked lozenges (8.35%), full single circles (8.63%) and plain spirals (8.35%) make up 39.6% of the total number of motifs represented. The dot and rays on orthostat 8, Site 14, have a counterpart in the more elaborate motif on one of the kerbstones on the east side of Site 1 (Eogan 1977, 48, Pl. 4b) and on a stone at Patrickstown, Loughcrew (Frazer 1893, 338, Fig. 76). Rayed circles from Sites K and Z, Newgrange, may also be noted (O'Kelly, Lynch and O'Kelly 1978, 323, 326, Figs 33, 35). There is slight evidence for motif combinations. At Site 16 all the designs are rectilinear. On one of the jamb stones (9) there are vertical serpentiform designs and on No. 13 chevrons near the top.

Pl. 58b–Site 17: orthostat 7, art.

These designs are to some extent comparable to stones 6 and 7 in the south tomb at Dowth (Lynch 1967, 18–19, Figs 9 and 10). Similar designs are also found outside Ireland, on stone 22 at Barclodiad y Gawres, Anglesey in Wales which has (amongst other designs) vertical zig-zags and multiple chevrons (Lynch 1967, 9); and the multiple chevron is the principal motif at the Dolmen du Petit Mont, Arzon, Brittany (Lynch 1967, 15, cf. Fig. 8). As on these sites outside Ireland the kerb of Site 16 (or the surviving portion) lacked art.

Fig. 69–Megalithic art, Site 17: 1–5–orthostats 6, 7, 16, 13 and 15.

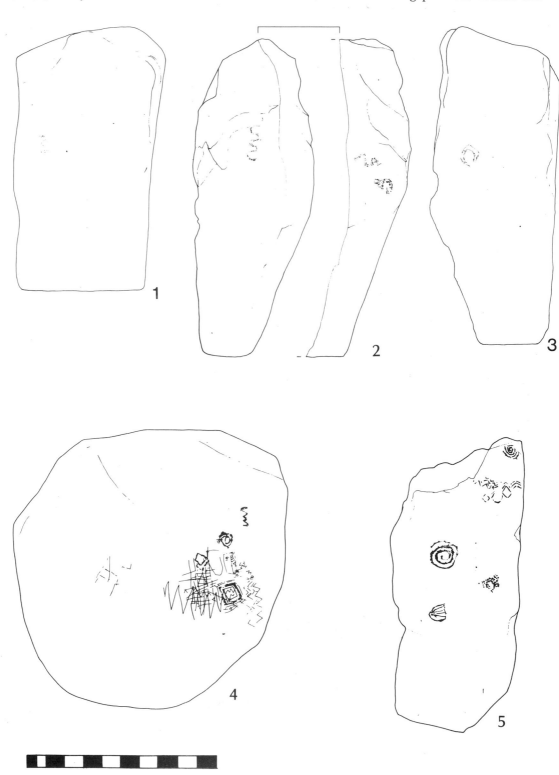

1METRE

Pl. 59a—Site 17: orthostat 13, inner face art.

Pl. 59b—Site 17: orthostat 15, inner face art.

There is no apparent difference in the pattern of decoration between the cruciform and undifferentiated sites. In general, the tombs to the north and north-east of Site 1 are more highly decorated than the others but this is probably due to better preservation in that area.

Pl. 60a–Site 17: orthostat 15 (left) and 16 (right), art.

As to *chronology,* C14 determinations (uncalibrated) are available for only two tombs, charcoal being the material dated. The determination for Site 2 is 4158 ± 126 B.P. (*c.* 2208 b.c.; B.M. 785); for Site 16, 4399 ± 67 B.P. (*c.*2449 b.c.; B.M. 1078). There are two determinations for dark soil underneath the mound of Site 17. These are 4875 ± 150 B.P. (*c.*2925 b.c.; U.B. 318) and 4795 ± 185 B.P. (*c.*2845 b.c.; U.B. 319). It cannot be established that this dark material dates from the period when the tomb was built. Neolithic domestic activity that predates Site 8 has a determination of 4852 ± 71 B.P. (*c.*2902 b.c.; B.M. 1076). For Site 1 charcoal samples have produced a determination of 4745 ± 165 B.P. (*c.*2795 b.c.; U.B. 357). As the number of dates available is very small, they cannot be relied on to give an absolute chronology for the cemetery. Dating from other passage tombs in Ireland falls within the Knowth range of dates.

Material dating from the time of construction of the Newgrange passage has given determinations of 4500 ± 45 B.P. (*c.*2550 b.c.), 4415 ± 40 B.P. (*c.*2465 b.c.; GrN–5462, 5463; O'Kelly 1969). Fourknocks II has a determination of 3480 ± 140 B.P. (*c.*1530 b.c.; D–45). Material from under the Mound of the Hostages, Tara, gave determinations of 4080 ± 160 B.P. (*c.*2130 b.c.), 4260 ± 160 B.P. (*c.*2310 b.c.) and 3880 ± 150 B.P. (*c.*1730 b.c.; D–42, 43, 44; McAuley and Watts 1961, 33). For the habitation layer beneath Townleyhall II there is a determination of 4680 ± 150 B.P. (*c.*2730 b.c.; B.M. 170).

Pl. 6ob–Site 18: orthostat 11, outer face art.

There is very little information available about relative chronology either. The size of Site 1 and the large number of sites that were erected in its immediate vicinity suggest that tomb building was spread over several centuries, possibly starting in the fourth millennium B.C. Parts of the kerbs and mounds of Sites 13 and 16 were removed to facilitate the erection of Site 1. This is clear evidence that these smaller sites predate at least the completion of the large mound. There is a hint that Site 17 may postdate it, since at least some of the kerbstones were placed on stones that may have been slip from Site 1. There is no evidence to indicate what the sequential relationship is between the large mound and any of the other smaller passage tombs. Among the smaller tombs themselves, Site 17 is later than Site 18 as its mound extends over the edge of that of Site 18. Sites 2 and 3 are close to each other but it is unlikely that the mounds

Pl. 61a–Site 18: orthostat 11, inner face art.

Pl. 61b–Site 18: orthostat 11, base art.

abutted, although the digging of a later drain destroyed the intermediate area.

It seems likely that undifferentiated passage tombs were among the first to be erected at Knowth. They were clearly the favoured type but it is quite possible that cruciform and undifferentiated tombs were built and used at the same time. The presence of two tombs of different types under the mound at Site 1 (Eogan 1967, 1969) points to the likely contemporaneity of the types.

Pl. 62a–Isolated finds of Megalithic art 1: souterrain 4, capstone 7

Pl. 62b–Isolated finds of Megalithic art 2: souterrain 9, capstone 3.

Knowth in relation to the passage tomb series

The principal problem investigated at Knowth was the chronological relationship between undifferentiated passage tombs and the more elaborate cruciform sites. The excavations have established the existence of both forms and the undifferentiated tombs must now be looked on as an integral part of the Irish series. Indeed, it is possible that the two forms were in use simultaneously and the excavation of Site 1 should help to elucidate this issue. It can be shown stratigraphically that two undifferentiated tombs (13 and 16) predate Site 1 and perhaps such tombs were amongst the first to be erected at Knowth. It may also be noted that the cruciform tombs have a different focus (Fig. 73B). At Newgrange the satellite tomb,

Fig. 70—Megalithic art, miscellaneous stones: 1–3 and 5–11.

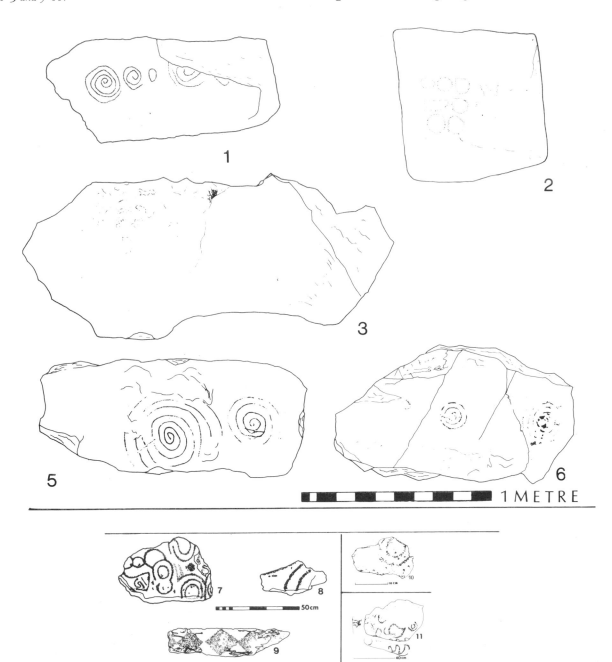

Site K, a small undifferentiated passage tomb, predates a cruciform tomb, Site L (O'Kelly, Lynch and O'Kelly 1978).

Knowth has the greatest concentration of undifferentiated passage tombs in Ireland but the relationship, if any, between this group and the tombs in the Tramore area has not been fully clarified. There are typological differences. In the Tramore group (Powell 1941a, 1941b; Hawkes 1941; Herity 1974, 179–80) the chambers are more strictly 'undifferentiated' than at Knowth, the tomb usually extends inwards beyond the centre of the mound and there is no cemetery concentration. The typical grave goods are absent as is the megalithic art. It has been thought that the Tramore tombs are a local group outside the mainstream of Irish passage-tomb development and this may indeed be so.

Pl. 63a–Isolated finds of Megalithic art 4: capstone 13, souterrain 1.

Pl. 63b–Isolated finds of Megalithic art 5: part of 'entrance' feature of Early Christian House J.

Apart from Knowth and the Tramore group, undifferentiated passage tombs are rare in Ireland, but there are two at Newgrange, Sites K and Z (O'Kelly, Lynch and O'Kelly 1978), and one example in each of the Loughcrew (Sliabh na Caillighe) (Site W, Herity 1974, 243, Fig. 35 bottom right) and Carrowkeel cemeteries (Site H, Macalister, Armstrong and Praeger 1912, 328–9, Pl. 22). Mageracar, Co. Donegal, is another example as is the small tomb under the Mound of the Hostages at Tara (Herity 1974, 215, 252, Figs 11 and 33, bottom).

Pl. 64a–Isolated finds of Megalithic art 6: from wall of 'modern' house in cutting 41.

The cruciform tomb is a characteristic Irish form. Sometimes the recesses open off a well-defined chamber (cf. Fourknocks I, Loughcrew T, Carrowkeel G and K) but in other examples there is no definite central chamber and the side recesses open off the passage. Examples of this variety are Site L Newgrange, Site A Kilmonaster in Co. Donegal, Belmore in Co. Fermanagh, Finner in Co. Donegal, and Sites F and H Loughcrew and Duntryleague, Co. Limerick. Often the right-hand recess is the largest (cf. Newgrange, Barclodiad y Gawres). The long end recess of Site 9 resembles that at Site A Kilmonaster and Duntryleague and the passage widening outwards from the chamber is another feature that is common to Knowth Site 9 and Duntryleague (Herity 1974, Fig. 60:3). A passage that widens inwards from the entrance is more common (cf. Site H Loughcrew, or G and K Carrowkeel). The double cruciform tombs or the stalled chambers which are best known from Loughcrew and Carrowkeel are not represented at Knowth.

Sillstones are frequently found in both cruciform and undifferentiated tombs elsewhere in Ireland. In addition to sillstones across the passage, cruciform tombs often have a transverse stone across the entrance to the recess, as at Loughcrew and Carrowkeel.

Paving is known from the passages of Fourknocks I and Slieve Gullion (Hartnett 1957, 205; Collins and Wilson 1963, 27).

Parallels for the various internal *mound features* are best found at Townleyhall where layering, a core and stone settings on the old ground surface and within the mound are known (Eogan 1963, 67–70). A sand core exists at Site L Newgrange, and the same site has a line of boulders within the mound (Lynch 1973, 149, Fig. 2; O'Kelly, Lynch and O'Kelly 1978). Short arcs of stones were also found in Sites K and Z (pp 277, 292). *Kerbstones* are usual and in some sites these

Pl. 64b–Isolated finds of Megalithic art 7.

curve inwards before the entrance (e.g. Newgrange). The circular *setting of quartz* outside the entrances to the western and eastern tombs at Site 1 and at Site 4, Knowth can be compared to the 'oval structure' close to the entrance to the main Newgrange mound. A similar feature near the entrance to Cairn T Loughcrew (M. J. O'Kelly 1973, 140, Fig. 2) can also be cited as a parallel as can the 'small platform of white quartz pebbles' at Bryn Celli Ddu in Anglesey (Lynch 1970, 63). Quartz spreads occur at other Boyne culture tombs such as Baltinglass and Loughcrew.

Cemetery concentrations, nucleate or dispersed, are common in Ireland. At least in the larger cemeteries more than one class of tomb is represented. Even within a class there are differences; for instance at Loughcrew and Carrowkeel one finds not only the classic cruciform tomb but also double cruciform tombs and stalled tombs. What may be called a focal site is also common. For instance, within the Brugh na Bóinne cemetery itself there are at least three small passage tombs close to Newgrange. At Loughcrew, on Carn Bán West there are two foci, Sites D and L; Cairn T forms the focus on Carn Bán East; while on Patrickstown, Cairn Y seems to have served a similar function (Herity 1974, 41–55). The large cairn on Knocknareagh, Co. Sligo, Miosgán Méadhbha, is a focus for four small tombs and nearby at Carrowmore, a tomb, Listoghil, around the centre of the cemetery may have served a similar function. Even in the dispersed cemetery of Kilmonaster, Co. Donegal, the tombs are overlooked by a site, L, which is situated on the prominent hilltop of Croaghan (Ó Nualláin 1968, 15).

The orientation of the entrances of the Knowth tombs, falling within an arc that extends from the north-east to the south-west follows the general orientation pattern of Irish passage tombs. In the Knowth locality Newgrange and its three nearby small tombs have a southerly orientation. The two tombs in the large mound at Dowth and the Site J tomb face westwards. At Fourknocks both sites face north-eastwards. Most of the Loughcrew (Sliabh na Caillighe) tombs

Pl. 65a–Isolated finds of Megalithic art 8.

face eastwards, focusing on Cairn T with its entrance facing eastwards. Perhaps the orientation was determined by a wish to site the entrance towards the rising sun but at Knowth and Loughcrew it may have been the existence of a focal point, perhaps an existing tomb, that determined the orientation.

Cremation is the predominant *burial rite* in Irish passage tombs. In the cruciform sites burials are known from the recesses, for instance at Fourknocks I. There'and at Fourknocks II burial also took place in the passage (Hartnett 1957, 206; 1971, 41). In Site S at Loughcrew burials took place in the two segments of the passage apparently on a flag which almost covered the floor of the segment (Conwell 1873, 66). Collective burial was common practice and as at Knowth other tombs were used on successive occasions. It cannot be proven that animal bones were part of burial deposits at Knowth, but it may be

noted that a thin scatter of animal bones was discovered over the floor of the chamber at Fourknocks I (Hartnett 1957, 249) and animal bones have also been recorded from burial deposits in English megalithic tombs (Daniel 1950, 98). Small flat stones covering burials are known from Fourknocks I (Hartnett 1957, 214) and Carrowkeel, Site K (Macalister, Armstrong and Praeger 1912, 336). The flag in the left-hand recess of Site 18 can be compared to the flags over the floor of the recesses in Fourknocks I (Hartnett 1957, 214). Stone basins occur in the neighbouring sites of Newgrange and Dowth, at Loughcrew and sporadically elsewhere in eastern Ireland (O'Kelly, Lynch and O'Kelly 1978, 341).

Pl. 65b–Isolated finds of Megalithic art 9: part of stone setting beneath the sod, 6m from Site 3 and 3.50m from Site 2.

The *small finds,* especially Carrowkeel ware, pendants, pins of bone or antler and chalk balls are characteristic and have parallels at other passage tombs in Ireland. The Knowth finds form a small but important addition to the general assemblage of Irish passage tomb artifacts. As already noted *megalithic art* is common in eastern Ireland, especially in County Meath.

While the Knowth tombs display native characteristics, the well-developed architecture of the earliest proven examples (13 and 16) indicates an already formed passage-tomb tradition. It is also unlikely that their *origin* rests within Ireland. There is a long tradition of passage-tomb building in Atlantic Europe; C14 determinations suggest that such tombs were being constructed from at least the fourth millennium B.C. (cf. Giot 1971; Jorge 1978). Therefore, the Knowth sites are best considered part of the wider Atlantic spread. Indeed, many of the Knowth features are common in that area. In Iberia, passage tombs were constructed on hill-tops or high ground. Cemeteries are known from Spain: Barranquete (Almagro Gorbea 1973b), Los Millares (Almagro and Arribas 1963) and Gandul (Leisner 1943, Taf. 170) are examples; while for western France, Forêt de la Boixe, Charente and Bougon, Deux-Sèvres can be cited (Burnez 1976, 33–36, 61; Mohen 1978).

Passage tombs with one or more side recesses are known from the Continent, for instance Tomb 7 at El Pozuelo, near Huelva in

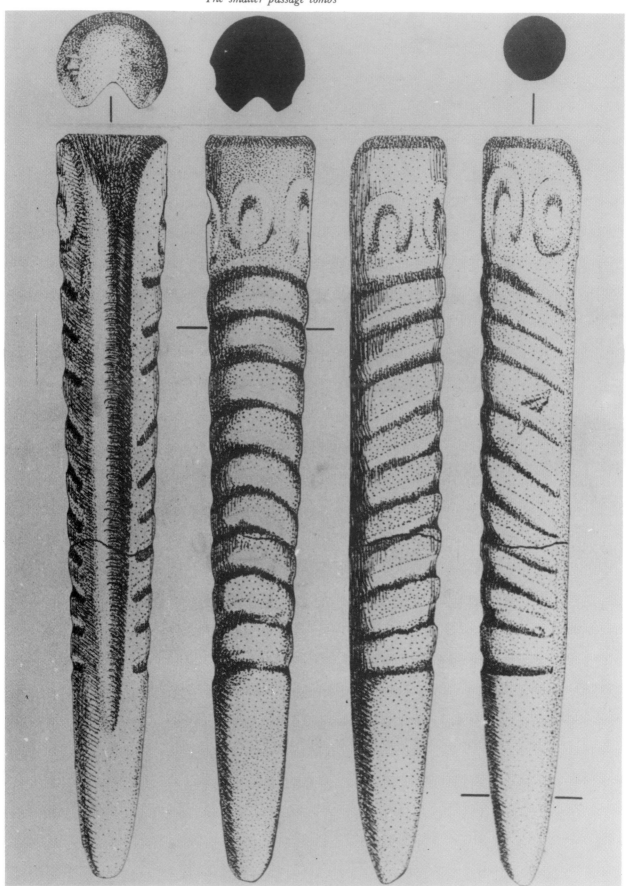

Fig. 71—Decorated stone object (3906).

Pl. 66—Decorated stone object (3906).
(Photo: National Museum of Ireland)

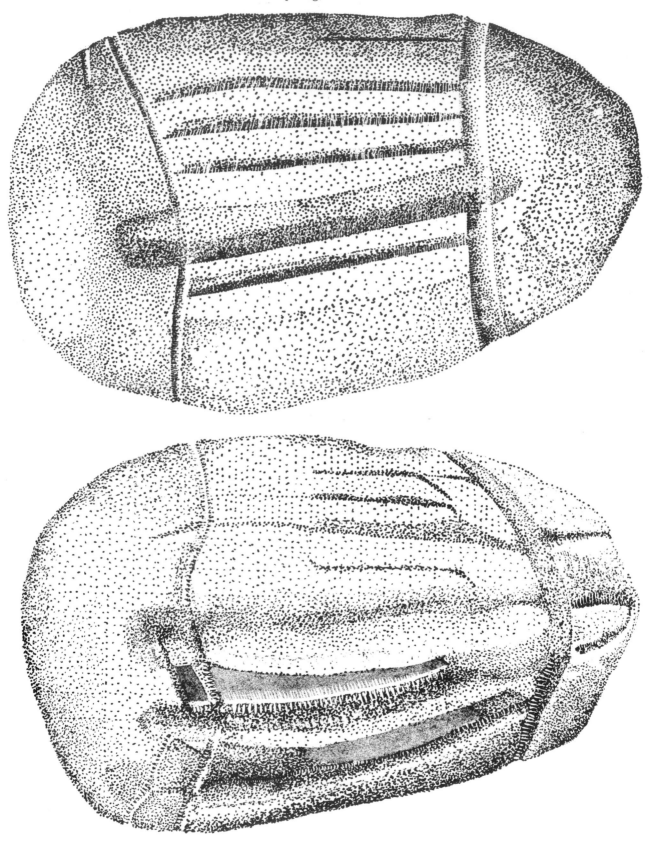

Fig. 72–Fashioned stone.　　　　　　　　　　　　　　　　　　　　30 cm

southern Spain has a cruciform plan (Márquez and Leisner 1952, 17, Pl. 6, bottom). In western France cruciform tombs are known, for instance La Planche à Puare en l'Ile d'Yea, Vendée (Burnez 1976, 55, Fig. 8:7), and in Brittany there is a variety of passage tombs with recesses or transepts (L'Helgouach 1965).

Undifferentiated tombs are also known abroad. Amongst these are the well-known Spanish sites of Cueva de Menga and Dolmen de Soto (Leisner 1943, Taf. 56, 70). In Brittany there are numerous examples varying in tomb plan and also in date (cf. L'Helgouach 1965, pp 159–64, 190–99). Even as far afield as northern Germany such sites as Mechelsdorf and Schwasdorf in Mecklenburg are undifferentiated (Schuldt 1972, Taf. 13). Nearer to home the Bargrennan group in south-west Scotland are also of the undifferentiated type (Henshall 1972, 2–14).

Pl. 67–Fashioned stone, as found.

Other features also found at Knowth occur in the Atlantic zone. Art is known in Iberia on structural stones (Leisner and Ribeiro 1968, 58–60; Shee n.d.) but more commonly on objects placed in the tombs such as the schist plaques (Almagro Gorbea 1973a, 181–223). Art on the structural stones is much more common in Brittany (Péquart and le Rouzic 1927; L'Helgouach *et al.* 1970). Art is an internal feature, either on objects placed in the tombs or on structural stones of the tombs on sites outside Ireland. External art as displayed on the kerbstones at Knowth is a peculiarly Irish feature.

The bone or antler 'pin' from Site 3 and the stone object already mentioned (p. 163) have fairly exact parallels in Portugal. Stone basins have been noted from a few Iberian tombs (Leisner 1943, 286) but they differ in shape from the basins of the Irish series.

These smaller passage tombs at Knowth, taken in conjunction with the large site, form a well integrated cemetery. Their 'culture' must be seen in the wider context of Atlantic Europe. A cult of the dead obviously played a big part in the lives of the passage-tomb builders. It is clear from the tomb construction that these people had considerable architectural and building skills and organisational abilities. Even were tomb construction spread over many centuries this would still imply a large population, some members of which must have been professional architects and engineers as even the small sites at Knowth must have been planned and designed beforehand. Such work and such skills were surely a by-product of a society with a sound economy the basis of which must have been the intelligent and efficient utilisation of the fertile lands of the region. Evidence from the small tombs, limited as it is, is not of mass burial deposits so perhaps only privileged members of society were buried in the tombs. While it is likely that this society was basically rural nevertheless the tomb concentrations may indirectly suggest proto-urban attitudes.

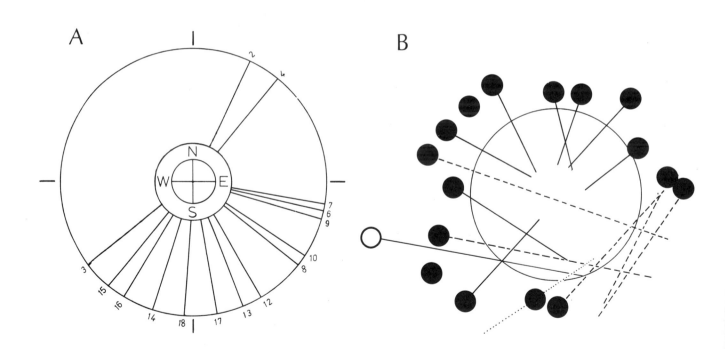

Fig. 73—Orientation diagram:
A—each radius represents a tomb;
B—the orientation and location of the smaller tombs in relation to Site 1.
Undifferentiated tombs have solid lines, cruciform tombs dashed lines.
Dotted line shows possible orientation(s) of Site 3 and the open circle is Site 7.

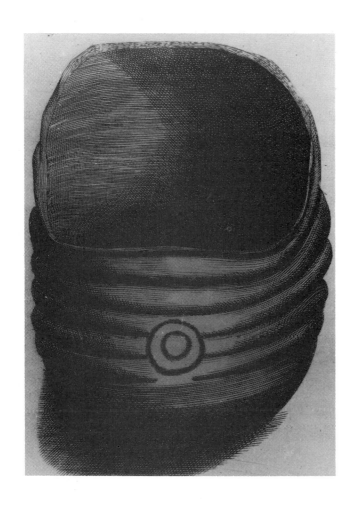

Pl. 68–Two views of 'stone urn', from Molyneux (1725, Figs iv and v).

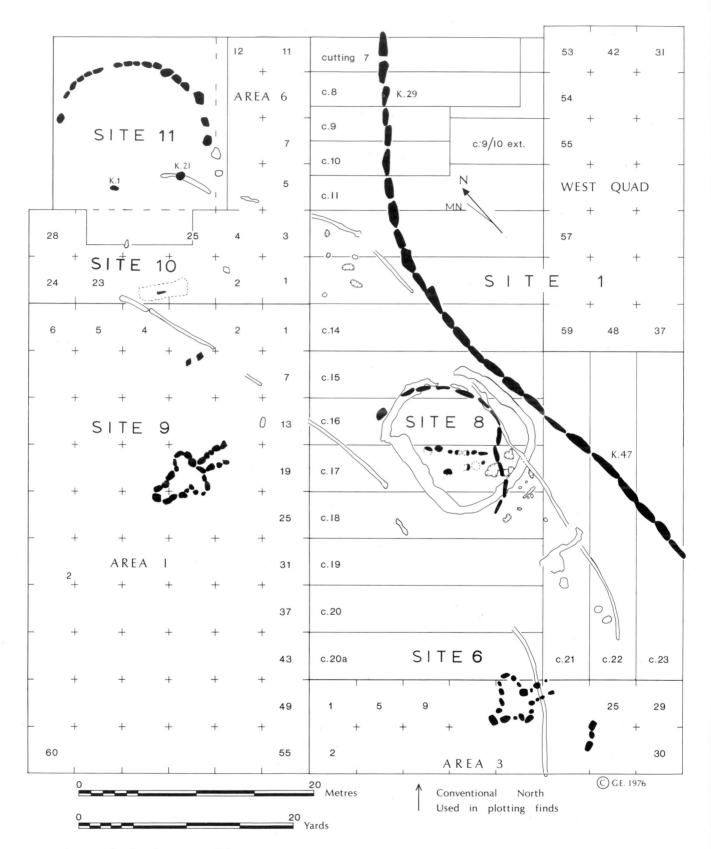

0   20 Metres

0   20 Yards

Conventional North
Used in plotting finds

*Fig. 74—Index plan of area to west of Site 1.
Neolithic occupation features are in outline,
overlying passage tombs (Sites 6, 8, 9, 10
and 11) and part of kerb of Site 1 in solid
shading.*

Part two

Neolithic occupation

To the west of Site 1 and underlying passage tombs 6, 8, 9, 10 and 11 (pp 41ff) was considerable evidence of Neolithic activity, probably domestic (Figs 74–84; Pls 69–72). The main features, not all of which are contemporary, are the foundations of a subrectangular structure, pits, fireplaces, pebbling, rough paving and palisade trenches. In the main, domestic refuse was confined to the fill of the trenches and pits. Apart from three isolated portions no natural sod layer survived over the area. At least part was removed at an early date as the mounds of the tombs in the area (Sites 6, 8, 9, 10 and 11) lie directly on the natural boulder clay. In more recent times damage was caused by the digging of drains, ditches and pits. Overlying the prehistoric remains was a layer of dark earth which contained artifacts of Early Christian date.

SUBRECTANGULAR STRUCTURE (Fig. 75; Pls 69a, 70a).

Description

This lay beneath the passage tomb, Site 8 (p. 48). The digging of sockets for the orthostats of Site 8 and a drain, probably of fairly recent date (Eogan 1974, 19–20), which runs across the structure from north-east to south-west, caused slight damage. The entrance area was also damaged by the digging of a large irregular pit.

The subrectangular structure is 10.70m by 9.10m internally and 12.30 by *c.* 10.10m externally. The principal feature is a trench that was dug into the subsoil with an undug gap in the north-eastern corner. The entrance area had been disturbed and the end of the trench on the north-eastern side removed. On the western side the end narrows almost to a point and has a pronounced inward curve. This is the entrance and was probably about 1m wide. The trench is largest and deepest on the western side. There a stretch 8.40m long was dug into the subsoil to a maximum depth of 97cm. In the base, closer to the western than to the eastern side, is a row of eleven postholes whose depths range from 7cm to 18cm.

Posthole	1	2	3	4	5	6	7	8	9	10	11
Depth (cm)	10	7	17	10	18	17	8	8	8	13	8

They tend to be circular at the mouth and average 15cm in diameter. Along the edge of No. 4 is a stone which probably served as packing. It appears that this western trench was really a large multiple post pit. Shallow holes were dug in the base to accommodate the tips of the posts. The posts were then placed in position, and the trench was backfilled. The fill consisted of dark earth and the lower part in particular had a considerable number of charcoal flakes. Ms Scannell has identified the wood as oak (*quercus*).

A few pieces of animal bone were also found in the fill (787). Ms Colette Dowling reports that these consisted of some teeth from the lower jaw of a small sheep (or goat) and some fragments of leg bone, including epiphysis (possibly cow). Pottery sherds and flints were also mixed through the fill (see below). In fact the material appears to have been largely derived from occupation debris. The sides are fairly steep and the bottom tends to be flat. The edges are irregular at the mouth and the width ranges from 1.50m to 80cm on the outside. Around the midpoint a U-shaped depression has been dug into the subsoil to a depth of 40cm. This is part of an area of disturbance, probably fairly modern, which was already noted when Site 8 was being excavated (Eogan 1974, 20–1).

Fig. 75–Ground plan and cross-sections of the sub-rectangular structure.

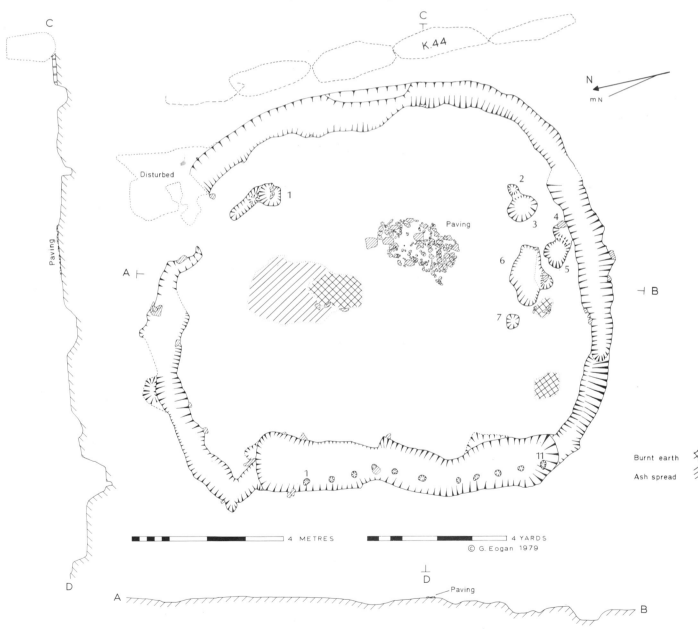

Pl. 69a–Neolithic occupation: air view from west of central portion, with sub-rectangular structure (centre) and kerb and mound of Site 1 beyond. White markers (right of centre) outline cruciform chamber of Site 6. (Photo: D. L. Swan)

Pl. 69b–Neolithic occupation: general view from south of sub-rectangular structure showing western trench (left).

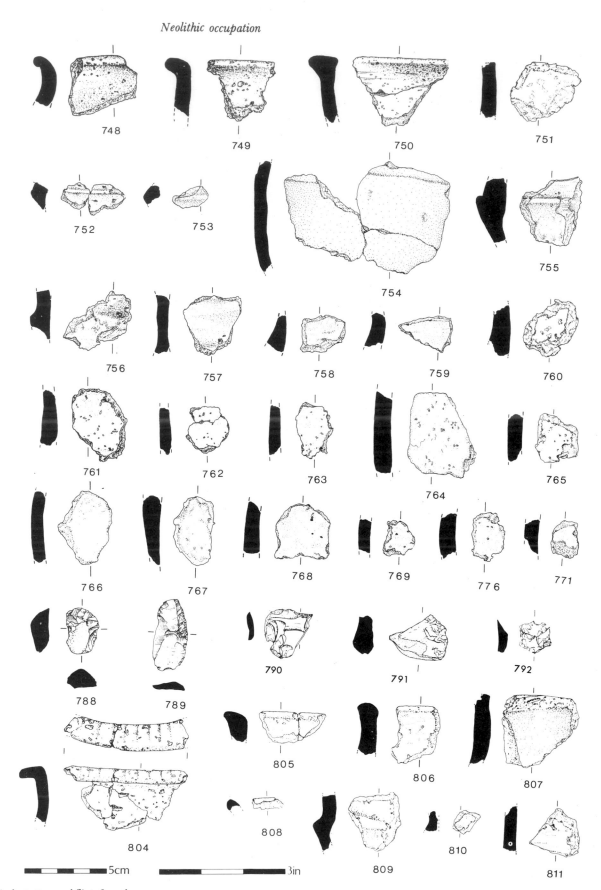

Fig. 76—Finds: pottery and flints from the
sub-rectangular structure (748–811).

The trench around the other three sides is much shallower. Again, the edges were somewhat irregular. They average 70cm in width and 30cm in depth. The cross-section tends to be U-shaped. The fill of dark earth overlay natural sod in the eastern trench which had an elbow bend at the north-west corner.

There were a number of features in the area enclosed by the trenches. Off-centre was an area of rough paving (already noted at the time of the excavation of Site 8, Eogan 1974, 21, 24) composed of a mixture of pebbles and stones over fist size. Originally it was more extensive, but parts were disturbed by the digging of sockets 10 and 11 of the tomb of Site 8 and on the north-western side by the digging of the later drain. The surviving portion had maximum dimensions of 2.40m by 1.70m. Between the paved area and the entrance was a fire-reddened area 1.5m long by 80cm in maximum width, termed Fireplace 1. An ash spread 1.6m by 1.5m is associated with it. There were two smaller areas of burning (Fireplaces 2 and 3) near the southern perimeter.

There were also seven pits within the structure. The fill in each was of soft dark earth.

DIMENSIONS OF PITS

Pit No.	1	2	3	4	5	6	7
Average width (cm)	60	30	70	60	70	130	35
Depth (cm)	20	15	20	40	40	30	15

1. The main portion is roughly circular. There are three stones in the base. A channel extends northwards from the pit for almost 1m. There is a depression in the base of this a short distance out from the pit. It has not been established if the channel is contemporary with the pit.

2–3. At present these are conjoined and their outline is irregular.

4. This pit was clearly earlier than the structure and part of it was cut away when the southern trench was dug. Beside it is Pit 5 which is of irregular shape.

6. This is the largest pit and is also irregular with a bulge on the southern side. This may be part of a small pit, but its chronological relationship to the large pit has not been established. Flakes of charcoal were mixed through the dark fill. This material produced a C14 determination of 4852 ± 71 b.p. (*c.* 2902 b.c.; B.M. 1076). This pit produced a number of finds.

7. Small pit, circular at the mouth.

Save No. 4, it has not been possible to establish the chronological relationships between the pits and the subrectangular structure.

Finds

Finds (Fig. 76) were made in the enclosing trenches and in Pit 6 but nearly all came from the basal portion of the fill of the western trench and it appears that they represent a period of activity that predates the erection of the subrectangular structure.

Pottery. The pottery from this structure, and also from the other parts of the area of occupation, belongs to the Western Neolithic family of wares, except possibly 941–5 which are a little coarser, although they too appear to be Neolithic. The following comments apply to the Western Neolithic from the entire area. In general the ware is of good quality with a smooth surface. A few sherds (e.g. 750, 757, 761) show evidence of burnishing but there was no indication of slip. Grits, usually crushed quartz and shale material which would have been immediately available, are present. Nearly all the sherds have small cavities and some have large cavities, almost exclusively on the exterior. Professor Brindley thought that these were due to the removal of large grits. Such grits could have become accidentally assimilated into the clay during the formation of the pots, but they would have been removed before firing, and after their extraction the surface would have been smoothed over, causing a lip to form over the cavities. The cavities not only affected the finish of the pottery but, in Professor Brindley's opinion, made it highly porous. He felt that such vessels could only be used for dry storage. Liquids could have been kept in the better finished, burnished vessels. The predominant colours are dark and brown. These usually vary between the inner and outer surfaces but the colour can also vary from one part of a surface to another, for instance 755 and 756 are dark above the shoulder and brownish below. Except 783–6 the pottery from the subrectangular structure came from the fill of the western trench.

Pl. 70a–Neolithic occupation: western trench of sub-rectangular structure from south. Scoop on left is a later feature.

748–51. Rimsherds, 748–50 out-turned; 748 tends to be beaded, 749 has a rounded outer face, and 750 has a flattish top. At the junction of the rim and the neck are some transverse striations. As only a small portion of 751 survives the shape of the rim cannot be determined but at least it expanded outwards. No. 752 has a ridge which may have come from the inner part of a rim rather than from a shoulder (cf. 750). The outer surface is missing. No. 753 comes from either a rim or a shoulder.

754–6. Shoulder sherds; 754 has a simple angle. At the angle on 755 the lower part of the body is pinched up to give a groove effect. No. 756 has a small step. Despite the difference in the shoulder step 755 and 756 may have come from the same vessel.

Pl. 70b—Neolithic occupation: general view from south showing line of eastern palisade trench.

757. Neck sherd of a shouldered vessel with an outwardly projecting rim. No. 758 is thicker at one end than at the other, and appears to have come from just above or just below the shoulder angle. Nos 759a–760 are neck sherds of shouldered vessels; 759a was associated with a few small pieces (b-e) but because they are so small it is not possible to say if they came from the same vessel. No. 760 was in the base of the trench and was overlain by a film of yellow earth 2cm–3cm thick. Above this film was the main basal layer of the trench fill, dark material with charcoal.

761–71. Bodysherds. The inner surfaces of 761 and 762 which may be parts of the same vessel as 750, are worn off. 766–7 may also have come from this vessel; 772–82 are small and poorly preserved bodysherds or fragments; 783 and 784 are also scraps but they were found in the northern trench.

785 and 786. Small bodysherd and fragments, found lying on the old ground surface in the structure 2m due east of the western trench and 2m south of the northern end of the eastern trench. None is illustrated.

Pottery was also found in Pit 6. 804 has a flat-topped rim which projects outwards at right angles to the wall. There is rippling on the top. On 805 the rim projects slightly outwards and is rounded on the inner side. The rim of 806 expands slightly on both sides, and the top is rounded. The shape of the rim of 807 cannot be determined as the outer part is broken away. The surviving portion of the top is flat. On the inside, immediately under the rim, the wall thins. The curvature at the bottom of the sherd suggests that it was part of a shouldered vessel. No. 808, a small fragment, is probably part of a rim; 809 is part of a shoulder; 810 also appears to have come from around the shoulder of a vessel. Nos 811–21 are bodysherds (Figs 76 and 77). 812–16 are of thin ware and at least 812–14 appear to have come from the same vessel. 822 is a collection of unidentifiable fragments, not illustrated.

Flints (Fig. 76). Except 802 and 803, all were found in the fill of the western trench. No. 788 is a rounded scraper formed from a piece detached from a pebble. On the upper side cortex survives. No. 789, another scraper, is made from a flake of chert. The working is mainly confined to one edge. Nos 790–803 are waste pieces, mainly chips. Only 790–792 are illustrated.

Four pieces of flint came from Pit 6 (Fig. 77). 823 is a leaf-shaped blade with pronounced medial line on one face. Both edges have been unifacially worked and the bulbar end has been trimmed. 824–6 are irregular. There is slight evidence for working on 825 and 826. No. 824 has been burnt.

The *animal bones* from the western trench (787) have already been described (p. 212).

Remarks

Although the purpose of this structure remains unknown, its general shape and size suggest a house. The reddened areas and the ash spread indicate that fires had been lit but there was no formal hearth. Apart from the small area of paving, really a stone spread, there was no evidence for a laid down floor; neither was there any occupation material within the structure. There is no counterpart in Ireland for the proportions of the structure, but rectangular Neolithic houses are known, such as Ballyglass, Co. Mayo (Ó Nualláin 1972), Ballynagilly, Co. Tyrone (ApSimon 1969), and Site A Knockadoon (Lough Gur), Co. Limerick (Ó Ríordáin 1954, 299–312). Wall trenches existed at both Ballyglass and Ballynagilly but these (and Knockadoon) had numerous postholes. There were also postholes within the houses. As in the Knowth structure the entrance to Knockadoon Site A was at one corner and a similar design may have existed at Ballyglass and Ballynagilly. On Site B Knockadoon, an L-shaped trench with an average width of 70cm and a depth varying between 12cm and 17cm occurred as part of a Neolithic structural complex. Ó Ríordáin (1954, 313–14) interpreted the trench as the remains of a groove for a wooden wall. As for parallels outside Ireland, a squarish enclosure with maximum dimensions of 9.1m by 8.8m was delimited by a shallow trench which had a maximum depth of 36cm and an average width of 82cm at the mouth, at Windmill Hill, Wiltshire. Dr Isobel Smith (1965, 30–33) proposed a Neolithic date for the Windmill Hill structure, on the basis of analogous wooden structures found under some long barrows, but wondered if it could have been a cattle pen.

There are difficulties in accepting that Knowth was a roofed building. Apart from the western wall, postholes were absent from the trench. The trench on the other sides is too shallow to have served as a continuous post trench, but it might have served as a bedding for planks with holes for uprights. Even if such walls, intended to bear a roof, did exist, internal supports would still be necessary but no evidence (i.e. postholes) for these came to light. However, if a wall had existed, we can tell from the size of the trench and the evidence for sunken posts that this would have been stronger on the western side, which is the side that would have been exposed to the predominant wind.

PALISADE TRENCHES (Fig. 78; Pls 70b, 71a, b)

Description

There are two such trenches. A small portion of the eastern trench was uncovered in 1963 but the extent of the complex was not then apparent (Eogan 1968, 324–7, 334). The trenches are curved and roughly parallel in a north-south direction. In the lengths exposed there are some gaps, including a fairly extensive one in the western trench. These gaps are the result of damage but even when evidence for the trench itself has disappeared its line is in some stretches continued by packing stones. However, about mid-way in the western trench there is a definite gap, 3.2m long. This 'causeway' is pebbled. The western trench, 59m long, extends further to the south than does the eastern one which is 58m long. The trenches are 8m apart at the southern end, 11m at the northern end. Excavation has not produced any evidence that the trenches extended further at either or both ends. The eastern trench is the better preserved. This is probably because it was closer to the large mound (Site 1) and therefore there was a deeper deposit of material over it than over the western trench. At many points, especially in the eastern trench, postholes were clearly identifiable. The more clearly defined postholes varied in depth from 10cm to 53cm. In the small number where fairly definite evidence was available the diameters averaged 25cm. Where there was positive evidence for posts they were not at the regular intervals which might suggest a post and horizontal beam fence. It is more likely that the trench had a series of closely-set posts, because throughout the fill of both trenches there are a number of smallish stones which may have served as packing stones for posts. If the posts were closely set throughout, and assuming that their diameter was up to 30cm, the eastern trench, for instance, would have had approximately one hundred and seventy posts. The height of the palisade cannot, of course, be determined but as the

Pl. 71a–Neolithic occupation: detailed view from north-west of eastern palisade trench in cutting 13, showing clear distinction between fill and surrounding material.

Pl. 71b–Neolithic occupation: eastern palisade trench beneath Site 8 from south, showing postholes and packing stones. Kerbstone 8 of Site 8 is on left.

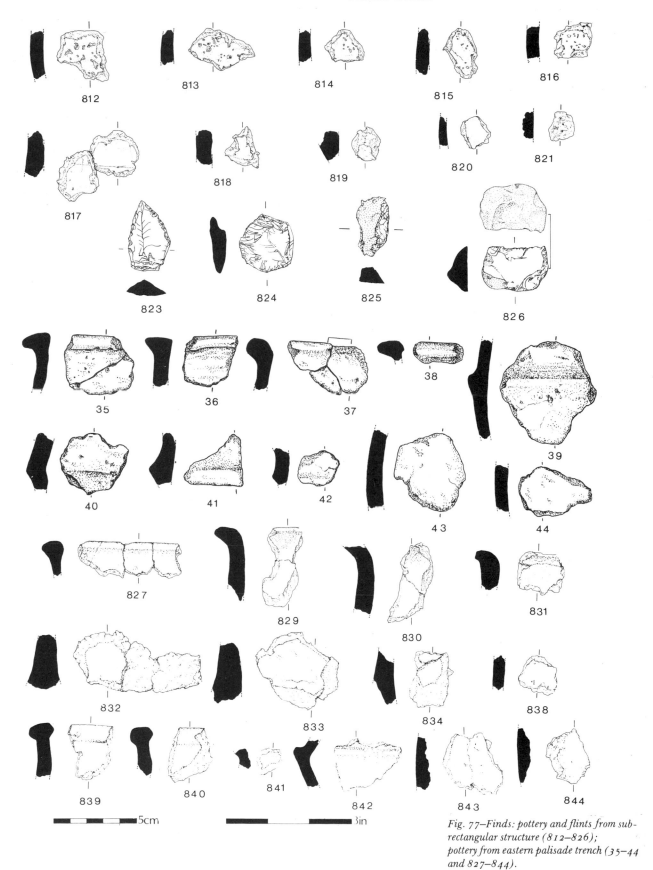

Fig. 77–Finds: pottery and flints from sub-rectangular structure (812–826); pottery from eastern palisade trench (35–44 and 827–844).

maximum depth of the trench is about 50cm, it is unlikely that it was more than 1.50m.

In the main the fill of the trenches consisted of dark or dark-brown earth with charcoal flecks. Pottery sherds and some flints were

Fig. 78–Neolithic occupation: ground plan of features.

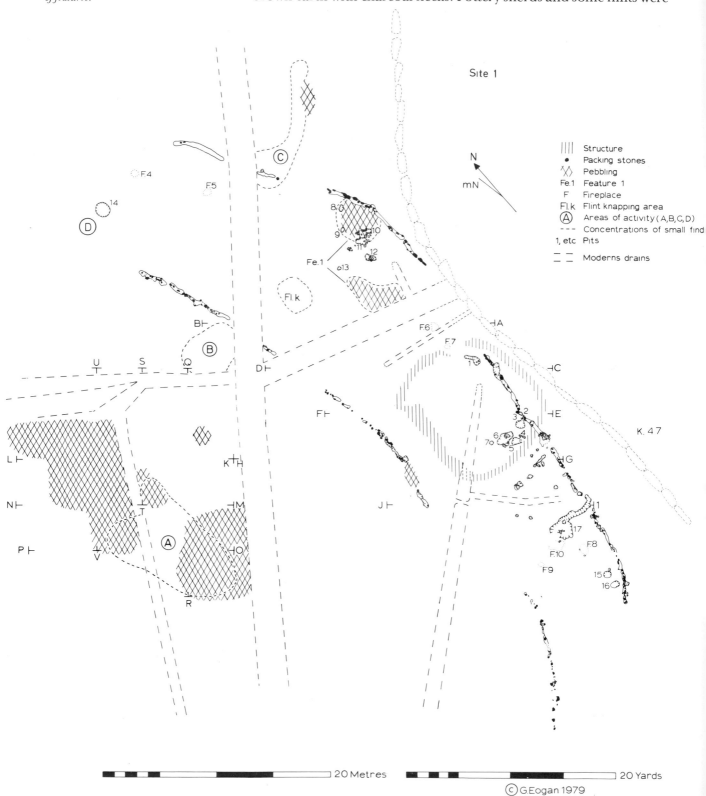

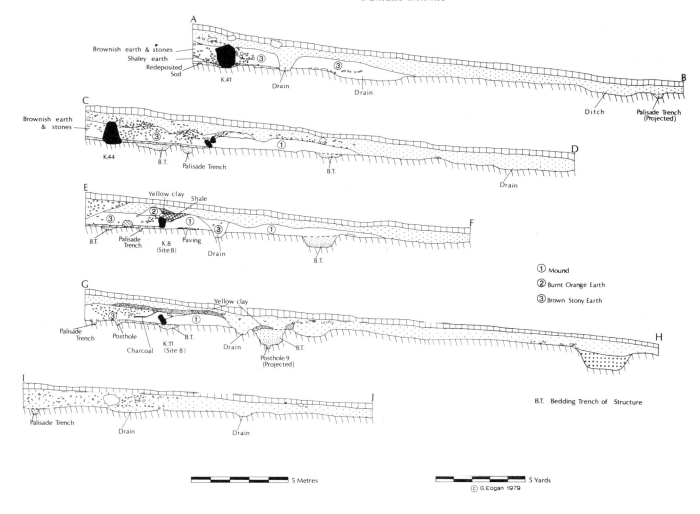

① Mound
② Burnt Orange Earth
③ Brown Stony Earth

B.T. Bedding Trench of Structure

5 Metres

5 Yards

© G. Eogan 1979

Fig. 79–Sections across Neolithic occupation (A–B to I–J).

mixed through it mainly in the eastern trench, suggesting that at least some of the fill was occupation debris. At one section of the eastern trench (under kerbstone 21 of Site 11) the upper layer of the fill consisted of wet and mushy charcoal (Eogan 1968, 324–5) It appears that a fire burnt in this section of the trench for a time. Perhaps this section of the palisade was destroyed by fire as happened at Mount Pleasant, Dorset (Wainwright 1979, 54) but the fire could not have been intensive as the sides of the trench were not reddened. A few small stones and a thumb scraper (36b) that came from the dark fill under the charcoal spread had been subjected to heat. The burning that caused the charcoal spread may have begun with the ignition of portion of the palisade. Ms Scannell has examined the charcoal and reports the presence of oak (*quercus*), 34 pieces; hazel (*corylus*), 1 piece; and grains of wheat (*triticum*). The wheat grains included one well-formed half grain, one damaged grain and fragments of others.

As the eastern trench cuts across the subrectangular structure it must be of later date (p. 211). However, the date of one trench relative to the other, and the chronological relationships between the trenches and the areas of activity around them have not been conclusively established. The trenches are roughly parallel; nearly all the activity is confined to the spaces between them, and the pottery from all areas is similar. Therefore the palisades may be contemporary, delimiting the area of activity, but if this is so their open ends seem odd.

Finds (Figs 77 and 81)

The eastern trench produced much more material than did the western. Starting with the eastern trench, the finds from each will be described separately, first the pottery and then the flints. The finds are described according to their find place starting from the northern end of each trench and continuing to the south.

The segment of the eastern trench largely under kerbstone 21 of Site 5 produced twenty-one sherds (35–44) over thumb-nail size (see Eogan 1958, 327, Nos 1–10, Fig. 21); 35–8 are rimsherds — these project outwards but they vary in form; 39 has a moderate step but 40–41 and possibly 42 are angular; 43a–f are bodysherds (only 43a is illustrated); 44a is a basesherd, while 44b–m are fragments, not illustrated.

Fig. 80–Sections across Neolithic occupation (K–L to U–V).

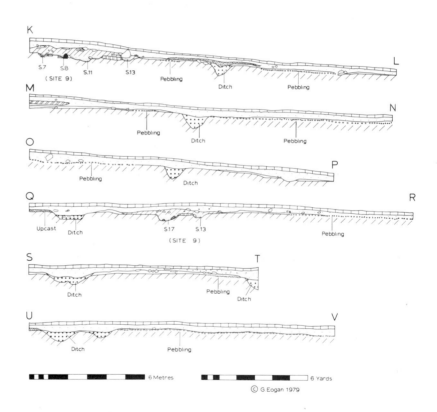

827. The rim is slightly rounded at the top. It expands to both sides but the expansion is more pronounced on the outside. Area 6, square 6, 3.40m from north, 2.60m from west; depth in trench, 7cm.

828. Fragments, perhaps from the body of a vessel. Cutting 12, 3.25m from cutting 11, 5.00m from west base line. Not illustrated. From the top of the fill.

829 and 830. Rimsherds from the same vessel. The rim projects outwards and is pointed. The tip is missing on 830. Cutting 16, 0.45m from north, 15.10m from west.

831–6. A group of sherds apparently all from the same vessel. The brownish ware is rather coarse and contains numerous quartz grits and some shale. One sherd (831) comes from a rim, is rounded on the inside, and projects upwards slightly on the other side. The remaining sherds are from the body. Three (832–4) are thicker along one side than the other and come either from around the shoulder of a carinated vessel or from near the base of a flat-bottomed vessel. Found with 837 and 838, in cutting 16, 2.05m from north, 16.00m from west. No. 837 consists of unidentifiable fragments, not illustrated and 838 is a bodysherd; although found with 831–7 it came from a different vessel. The ware is thinner, with some cavities and grits of quartz and shale.

839–41. Two rimsherds and a rim fragment of the same vessel. The rim projects outwards and inwards, and is rounded on the outside and on the top. The inner projection is faceted on the top and bottom. 842 is a shoulder sherd with steep step. In colour and ware this sherd is similar to 839–41 and is probably part of the same vessel. The original inner surface of 843–4 seems to have been worn away.

845–63. Nineteen fragments, apparently from the body of a vessel; not illustrated. No. 864 is represented by unidentifiable fragments; not illustrated.

839–64. Found close to 892 and 893 (flint) in cutting 16, 2.00m from north and 15.85m from west; 839–42 appear to be part of the same vessel but it is not certain if the others are.

865–80. Sixteen sherds found together and of similar ware with cavities and grits of quartz and shale. The colour varies from brown to dark. The group may have been part of the same vessel with an out-turned rim and concave neck. Nos 866–72 are rimsherds, 866 and 867 are similar in shape. The rim projects outwards and downwards slightly. On 866, just below the rim, is a slight but irregular channel. The rims of 868 and 869 project outwards only. On No. 870 the rim projects outwards but also slightly inwards. Nos 871 and 872 appear to be fragments from the inner face of the rim. Only one face of 873 survives. It has a slight channel rather like that on the inner face of 866 below the rim. The slight curvature on 874 shows that it is a neck sherd. Nos 875–9 are plain bodysherds. No. 880 is a collection of unidentifiable fragments found together in cutting 17, 0.60m from north, 17.8m from west; not illustrated.

881. Rimsherd projecting outwards and inwards. The outer expansion is rounded; the inner is 'stepped' near the base, probably because the clay, when wet, was spread over part of the inner face below the rim. Found with 882–4 and 892 in cutting 16, 2.3m from north, 16. 5m from west. No. 882 is a small sherd, probably part of the same vessel as 881. 883 is a fragment (not illustrated). 884 is a rimsherd of similar ware to 882, and at the time of manufacture it appears that wet clay was spread over the inner wall for a short distance below the rim. The rim projects outwards only, so it does not appear to come from the same vessel as 882.

885. Shoulder sherd of dark ware with cavities. The top of the shoulder is slightly concave. Found at a point where cutting 21–22 crosses the trench. 886 is a small portion of expanded rim, poorly preserved, from cutting 21, 26.68m in from south base line, 3.50m

from west. 887a–b are two small pieces of ware similar to 886 with which they were associated. All three probably came from the same vessel.

888 and 889. Two small bodysherds. There were two fragments of similar ware found with the sherds (889b–c). Cutting 21, 25.50m in from south base line, 0.55m from west; only 889a is illustrated.

890. Shoulder sherd. The top of the shoulder slopes downwards. Found with 891 and 896 (flint). Cutting 22, 23.00m from north, 1.65m from west. 891 is represented by small bodysherds; not illustrated.

28–32. Flint scrapers found in the segment of the eastern trench under Site 5, kerbstone 21 with sherds 35–44. Nos 28 and 29 are thumb scrapers, both made from a piece detached from a pebble. On one face of each is a considerable amount of cortex. 29 had been burnt. In scraper 30 only the bulbar end is unworked. The striking platform is triangular and is inclined at an angle to the working edge. In 31 the working has been confined to the concave side. It may have been made from a chip derived from a polished flint axehead. No. 32, found on the edge of the trench, is also a side scraper but the worked edge is straight.

The fill also produced four chips of flint (33a–d) and three fragments of quartz (34a–c); not illustrated.

On 892 the crude scraping edge has been formed around the broad end. An unworked chip of chert, 893, was found with it; both were found with pottery (839–64). Nos 894–5 are unworked pieces derived from pebbles with smooth cortex; 894 was found with pottery sherds 881–4 and 895. No. 896 is rough and also derives from a pebble, as it has smooth cortex. Found in cutting 17, 0.20m from north, 17.40m from west. No. 897 is a chip of chert which came from the top of the fill in cutting 21, 17.30m from south, 3.20m from west.

Pl. 72a–Neolithic occupation: general view from south of feature 1, showing large pit in centre (11), partially covered by a dump of stones, during excavation, pit 12 below it on right and later pit containing Inhumation Burial 17 below it on left.
Areas of pebbling lie on north and south-east of Pit 11.
Portion of eastern palisade is visible (top right).

898. Pottery fragments from western trench too poorly preserved to identify; not illustrated. Area 1, square 3, 3.25m from north, 3.20m from west.

899 and 900. Bodysherds, perhaps from the same vessel; associated with unidentifiable fragments (901) in Area 1, square 3, 3.50 from north, 3.25m from west; none is illustrated.

902. A group of small sherds. One sherd is part of a rim that projected outwards and two fragments (902a–c) appear to be part of a similar rim. The remainder are bodysherds. Area 3, square 22, 2.00m from north, 0.55cm from west; depth 0.25cm below lip of trench; only 902a is illustrated.

Pl. 72b–Neolithic occupation: pit 17 and posthole trench. This may form southern wall of a possible structure (see p. 233).

AREA DELIMITED BY PALISADE TRENCHES

Possible living areas (Feature 1) (Fig. 78; Pl. 72a)

This may have been a living area but no house plan came to light. The features consisted of six pits (8–13) and two areas of pebbling. All the pits were irregular and 11 and 12 were the largest, the fill consisting of soft dark earth.

DIMENSIONS OF PITS

Pit No.	8	9	10	11	12	13
Width (cm)	50	35	40	80	80	30
Depth (cm)	5	12	20	20	20	10

The pebbling occurred in two areas, one to the north and one to the south of Pits 10 and 11. Both patches consisted of very small stones that were set into the surface of the boulder clay. There were some flakes of charcoal and minute fragments of unburnt bone, too small for identification, lying on the spreads. The southern spread measured 1.50m by 60cm and the northern 80cm by 40cm. Pits 10 and 11 interrupted the continuity of the spreads but it was not possible to establish if they were a later intrusion.

Finds (pottery) (Figs 81, 82)

A considerable number of pottery sherds were found on top of and immediately around the southern area of pebbling and the large irregular Pit 12. The majority of the sherds appear to have come from round-bottomed vessels. There is some variation in rim and shoulder shape, and evidence for the presence of lugs. Other sherds are of coarser ware (942–44). These have an internal cordon and the rimsherd (942) has an outward projection.

903. The rim projects outwards and downwards to give a barbed effect. The surface is worn all over. No. 904 is another rimsherd with no inward expansion. The outer surface is worn away, so it cannot be established if there was a projection on that side. Two shoulder sherds (905 and 906) may have been part of the same vessel. Sherds 907a–b and 908 are from a curved neck. 907b, a fragment, is not illustrated; 909 is a bodysherd. As the ware of 904–9 is similar, generally dark-brown with some cavities, all may have been part of the same vessel. Nos 910–12 are rim fragments, 910 is out-turned but the tip has been damaged. The small size of 911–12 makes it impossible to be certain about the type of rim. Nos 913–14 may also be rimsherds. No. 915 has a slight projection along the fractured edge. It cannot be determined from what type of vessel or from what portion of the vessel this sherd came but it may have been a cordoned vessel like 943. In 916 the rim projects slightly outwards. All appear to be from the same vessel.

917–28. Shoulder sherds; 917–25 have a 'gutter' and 917 also has an elongated lug. As the shape of the shoulder and the ware are similar it appears that these sherds are part of the same vessel. Nos 926 and 927 are of similar dark ware. The 'gutter' on 926 is damaged and 927 has no 'gutter'. It is not certain if they are part of the same vessel. No. 928 also has a 'gutter'.

929. Curved sherd with one face missing, part of either a rim or shoulder. 930, also damaged, may have been part of a rim; 931 could have come from a shoulder and has a projection along one of the fractured edges. There is a broad channel on one side of 932.

933–9. Seven sherds thicker along one edge than along the others, possibly from near the shoulder of a vessel. The ware is dark and compact. It is not unlike that of 917–25. 940 is a pointed rimsherd. 933–40 may have come from the same vessel.

941a–b. Rimsherds. No. 941a has an internal bevel and outward expansion. As the outer part has been broken away the extent of the expansion cannot be determined. No. 941b is damaged but may be part of a similar rim. The ware is flaky and has quartz grits. These sherds may have come from ware that is slightly coarser than the normal (cf. 943).

Fig. 81–Finds: pottery (865–890) and flints (28–32 and 892–897) from eastern palisade trench;
pottery (898–902) from western palisade trench and pottery (903–921) from Feature 1.

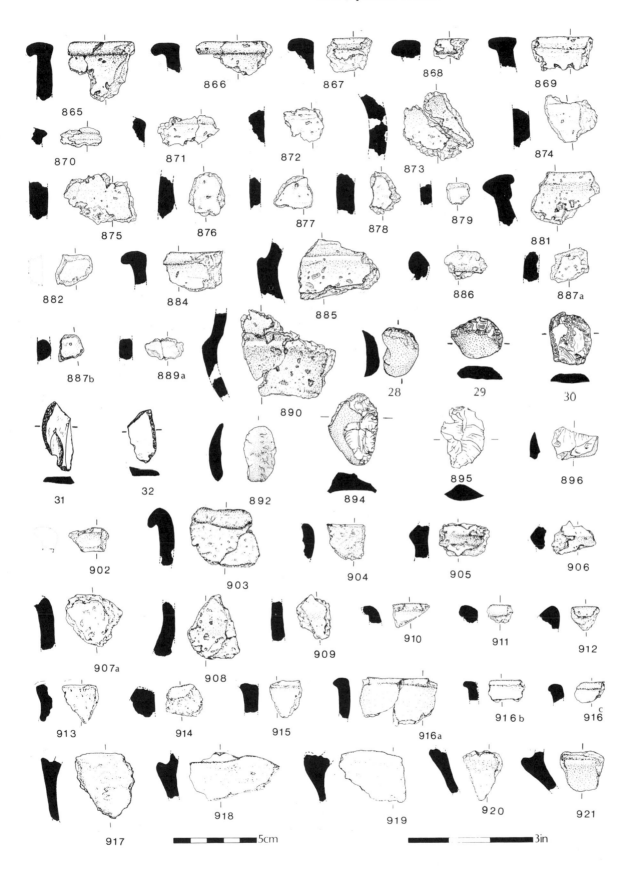

5cm

3in

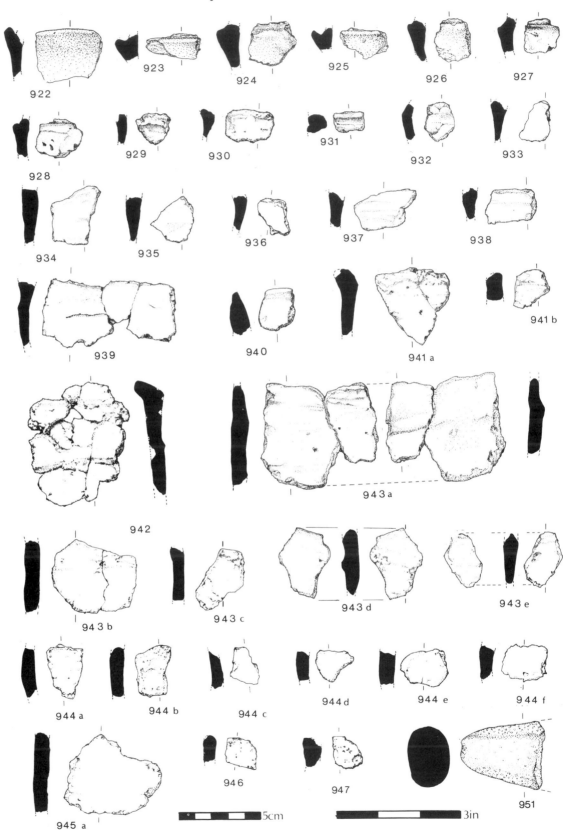

Fig. 82—Finds: pottery (922–947);
stone axehead (951) from Feature 1.

942. The rim has an internal bevel and outward expansion. There is an internal horizontal ridge 3cm below the rim. The darkish, somewhat flaky ware resembles 941a–b but it is not certain if they come from the same vessel (illustration shows interior).

943a–e. Bodysherds. 943a has an internal horizontal ridge from which the ware narrows on one side and thickens slightly on the other. Along the fractured edge of the latter are the remains of a slight expansion (cf. 915). The ware is compact and dark-brown. Internally one part of the sherd is worn. Striations on the outer surface are probably due to smoothing down when the clay was soft. Nos 943b–e are bodysherds with a ridge. The ware of all sherds is similar and they may be from the same vessel. The illustration shows the external face on left, the internal face on right. The inner face only of b and c is illustrated.

944a–f. Six bodysherds of ware that is not unlike 943. The inner surface of d and f has a dark encrustation.

945a. Bodysherd of greyish ware with a dark encrustation on the inside. Nos 945b–c are small pieces of similar ware; not illustrated.

941–4 and possibly 945 differ in texture, in the out-turned rim on 941a–942, and in the cordons on 942–3, from the main bulk of the sherds. Their precise affinities cannot be determined but they may be a variation of the normal Western ware.

946. Rimsherd that curves outwards slightly, rounded at the outside but unexpanded, with cavities in the ware.

947. Sherd from either the shoulder or the rim of a vessel. The inner face is missing and the outer surface is dark. There are cavities in the ware.

948. Under this number are grouped forty-four small sherds over thumb-nail size and small indeterminate fragments. These are featureless but all appear to have come from the bodies of vessels. Two main wares are represented, hard compact ware and 'corky' ware, but only about seventeen sherds can be assigned to the latter category. Not illustrated.

Stone finds

951. Axehead (Fig. 82), only the butt of which survives. This is narrow at the top and its cross-section is oval at the fractured end. The broad surfaces have been polished but the sides are abraded. The axe was found in the southern area of pebbling. Dr John Jackson who has examined the axe and also a thin section (prepared by Mr P. O'Donoghue, Department of Geology, University College, Dublin) reports: 'The rock is a deeply weathered basalt with an interesting mineral assemblage, indicating extreme basic affinities. This is reflected, for example, in the felspars which exhibit very high extinction angles, ranging from 46° to 49°, the majority of readings being at the lower end of the range, indicating anorthite which occupies a position at the extreme basic end of the albite-anorthite series. Leocoxene is also present in limited amounts, indicating the presence originally of ilmenite, a mineral usually associated with the more basic holocrystalline rocks such as gabbro and norite.

'The ground mass consists of a felted mass of haphazardly oriented felspar crystals (anorthite) all exhibiting lamellar, or multiple, twinning. Kaolinisation is evident but alteration of the felspars is limited; extinction angles can be measured without difficulty and the majority of the crystals are surprisingly fresh.

'The ferromagnesian minerals have been altered to chlorite almost throughout the thin section, exhibiting the typical "ultra-blues" between crossed nicols. Chlorite pseudomorphing augite crystals can be detected but the intermediate stage of amphibolisation to pseudomorphic hornblende was not noted. A considerable amount of calcite is present due, no doubt, to the chemical alteration of anorthite. The calcite forms a mosaic of crystals filling small veinlets in the rock and also occurs with chlorite and quartz as crystal mosaics filling vugs. The presence of quartz in such an extremely basic mineralogical context is of interest.

'The rock could have been derived from outcrops of the Tertiary basic igneous intrusive complex of the Kingscourt area to the north of Knowth where sills and dykes of basalt and dolerite are of common occurrence. However, its extremely weathered nature suggests that the material could have occurred as an erratic cobble in the glacial drift of the area and initially derived from outcrops in the vicinity of Kingscourt. The provenance, in the context of Knowth, could therefore have been immediately local.'

Flint-knapping area (Fig. 78, Fl. k)

This consisted of a scatter of eighty-two pieces of flint which occurred over a limited area (952–1034, Fig. 83). It appears that pebble flint was the predominant raw material used. There is one unused pebble with a very smooth cortex. Two other pieces are the remains of pebbles and others the pieces that were knocked off pebbles. Sixteen of the pieces (including the pebbles) are honey-coloured flint (969–84). The remaining pieces are grey. Forty-nine have been burnt. Seventeen are artifacts (952–68). The others (except for the pebble) are waste scrap, pieces knocked off pebbles and various pieces and scraps, the by-product of flint-working (969–1034).

Among the artifacts 952 is a bi-facially flaked leafshaped arrowhead. A small portion is missing at the base. Eleven (953–63) are rounded scrapers. Most are well formed and 953, 954 and 960 have steep scraping edges. Two (962 and 963) are small inferior scraps; 964 is pointed and bifacially worked. Nos 965–8 are blades: 965 has a triangular cross-section and definite working along the edges; 967 and 968 tend to be parallel-sided. There is slight evidence of working along the edges; 966 has slight evidence of utilisation along the convex side. Only 952–71 are illustrated.

Twelve rough pieces of quartz and two of shale (1035) also turned up but these could be fortuitous intrusions. Three sherds of pottery were found together, associated with the flint scatter. None is illustrated.

949. Small sherd of fairly compact ware, poorly preserved. From the portion of surfaces surviving it appears that it came from around the shoulder or rim. Found between Pits 10 and 11 amongst the spread of stones. Not illustrated.

950a–b. Sherds. No. 950a is of fairly compact ware, brown on the outside and dark on the inside, with grits in the ware; 950b is of 'coarse' ware (cf. 943) brownish and with grits. What appears to be the remains of a cordon occur on one face; the other face has been worn away.

TRENCH, HOLES, ETC. BETWEEN SUBRECTANGULAR STRUCTURE AND PIT 17

Immediately to the south of the structure was a series of nine holes, three conjoined to form a short trench 1.40m long. Between this trench and the structure are two holes, and there are two further holes close to it on the south side. The three conjoined holes and two more to its west form a straight line. Parallel to this line, to the south, is a continuous trench, more substantial than the holes. The edge is irregular and averages 45cm in diameter at the mouth. At the western end is a pit (17), while at the eastern end the trench curves to the north. The relationship between this trench and Pit 17 on the one hand and the palisade trench on the other has not been determined, although the 'extension' of the trench through the line of the palisade suggests that the trench is the earlier feature. The original surface of the area between the two rows has been damaged and a drain was cut across part of it. This could have destroyed internal features and may also explain the scarcity of structural evidence along the western edge. There is a circular hole in an approximately central position (diameter at mouth 30cm, depth 15cm). Some flat stones on the old ground surface give the appearance of paving. The maximum external distance between the trench and the row of holes is 6.60m, internally it is 5.50m. To the west are two isolated holes. No finds have been definitely associated with these features.

It has not been established that any of the features described above are contemporary, but if they were then they could represent the remains of another rectangular structure possibly a house or hut which measured about 5.5m by 4.5m externally. The Knowth features can be compared to the foundations of a rectangular house, 7m by 8.5m, from the Padholme Road site, Peterborough, England. These remains consisted of a trench with irregular edges. The finds included round-bottomed shoulder pots in the Western Neolithic tradition (Pryor 1974, 6–13, 34).

PITS

In all, seventeen pits were found. The seven (1–7) within the large, subrectangular structure and the six (8–13, Fig. 78) that were associated with a spread of Neolithic pottery have been described already (p. 215). 14–16 are roughly circular at the mouth and the fill of darkish material could be clearly distinguished from the surrounding soil.

DIMENSIONS OF PITS

Pit No.	14	15	16
Average width (cm)	125	60	80
Depth (cm)	40	20	10

The largest in the group is Pit 17 (Pl. 72b). The mouth is irregular and its maximum dimensions were 2.00m by 1.30m. It was dug into the subsoil to a depth of 40cm. The edges were steeper along the eastern side and the floor of the pit sloped downwards from west to east. The basal part of the fill consisted of stones mixed with compact earth (1). Above this was compact dark earth (2), overlain by a layer of charcoal which occurred a short distance below the mouth of the pit (3). It appears that the charcoal was derived from fireplace 10 which indicates that the use of the fireplace continued longer than the pit. Two holes which might have held posts occurred in the layer of compact dark earth, but if there were posts they were removed before the spread of charcoal occurred.

Some fragments of animal bone (1036) were found in layer 1. Ms Dowling reports that these consisted of fragments of a vertebra and a top pre-molar of a cow. Artifacts were discovered in the three levels in the pit (Fig. 83).

1037. The single find from *layer* 1 was a sherd of pottery. This is part of an out-turned rim that has a slightly convex top.

1038a. Shoulder sherd from *layer* 2. The inner face is missing. The shoulder step is not pronounced. Four fragments (1038b–e, not illustrated) of what seems to be the same ware were also found.

1039a. Round flint scraper. The scraping edge is confined to the nose, and along one side. A small chip was found beside the scraper (1039b, not illustrated).

1040. Unworked chip of chert from *layer* 3. Not illustrated.

1041. Rimsherd that projects outwards slightly convex at the top.

1042. Shoulder sherd. The outer part projects upwards and forms a channel. No. 1043, fragments of pottery too poorly preserved for precise identification, are not illustrated.

1044. Flat stone bead of irregular outline. The perforation, close to the centre, was formed by boring from both sides (hour-glass technique), but the boring was concentrated more on one side. The surface is smooth, possibly due to polishing.

1045. Flat stone bead, fairly similar to the previous example, sub-triangular. The surface is also smooth. This bead was found on the lip of the pit at the same level as layer 3. Originally the layer might have extended over the lip.

Professor J. C. Brindley has examined the beads and reports: 'These two beads are *serpentine*. Normally this has a much richer green or yellow colour and so it appears to have been bleached—an effect which might develop by heating or burning, or under some conditions, such as acidity, in the soil. It does not now resemble any of the Irish serpentines nor that of Cornwall, but I have seen material like it in north-west Scotland and on the Continent. However, a distribution map of these serpentine bead occurrences is more likely to point to the source than is geological reasoning, since the mineral type occurs rather widely.'

Both beads have counterparts in shape and in material in the two beads from the central area of the cairn at Lyles Hill (Evans 1953, 56–7, Fig. 24). They can also be compared to a bead that was found on the old ground surface at Site C, Knockadoon, Lough Gur, Co. Limerick (Ó Ríordáin 1954, 347, Fig. 23:18; Pl. 32b:10). Piggott (1954, 273) states that serpentine beads were found at Lough Gur, but he gives no further details.

Fig. 83–Finds: flints (952–971) from flint-knapping area;
pottery and flints (1037–1042) and stone (1044 and 1045) from Pit 17;
pottery and flint (1046–1051) from fireplace 10;
isolated finds of pottery and flint (1053–1063).

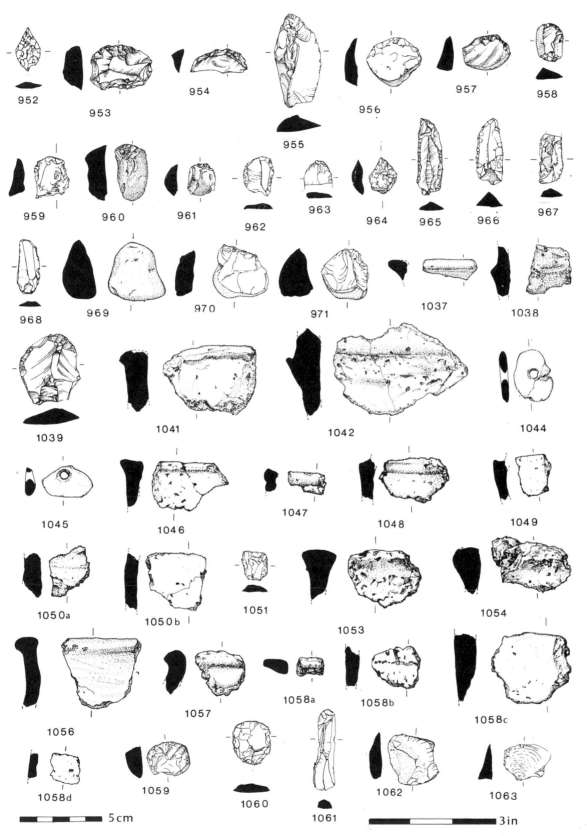

952
953
954
955
956
957
958
959
960
961
962
963
964
965
966
967
968
969
970
971
1037
1038
1039
1041
1042
1044
1045
1046
1047
1048
1049
1050a
1050b
1051
1053
1054
1056
1057
1058a
1058b
1058c
1058d
1059
1060
1061
1062
1063

5 cm
3 in

As layer 3 (charcoal) appears to be derived from fireplace 10, it is likely that the foregoing finds are *contemporary* with the finds from the fireplace (1046–51).

FIREPLACES

This name is applied to any place where a fire had been kept burning for some time, but where there are no structural features such as a stone setting. There were ten of these, all on the old ground surface, varying in size and in the intensity of burning. The three which occurred within the subrectangular structure (1–3) have already been described. The other fireplaces were isolated features.

During the excavation of Site 11 three fireplaces were found. These have already been described (Eogan 1968, 363, Fig. 15) and numbered 3–5. Fireplace 3 of that report is outside the palisade area and is not included here. Fireplaces 4 and 5 retain their original numbers in this report. The digging of a drain removed part of 6.

Fireplace 10 was much larger than the others and from the intensity of burning it appears that it was used over a greater length of time. It was the only fireplace that had a spread of charcoal associated with it. This spread produced sherds of pottery and a flint.

1046 (Fig. 83). The flat-topped rim projects outwards and it tends to be pointed. The inner face has worn away. No. 1047 is a rounded rimsherd; 1048 may have come from a shouldered vessel with steep step; 1049 has a slight channel along one side and may have come from a shouldered vessel; 1050 is a collection of bodysherds. The ware is dark and most of them could have come from the same vessel as 1048. Two are illustrated (1050a–b).

1051. Part of a flint blade.

ACTIVITY OUTSIDE PALISADE TRENCHES

Evidence for Neolithic activity was found in four places outside the palisade trenches. Two of these are to the west and the third is to the north-east (A, B, C and D on Fig. 78).

A, 25m long by 9.6m in maximum width, is centred on a point about 18m outside the western trench. It consists of a broken area of pebbling, composed of pebbles *c.*2cm in diameter with a small number of larger ones embedded into the old ground surface. The quality of the pebbling varies but in general it presents an even surface. It extends over an irregular area, 24m by 15m. It is discontinuous but this seems to be due to damage. Pebbling is absent in the area of the tomb of Site 9, which stood above this feature, except for a small patch in the right-hand recess. It was probably removed when the tomb was built. Other damage was more recently caused by the digging of ditches. There were no traces of structures or any other contemporary features.

Two bodysherds (3827 and 3828) of *pottery* were found. On the former the outer surface is damaged and on the latter the inner face is worn. Not illustrated.

Fifty-two pieces of *flint* (Fig. 84) were found. Twenty-two are artifacts and five are utilised pieces (3829–55). 3829 is a bi-facially

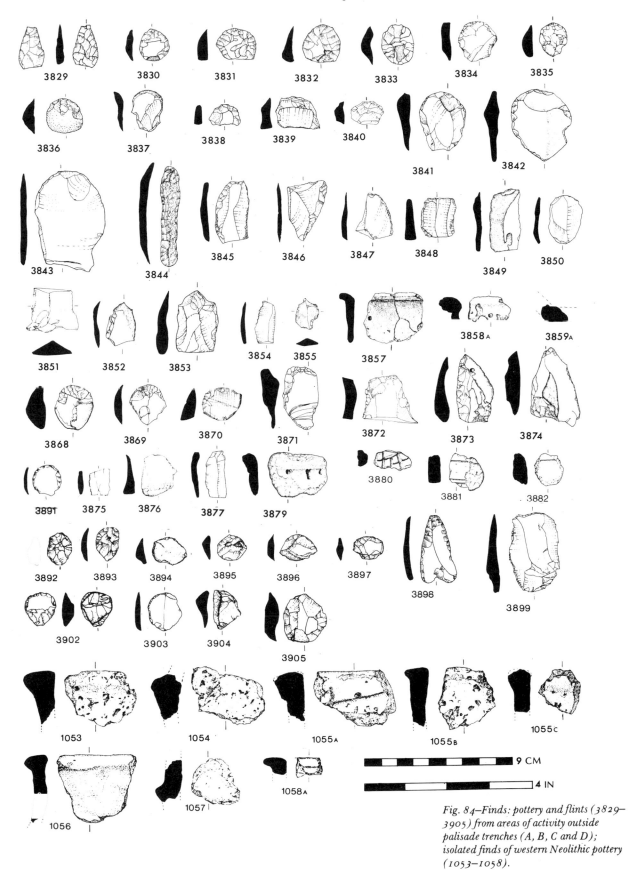

Fig. 84—Finds: pottery and flints (3829–3905) from areas of activity outside palisade trenches (A, B, C and D); isolated finds of western Neolithic pottery (1053–1058).

237

worked leaf-shaped arrowhead. The tip and bottom are missing. Amongst the other artifacts scrapers predominate (3830–43). In general these are round or thumb scrapers (3830–39), well-worked except 3839 which is crude. No. 3840 may be part of a thumb scraper, and has been crudely worked; 3848 had been broken and burnt; 3841 and 3843 are much larger and more elongated than the thumb scrapers; 3841 and 3842 have considerable working around the sides, while 3843 has rough working along one edge only. The remaining artifacts (3844–50) are blades: 3844 is elongated, D-shaped in cross-section and worked all around the edges; 3845 is worked along both edges but this is more pronounced along the convex edge; 3846 is a somewhat triangular piece with definite working along one long side and limited working on the short side; 3847 has working along the convex edge. The other five pieces (3851–5) vary in form. They have limited working along one or more edges. The unworked flints consist of twenty-five scraps, (3856a–y) two of which had been burnt.

B is a spread of pottery and flints found lying on the surface of the boulder clay and occupying an area of 20 square metres. There were no associated structures such as fireplaces or postholes.

There are fifteen sherds of *pottery* of above thumbnail size and three fragments. No. 3857, a rimsherd, expands outwards and is slightly rounded. A slight expansion at the base of the sherd suggests that the vessel was shouldered. Nos 3858a–b came from the same vessel; 3858a, a rimsherd, expands on both sides but the expansion is more pronounced on the outside. A basesherd (3859a) and three undecorated bodysherds (3859b–d) are part of the same vessel. Nos 3860–7 are undecorated bodysherds (none are illustrated): 3862a–b are probably from the same vessel; 3867a–b are from a single vessel, but not the same one as 3862.

Twenty-five pieces of *flint* were found (Fig. 84). Nine are artifacts: 3868–70 are thumb scrapers; 3870 is less finely worked than the other two; 3871 is a scraper with working on one long side and the broad end; 3872 has more limited working on two sides. 3873 and 3874 are pointed, have working along one edge and may have been used as scrapers; 3875 is a portion of a blade with a serrated edge; 3876 is a utilised flint with some working along one edge. Although 3877 is unworked it may have been used as a blade. There are fifteen scraps, one of which had been burnt (3878a–o).

C lies immediately to the north-east of the eastern palisade. It consists of a small, oval area of pebbling, 3.50m in maximum length by 1.30m in maximum width. To the north and west of this feature was a spread of pottery and flints over an elongated area 11.50m long and 1.50m in maximum width at the bulbous western end. At one point this spread abuts onto the pebbling which was probably contemporary.

The spread produced eleven sherds of *pottery* of above thumbnail size and two smaller sherds (Fig. 84).

3879. A slightly rounded rimsherd, which expands outwards. It is very worn on the outer face and has cavities. This face has the remains of what appears to have been an applied layer, rusty in colour. The following sherds (3880–90) came from the bodies of vessels but only the three decorated sherds (3880–2) are illustrated. No. 3880 has a criss-cross pattern formed by grooved lines. This is delimited on one side by a single horizontal line at which point the sherd is broken. On 3881 the decoration consists of three parallel horizontal lines and one oblique line. Two of the parallel lines are set close together and the lower one is cut by the oblique one. No. 3882 has a single line of incised decoration on the outer face. These three decorated sherds are unusual amongst the Neolithic material. However, their ware, if not their decoration, is closer to the Neolithic than to the Beaker wares. Nos 3883–90 are undecorated; 3883a–b are from the same vessel.

Twenty-three pieces of *flint* and one of chert were found (Fig. 84). Ten of these are artifacts. Thumbnail scrapers predominate (3891–7). Nos 3891 and 3892 are well finished while others like 3895 have been broken or damaged; 3893 is chert; 3898 is a triangular piece with working along the two longer sides and a natural hollow at the base; 3899 is a blade with rough working along two edges. The unworked flint consists of thirteen scraps (3900a–m).

D consists of a scatter of pottery and flints north of the end of the western trench. The scatter only covered an area 3m by 5m. There are five poorly preserved sherds (3901a–e). None is illustrated. The *flints* consist of four thumb scrapers (3902–05; Fig. 84) and six unworked scraps (3906a–f). No. 3902 is a bifacially worked thumb scraper.

DISCUSSION

The evidence described indicates that fairly large-scale activity took place over a period of time. The exact nature of the activity remains unknown, but the various structural remains, fireplaces, pits and finds indicate occupation. The finds can all be paralleled on habitation sites of the Neolithic period in Ireland. The number of flint chips, especially the concentration marked Fl. k on Fig. 78 indicates a centre of flint-knapping. The meagre evidence available shows that the inhabitants had cattle and sheep (or goats) and that they grew wheat. Hunting, at least by bow and arrow, may have been practised but not widely; there were only three arrowheads, two leaf-shaped. Palisades indicate woodworking but only one stone axehead was found. Two beads of serpentine provide evidence for personal ornament.

There is evidence for sequential use of some features. The occupation material in the fill of the trench on the western side of the large subrectangular structure shows that the structure is not the earliest feature. As part of Pit 4 was removed by the diggers of the southern trench, it is also earlier than the structure. In turn the eastern palisade trench is later than the structure. Portion was inserted into the fill of the southern trench and its construction also damaged the edges of the trench.

The single homestead, as far as is known, seems to represent the characteristic occupation site of Neolithic Ireland. At Ballynagilly, Co. Tyrone, such a homestead was the 'focus of a settlement proved to extend over an area some 60m across' in which there were numerous hearths, pits, postholes and occupation debris (ApSimon 1969, 166).

The palisades have no counterparts in Ireland. If they were intended to delimit the area of pits, etc., it is odd that neither end had apparent evidence for permanent closure. There is no evidence that they continued further although ploughing, etc. may have obliterated all evidence, traces surviving only where there was a greater build-up of surface material. Perhaps what has been discovered is only part of an arc of palisades that enclosed a much larger area. If the curvature of the palisades was maintained the western (inner) palisade would have enclosed an area close to 100m in diameter. As the palisades are roughly concentric they may be contemporary, but there is also the possibility that the eastern (outer) palisade might represent an expansion of the area of occupation. This cut across the then defunct subrectangular structure. It is, of course, possible that the pits and other features in close proximity were associated with the structure and were not features protected by the palisades. However, it may be pointed out that over the fairly large area excavated to the west of the palisades only limited evidence for activity came to light.

Definite evidence for enclosures of the size that might be indicated by the palisades are not known in Neolithic Ireland. At Langford Lodge, Co. Antrim, an area of activity with pits, stake-holes and stone settings may have been enclosed by a ditch measuring *c.* 1.38m wide at the top and *c.* 75cm deep. Only a tiny portion of the site was excavated but it seems that the area occupied would have been relatively small, probably around 6.5m in diameter (Waterman 1963).

Settlements enclosed solely by palisades are known on the continent. In Germany such settlements go back to an early date in the Linear Pottery culture. At a later stage, palisades in combination with ditches occur (Whittle 1977, 329). Palisaded and ditched enclosures were constructed by the Funnel-Necked Beaker culture in Denmark and Schleswig-Holstein (Andersen 1975; Hingst 1971). In Britain some of the causewayed camps have palisades (Hedges and Buckley 1978, 237–8). At a later stage, about 1700 b.c., a huge palisade that enclosed about eleven acres was constructed at Mount Pleasant, Dorset (Wainwright 1979, 48–64, 237–45). The predominant pottery types belong to the Western Neolithic tradition, that is round-bottomed vessels with shoulders and expanded rims. Out of thirty-five rimsherds out-turned rims predominate and form 50% of the total. T-shaped rims account for a further 25%. The remaining rim forms include bulbous and beaded types and rims with slight expansion to both sides. There are three main varieties of shoulder amongst the thirty-one examples found. About 45% are grooved, 32% medium stepped and the simple angle accounts for almost 23% (cf. Case 1961).

Amongst the flints there are about seventy-five definite artifacts. What in general terms can be called rounded scrapers predominate (*c.*70%), and there are also side scrapers (*c.*11%) and blades (*c.*11%). Arrowheads are represented by only three specimens. Scrapers clearly dominated the industry. Bradley (1978, esp. p. 56) has suggested that scrapers in Britain may be associated with an economy based on livestock as the sites where they most frequently occur have an abundance of animal bone.

The forty-one rounded scrapers were measured for length, breadth and thickness and the results are presented in Table B. These show that in general there was a preference for smaller scrapers: 81% are 30mm or less in length and a third are 20mm or less; 90% are not broader than 30mm and 51% are not more than 20mm broad; 91%

are 10mm or less thick and 20% are 5mm or less. Within the Knowth assemblage the scrapers from C tend to be smaller than those in the other areas. None of this group is longer than 30mm and 67% are 20mm or less in length; 83% are not wider than 20mm and none exceeds 10mm in thickness.

Table B—Comparative sizes of Neolithic scrapers from Knowth and Townleyhall

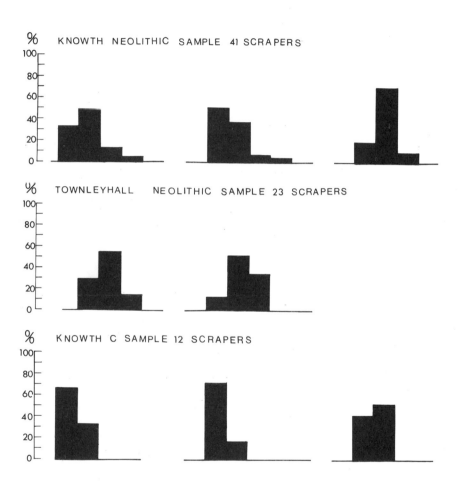

A comparison between the Knowth round scrapers and those from the nearby site of Townleyhall (Eogan 1963) shows that the former are generally smaller (Table B). While 81% of the Knowth group are 30mm or less long, only 30% of the Townleyhall scrapers fall into this category. Only 13% of the Townleyhall scrapers are 20mm or less wide. 51% of the Knowth group are in this category.

There is only one C14 determination and it centres on 2900 b.c. (4852 ± 71 b.p.; B.M. 1076). This was obtained from charcoal in Pit 6 which is within the subrectangular structure. A date some while before the end of the Neolithic would be indicated for tomb building if it commenced soon after the abandonment of the occupation.

However, the expanded rims of the pottery may suggest that they are not amongst the earliest varieties of Irish Neolithic pottery (Case 1961).

OCCUPATION AND THE TOMBS

The domestic activity predates six passage tombs. Occupation material has already been recorded from beneath megalithic tombs in Ireland, both court tombs (cf. Ó Nualláin 1972) and passage tombs. For the latter the best evidence comes from Townleyhall II where hearths, numerous stake holes and artifacts were found. The artifacts included rounded and hollow flint scrapers. The predominant pottery type was Sandhill ware but Carrowkeel ware was well represented. The Western Neolithic element was negligible (Eogan 1963, 40–63). There was a related site nearby, Townleyhall I, which was covered by a low unchambered mound (Liversage 1960). Blackened earth under the small passage tomb, 'Druid's Stone', Ballintoy, Co. Antrim, produced sherds of Western Neolithic pottery as well as a broken kite-shaped arrowhead, two rough scrapers and a long flint blade (Mogey 1941). At Baltinglass there were two areas of dark material. The contemporary finds were a polished stone axehead, a flint javelin head and five rounded scrapers (Walshe 1941). At Site L, Newgrange, the habitation features consisted of a large depression and a few small pits sealed by a natural sod layer which formed prior to the construction of the overlying passage tomb. The finds consisted principally of pottery, round-shouldered bowls, and flints. Ten of these were worked, five were round scrapers, two double hollow scrapers and the other three were flakes or blades (O'Kelly, Lynch and O'Kelly 1978, 263–9).

At Townleyhall there was no evidence for a time lag between the desertion of the habitation and the construction of the tomb; no discernible natural sod had formed over the habitation for instance. This may have been so at Baltinglass and Ballintoy also. However, the stratigraphical evidence at Knowth is more complex. Natural sod was absent from virtually all over the occupation area. Its absence from beneath the tombs shows that it was removed or destroyed by tillage, at least in those areas, in antiquity. It survived in only three places: between the kerbs of Sites 1 and 8, within the chamber of Site 9 and over the spread of finds (C) which occurred on the northeastern side of the occupation area. The latter area, however, does not throw any light on the relationship between the occupation and the tombs. The sod between Sites 1 and 8 seems to be homogeneous. It extends from beneath kerb 10 of Site 8 over the eastern palisade trench and continues over the eastern trench of the structure and under the kerb of Site 1. It is thicker (*c.*15cm) under the kerb of Site 1 than under kerb 10 of Site 8 (*c.*5cm), so it appears that the structure had been abandoned when at least the nearby portion of the Site 1 kerb was built, and indeed the thickness of the sod suggests that a considerable interval had elapsed.

At Site 9 sod survived only in the end recess where it formed the floor of the chamber. There was a small patch of pebbling on the boulder clay in the right-hand recess. Although the sod did not survive here the stratigraphical evidence suggests that the pebbling predates the growth of the sod. However, it was not possible to relate it to the other areas of pebbling (pp 227, 236, 238).

On the other hand, the smallish stones in the fill of the eastern palisade trench under kerbstone 21 of Site 11 appear to have acted as a foundation and to give consolidation to the kerb. The fill of the trench was mushy charcoal but a 'foundation' would hardly be required if a long period elapsed between the use of the trench and the construction of the kerb. The very limited evidence at our disposal suggests that Site 11 may have been built shortly after the trench went out of use but that a longer interval may have elapsed between the use of the trench and the construction of Site 8.

At least on the pottery evidence (round-bottomed shouldered bowls) the assemblage of material from the occupation differs from hat of the tombs that had Carrowkeel pottery. Indeed, the finds from the occupation can more readily be compared with those from court tombs (de Valera 1960, 48–59) though the absence of hollow scrapers from the Knowth occupation and incidentally from Dalkey Island and Feltrim Hill, both in County Dublin (Liversage 1968; Hartnett and Eogan 1964, 5–19) should be noted. Perhaps there was a settlement by court-tomb people at Knowth and the passage-tomb builders were later arrivals. On the other hand, it is possible that this was an occupation site of passage-tomb people who used round-bottomed bowls of fairly fine ware for domestic purposes. Unfortunately the evidence available does not resolve the problem. Incidentally, it may be remarked that round-bottomed bowls, sometimes with slight shoulder have been found in passage tombs in Spain (cf. Almagro and Arribas 1963, 109 ff) and in Brittany (L'Helgouach 1965).

ISOLATED FINDS OF WESTERN NEOLITHIC POTTERY (Fig. 84).

In addition to the group of sherds described below (p. 252 under *Beaker Activity—Concentration A*) the following sherds were discovered.

1052. A couple of small fragments, not illustrated. Found on the old ground level in Area 6, square 23.

1053–5. A scatter of sherds most of which are in poor condition: 1053 is a rimsherd with an outward expansion and slightly convex top; 1054 is a shoulder sherd; 1055a–c are rimsherds. 1055a has an angular flattish profile with an outward expansion and a channel or groove beneath the rim on the outer face, 1055b–c have outward expansions and may be parts of the same vessel as 1053 and 1054. All were found on the old ground level in Area 6, square 25.

1056. Rimsherd with slightly convex top. The outward expansion is marked, the inner is slight. From the edge of fireplace 7 close to the entrance to the structure.

1057. Shoulder sherd whose inner surface has been broken off. Found on the old ground surface in cutting 16, 6.12m from west 0.70m from north.

1058a–d. These four sherds and 1063a–b were found together close to fireplace 8 (Fig. 78). No. 1058a is a rimsherd of uncertain type, poorly preserved. The ware is brownish and has some cavities. No. 1058b is a neck or body sherd of similar ware. The ware of 1058c is grey/brown, with cavities and grits. Its inner surface has been almost completely broken away and the surviving surface is smooth. No. 1058d is of similar ware.

1295–1308. A group of twelve sherds found on the old ground surface in Area 4. With one exception all were from square 24. This area is part of Beaker Concentration A; accordingly the sherds are dealt with in that section (p. 252).

Part three

Beaker activity

Evidence for Beaker activity at Knowth consists of four areas where finds of pottery and flint were concentrated (here termed A, B, C and D), a burial and a number of isolated finds of pottery (Fig. 85). Apart from some shallow pits and two fireplaces associated with Concentration A and a fireplace and postholes at Concentration D no other definite evidence for structures came to light. Nevertheless the material from the concentrations appears to represent domestic debris.

CONCENTRATION A (Fig. 86; Pl. 73a)

This concentration occurred on the north-eastern side of Site 1. In this area, where the old ground surface slopes downwards very gently from south to north, pottery and flint were found in a layer of soft, dark earth containing flakes of charcoal and small stones. This layer averaged 24cm in thickness and covered an irregularly shaped area, approximately 19m by 14m. The western side is concave. This shape is due to the presence of a passage tomb (Site 15) which bounded the material on that side. Later interference, especially the digging of drains, may have removed some of this layer on the northern side. From a maximum thickness of 40cm at the western and northern sides it thins out to the south and east. The layer of dark earth overlay a layer that was sticky when first exposed. This layer, which averages 10cm in thickness, directly overlies the subsoil and appears to have been a layer of sod that formed naturally in antiquity. At the top, the dark layer was sealed by a layer of yellowish clay. This material might have been derived from the mounds of one or more of the smaller passage tombs (e.g. Site 15) which were scattered when the mounds were being lowered.

Underneath the dark earth layer thirty-seven pits penetrated the natural sod and subsoil. These pits were artificially dug and occurred mainly over the southern portion of this area. Two of them were conjoined. The single pits varied in shape and depth; some were circular, others tended to be sub-rectangular while yet more were irregular. They varied in size from 20cm in diameter to 80cm in length and were between 16cm and 32cm deep. One pit (No. 1) was much larger than the others. It tended to be oval and occurred about three metres north of the main concentration of pits. It measured 2.80m by 1.50m by 22cm deep. The southern and eastern sides were fairly steep but the western side had a gentle slope. A paving of small stones extended over the base and sloping western side (Pl. 73b). The fill of the pits consisted of a mixture of soft dark earth and stones (Pl.

74a). Sherds of pottery were found in Pits 1 (1315) and 2 (1419a-d, Pl. 74b), but in general the distribution of finds is outside the main concentration of pits.

There are two fireplaces or hearths that appear to be contemporary with the Beaker activity. Neither had a formal edging. Hearth 1 consists of a reddened area on the old ground surface. It is sub-rectangular and is 47cm by 25cm. Hearth 2 is oval. The base is on the old ground surface but the hearth continued in use as the debris was forming around it. It is 1.30m by 1.20m by 4cm thick. The centre consists of charcoal and was surrounded by ashes:

Fig. 85–Positions of Beaker Concentrations A, B, C and D and isolated finds of Beaker pottery (Roman numerals).

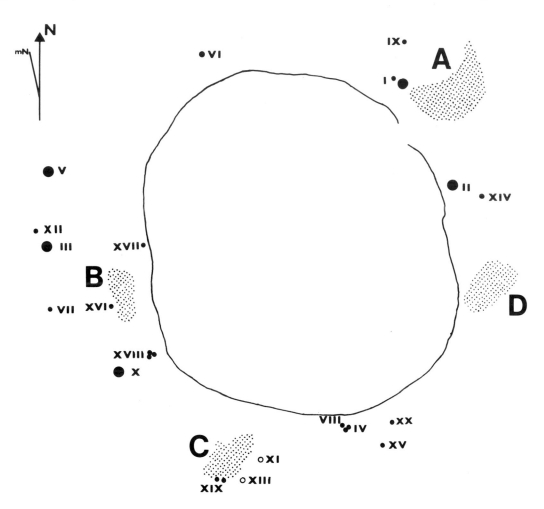

• **Single sherd**
● **Over 4 sherds**
○ **Exact findplace unknown**

50 metres   50 yards
© G.Eogan

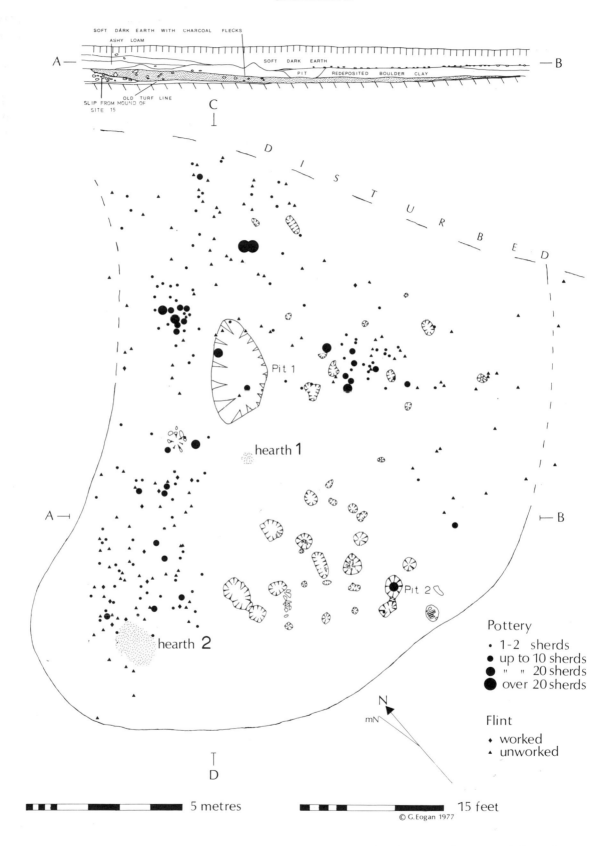

SOFT DARK EARTH WITH CHARCOAL FLECKS

ASHY LOAM

SOFT DARK EARTH

PIT REDEPOSITED BOULDER CLAY

OLD TURF LINE

SLIP FROM MOUND OF SITE 15

C

D I S T U R B E D

Pit 1

hearth 1

hearth 2

Pit 2

Pottery

· 1-2 sherds
● up to 10 sherds
⬤ " " 20 sherds
⬤ over 20 sherds

Flint

◆ worked
▲ unworked

N

mN

5 metres

15 feet

© G. Eogan 1977

PIT 1

SOFT DARK EARTH

REDEPOSITED BOULDER CLAY

OLD TURF LINE

Fig. 86—Concentration A: ground plan and sections.

Along the eastern edge of the concentration is a rough scatter of small stones. These cover an irregular area that measures 6.80m (north-south) by 4.50m (east-west). The relationship between the Beaker layer and the scatter is uncertain. A sherd of coarse pottery (1498) was found amongst the stones but the date of the scatter is uncertain, as is its function. The stones have an uneven surface and so cannot be considered as a floor of a structure or part of a yard.

Pl. 73a–Concentration A: general view from north.

Pit 1 (foreground) during excavation. The knoll (also in foreground) is unexcavated portion of a baulk. Stone scatter in the background is probably a later feature.

Stone finds (Fig. 87; Nos 1064–1109)

With one exception, a piece of chert (1086), the material was flint. Two hundred and thirty-two pieces were found but of these only nineteen (1064–82) were artifacts. There is evidence for utilisation on twenty-seven other pieces (1083–1109). There is considerable variety in the unworked pieces: some are tiny fragments while others are crude lumps (1110–1294, none illustrated). Pebble flint was undoubtedly used as a number of flakes with smooth cortex show, but a small number (e.g. 1067 and 1068) have a coarse cortex and may have been made from flint derived from a natural deposit. The large number of fragments indicates that flint was worked on the site. No definite cores survive. Six pieces have been burnt.

The following are artifacts.

1064. A bifacially worked and well-finished hollow-based arrowhead. In cross-section each face is slightly convex. A flake (1065) has a definite scraping edge on each long side. There is also some rough working at the broader end. As the surface is covered with a distinctive white patination which had been chipped away by the working it appears that the flake was for long exposed to weathering. On 1066, also a flake, both edges and the broader end have been crudely worked. No. 1067 is a scraper fashioned from a somewhat oval, flattish piece. There is a bulb of percussion at one end and along one side there is cortex with a rough surface suggesting that the piece was struck from a core that was derived from a natural flint deposit. The scraping edge has been formed on one convex side. Nos 1068–9 are end scrapers: 1069 also has slight working along the sides and 1068 is made from an outer flake of dark-coloured flint. The cortex, which has survived on one face, is rough. No. 1069 is a short flake with a triangular cross-section. Nos 1070–79 are rounded scrapers, generally thumb-shaped and varying in size: 1070 is a flake struck off a pebble. The working is crude and confined to a limited area along one side; 1071–3, 1075 and 1076 are also outer core flakes. No. 1080 appears to have been

Pl. 73b—Concentration A: Pit 1, upper level before excavation.

part of a somewhat oval flake. There is a bulb of percussion at one end and fine unifacial working along one edge. As part of the flake is missing the extent of the working cannot be established. No. 1081 is a small portion of a well-worked edge. The working was unifacial. This may be part of a scraper or a flake like 1082 which has good unifacial working along one long edge. The shape suggests that it could be a broken-off part of a scraper but slight working along the other long edge indicates that this is not so unless it was applied after detachment.

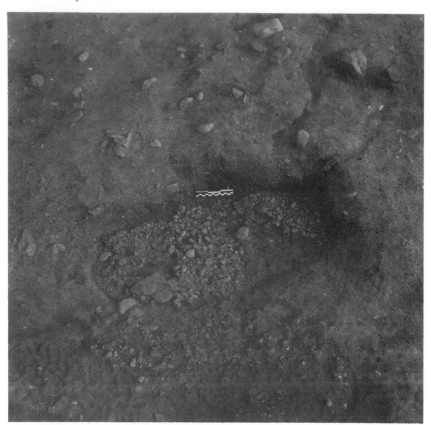

Pl. 74a–Concentration A: Pit 1 after excavation.

Pl. 74b–Concentration A: Pit 2 with sherds of coarse ware (1419a–e) in situ.

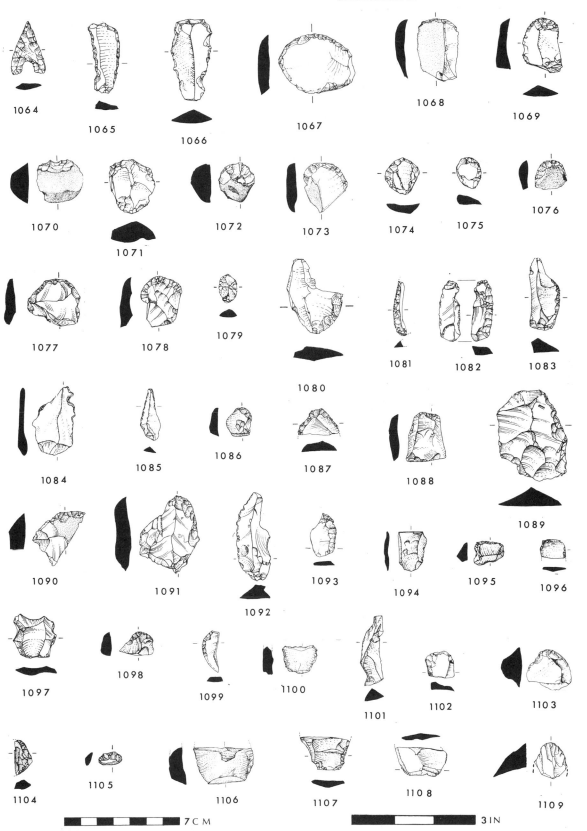

1064

1065

1066

1067

1068

1069

1070

1071

1072

1073

1074

1075

1076

1077

1078

1079

1080

1081

1082

1083

1084

1085

1086

1087

1088

1089

1090

1091

1092

1093

1094

1095

1096

1097

1098

1099

1100

1101

1102

1103

1104

1105

1106

1107

1108

1109

7CM

3 IN

Fig. 87—Concentration A: flints, mainly artifacts (1064–1109).

1083–1109. These twenty-seven utilised pieces have some evidence of working along the sides but none is a definite artifact. Sometimes the working is fairly pronounced (e.g. 1083–5 which have working along one side) but on other examples (e.g. 1092, 1097) there is only slight nibbling. 1109 has a steep edge and may have served as a scraper. 1082 was found just on the outside of kerbstones 2–3 of the passage tomb on Site 15 and was not definitely sealed by or in the Beaker layer.

Pottery finds[1]

The pottery assemblage consists of some four hundred sherds which may represent about thirty-four vessels. Three varieties of pottery are represented. One small group of sherds (1295–1308) can be regarded as Western Neolithic pottery. Another small group (1309–84) appears to have derived from fine beakers, probably Bell-Beakers.[2] The majority (1385–1510) come from coarse, flat-based vessels. These two groups appear to form a Beaker assemblage. While it is possible to divide the groups on grounds of ware, the distinction is not absolute. Even in the fine wares variation occurs in the fabric; for example, 1318 is rough in texture and thick in comparison with 1332. A lump (1511) appears to have been unused but prepared clay.

Western Neolithic (Fig. 88; Nos 1295–1308). These sherds were found fairly close together at the base of the dark earth layer in Area 4, square 24. No. 1306 was some distance from the others in square 22 and was found directly on the old ground surface. The group probably represents a scatter of sherds which were on the old surface when Beaker activity started. All the sherds are undecorated and of similar ware, orange or black, of smooth paste with many cavities and on average are 6mm thick. Probably two or three vessels are represented.

1295–7 Rimsherds of rounded, unexpanded profiles, curving slightly outwards.

1298. Shouldered sherd with medium step. The inner face is badly worn. No. 1299 is also a shouldered sherd. It has a small step and is probably a different vessel from 1298. No. 1299a is a fragment of a shoulder sherd (not illustrated). Nos 1300–08 are featureless bodysherds. Portion of the outer surface of 1300 is missing.

Fine Beaker (Fig. 88; Nos 1309–84). In the fine ware, none of which is of very high quality, the surface is smooth and while there are grits, mainly of granite and quartz, they are well crushed. The fabric is compact and hard, and the colour varies from grey to orange-brown and buff. The thickness of the bodysherds ranges from 5mm to 9mm but averages 6mm. It is not possible to reconstruct any vessel because the sherds are so small but the curvature on some pieces, especially 1331–8, suggests that Bell-Beaker type vessels are represented. A count of rim forms, decorative motifs and fabric indicates that there are about fifteen vessels, at least

---

[1] Because the sherds are so small it is not possible to offer a classification. Accordingly, in the description of the pottery, decoration is the criterion generally used. In the main the accounts of the fine ware follow the order – cord, comb, incision, other decoration and plain. This is simply to facilitate description and in no way implies a typological or chronological ordering.

[2] In this report the term 'Bell-Beaker' is used in the widest sense and embraces regional variations.

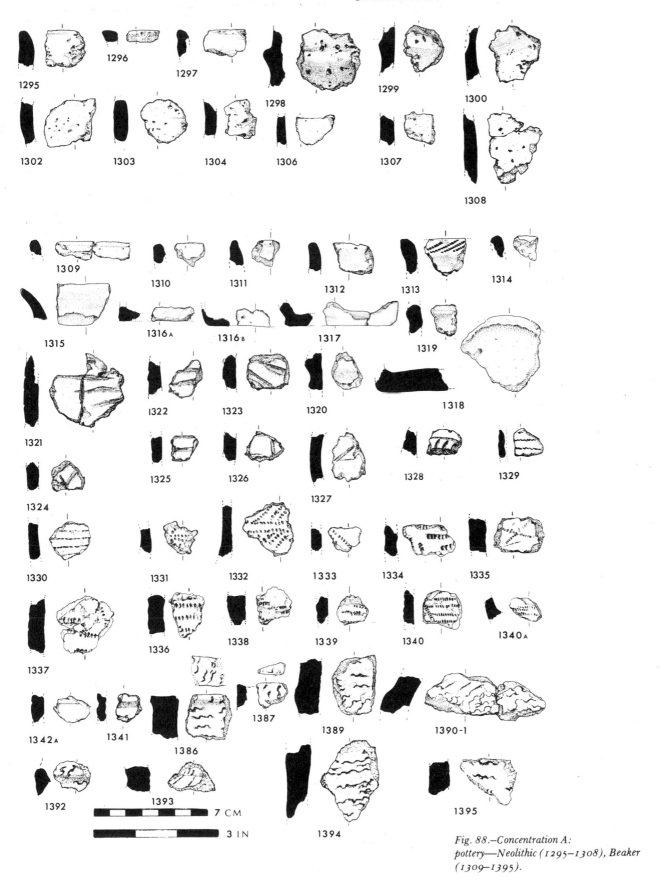

*Fig. 88.—Concentration A:
pottery—Neolithic (1295–1308), Beaker
(1309–1395).*

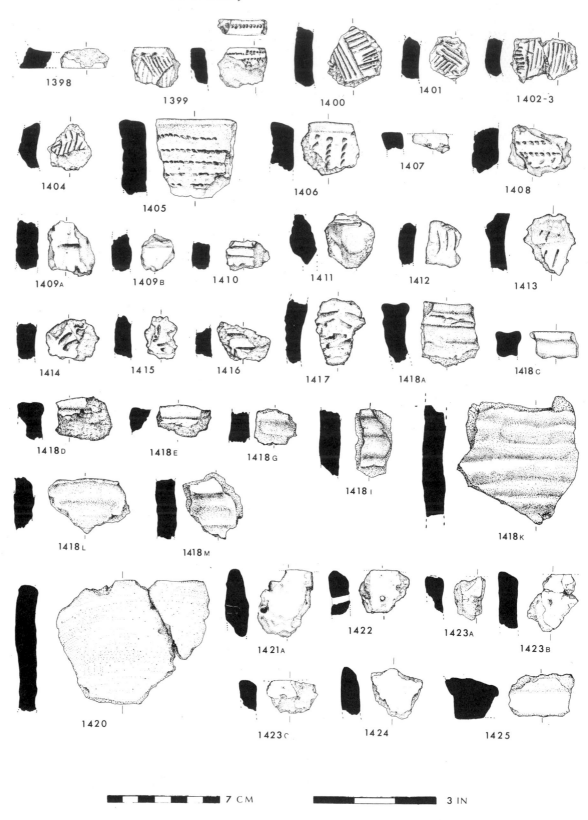

Fig. 89—Concentration A: pottery
(1398–1425).

1385

1386

1389

1321

1391

1394

1400

1404

1403

1406

1422

1401

1402

1454

1439

1405

1418

1418

5 CM

Pl. 75—Concentration A: pottery, coarse ware.

nine of which are decorated with cord (1329), comb (1313, 1330, 1339, 1340, 1340a), incised lines (1342, 1342a), groove or channel (1341), dots or small stabs (1331–8) or cordons (1319–20). One sherd (1328) has a horizontal incised line with a fringe of short vertical impressions on one side. However, because there are so few sherds they have not been primarily described under their ornamentation.

1309–15. Rimsherds. All have a rounded profile. The ware of 1309 and 1314 is brown, that of 1310–12 and 1315 buff and of 1313 grey. The rim of 1309 was probably rolled over and there is an external channel; 1312 is slightly flared. On 1313 there is an internal bevel and on the outside is a band of oblique comb decoration; underneath this is a depression which appears to be part of a broad channel. No. 1313a (not illustrated) is similar. No. 1315a was found in the large pit (1) together with six bodysherds and fragments (1315b–g, not illustrated).

1316a, b–18. Basesherds. All are badly worn and it was possible to estimate the basal diameter, about 7cm, only of 1318. They are either buff (1317 and 1318) or orange (1316).

1319–42a. Decorated bodysherds. Nos 1319 and 1320 have cordons but it is not clear whether these are applied or pinched-up; 1321–7 are sherds of orange-brown ware with haphazard decoration of 'smear' lines and very little curvature. They appear to be parts of the same vessel. No. 1328 is decorated with an incised horizontal line and with deep vertical impressions on one side which form a fringe. On 1329 are horizontal lines, 5mm apart, of fine cord impressions. The inner surface is missing. A similar lay-out occurs on 1330 but the decoration was formed with comb-like impressions. The decoration on 1331–8 consists of small stabs in a pattern of horizontal and diagonal lines, possibly based on triangles. These sherds probably came from the same vessel and the curvature suggests a Bell-Beaker form. Nos 1339, 1340 and 1340a are decorated with comb impressions, but the differences in colour and technique indicate that they came from different vessels; 1341 has a deep groove and the inner surface is missing. The surface of 1342 (not illustrated) is worn but there are remains of three incised lines. Another sherd (1342a) has a short depression which may be the remains of an incised line.

1343–84. Undecorated bodysherds, not illustrated. They include a concentration of about thirty sherds from Area 4, square 24, most of which are of a fairly high quality ware with smooth surfaces (1375–84). The outer face is brownish, the inner dark. The similarity in the ware suggests that most of the sherds came from the same vessel. The ware is comparable to 3772, associated with the cremation burial.

Coarse ware (Figs 88–91; Nos 1385–1510). The surface is uneven and occasionally rough, but in some instances there is a rudimentary smoothing of the walls of the vessel (e.g. 1418). There is a high grit content. The grits, mainly of granite, shale and quartz are large and angular, and some are over 1cm across. The fabric is brittle and not compact. The colour varies from a blotchy grey to orange-brown; it is usual for inner and outer surfaces to differ, often with grey on the exterior and orange-brown inside. The thickness of the bodysherds ranges from 9mm to 15mm but the average is *c*. 11mm. A count of rim forms, decorative motifs and fabric indicates that about

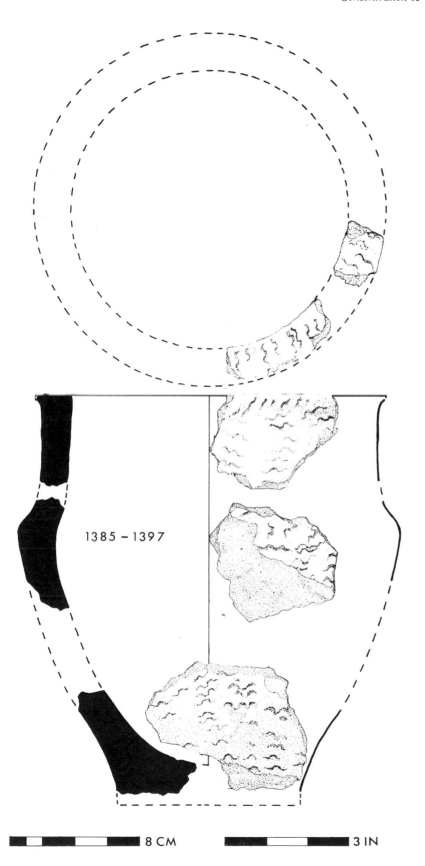

1385 – 1397

■■■ 8 CM   ■■■ 3 IN

Fig. 90–Concentration A: suggested reconstruction of coarse ware vessel (1385–1397).

Fig. 91—*Concentration A: suggested
reconstruction of coarse ware vessels
(1418, 1419).*

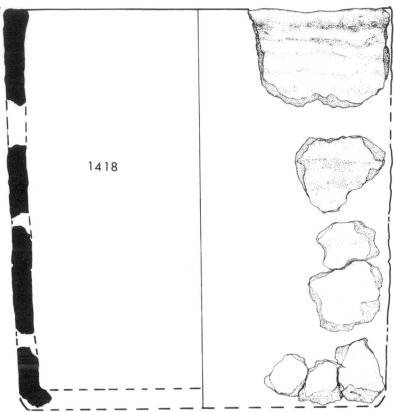

1418

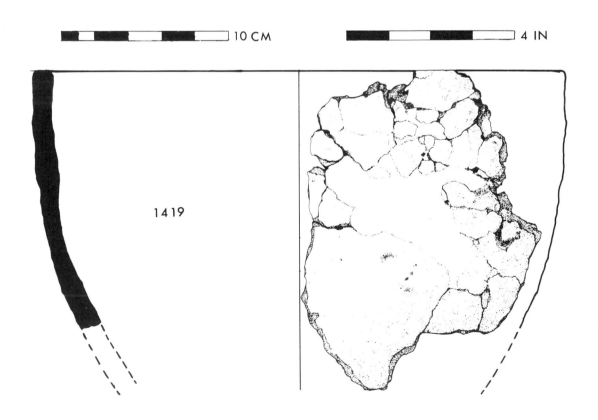

1419

10 CM

4 IN

seventeen vessels are represented of which at least ten are decorated. The decorative techniques vary from cockleshell impressions to cord, incised lines, and broad channels possibly produced by running the fingers horizontally on the wet clay. The shapes also vary. Amongst the decorated sherds it is possible to determine the profile of two vessels. One has a flat rim that expands outwards slightly, probably a straight neck which merges with a shoulder underneath, and at the base there was a slight outward expansion and its height was probably around 18cm (Figs 88 and 90; Nos 1385–97) with a rim diameter of about 15cm. The other vessel appears to be straight-walled or bucket-shaped with an unexpanded base, and a diameter of about 24cm (Fig. 91; Nos 1418–26). Amongst the undecorated sherds the shape of two vessels (1419, 1420) can be suggested. These have an internal bevel on the rim and a slightly bulging body tapering to the base, possibly like the vessel from Site D, Lough Gur (Ó Ríordáin 1954, Pl. 46a). The basesherd (1425) appears to be part of a similar vessel. In 1421–2 there are perforations a short distance below the rim.

Decorated vessels. 1385–97. Part of same vessel, orange-brown on the outside and dark on the inside. The sherds average 11mm in thickness and have many large grits. Cockle-shell impressions occur all over. Although basically horizontal, these occur radially on the rim and vertically on the shoulders. The rim was flat-topped and projected slightly outwards. The neck appears to have been straight and below was a shoulder. At the base the sides expanded outwards slightly. Nos 1385–7 are rimsherds, 1388–93 shoulder sherds and 1394–6 bodysherds. On 1397, a basesherd, part of a charred deposit occurs. No. 1396 is not illustrated.

1398. Basesherd, brown externally, of thinner ware than 1397.

1399–1404. Sherds of a hard dark ware averaging 10mm in thickness and having large grits. The rim is flat-topped and decorated (1399) on the top with a row of comb impressions and on the outside with two horizontal lines of similar impressions and what is probably the apex of a triangle. On the inner face are three depressions and below a basket pattern based on triangles and executed in narrow even grooves. The exterior of the bodysherds is decorated with a similar basket-work type pattern (1400–04). The bodysherds are similar, and despite the difference in ornamental layout on the rimsherd it, too, may have come from the same vessel. No. 1404a (not illustrated) is a bodysherd with remains of an incised design similar to that on 1399–1404.

1405–08. Sherds of orange-brown ware with large angular grits almost certainly parts of the same vessel. The rim was flat-topped and straight (1405–07). Decoration consists of horizontal or vertical lines of fairly large cord impressions. On 1408 there are horizontal lines and an oblique fringe of deep fingernail impressions.

1409a–c. Orange ware; a–b are decorated with broad shallow grooves; c is not illustrated. The decoration on 1410 consists of incised parallel lines; some fragments (1410a) of similar ware were associated with this sherd. No. 1411 has two deeply scored lines and what is probably a boss, 1412–15 have shallow stabs, perhaps fingernail impressions. One sherd (1413) has a cordon. Associated with 1412 were four featureless body sherds 1412a–d (not illustrated). No. 1416 is badly worn but decoration consists of two parallel grooved lines. There are stab-like marks on 1417.

1418. The sixty sherds of this group were found near each other. They are all of a similar ware with large angular grits mainly of granite and crushed quartz. The finish is uneven and the colour varies from grey to orange-brown on both the interior and exterior. The vessel itself was straight-walled with a flat base. The rim was flat with a tendency to a slight inward and outward expansion. Externally the vessel had a series of broad shallow channels arranged horizontally, as if formed by running the fingers around the wet clay. The channels are more definite and closely set towards the top than at the base. The estimated rim diameter is about 24cm. Nos 1418a–e are rimsherds, 1418f is a basesherd and 1418g–m are bodysherds. Seven other decorated bodysherds (1418n–t) are not illustrated.

Undecorated sherds. 1419a. A piece of friable grey-black ware with rough surface and charred deposit inside and many large angular grits, averages 13mm thick. The rim has a slight inward slope and the body profile was slightly curved and barrel-shaped. The rim diameter was *c.* 32cm. Found along the western edge of the eastern portion of a pit numbered 2, on the southern side of the concentration, which contained three other sherds and some fragments of similar ware, maybe part of the same vessel (1419b–e).

1420a–b are similar to 1419. The rim is flattish and the sherds come from a slightly barrel-shaped vessel. The rim diameter is smaller than in 1419, about 15cm, and seems, therefore, to be from a different vessel. No. 1420b is not illustrated.

1421a–e. Sherds and fragments found together, apparently part of the same vessel. The ware is brownish on the outside, and dark on the inside, with a thin accretion of uncertain origin on the inner surface. The rimsherd (1421a) has a rounded profile and an incomplete perforation 21mm below the rim top. The remaining sherds, from the body, are not illustrated.

1422. Rimsherd with an internal bevel and perforation underneath.

1423a–c. Rimsherds bevelled on the inner face, part of a group of seventeen sherds found together. The rim profiles are similar and probably from the same vessel. The associated bodysherds are of a generally similar ware, but it cannot be established that they came from the same vessel as the rims (1423d–q). No. 1424 is also a rimsherd with an internal bevel, less pronounced than 1423; 1425 is a basesherd of brownish ware. Just above the base the wall is straight and then the body curves outwards.

1426–1510. About ninety featureless bodysherds, only two illustrated. More than one vessel is represented but it is likely that they form parts of vessels already described.

CONCENTRATION B (Fig. 92)

This was on the western side of Site 1 and consisted of a thin layer of dark earth in which pottery and flints occurred. This layer, about 7cm in maximum thickness, extended over an irregularly shaped area, 15m by 17m at its extremes, covering about 18 square metres, and overlay a natural surface, mainly boulder clay, but there was a greater concentration at the northern end. There was a shallow depression near the northern end but otherwise no structural features or fireplaces came to light. The Beaker horizon was overlain by features of Early Christian date, including a paved area (publication pending).

Stone finds (Fig. 93; Nos 1512–48b)

Apart from four struck but unworked pieces of shale (1512a–d, not illustrated) the material was flint. Flint was worked on the site as fifty-eight pieces of scrap (1512e–1520h, not illustrated) show. Both

Fig. 92–Concentration B: ground plan.

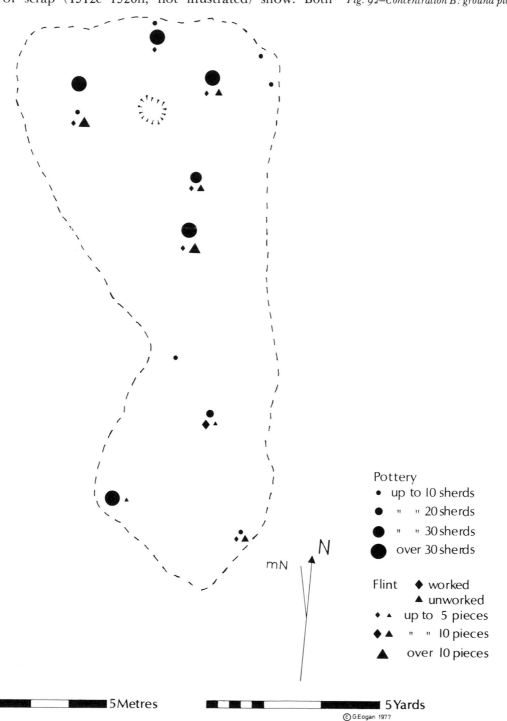

Pottery
- • up to 10 sherds
- ● " " 20 sherds
- ⬤ " " 30 sherds
- ⬤ over 30 sherds

Flint ◆ worked
▲ unworked
◆ ▲ up to 5 pieces
◆ ▲ " " 10 pieces
▲ over 10 pieces

mN   **N**

5 Metres

5 Yards

ⓒ G.Eogan 1977

pebble and deposit flint were used. Amongst the scrap at least 1517a and 1518a–b are pieces detached from a pebble to form a striking platform. No. 1515b appears to be part of a core while 1519b is a rough blade. The following twenty-nine pieces (1521–48b) are artifacts. Blades and rounded scrapers predominate.

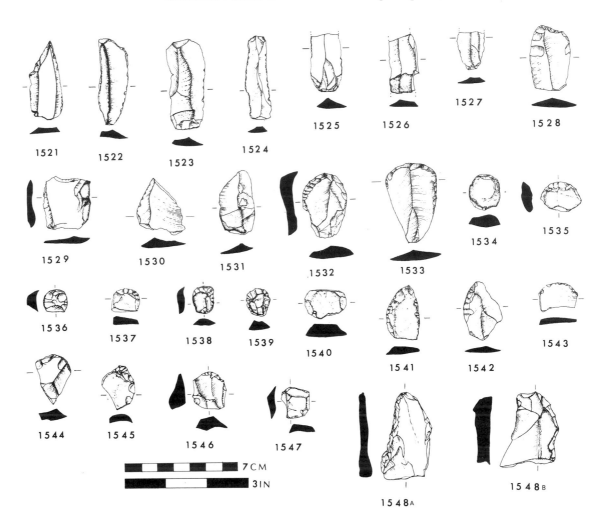

Fig. 93–Concentration B: flints, mainly artifacts (1521–1548).

1521–31.   Blades or flakes; cortex remains on 1522 and 1529 and there is a bulb of percussion on 1521–5 and 1527. The butt has been trimmed on the outer face on 1523 and 1525. The outer surface of 1523 is rough and has flake scars. The shapes vary: 1521 is pointed, 1523–4 are parallel-sided, 1531 tends to be leaf-shaped and 1527 may have been similar but the upper part is missing; 1523, 1525 and 1528 have a triangular cross-section. The working is generally faint and confined to the long edges; in 1521, 1523–5 and 1527 it occurs on both edges. There is limited working along one end of 1522 and 1528.

1532 and 1533.   End scrapers, both with the bulb of percussion at the narrow end, and 1533 has a patch of cortex. The scraping edge is well formed and the working extends down both sides. Nos 1534–9 are thumbnail scrapers, 1534–5 and possibly 1538 were made from outer flakes struck off a pebble. Part of 1537 is missing. No. 1540 is damaged by heat but it may be the remains of a thumb scraper; some cortex survives.

1541–8b.   Miscellaneous pieces: 1541 is part of an outer flake with working along the convex and the straight edge, 1542 is irregular and has working on the convex edge; 1543 and 1544 have working along the convex edge; this is more refined on 1543; 1545 has a bulb of percussion. The working is confined to a convex edge to one side of the bulb. Nos 1546 and 1547 are rough pieces with working along part of the edge, 1548a is a flake with remains of a bulb of percussion at the broad end. There is slight trimming along part of this and on the bulbar face. No. 1548b is a flake of honey-coloured flint that may have been part of a large round-nosed scraper.

Pottery finds

Approximately 300 sherds, representing about thirty vessels, were found. The pottery is evenly fired and well bonded and characterised by a hard, smooth and, in some cases, slightly shiny ware. The assemblage as a whole is of a high standard of manufacture but the fabric of a few sherds (1638, 1644–8, 1652a–b and 1657a–g) is of coarser quality. The colour varies but buff and brown are the commonest. Professor Brindley has shown that the grits, mainly of sandstone, quartz and shale, are small and unobtrusive. Surface protrusion occurs but is not a feature of the group (p. 341). Grog was also used. The thickness varies from 4mm to 11mm but the average is 7mm. Some sherds (e.g. 1655a) indicate that vessels were built up by the coil method. No vessels could be reconstructed but the sherds appear to represent Bell-Beakers with elongated S-profiles, and in some cases with relatively upright necks (e.g. 1567). Bowls may also be present (1655). There do not appear to have been any great extremes in size with vessels probably corresponding to the undecorated beaker from the burial (p. 308). The profiles of the rims varied, most were rounded or pointed, but on 1657 the rim was rolled. At least twenty-three vessels were decorated, usually externally but there is limited evidence for decoration on the inside of the rim (1552 and 1637). Incision was the principal technique but comb, cord and fingernail impressions were also employed, and there are also cordons. The decoration is mainly horizontal but fringe decoration and oblique impressions were used on some vessels, and there is one instance of a metopic pattern (1635). There is evidence that ornamentation occurred in zones (e.g. 1552–5).

Cord decoration (Fig. 94; Nos 1549–51). 1549 is a flat-topped rimsherd with three horizontal lines, the lower two closely-set. There may be the remains of a fourth line at the bottom. No. 1550 is also a rimsherd with rounded profile. The cord decoration, which is internal, is worn and consists of two horizontal lines on the inner face. Externally, there is a band of oblique impressions under the rim and a short distance below is a low cordon with a band of oblique impressions, arranged in opposed directions, on each side of it. The decoration on this sherd is similar to 1637. 1551 is a bodysherd with two parallel lines. One is a slight channel but the other appears to be 'simulated' cord.

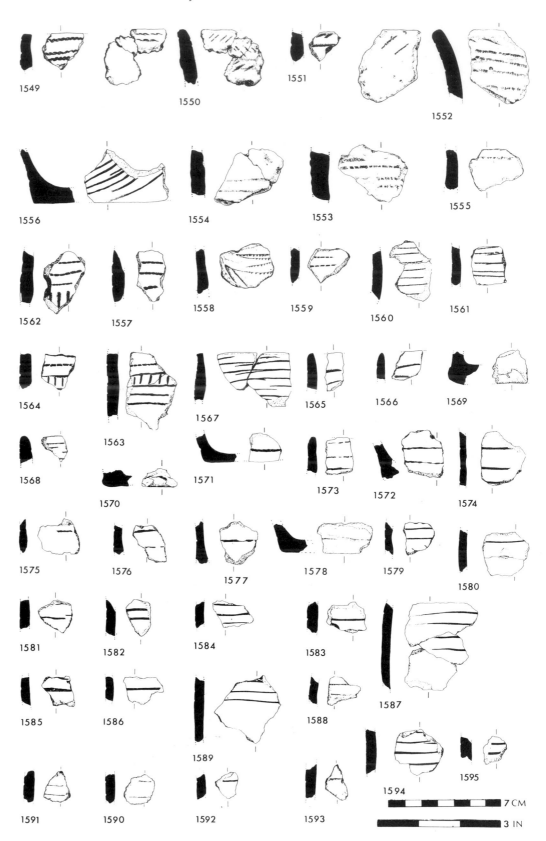

Fig. 94—Concentration B: pottery
(1549–1595).

Pl. 76–Concentration B: pottery.

Comb decoration (Fig. 94; Nos 1552–64). 1552–6 are a rim, a base and three bodysherds. The rim (1552) has a rounded profile and is flared, with a band of oblique impressions on both the inner and outer faces. Like bodysherd 1553 it has fairly closely set horizontal lines, but 1554 and 1556 have blank zones. On the basesherds the lines slant. This group of sherds and 1659 and 1690a–j were found together; 1552–5 could be part of the same vessel. It is less certain that 1556 is, as it differs in colour; because of wear, the technique of decoration is not clear, but there is a hint of comb impressions or hyphenated lines.

1557–64. Bodysherds. The decoration is worn on 1557–9 and 1562; 1557–61 have horizontal decoration. On 1558 the lines were carelessly executed and are not distinct comb impressions. In addition to horizontal lines, 1562–4 have vertical stabs or fringe decoration. Nos 1563 and 1564 are part of the same vessel and there is evidence for a blank zone on 1563.

Incised decoration (Figs 94–95; Nos 1565–1618). Unless otherwise stated the following sherds are all decorated with horizontal lines. 1565–8 are rimsherds; two (1565 and 1568) have a rounded profile. 1566 is slightly pointed. 1567 is slightly flattened and appears to have come from a vessel with a fairly upright neck.

One rimsherd (1573), four basesherds (1569–72) and four bodysherds (1574–7) appear to be part of the same vessel. However, 1569 has a spread of clay on the body and further up is a grass impression. On the base of 1570 are two impressions, but these are fortuitous.

No. 1578 is a basesherd with a horizontal line and part of a line at an angle; 1579–1618 are bodysherds. Nos 1578–1601 have unevenly incised lines but 1603–7 are more finely incised. Several vessels are represented amongst these sherds.

Bodysherds decorated with horizontal and other lines (Fig. 95; Nos 1619–36). A number of different motifs occur in this category. The decoration is executed in incised lines, fingernail (1624 and 1625) and bone impressions (1631–4). The most common motif is a fringe, oblique or vertical. Decoration was not confined to the upper parts of vessels but occurred in at least one example (1635) at the base. Rimsherds 1637a–b are included in the category *Sherds with cordons*. Rimsherd 1550 is described above under *Cord decoration*.

No. 1619 is decorated with a horizontal line and oblique impressions, probably fingernail; 1620 may have been similarly decorated but the impressions could be vertical. The decoration on 1621 consists of a blank zone bordered on both sides by a pair of incised lines with oblique impressions running from these. No. 1622 also has a pair of closely set horizontal lines with oblique impressions. The decoration on 1623 consists of a band of oblique fingernail impressions bordered by an incised line on each side. The pattern is fairly similar on 1624. 1625 has oblique impressions below a horizontal line, 1626a has the remains of impressions below a horizontal line, and there are rough diagonal jabs on 1626b above which is a horizontal line of comb decoration. Nos 1627 and 1628 have horizontal incised lines with oblique impressions which form a herringbone pattern, the decoration continuing through at least

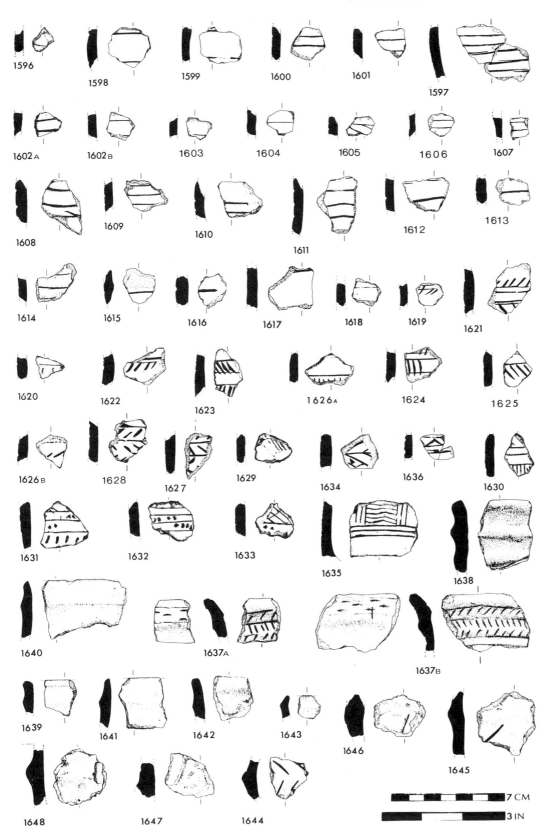

Fig. 95—Concentration B: pottery
(1596–1648).

three bands; 1629 has fingernail impressions obliquely applied and there are horizontal lines with a band of vertical lines below on 1630; 1631–4, which were found together and are probably from the same vessel, have alternating bands of criss-cross pattern, small bone or stick impressions, and on 1631 deep vertical stabs forming a fringe. Sherd 1635 came from close to the base of the vessel. The decoration consists of an incised metopic pattern of vertical and wavy horizontal lines. There are the remains of a charred deposit inside. In comparison with the other sherds from this assemblage the excellent quality of the ware and decoration makes this sherd exceptional. There is some resemblance between the decoration and that on a beaker from Site D, Knockadoon (Ó Ríordáin 1954, 398, Fig. 37). No. 1636 has decoration of horizontal lines and probably part of a zig-zag pattern.

Sherds with cordons (Fig. 95; Nos 1637–48). Thirteen other sherds (as well as 1550) have cordons and there is also a broad ridge on 1666 (not illustrated). Nos 1637–43 are rimsherds and 1644–8 are bodysherds. It appears that the cordons occurred near the rims of the vessels and were pinched up except on 1648 where the cordon was applied, part of it has fallen off. A small number of cordons 1550, 1637, 1644–6, were decorated with oblique impressions. 1647 has a 'smear' line comparable to the lines on sherds 1321–7 from Concentration A.

Nos 1637a–b have a rim with rounded profile and are probably part of a flared vessel. Decoration occurs on both sides. On the inner face of the rim it consists of a band of horizontal fingernail impressions. On the outer face beneath the rim is a horizontal incised line and below it a band of oblique fingernail impressions. The cordon has two rows of opposed impressions, probably fingernail, bounded by a horizontal incised line. Below these are the remains of another incised line. Rimsherds 1638, 1639 and 1642 have a rounded profile while 1640, 1641 and 1643 have pointed profiles. Apart from the cordon these sherds have no other decoration. The surface of 1640 appears to have been burnished. 1640 and 1641 may be parts of the same vessel with a rim diameter of *c.* 12cm, 1644–8 are bodysherds.

Undecorated sherds (Fig. 96; Nos 1649–61). 1649–58 are rimsherds; 1649a–c are excellent ware and were probably part of the same flared vessel with a pointed profile; 1650a–d may have come from the same vessel. They are related in form and ware to 1649 but they appear to come from a different vessel. In 1651 the top of the rim is flattish, and the ware has been pinched up beneath to form a slight outward expansion. 1652a–b have a rounded profile, come from the same vessel and are much coarser than the previous sherds; 1653 has a similar profile but appears to be from a different vessel. It is difficult to know from what part of the vessel 1654 came. One side is missing and the smooth patch on one of the narrow faces appears to be due to damage after breakage. If it was part of a rim it would have been pointed. The group of sherds 1655a–f are part of the same vessel, which had a slightly incurving rim and perhaps a round base. There is a large grit content in the ware. 1656a–e are part of the same vessel and were found beside each other, 1656a is a rimsherd with a flattened profile, and the vessel appears to have had a flared neck. Sherds 1657a–g were found together and are part of the same vessel. This had a flat base and the rounded rim was rolled over. There were at least two horizontal cordon-like features underneath. There are numerous small grits and cavities in the ware. No. 1658 has a flattened and expanded profile, a form unusual for Beaker ware. The ware was well-made, is buff and has numerous tiny cavities. Nos 1655f, 1656c–e and 1657c–f are not illustrated.

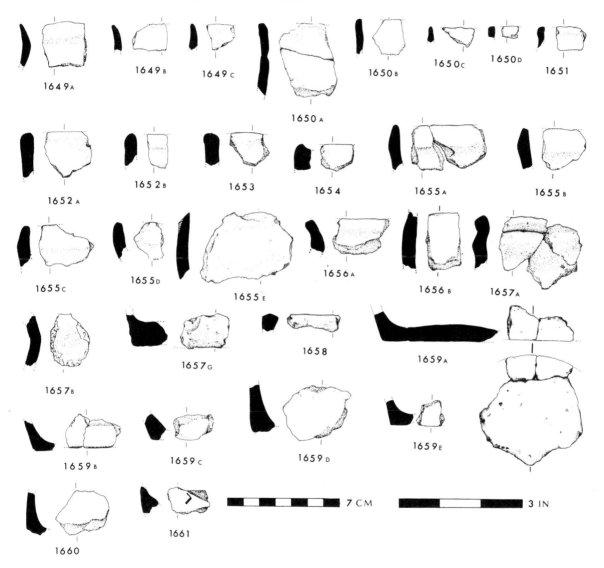

1659–61 are basesherds: 1659a–e were found close to each other and appear to be part of the same vessel, which would have had a basal diameter of *c.* 10cm, 1660 is thinner and the ware is more compact than that of 1659, the interior is dark and it seems to have come from a different vessel; 1661 also represents an individual vessel. The impression does not appear to be a deliberate design.

In addition to the undecorated bodysherds already described as parts of vessels there are about 150 bodysherds and pieces (1662–1703) which cannot be easily associated with those already described.

Fig. 96–Concentration B: pottery (1649–1661).

CONCENTRATION C (Figs 97–98)

The principal evidence for Beaker activity in this area is provided by a concentration of artifacts which occurred over an irregular area of 51 square metres on the south-western side of Site 1. A density of ten or more sherds was restricted to a much smaller area of 34 square metres.

Fig. 97–Concentration C: ground plan. Area 3, squares 70–72 and 75–83. Numbers in top left-hand corner refer to sherd density per m² and those in bottom right-hand corner to flint density.

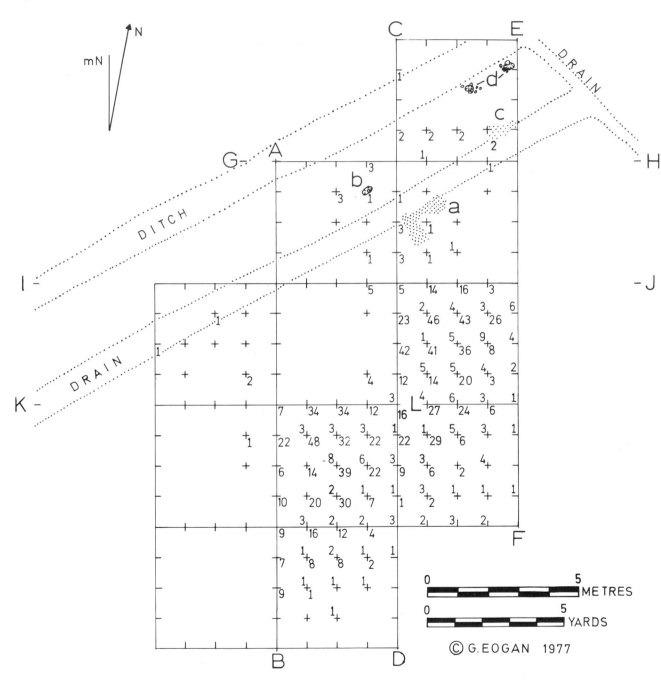

The artifacts occurred in a layer of dark grey soil averaging 17cm in thickness and overlying the old ground surface. In the area of the Beaker concentration the dark grey soil was overlain by a deposit of sterile brown soil. This layer also occurs outside the Beaker concentration; perhaps it is material scattered at the time of the destruction of nearby mounds. This brown soil extended over approximately half of the area of the Beaker concentration. South of it, the dark grey soil lay immediately below a layer of soft dark earth.

Professor G. F. Mitchell reports: 'The brown soil contained small crumbs of iron oxide, which suggested it had once been gleyed; it contained few stones, and little shale debris. There were a few charcoal crumbs, but no identifiable plant debris.

'The dark-grey soil was heavy in texture, rich in shale debris, and also contained a few stones. It was rich in charcoal, and also yielded five carbonised cereal grains, a broken seed of *Polygonum lapathifolium* and one unknown seed.

'The two materials appeared to be different in origin. The dark-grey soil had fragments of the underlying shale bedrock worked up in it, and also contained occupation debris. The overlying brown material was very different, and could not, in my opinion, have been derived from the lower material by simple weathering processes.'

While the dark grey soil contains material that could have been derived from an occupation layer, there is a considerable amount of broken shale mixed with it. It seems, therefore, that the dark grey soil contains occupation debris scattered by subsequent activity.

There was no positive evidence for structures in this area. However, a small number of features occurred a short distance north of the main bulk of the Beaker concentration, on the old ground surface (Fig. 97):

A. An L-shaped area of rough cobbling 180cm by 130cm at its extremes.

B. An oval pit 20cm by 15cm by 10cm. A small stone was found embedded in its side.

C. A subrectangular area, reddened by burning, 60cm by 100cm. No ash or charcoal was found in this area.

D. Two oval holes 30cm by 40cm by 13cm and 30cm by 40cm by 17cm respectively. A small scatter of stones occurred in the vicinity of both.

No pottery or flint was associated with these features, nor could it be established conclusively that they were the result of Beaker activity in the area.

Stone finds (Fig. 99 artifacts only; Nos 1704–1879)

One hundred and seventy-six stone objects were discovered within the area of the Beaker concentration. Apart from two pieces of black chert (1706, 1807), they were all flint, of poor quality and derived chiefly from pebbles. Cortex survived on many pieces. The colour varies: grey is predominant but honey-coloured pieces also occur and a few pieces are reddish. Thirty-seven pieces had been burnt. Two-thirds of the assemblage consists of waste material, mainly small pieces and scrap. However, there is limited evidence for large flakes (1733–6, 1765 and 1766). No definite cores have survived but there is one fairly large piece (1704) from which flakes have been detached. A portion of its surface is smooth and curved but these features may be natural. Another piece may be the remains of a worked-down core (1705).

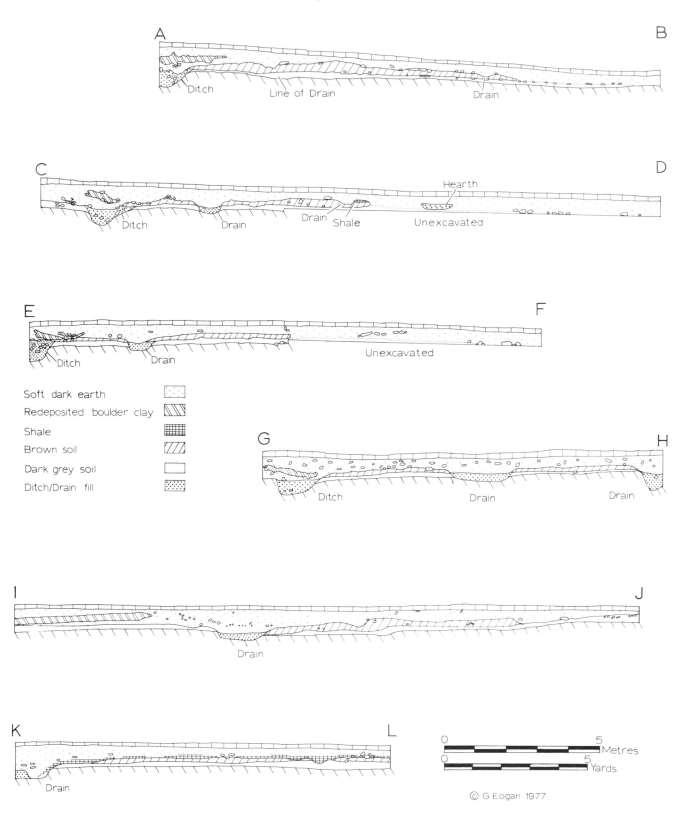

Soft dark earth
Redeposited boulder clay
Shale
Brown soil
Dark grey soil
Ditch/Drain fill

Fig. 98—Concentration C: sections.

© G Eogan 1977

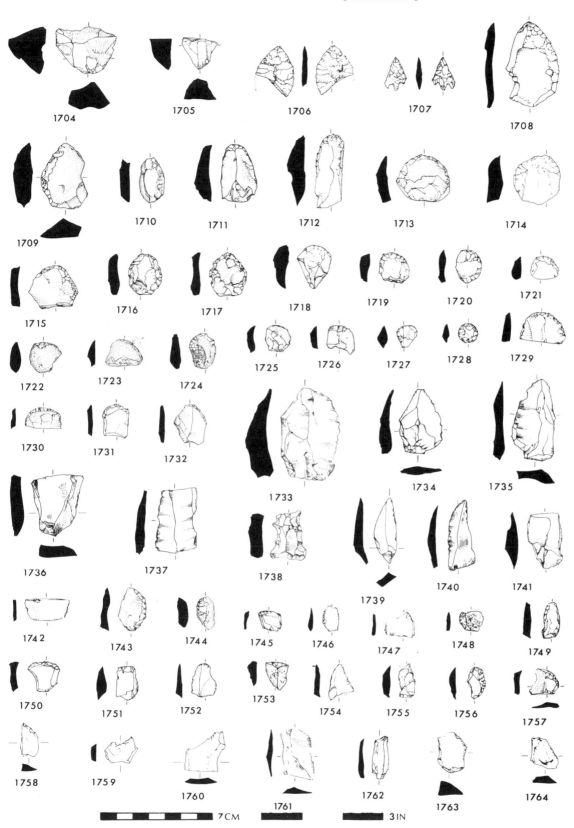

1704 1705 1706 1707 1708
1709 1710 1711 1712 1713 1714
1715 1716 1717 1718 1719 1720 1721
1722 1723 1724 1725 1726 1727 1728 1729
1730 1731 1732 1733 1734 1735
1736 1737 1738 1739 1740 1741
1742 1743 1744 1745 1746 1747 1748 1749
1750 1751 1752 1753 1754 1755 1756 1757
1758 1759 1760 1761 1762 1763 1764

7CM   3IN

Fig. 99—Concentration C: flints
(1704–1764).

One third, fifty-nine objects, showed signs of utilisation. Amongst these are twenty-seven artifacts, two of them arrowheads: 1706 is part of a bifacially worked leaf-shaped arrowhead and is the only utilised piece made from chert; 1707 is barbed and tanged and is bifacially worked. The tip of one of the barbs is missing. Amongst the remaining artifacts scrapers of different varieties predominate: 1708–10 are side scrapers, 1711–12 are end scrapers and there are twenty rounded scrapers (1713–32), some made from an outer piece knocked off a pebble (e.g. 1713 and 1714) and others fashioned on flakes (1729–32). The size varies from largish examples like 1713 down to the tiny 1728. In 1716 the entire edge is worked, in others working is confined to portion of the edge (e.g. 1713–15) and 1729 and 1730 in particular are D-shaped. There are also thirty-two pieces with secondary working or utilisation (1733–64) which vary considerably in shape and in the nature of the working: 1733–6 tend to be leaf-shaped flakes, 1737 is part of a parallel-sided blade, 1738 is part of a somewhat similar blade but much rougher and 1739 and 1740 are points. The other pieces (1741–64) vary considerably in shape but less in size. The working ranges from faint nibbling (e.g. 1741) to more definite working (e.g. 1743). 1765–1879 (not illustrated) are waste pieces.

Pottery finds (Figs 100–105: Nos 1880–2825, Pl. 77)

Over 1000 sherds of pottery were recovered. Probably about eighty separate vessels are represented but in the absence of any complete or reconstructable pots this number is a very rough estimate. Only one definite coarse ware vessel (2168) was present. The sherds of this pot are 17mm thick. Four vessels of a somewhat similar fabric but less coarse and thinner are represented by sherds 1956–61, 1962, 2131 and 2169–73. In contrast to the coarse wares of Concentration A the grits are usually small.

The other sherds from this assemblage are of fine ware and in the main appear to represent Bell-Beakers with elongated S-shaped profiles. The fabric consists of a paste with small grits, evenly fired and well bonded. Analysis of a small section of sherds by Professor Brindley (p. 338) showed that grog was used extensively and that the grits were sand-like inclusions chiefly of sandstone and various minerals, in particular quartz. It seems clear that the immediate source of these grits was local but their primary source is in the north of Ireland. Features on a small number of sherds revealed that at least some of the pots were coil built (1943, 2197, 2235, 2246, 2253). The thickness of the walls varies from 4mm to 7mm. The colour ranges from buff to orange and yellow. Usually the colour of the interior differs from that of the exterior and the core is usually dark. Variations in the ware occur. Some sherds are soft and 'dusty' to touch; others have grits visible in the surface. Some have small cavities (1890–7) and 2197–9 are cinder-like. The ware has a tendency to split parallel to the surface in 2097–2106 and 2117a–b. Generally the surfaces have been smoothed down. In some sherds the outer surface is rougher than the interior (2094 and 2095). None shows evidence of having been burnished and the assemblage as a whole is characterised by its rather sandy texture.

Because there are no complete or nearly complete vessels it has not been possible to estimate size but differences in rim and base

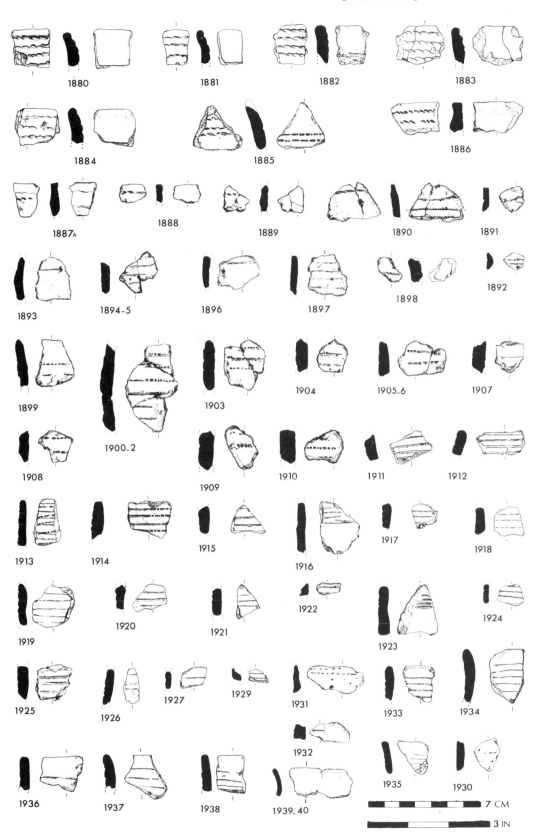

*Fig. 100—Concentration C: pottery
(1880–1940).*

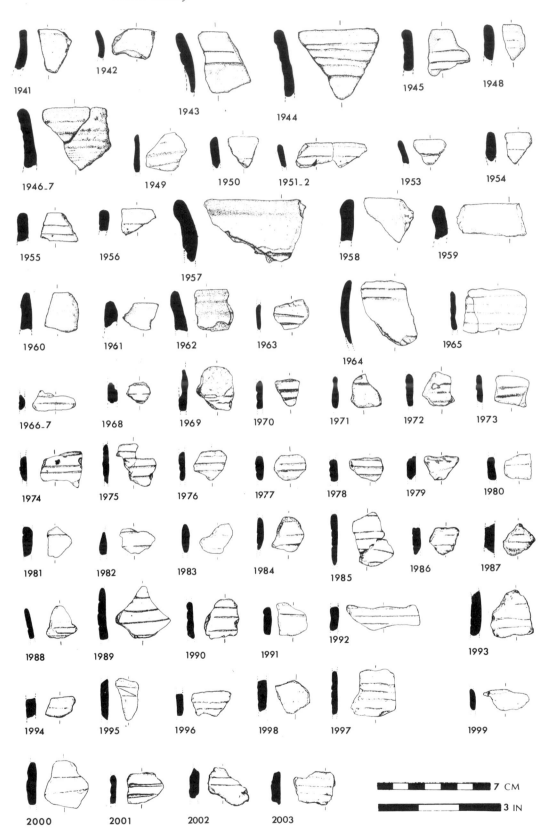

Fig. 101—Concentration C: pottery
(1941–2003).

diameters and wall thickness show that it varied considerably. At least one rim represents a fairly large vessel with a rim diameter of *c.* 26–28cm (1957–62); some of the smaller and thinner sherds could only have come from diminutive vessels (2186, Fig. 104).

Eighty-three rimsherds are present. These belong to a variety of forms amongst which rounded profiles predominate (fifty-seven examples), but flattened (ten) and pointed (three) examples are also present. There were also some other forms. Forty-eight had decoration, in a few cases on the inner face (1880–84, 1886–8; Fig. 100). None of the thirty-one basesherds had any particular characteristics and none was decorated.

Two hundred and seventy-eight sherds representing about thirty-three vessels have decoration, basically horizontal in character and, in some cases, confined to zones. It was executed chiefly by incised lines or impressed comb. Impressions of cord, fingernail, small sticks (or bone) and shells also occur. Eighteen sherds had low cordons beneath the rims, at least one of which was applied (2131). Decoration is external except that on the inner faces of 1880–90.

For descriptive purposes the sherds are grouped into seven categories according to their decoration, or, in the absence of this, some other diagnostic trait.

I. *Horizontal lines* (Figs 100–102; Nos 1880–2081)·

These are executed with cord impressions, comb impressions or, most frequently, with incised lines. On occasion the lines were irregularly formed and they sometimes overlap (e.g. 2006–12, 2025–9).

Cord impressions (Fig. 100; Nos 1880–98) are restricted to the inner faces of 1880–90, all rims except 1889 and 1890–7. Cord-impressed sherds come from a number of vessels whose bodies are decorated with either comb or incised lines.

1880–84. Five rimsherds with rounded profile, very likely from the same vessel. The decoration consists of four horizontal lines of impressed cord.

1885. Bodysherd decorated with two lines of comb impressions on the exterior and three lines of cord impressions on the interior face. It may belong to the same vessel as 1880–84.

1886. Flat rim with low external cordon, probably pinched up. Two lines of cord impressions occur on the inner face and the remains of a third are visible along the fracture line.

1887a. Rimsherd with flat top and low external cordon, probably pinched up. There is a single line of cord on the inner face. A small undecorated sherd of similar ware and cordon is probably part of the same vessel (1887b, not illustrated).

1888. Flat rim, probably with cord ornamentation underneath internally. The ware is similar to 1887a but the decoration is closer to the rim. It is not possible to say if this sherd came from the same vessel.

1889. Bodysherd of similar ware to 1887a–b. There are two lines of cord impressions on the inner face.

1890–97. Eight bodysherds of light corky ware with outer orange face and buff inner face, apparently from the same vessel; 1890–92 have three lines of shallow incised decoration on the outer face; 1890 has a single line of impressed cord on the inner face; 1894–7 are

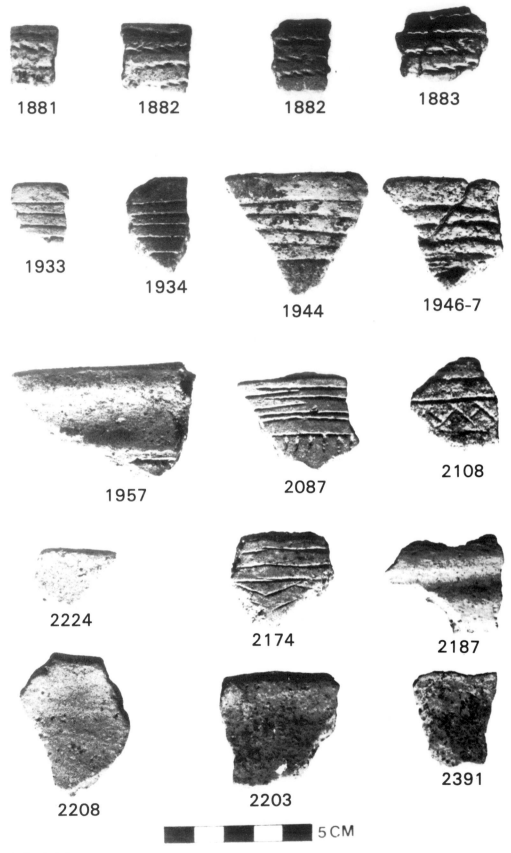

1881   1882   1882   1883

1933   1934   1944   1946-7

1957   2087   2108

2224   2174   2187

2208   2203   2391

5 CM

Pl. 77—Concentration C: pottery.

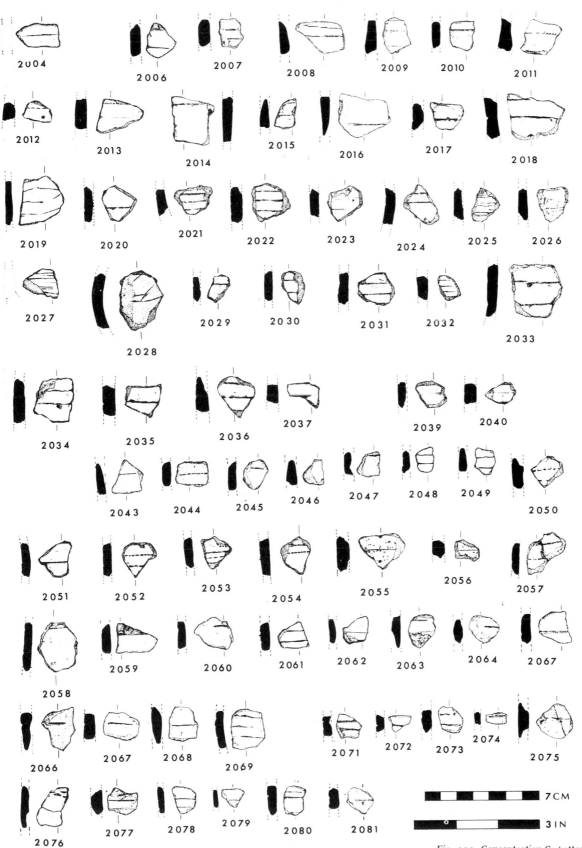

Fig. 102—Concentration C: pottery (2004–2081).

decorated with shallow incised lines on the outer face only.

1898. Rim with two lines of cord impressions (one on fracture line) 4mm apart.

Comb impressions (Fig. 100; Nos 1899–1932). As well as 1885 and 1890–92 the following sherds have decoration of comb impressions and unless otherwise stated are bodysherds.

1899. Rimsherd with rounded profile. Two fairly broad lines, 5mm apart. 1900–08 may be part of the same vessel as 1899. The decoration consists of fairly broad lines, 8mm apart.

1909–10. The lines were applied with a fairly coarse-toothed comb.

1911–29. The decoration was executed by dragging a comb through the damp clay and pausing at irregular intervals. This results in an evenly incised line broken by short stretches of comb impressions – 1914 is a clear example of this technique, 1913 and 1916 show the overlap of lines, and 1916 and 1923 indicate that the decoration did not cover the whole vessel. It is possible that more than one vessel is represented by these sherds but 1913–21 almost certainly represent the same vessel as 1880–84. 1928 is not illustrated.

1930 has two lines. 1931 is badly worn and has one line, and possibly another 4mm away. It is difficult to know whether this is a rimsherd or a junction of a coil-built vessel. On 1932 is a comb impression at right angles to what may be an incised line.

Incised decoration (Figs 100–102; Nos 1933–2081) is the commonest method employed in the assemblage. In all instances the decoration occurs on the outer face and the lines encircle the vessel horizontally. The full extent of the decoration cannot be determined but there is evidence that it did not cover the whole vessel in some instances (e.g. 1944, 1964). The lines were usually closely spaced, about 5mm apart on average. The decorative technique varies in detail. In some cases the lines were lightly incised and narrow (2067–9), in others they were deeper or broader (e.g. 1969–73). Sometimes the lines were regularly executed (1933, 1934 and 1937) but in others they were roughly formed with slashing, overlapping and gapping (1965, 2019 and 2025). The fine lines on 1939–40 may be fortuitous. 1933–62 are rimsherds usually of a rounded unexpanded profile, and 1963–2081 are bodysherds, but 1988 is worn and may be from a rim. Groups of sherds forming individual vessels can be distinguished such as 1939–42, 1946–54, 1964–5, 1979–84, 2000–04, 2006–12, 2021–2 and 2035–40. The most definite group is formed by 1957–61 which are much coarser than the others; all have a broad channel below the rim and on 1957 are the remains of an incised line. No. 1992 seems to have been part of a large vessel. The ware of 1944 is similar to 1964–5 and these may have formed part of the same vessel. No. 2018 probably came from the same pot as 2110.

II. *Specific motifs* (e.g. criss-cross) frequently combined with horizontal lines (Fig. 103; Nos 2082–2130)

All are bodysherds and unless otherwise stated the decoration is incised.

2082–4. Apparently part of the same vessel. The decoration is deeply set vertical lines with horizontal lines below. In addition 2083 has a band of lentoid depressions adjacent to the horizontal lines. The curvature and increasing thickness suggest that the sherds came

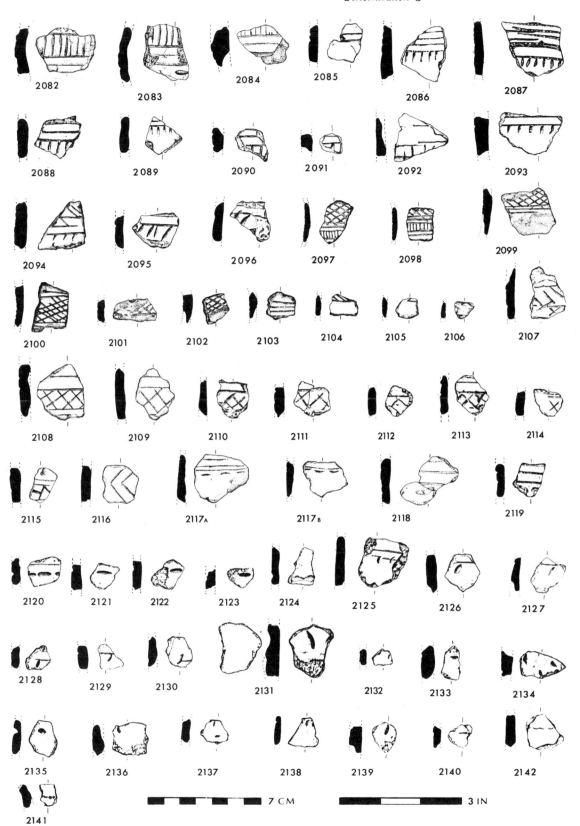

Fig. 103—Concentration C: pottery
(2082–2142).

281

from close to the base. No. 2085 has two deeply scored horizontal lines, and is possibly from the same vessel as 2082–4.

2086–91. The decoration consists of horizontal lines of comb decoration in a zone bordered by a fringe of short vertical impressions. The technique of decoration does not appear to be simply impressed comb. Rather the comb appears to have been dragged through the damp clay to give a continuous or nearly continuous line around the vessel. The result is a combination of comb and incised line. This is clearly demonstrated on 2086 in which the comb was removed, dragged and replaced on the wet clay surface. 2087 shows an overlap of comb impressions.

2092. Probably from the same vessel as 2089. One of the two horizontal lines is gapped, the other overlaps. Below this is fringe decoration.

2093. Has two lines and a border of short vertical lines; 2094 is similarly decorated but it also has a band of diagonal lines. These two sherds may have come from the same vessel. 2095 and 2096 are decorated with horizontal lines and diagonal impressions.

2097–2103 and 2104–06. Perhaps parts of the same vessel. The decoration is executed in fairly broad even lines. On 2097 and 2098 it consists of a zone of short, closely set vertical lines and a zone of tight criss-cross pattern combined with horizontal lines; 2099 and 2100 have a criss-cross band with vertical lines on both sides; 2102 has criss-cross decoration, 2103 has horizontal lines and 2104–06 are tiny but each has the remains of a horizontal line and diagonal or criss-cross decoration above.

2107–13. Have criss-cross pattern bordered by horizontal lines, 2114 and 2115 may have been similarly decorated, 2116 has a herring-bone pattern.

The decoration on 2117a–b and 2120–30 is characterised by impressions, probably fingernail. On 2117a–b these occur in a line close to and parallel to horizontal lines. These sherds are similar and may have come from the same vessel. On 2118 and 2120–30 the impressions are lentoid. They are set horizontally and in combination with horizontal lines on 2118–20. On 2125–30 they are set diagonally in relation to horizontal lines, not unlike the arrangement on 2095. The diagonal impression on 2130 may not be original. Nos 2120–23 may have come from the same vessel.

III. *Scattered impressions* basically arranged horizontally (Figs 103–104; Nos 2131–58)

All are bodysherds: 2131 has a pair of fingernail impressions and an applied cordon has fallen off; 2132–9 are decorated with small stabs, but that on 2135 may be a cavity; 2140 may have a single fingertip impression. There is a row of three slight impressions on 2141. Nos 2142–6 appear to be part of the same vessel and are decorated with shell impressions. 2146 is not illustrated. Nos 2147–58 have dot decoration, scattered on 2148–9 and 2157 but in lines on 2150 and 2152–6. There is a single dot on 2147, 2151 and 2158. It is difficult to know whether the scattered dots on 2157 are intentional or due to grits having fallen out. The inner surface of 2148 is missing.

IV. *Other decorated sherds* (Fig. 104; Nos 2159–2196)

This category includes a number of sherds which do not fit into the above categories.

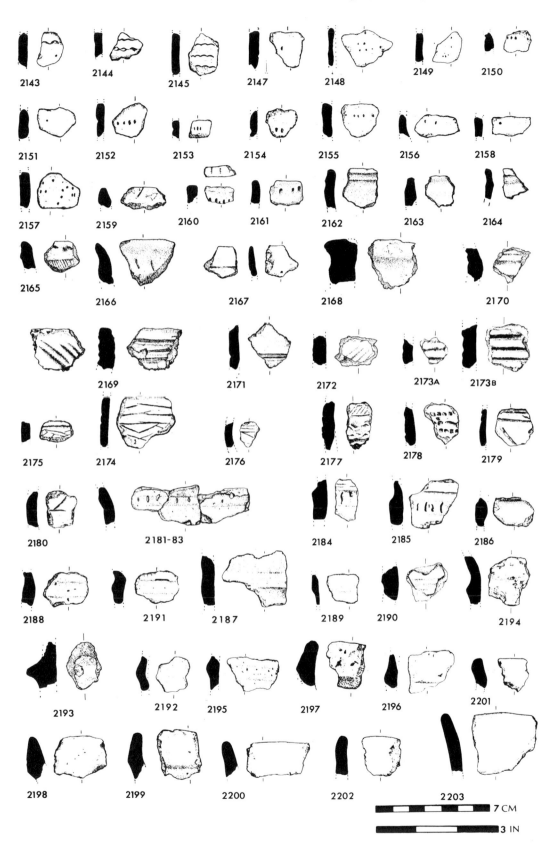

Fig. 104—Concentration C: pottery
(2143–2203).

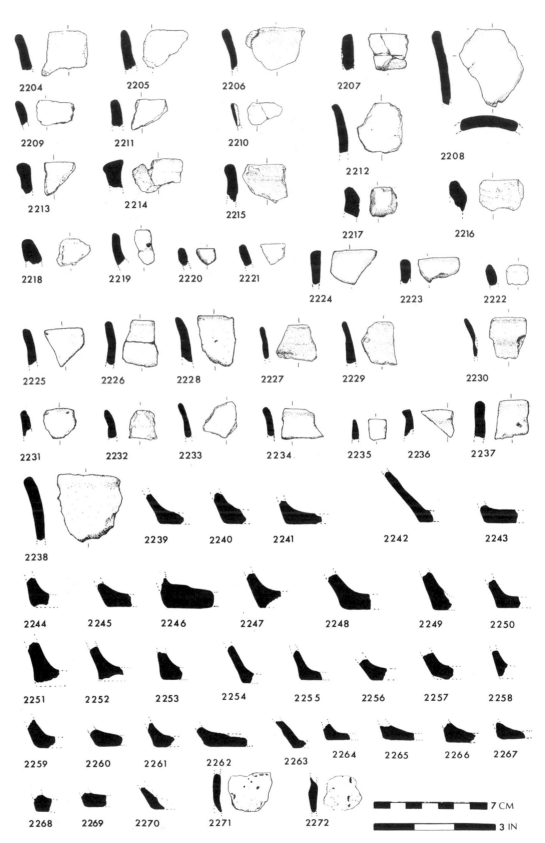

Fig. 105—Concentration C: pottery
(2204–2272).

Rimsherds (Nos 2159–2173). 2159. Rounded profile with a single diagonal stroke on the outer face.

2160. Flattened profile with a slight outward expansion and radial strokes along the rim top. The remains of decoration consist either of small dots or vertical lines, the tops of which occur along the break line.

2161. Rounded profile and three small dot-like impressions on the outer face.

2162. Rounded profile and possibly from a bowl-shaped vessel. Two closely set, evenly defined 'grooves' occur immediately below the rim on the outer face.

2163. Flattened profile and a shallow 'groove', poorly defined, beneath the rim.

2164. Rounded profile and a very shallow groove-like depression below the rim.

2165. Immediately below the rim are two horizontal lentoid depressions underneath which is a low ridge, and below this is a band of fine, closely set incised diagonal lines. The sherd is possibly from the same vessel as 2177.

2166. From a vessel with a cordon below a rounded rim. Diagonal strokes occur on the upper side of the cordon.

2167. Rounded profile and two small depressions, which might be natural, on the outer surface. A horizontal line, possibly decoration, occurs on the inner face.

2168. Of coarse ware with a flat rim top, beneath which, externally, is a broad channel.

2169–73. Apparently from a vessel with a flat rim (2169) and horizontal incised lines externally. Internal decoration on 2169 consists of diagonal lines. These sherds are comparable to 1399–1404.

Bodysherds (Nos 2174–92). On 2174 the decoration consists of incised horizontal and zig-zag lines; 2175 is similarly decorated but on a smaller scale. The ornament on 2176 may also be similar.

2177. Decorated with bands of closely spaced diagonal lines, blank bands and a band of lentoid depressions.

2178. Decorated with lines of broad comb-like impressions.

2179. Has two broad horizontal lines, a diagonal line and possibly the remains of another.

2180. Has a Y-shaped motif, but it is difficult to establish whether this is decoration.

2181–3. Decorated with short vertical stabs, probably made by a fingernail.

2184–6. The low cordon is decorated with short vertical stabs and on one side is an incised line. These sherds are similar in ware to 2181–3 and may have come from the same vessel.

2187–92. Light brown surface and a dark core, and characterised by a broad shallow channel and, on 2192, a cordon. All may have come from the same vessel. No. 2193 has a pronounced pinched-up cordon. The ware is dark brown.

2194. Has a cordon and broad channel. The ware is darkish with cavities. It may have affinities with Western Neolithic wares and has a resemblance to that of sherds 1657a–g from Concentration B.

V. *Undecorated rimsherds* (Figs 104–105; Nos 2195–2238)

Considerable variation in detail occurs in the rim forms but nearly all have rounded profiles; 2206 and 2236 are flat-topped, 2216 expands outwards, 2197 is rounded but it is not possible to say whether it was part of a vessel with an inward bevel or a distinctive out-turned rim. 2195 and 2196 are bodysherds with a low smooth cordon and as the ware is similar, darkish with tiny cavities, these sherds, and perhaps 2194, appear to have formed part of the same vessel. No. 2236 is similar in rim profile and ware to 1887 and 1888. A number of vessels are represented in this category but matching sherds are rare. Nos 2195 and 2196 are from the same vessel, another vessel is represented by 2198–9 and another by 2200–02.

VI. *Undecorated basesherds* (Fig. 105; Nos 2239–70)

Several vessels are represented. Most of the sherds come from vessels with a slight incurving at the base, but one or two may have had a sharper angle.

VII. *Undecorated bodysherds* (Nos 2271–2825)

There are approximately six hundred undecorated and featureless bodysherds, representing sixty per cent of the total assemblage. This figure should be taken as a minimum percentage: undecorated rim and basesherds are not included as they have been dealt with already (2197–2269). It seems likely that the assemblage consisted of a large number of undecorated vessels of varying sizes but in the absence of any specific features it is not possible to group them.

CONCENTRATION D (Figs 106–107; Pl. 78)

This concentration is on the south-eastern side of Site 1. Flint and pottery were found over a trapezoidal area 16.5m by 11m at the north-eastern and 8.5m at the south-western end. Except for a strip averaging 1m in width which had a fence on it, this concentration was excavated in 1978. When further lands were acquired it was possible to complete the excavations in 1980. By this time this report had been submitted for publication so the finds, pottery (3907–55) and flint (3795–3805), were inserted at the relevant parts of the text, but not illustrated.

When this settlement commenced most of the area used was flat and grass-grown as the presence of a natural sod layer over most of the area shows (Fig. 107). Material which appears to have been primary slip had built up immediately outside the kerb of Site 1. The settlement took place on the surface of the sod and to a limited extent it continued up over part of the Site 1 slip. The layer that represents Beaker activity is not as well defined as in Concentrations A and B and the edges were difficult to delimit. It consisted of darkish gritty earth ('Beaker layer' in section), 10cm in maximum thickness, with a considerable quantity of pebbles mixed through it. The pebbles were more plentiful in the western part. Finds were made throughout this layer but the greater number occurred towards the base, The northern end of this material was covered by a layer of brown earth. This layer corresponds to the layers of yellowish and brown material already noted at A and C. The source of this layer has not been established but it may represent the spreading of mound material over the concentration.

No definite structures turned up. A hearth consisting of a shallow pit, 16cm in maximum depth, dug into the subsoil was the most prominent feature. Its edge was slightly irregular and it had maximum dimensions of 1.21m by 1.08m. The inner edge was reddened by burning and the centre was filled with charcoal and ash. Five small stones at the base were not set to form a floor. The hearth contained pottery and flint, which concentrated most thickly in its

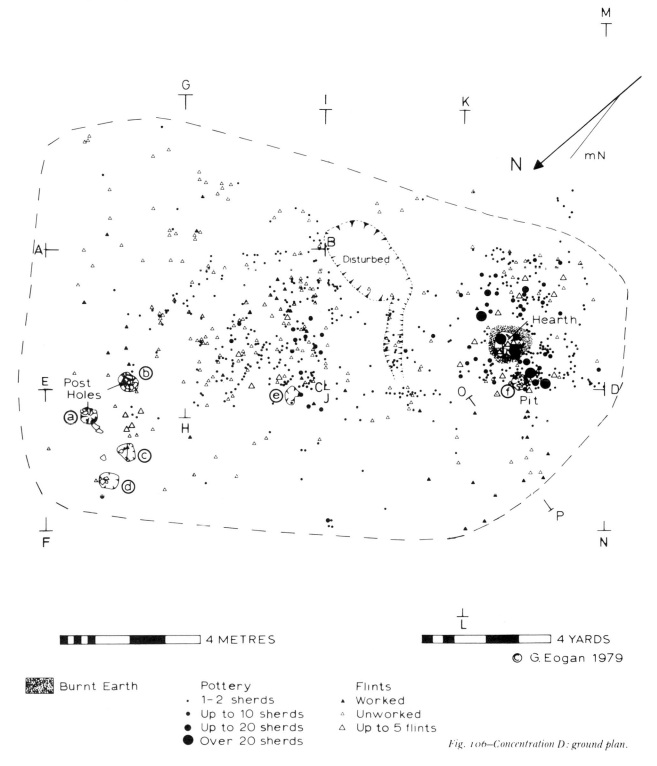

4 METRES

4 YARDS

© G. Eogan 1979

Burnt Earth

Pottery
- · 1–2 sherds
- • Up to 10 sherds
- ● Up to 20 sherds
- ⬤ Over 20 sherds

Flints
- ▲ Worked
- △ Unworked
- △ Up to 5 flints

Fig. 106—Concentration D: ground plan.

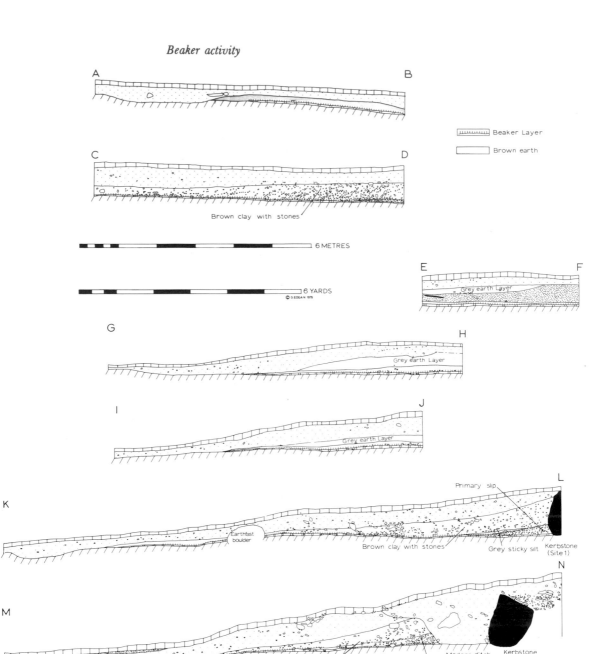

Beaker Layer

Brown earth

Brown clay with stones

6 METRES

6 YARDS
© G EOGAN 1979

Grey earth Layer

Grey earth Layer

Grey earth Layer

Primary slip

Earthfast
boulder

Brown clay with stones

Grey sticky silt

Kerbstone
(Site 1)

Brown Clay with stones

Primary slip

Modern ditch

Kerbstone
(Site 1)

Ditch

Brown Clay
with stones

Primary slip

Kerbstone
(Site 1)

Fig. 107—Concentration D: sections.

immediate area. There were two postholes near the northern end of
the area. Posthole *a* was 42cm deep and 50cm at the mouth. There
were packing stones around the mouth and further down along the
sides. Posthole *b* was 71cm deep and 55cm in diameter at the mouth.
There were also four depressions, *c–f; f,* 30cm, was the deepest but *c*
was only 10cm deep. A little to the south of the centre of the site was a
gully which expanded into a pit at the eastern end. Both were later
features which cut through the Beaker layer and into the subsoil.

Near Site 1, where it overlay primary slip, the Beaker layer was
covered by a layer of grey sticky silt which may be the remains of a

natural sod layer (see sections K–L). A layer of brown earth over the north and east of the concentration had been cut through by later activity over the remainder of the Beaker area. Its counterpart on the south and west sides was a layer of brown clay with stones, probably throw-out from the Iron Age ditch inside the kerb of Site 1. Above this layer and the brown earth was a layer of soft dark earth, directly below the humus, and of Early Christian and Norman date.

Stone finds (Fig. 108, artifacts only; Nos 2826–3092, 3795–3805)

Flint was the only material used and over three hundred pieces were recovered. The predominant colour is greyish, but dark and to a lesser extent honey-coloured flints also occurred. A limited number have coarse cortex (e.g. 2836, 2840, 2863) but usually the cortex is smooth. No. 2826 is a flint pebble, 2827 and 2828 are pebbles with pieces knocked off, and on 2827 cortex has formed over the fractural scars. The removal of pieces could, of course, be due to natural causes. No. 2829 is half a pebble; 2830 is similar but has a striking platform and part of the edge has been trimmed; 3795 is a core with striking platform and flake scars; 2831–3 are uneven pieces with flake scars, 2833 with a striking platform and a bulb of percussion. Only thirty-one are artifacts and there are also twelve pieces (2865–74, 3798–3800) that have slight evidence of utilisation. The remainder (2875–3092, 3801–3805) are scraps and waste pieces. Nos 2826–9, 2832 and 2875–3092 are not illustrated.

Artifacts form only about ten per cent of the flints. They are nearly all scrapers, mostly rounded: 2834 and 2835 are thin pieces with a concave edge worked from one side only and appear to be parts of hollow scrapers; 2836 was made from an outer core flake and working is confined to one end; the other having a bulb of percussion; 2837, also a flake, has working around one end and along the sides; 2838 may be part of a long scraper. It has working along both sides and was made from pebble flint.

Nos 2839–51 are good examples of rounded scrapers: 2839–43 are worked along the entire edge, and portion appears to have been broken off 2842; 3796 is also D-shaped and this seems to be its original form. In size they vary from 2839, 34mm across, to 2843, 15mm across. Nos 2844–50 tend to be longer and more irregular; 2851 is a broken-off piece; 2852–5 have working along part of a concave side, and part of 2852 may have been broken off. Nos 2856–61 generally have working confined to a straight edge but they do not form a coherent group. Nos 2862 and 2863 are irregular; 2863 which has some crude working along the edge may be part of a large scraper. No. 2864 is part of a pointed blade with faint working along the edges and 3797 is of similar shape and has definite working along both long edges.

Pottery finds (Figs 109–15, Pl. 78)

This site produced about 2000 sherds, all small, some fragmentary, and it was not possible to reconstruct any vessel. However, about eighty vessels are probably represented. Five crude lumps of pottery-like material may be paste, suggesting that pottery was manufactured on the site (3729–35). The great majority of sherds came from fine ware vessels averaging 6mm thick. The ware is fairly compact and nearly all sherds have a liberal supply of small grits, mainly of shale, quartz and sandstone. Grog was also used. In most sherds the grits are visible on the surface. The thickness of the walls varies from very thin ware as in 3259–61 (4mm) to thicker ware as in 3282 (9mm). The nature of the break on 3282a, 3377 and 3721 indicates that at least some vessels were built up by the coil method. On 3284 the rim was folded inwards.

Most of the sherds are brick-red externally. Some of these are also red internally and have a black core (e.g. 3283 and 3326–3331); others have a dark core and inner surface (e.g. 3422–88). A smaller number are cream-coloured throughout (e.g. 3180) while others have a darker inner surface (e.g. 3181). Sherds 3700, 3701 and 3707 are distinctively dark throughout and 3699 has a definite black incrustation on the inner surface. Some sherds are well finished and have smooth surfaces. Probably the best finished vessel is represented by 3247 where the outer surface appears to have been finished off by a red slip.

As the sherds are fragmentary it is impossible to estimate either the diameter of the mouth or base or the shape of the vessels. However, sherds 3235a–j suggest that the vessel of which they formed a part had a diameter of about 12cm–13cm at the mouth. The basal diameter of 3301 was *c.* 7.7cm, that of 3311 was *c.* 7.9cm and that of 3312 was *c.* 9.3cm. Judging by the decoration, most vessels may have had a soft S-shaped profile, but bowls were also represented (e.g. 3282 and 3283). There are fifty-three rimsherds of different forms, but the unexpanded variety, whether rounded (thirty-four examples), pointed (ten) or flattened (five), predominates. Only 3262 has an expansion. Apart from 3300, definite expansion at the base (foot) does not occur.

Two hundred and eighty sherds, fourteen per cent of the total, were decorated, in the main only with incised horizontal lines. Cord has been found on only ten sherds (3093–5, 3244a–e and 3907–08), on the inner surface just below the rim. Comb alone occurs on thirteen sherds (3096–3108) and comb with incision occurs on sherds 3209, 3217–20 and 3235a–i. Incision only is found on sherds 3109–3207 and 3842–55. Sherds 3208–45 have horizontal lines, usually incised, and frequently combined with other motifs including oblique lines (3211, 3217–20, 3922), short stabs (3212, 3232) and zig-zags and broken lines (3233 and 34). Impressions forming horizontal lines but applied at least in some cases with a shell occur on 3236–43 and 3923. Scattered impressions, basically arranged horizontally, occur on sherds 3244, 3245, and 3924–6; 3246 may have 'barbed-wire' decoration. Cordons have been found only on sherds 3245a, 3247a-d (same vessel), 3251, 3252 and 3711. The remaining sherds show that large portions of vessels and probably whole vessels were undecorated.

There is one sherd of thick ware (3929) but coarse ware, like sherds 1385–1510 from Concentration A, is not represented. However there is a limited amount of fairly coarse ware (3710–27, see p. 303). The ware of these sherds tends to be brown, and grits, though not large, are common. There may be no more than four vessels. The distinction between some of the sherds (e.g. 3722) and a few that have been left in the fine-ware category is very slight. Sherds 3710 and 3711 show that at least one vessel had a flat rim and a cordon. Most were decorated with incised lines, usually obliquely but sometimes horizontally.

Because of its fragmentary state the *fine pottery* is being described

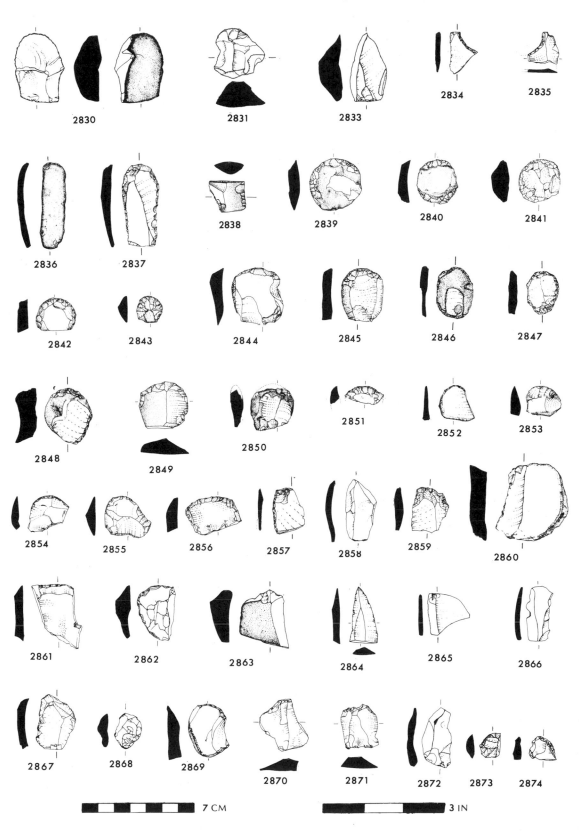

Fig. 108–Concentration D: flint (2830–2874).

7 CM

3 IN

3094

3109

3113

3181C

3188

3211B

3217A

3230A

3235

3235G

3244G

3245A

3247A

3256A

3282A

3710

3711

3726A

3722

5CM

Pl. 78—Concentration D: pottery.

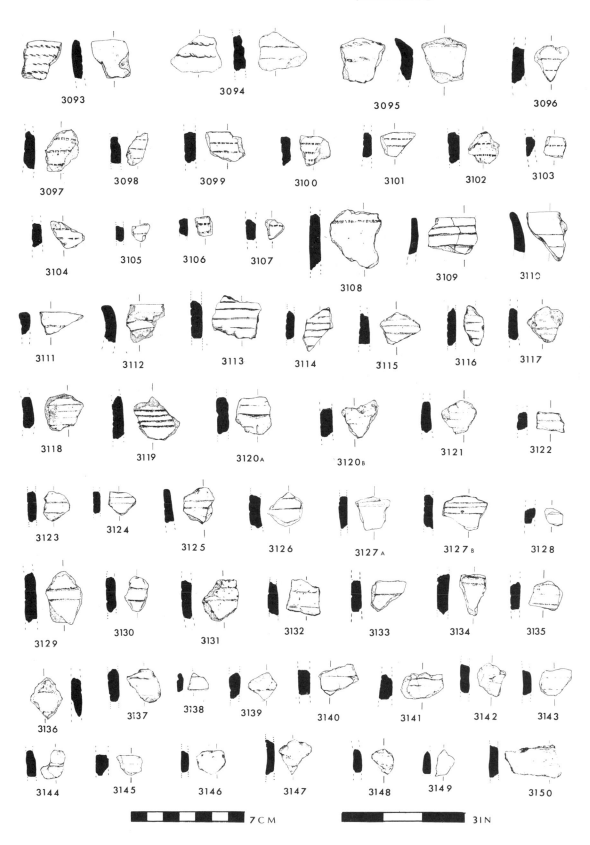

3093

3094

3095

3096

3097

3098

3099

3100

3101

3102

3103

3104

3105

3106

3107

3108

3109

3110

3111

3112

3113

3114

3115

3116

3117

3118

3119

3120A

3120B

3121

3122

3123

3124

3125

3126

3127A

3127B

3128

3129

3130

3131

3132

3133

3134

3135

3136

3137

3138

3139

3140

3141

3142

3143

3144

3145

3146

3147

3148

3149

3150

7CM

3IN

*Fig. 109—Concentration D: pottery
(3093–3150).*

on the basis of decorative features, as in the accounts of the other concentrations.

I. Horizontal lines

Apart from the cord decoration all decoration occurs externally.

Cord decoration (Fig. 109, Nos 3093–3095). (As well as the three sherds described in this category, cord also occurs on 3244a–e described below.) The cord is on the inside face: 3093 is a rimsherd with a flattened profile and four lines of decoration; 3907 (unillustrated) is fairly similar in profile and decoration but the ware is paler and it is not clear whether scratches on its outer surface form decoration; 3094, also a rimsherd, has, in addition to two lines of cord on the interior, two lines of vague jab-like impressions on the exterior and the ware is cream-coloured throughout; 3095 is part of a rim with a distinctive outward turn. No. 3908 (not illustrated) may be part of the same vessel; the fabric resembles 3093 but it is from a different vessel. The two lines of decoration are formed by impressions resembling cord. The outer part of the rim is missing.

Comb decoration (Fig. 109; Nos 3096–3108) is found on thirteen bodysherds. The lines are closely set except on 3108 where there is a considerable black area. The impressions are not distinctive. Comb impressions also occur on sherds 3209, 3217 and 3235 in combination with other motifs.

Incised decoration (Figs 109–111; Nos 3109–3207, 3910–21) is the commonest method used. Except on 3109, 3113, 3117, 3118, 3910 and 3911, blank spaces occur, suggesting that overall decoration was not a feature of any vessel. On 3109–65, 3910 and 3911 the lines tend to be closely set whereas on 3166–86 and 3912–21 they are more widely spaced. On 3187–3207 the lines are discontinuous. On sherds 3189–91c and 3195 the decoration, although incised, is oblique; 3191a is similar to 3722 (see below). On some sherds (e.g. 3140, 3141, 3148 and 3158) the incision is light. Deeper lines are found on sherds such as 3122, 3131, 3155 and 3181b. There are six rimsherds, 3109–12, 3181a and 3187a: the latter is described below; 3109 and 3111 have flattened profiles but 3110 is more rounded; 3112 has a slight shoulder. Only three basesherds are present (3180a, 3186 and 3909). There are incised lines directly above the foot.

There are differences in ware but the majority have a rustcoloured surface with a dark core. Sometimes the inner surface is also rust-coloured or dark. Nos 3162 and 3163 seem to be part of the same vessel; 3113 is light brown throughout; 3180a–m and 3909 are cream-coloured and may be part of one vessel; 3181a–o are of similar ware, consisting of an outer and inner cream surface and a dark core, possibly part of a single vessel; 3182a–m also tend to be cream coloured and most have a dark core. However, it is difficult to know if they are part of the vessels represented by 3180 and 3181. The basesherd 3186 is of soft, greyish ware.

II. Specific motifs (e.g. criss-cross) frequently combined with horizontal lines (Figs 111–112; Nos 3208–3235, 3922)

Unless otherwise stated all are bodysherds and incision is the technique used.

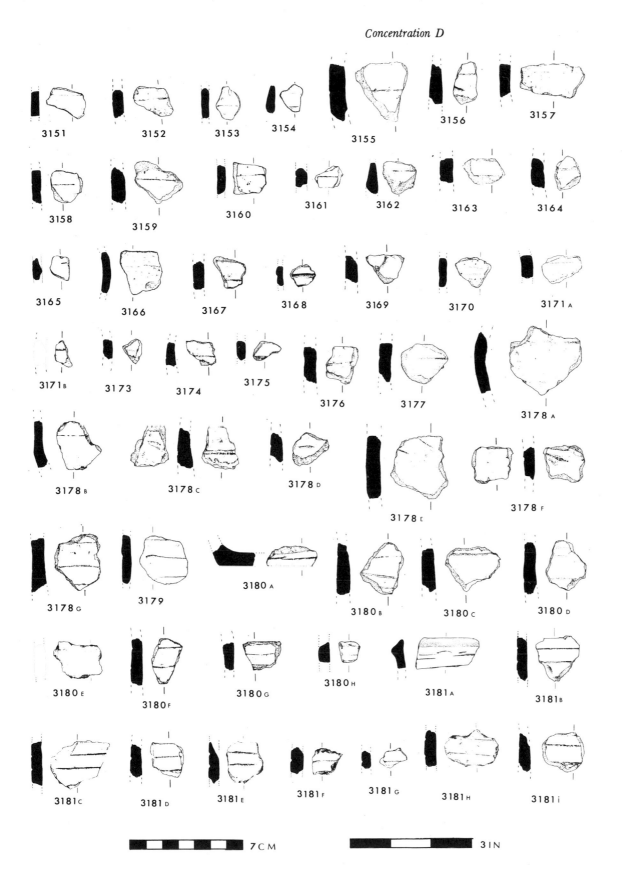

Fig. 110—Concentration D: pottery (3151–3181i).

*Fig. 111–Concentration D: pottery
(3181l–3215).*

No. 3208 is a rimsherd tending to have a flattened profile and an outward expansion. Underneath are two worn oblique impressions which seem to indicate comb decoration, although there is no horizontal line. No. 3209 has a band of closely set, horizontally incised lines with oblique impressions possibly formed by a comb along one side and a row of impressions along the other. No. 3210 has a band of oblique lines bounded on the top and bottom by a horizontal line. Sherds 3211a–b have a band of deep, almost vertical lines bounded by horizontal lines. The ware of 3211c–f is similar, being brick-red internally and externally; 3211a is thinner and darker but may also be part of the same vessel. Nos 3212–14 have similar decoration, horizontal lines and a row of stabs, and may be part of a single vessel; 3215–17 seem to be from a vessel decorated with horizontal lines and somewhat triangular impressions; 3217a–b and 3218–20 have horizontal rows of comb decoration with oblique impressions, perhaps fingernail below; all may have come from the same vessel. Nos 3221–4 and 3855 have similar decoration except that the horizontal lines are incised; 3225–8 are similarly decorated with horizontal lines, and short impressions beneath. On 3225 the bottom line overlaps and part of it may be worn impressed comb; 3225–7 are probably from the same vessel. 3229 has horizontal lines and impressions haphazardly arranged; 3230a has horizontal lines and criss-cross ornamentation. The criss-cross pattern is also found on 3230b–d. Nos 3231 and 3232 have diverging lines while 3233 and 3234 have a V-shaped motif, with a horizontal line above on 3233.

3235a–j appear to be part of the same vessel which has a dark brown outer surface and is generally dark on the interior. The outer surface feels sandy. It was decorated with horizontal lines of comb impressions, bands of oblique impressions, zig-zags and horizontal stabs. The rim (3235a–b) is slightly rounded and flared and the vessel had a diameter of *c.* 12–13cm at the mouth.

III. Scattered impressions basically arranged horizontally (Figs 112–113; Nos 3236–46, 3924–6).

No. 3236 is a rimsherd with the remains of faint horizontal decoration under the rim perhaps made by impressing a shell into the wet surface. A similar technique was used in the decoration of 3856. No. 3237 has two impressions; 3238 has interrupted horizontal lines and the ware tends to be cream-coloured; 3239–43 are similar in ware and decoration to 3238.

Sherds 3244a–o and 3924–6 are all decorated with impressions arranged horizontally if in a somewhat haphazard manner. No. 3244a is a rimsherd with an outward bevel and a slight expansion. On the outer surface are faint oblique impressions. Internally this sherd and 3244b–d are decorated with a cordon, apparently pinched-up, with two horizontal rows of circular impressions below it. The rim profile of 3245a shows a slight inward slope and an outward expansion; 3245a, the cordoned sherd 3245c and the bodysherd 3245d are very similar in ware; 3245b also a rim, has less pronounced features than the rim of 3245a and is lighter in colour; nevertheless it appears to be part of the same vessel. Sherds 3245e–k with their horizontal rows of impressions may also be parts of the same vessel.

No. 3246a is decorated with short stabs apparently transversely placed across a lightly incised line. It probably represents 'barbed-wire' decoration. It was found with a sherd (3246b) of similar but undecorated ware.

Fig. 112–Concentration D: pottery (3216–3244d).

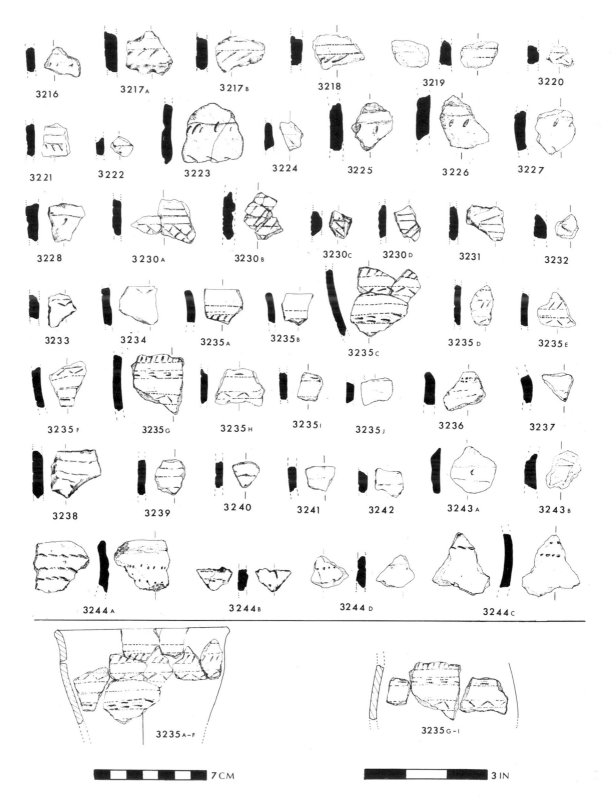

3216 3217ᴀ 3217ʙ 3218 3219 3220

3221 3222 3223 3224 3225 3226 3227

3228 3230ᴀ 3230ʙ 3230ᴄ 3230ᴅ 3231 3232

3233 3234 3235ᴀ 3235ʙ 3235ᴄ 3235ᴅ 3235ᴇ

3235ꜰ 3235ɢ 3235ʜ 3235ɪ 3235ᴊ 3236 3237

3238 3239 3240 3241 3242 3243ᴀ 3243ʙ

3244ᴀ 3244ʙ 3244ᴅ 3244ᴄ

3235ᴀ₋ꜰ 3235ɢ₋ɪ

7 CM 3 IN

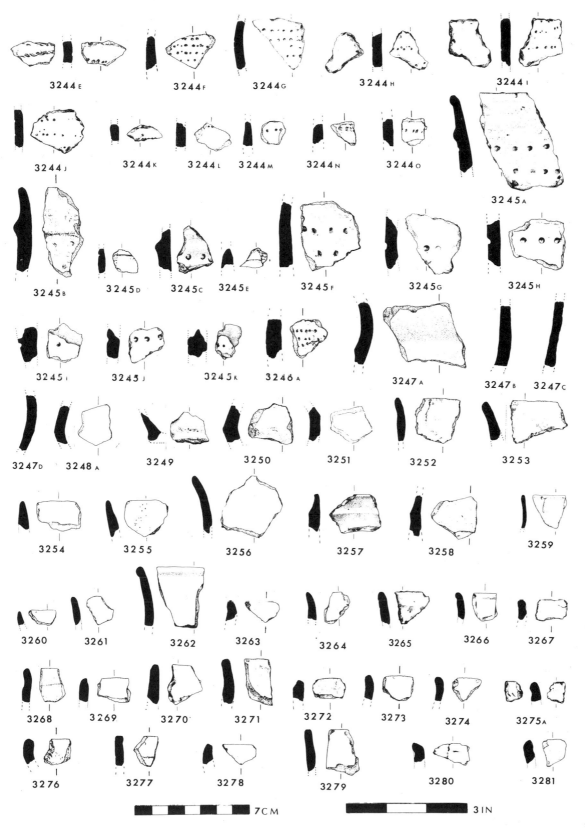

IV. Cordoned and shoulder sherds (Fig. 113; Nos 3247–51)

Cordons also occur on 3245a–c already described.

No. 3247a is a shoulder sherd of good compact ware. The outer surface is rouge. It is smooth and well finished and may have had a slip. The interior is dark and grits are rare. The bodysherds 3247b–k appear to be part of the same vessel and are included here. No. 3248 came from the junction of the neck and body of a vessel. The ware is cream to red on the outer and grey-brown on the inner surface. Sherds 3249 and 3250 are cordoned. On 3249 the cordon is at a pronounced angle to the body while on 3250 the angle is slighter. No. 3251 has a facet along one fractured edge. Because of damage and its small size it is uncertain whether this is a cordoned or a rimsherd. In form it is similar to the rim of 3095 and is also comparable to 3298.

V. Undecorated rimsherds (Figs 113–114; Nos 3252–98, 3927–8)

In addition to the decorated rimsherds (3093–5, 3109–12, 3181a, 3187a, 3208, 3235a–b, 3236, 3244a, 3245a, 3245b and 3907) there are fifty-three undecorated rimsherds.

No. 3252 is a sherd of light brown ware with a pointed profile and a flared neck; 3927 is fairly similar; 3253 is also light brown and tends to have a flattened profile; 3254 has a pointed profile and is reddish brown; 3255 has a similar profile but is cream and has more grits than 3254; 3256 has a rounded profile and a flared neck and is of similar ware to 3255. Nos 3257 and 3258 are of similar, cream-coloured sandy ware. Both have pointed profiles and flared necks but are probably not from the same vessel. Nos 3259–61 are small sherds of thin ware with pointed rims. There is a vertical stab, probably accidental, on 3259. A similar stab occurs on 3252. Nos 3262–76 generally have rounded rims and the colour varies from red (e.g. 3264 and 3270) to dark grey-brown (3273); 3262 is of compact greyish ware and the rounded rim projects outwards. Nos 3277–9 have flattened profiles; 3278 and 3279 are red throughout and may be part of the same vessel. Nos 3280 and 3281 have inward bevels and can be compared to 3095.

Nos 3282–4 are brick-red, average 8mm in thickness and may be part of a bowl; 3282a is slightly rougher than the others and has a dark core. The nature of the break on the outer surface indicates that the coil method of construction was used. It was found with 3282b, a sherd of similar ware from the same vessel (not illustrated). Nos 3283a–d also appear to have come from a bowl, but a different one. The rim profile is rounded but there is a slight inward expansion. The ware contains grits and some grog. 3284 is of similar ware, has a somewhat flattened profile and the edge folded inwards. Nos 3285–7 also have slightly flattened profiles and there is a slight external ridge beneath the rim of 3285; 3288 and 3289 have flattened rims and may have come from the same vessel; 3290 is similar to 3288 and 3289 but the ware is somewhat coarser; 3291 and 3292 have a slightly pointed profile and may be part of the same vessel; 3293 has a somewhat rounded profile, and the creamy ware is similar to that of 3180. Sherd 3294 has a rounded profile and a pronounced inward expansion beneath the rim; the fragmentary sherds 3295 and 3296 are part of a broadly rounded rim and may belong to the same vessel, 3297 is a fragment of a slightly more pointed rim than 3295 and 3296;

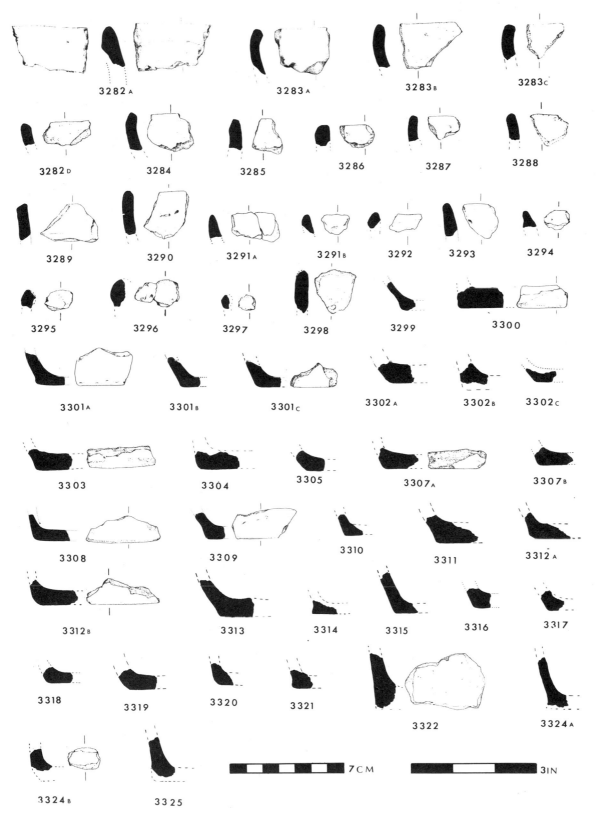

*Fig. 114–Concentration D: pottery
(3282–3325).*

3298 has a facet or bevel on the inside but it is not certain what form the rim profile took.

VI. *Undecorated basesherds* (Fig. 114; Nos 3299–3325)

In addition to the decorated basesherds already described (3180a, 3186 and 3909) thirty-two undecorated basesherds are also present. The foot is unexpanded except for a slight protrusion on 3300, some pinching at the base of the wall of 3301a–c and a slight rounded expansion on 3299. Nos 3301a–c are cream to red throughout and may be from the same vessel; 3302a–b are a similar colour but they are thicker than 3301 and contain a considerable amount of grog; 3303 is cream on the outer surface but the core and inner surface are darker; 3304–6 have a red outer surface with a dark core. The ware contains quartz grits and 3305 also contains grog. Nos 3307a–b are of finer ware; the red outer surface is worn. No. 3308 has a brick-red inner and outer surface and a dark core. There are few grits and the ware has a smooth, dusty texture. Nos 3309–19 have a red outer face with a dark core and an inner face that varies from red to grey; 3312a–b and 3313 may be from the same vessel which would have had a basal diameter of *c*.9.3cm. No. 3320 is rounded but because it is broken immediately above the foot it is not possible to say if it was expanded. Sherds 3322–5 come from the foot of the wall where it thickens towards the base.

VII. *Undecorated bodysherds* (3326–3709, 3930–3955; none illustrated)

These form the largest group. A large number of vessels are represented but it was difficult to establish how many. However, the sherds do fall into several broad categories.

Sherds 3326–82 are characterised by a brick-red inner and outer surface and have a dark core. Some of these, such as 3326–9 may be from vessels represented by rimsherds 3282 or 3283. Others (e.g. 3335–9) are more similar to 3318 and have a liberal supply of grog. Nos 3326a-k are probably from the same vessel as 3238a-t. The average thickness is 6mm. There is a possible grain impression in the outer face of 3364. The nature of the break on 3377 indicates that it comes from a coil-built vessel. The ware of 3383–3409 is rougher and has more grits than the preceding group. They tend to be thicker (average thickness 9mm) than the other sherds and are more similar to the coarse ware described below.

A small group of sherds, 3410–21, are also red with a darker core but they tend to be thinner (average thickness 4mm) than the other sherds. These may come from a vessel or vessels represented by rimsherds 3259–61.

A large group of sherds, 3422–3558, have a red or light brown outer face and a dark inner face. On some, such as 3422 and 3430, the inner surface is black, while on others, e.g. 3519 and 3531, it is grey-brown. The ware tends to be gritty and some sherds, such as 3442 and 3520, also contain grog.

Sherds 3559–3608 are characterised by a creamy red colour throughout. The ware is 'dusty' to the touch. 3559a–o are from a single vessel which may be represented by rimsherds 3266 or 3279, or basesherds 3301a–c. There is a grain impression in the exterior of 3597a. The average thickness is 6mm. Nos 3610–55 have a similar outer and inner surface but the core is dark; 3611a–p appear to be from the same vessel and are similar to rimsherd 3254 and basesherd 3308. The ware of 3656–72 is also similar to 3559 but they are slightly thicker (average 8mm) and have a dark core.

Nos 3673–91 are characterised by their creamy colour. Some, such as 3673a–e are the same colour throughout and have the same gritty ware as rimsherds 3257 and 3258. Others, such as 3683, have a dark core and are more similar to 3181.

The outer surface of 3692–3708 varies from red to cream but all have a very dark, or even black core and inner surface. The ware contains few grits; 3699a–d have a black, burnt accretion on the inner surface.

A number of sherds either too small or too poorly preserved for categorisation were also recovered. These have been given a single number, 3709.

Coarsish ware (Fig. 115; Nos 3710–27)

A group of thirty-six sherds is being termed coarsish ware. However, none is as rough as those from Concentration A and can only be called coarsish when compared with the other, generally finer, sherds of this concentration. The five rimsherds 3710a–e appear to come from the same vessel despite differences in coloration. They are characterised by a flat-topped rim with decoration in the form of oblique stabs. Underneath, on the outer surface are more oblique stabs. Grit is fairly liberally applied. In the main this has been well crushed down but it does protrude through the surface of some sherds. Quartz was the principal material. The average thickness is 9mm. 3711 has a very slight cordon with rows of opposed oblique lines above and below it. These form a pattern like herring-bone. This sherd comes from the same vessel as the rimsherds.

Sherds 3712–14 come from the bodies of vessels, and have line decoration, apparently obliquely set. All are decorated, and the ware is similar to that of 3711 and all may come from the same vessel. Sherds 3715–19 while of similar ware to 3711, have horizontal incised decoration which suggests that they may be from a different vessel. Nos 3720 and 3721 (not illustrated) are red to brown; 3720a has a slight cordon, below which are the remains of three oblique stabs; the break on 3721 indicates that it came from a coil-built vessel. No. 3722 is of light brown ware and is decorated with two opposed rows of oblique lines. Nos 3723–5 have redbrown ware. There is a single stab on 3723a. Nos 3723b and 3724 are undecorated bodysherds. There are three vertical stabs on 3725; 3726a–h have a red outer face on a dark core and inner surface, 3726a has two oblique stabs elongated by incised lines; 3726b has a horizontal pattern consisting of a blank area bounded on one side by two closely set incised lines and the other side is bounded by a line of fingernail-like impressions and the remains of an incised line, 3726c has two parallel oblique incised lines and a third, converging line. There are two faintly incised oblique lines on 3726d and g, and a single one on 3726e and h.

The ware of 3727 differs from the wares previously described in any of the concentrations. It is of hard compact black ware with a smooth outer surface, leathery to the touch. The rim is flat-topped. A

Fig. 115–Concentration D: pottery (3710–3727).

perforation a short distance below the rim is broader on the outer than the inner face. It appears to have been bored into the vessel after firing. Internally there is a groove a short distance below the rim. This vessel can be compared to 3773 and 3774 found at Sites 6 and 18 (p. 312).

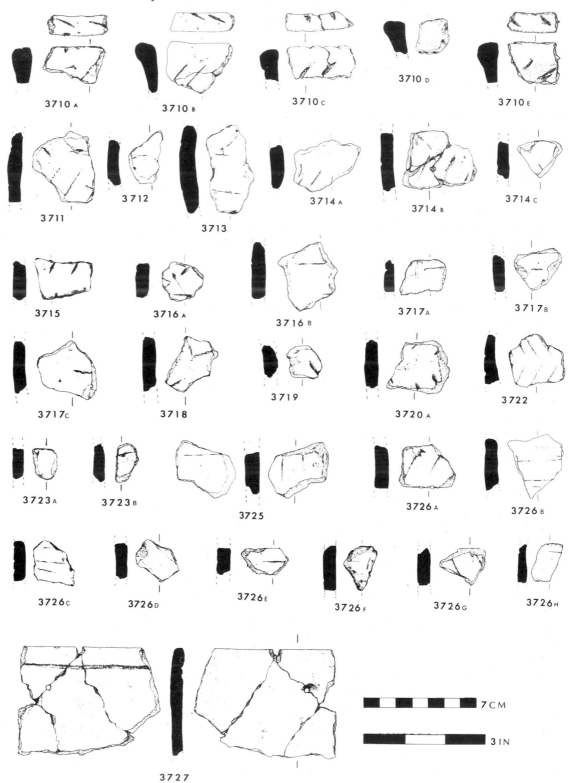

3710 A   3710 B   3710 C   3710 D   3710 E

3711   3712   3713   3714 A   3714 B   3714 C

3715   3716 A   3716 B   3717 A   3717 B

3717 C   3718   3719   3720 A   3722

3723 A   3723 B   3725   3726 A   3726 B

3726 C   3726 D   3726 E   3726 F   3726 G   3726 H

3727

7 CM

3 IN

ISOLATED FINDS OF BEAKER POTTERY (Figs 85 and 116; Nos 3728–3774)

In addition to the large concentrations A, B, C and D, a small number of isolated finds of Beaker pottery were made. These consist of single sherds of pottery or small groups of sherds. In all about fifteen vessels of fine ware, one of coarsish ware (3738) and two of hard dark ware (3773 and 3774) are represented. Finds of isolated sherds are absent from the north-western side of Site 1 and, with one exception, from Site 1 itself.

Some of the isolated finds of flints must be the result of Beaker activity. But with the exception of the barbed and tanged arrowheads (Eogan 1968, 323) our knowledge of flint artifact typology is not sufficient to enable us to separate Beaker from Neolithic flints. Accordingly, all isolated finds of flint will be described together and published in a subsequent volume.

The Roman numerals preceding the museum numbers refer to location on Fig. 85. All are of fine ware unless otherwise stated.

I. A group of sherds found together in a brownish, charcoal-flecked clay layer in Area 4, square 9, just above the old ground level. No. 3728 is a bodysherd, brick-red on the outside, with a darkish inner face. The external surface is decorated with a low cordon and a multiple incised chevron motif. The decoration is not comparable to any of the sherds from Knowth. The ware has many smooth grits which protrude through the surface. Bodysherds 3729–34 are undecorated but the ware is rather like 3728. It is possible that some, if not all, form part of the same vessel as 3728. No. 3729 is of slightly thicker ware than the other sherds and has a slight thinning along one of the fractures. No. 3736 is a group of poorly preserved fragments from a coarseware vessel different to the preceding example. One of the faces is blackened. A grit in one of the sherds is 20mm long.

II. A group of sherds found on the old ground level in the recess caused by the removal of kerbstone 8 from the kerb of Site 17. Two different vessels are represented: 3737 is a base from a fine-ware vessel and 3738 is a group of sherds of rougher orange-brown ware. These include a flat-topped rimsherd 3738a and a basesherd 3738b. The rest are bodysherds.

III. 3739–3743. Found within the 'curved trench' (see Appendix I), but there is insufficient evidence to establish any association with it; 3739–41 are of fine ware and 3739 is a basesherd; 3742 and 3743 are of rougher ware, poorly preserved.

IV. 3744a. Rimsherd of thin, well-made and well-fired orange ware. The rim tends to be pointed and slightly flared. The body is decorated with irregularly applied parallel rows of comb. There is a blank zone beneath the decoration. No. 3744b is of coarser ware than 3744a. It is a bodysherd with an orange outer and inner face and a dark core. There are quartz and granite grits in the ware and a high grog content. The outer face has irregularly applied fingernail impressions. These two sherds were in a charcoal spread on the old ground surface in the gap left by the removal of the kerbstone between Nos 16 and 17 of Site 2. The charcoal spread has been dated to *c.*1235 b.c. (3185 ± 255 B.P. B.M. 786).

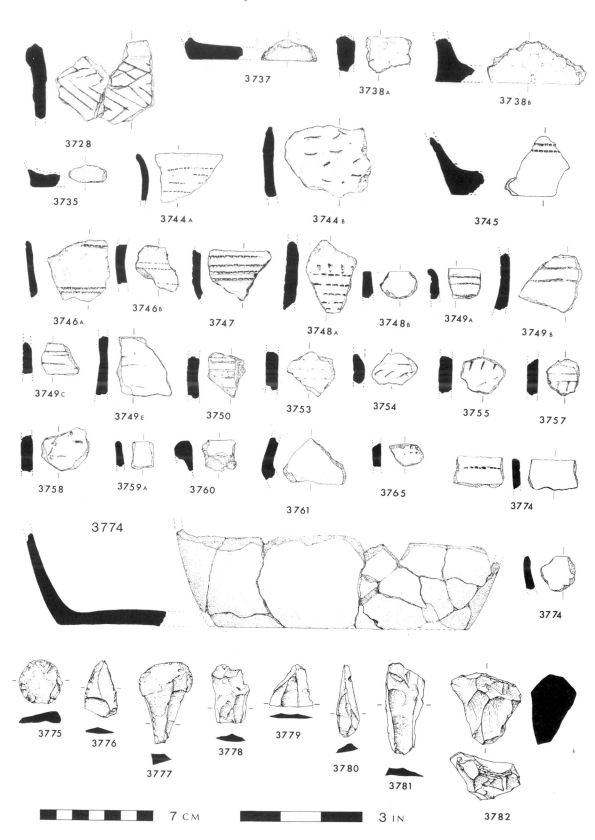

Fig. 116—Isolated finds of Beaker pottery (3728–3774) and flint (3775–3782).

V. 3745a. Basesherd with the remains of two closely set rows of comb decoration 2.5cm above the foot. The outer surface is red to cream, the core is black and the inner face grey. No. 3745b may be part of the base of the same vessel as 3745a; 3746a is a bodysherd with two rows of comb decoration, closely set and separated from a third row by a blank space; 3746b also has the remains of two closely set rows of comb decoration; 3746c is a plain bodysherd of the same ware and colour as 3746a. From the disturbed fill of the sockets of Site 9.

VI. 3747. Bodysherd of fine, well-made ware. It has four closely set horizontal rows of well executed comb decoration. The comb had different sized teeth. Found in Area 6, square 17.

VII. 3748a. Decorated with parallel rows perhaps formed by angled stabs or by impressing a comb at an angle, above which are short vertical depressions, perhaps bone impressions. No. 3748b is a rimsherd with a flattened profile and may be from the same vessel as 3748a. Found on the old ground level in Area 3, square 15.

VIII. 3749a–f. Rimsherd and fine bodysherds of well-made and well-fired ware, brown in both faces with a dark core. The rim is rounded and the decoration consists of horizontal incised lines and blank bands. From Area 7, square 47.

IX. 3750. Bodysherd of light brown ware with dark core and liberal mix of grits. The decoration consists of closely set parallel incised lines. From Area 7, square 47.

X. 3751a–b. Bodysherds of coarsish ware, brick-coloured and with fairly prominent quartz grits; 3751a has an incised line; 3752a and 3752b are of similar ware to 3751.

No. 3753 is a bodysherd with brown external surface and dark inner surface. There are three incised lines. The ware of the next two sherds is similar; 3754 has an incised line and a fringe of short oblique lines beneath; 3755 has similar oblique lines. No. 3756 is a plain bodysherd. Nos 3751–6 all came from the old ground surface in Area 3, square 35.

XI. 3757. Brownish ware, decorated with horizontal incised lines with a fringe of vertical lines. From a modern spoil heap in Area 3, square 83.

XII. 3758. Light brown externally and dark internally, and decorated with fingernail impressions haphazardly arranged. Found in a layer of dark sticky earth immediately above the old ground surface in cutting 20a.

XIII. 3759a–d. A group of small buff sherds, probably parts of the same vessel; 3759a is a rimsherd with a slightly pointed profile and the others are undecorated bodysherds. Found in a modern spoil heap in Area 3, square 21.

XIV. 3760. Rimsherd of flattened profile. The orange ware is blackened. From the old ground surface, Area 4, square 61.

XV. 3761. Seems to be from the junction of the belly and the upper part of a vessel. The ware is compact and buff-coloured throughout. It came from the passage of one of the smaller passage tombs (Site 2) above the old ground surface.

XVI. 3762. Plain bodysherd of darkish ware throughout, found on the old ground surface in cutting 22.

XVII. 3763. Undecorated bodysherd with a buff outer face and a dark core and inner face, from cutting 21.

XVIII. 3764–6. Plain bodysherds, of red-brown ware; 3766 has a dark core. Found in the same layer in Area 3, square 41.

XIX. 3767a. Brown on the outer and red on the inner surface, from near the base of a vessel where the wall thickens; 3767b is a fragment. No. 3768 also comes from near the base of a vessel and is similar in colour and texture to 3767a.

XX. 3769. Plain bodysherd with an orange outer face on a dark core and inner surface. No. 3770 is a plain bodysherd of orange ware, 10mm thick. The inner face is worn. Both 3769 and 3770 were found on the old ground surface at the junction between cuttings 39 and 40 opposite the entrance to Site 2.

BURIAL (Fig. 117; Pls 79a and 80)

This burial was in the passage of a passage tomb, Site 15 (p. 90 above). The fill of the passage around where the burial took place

Pl. 79a–Beaker burial in passage of passage tomb (Site 15) showing cremation deposit and sherds of Beaker vessel (3772) in situ.

consisted of two main layers. The bottom layer (1), which directly overlay the old ground surface, was silt-like in composition and about 40cm thick. This layer may have accumulated naturally as a result of material filtering through cavities between the roof stones or orthostats. The overlying layer (2) consisted of soft dark earth and stones, probably material that accumulated after the removal of the roof stones.

The burial, the cremated bones of an adult and a young child, extended over an area 44cm by 30cm and 5cm in maximum thickness (3771). It was in layer 1 and its base was 30–40cm above the floor of the tomb. There was no evidence for a pit so the disposition of the layer may have occurred after the placing of the burial. It appears that the burial was in a sort of compartment. It was placed in the corner of a segment of the passage. There were some flattish stones immediately underneath it, probably deliberately inserted and it was bounded on the northern side by sillstone 1, on the eastern side by orthostats 17 and 18, on the southern side by two stones (one of which partly overlay the other) and on the western side by two stones. However, the deposit did not extend as far as the presumed edging on the southern side. Some flattish stones covered the burial on the southern side and there were a couple of fairly small stones over it at other points.

Sherds of a beaker were found in and close to the burial, not all at the same level. Some were associated with the deposit, others were in the fill above it but the main concentration was outside the compartment on the south, 20–25cm from the edge of the cremation.

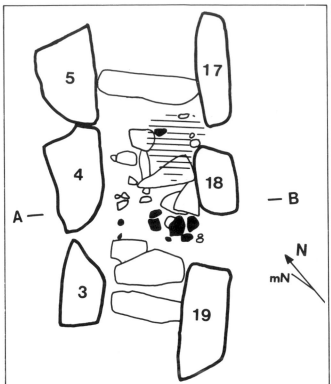

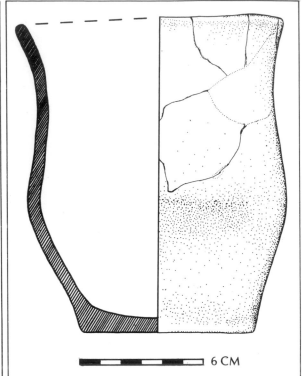

6 CM

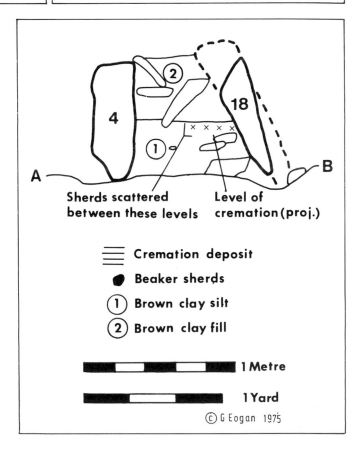

Sherds scattered
between these levels

Level of
cremation (proj.)

≡ Cremation deposit

⬤ Beaker sherds

① Brown clay silt

② Brown clay fill

1 Metre

1 Yard

© G Eogan 1975

*Fig. 117—Plan and sections of Beaker
burial, Site 15;
Beaker vessel (3772) from burial.*

This concentration was at about the same height as the larger stones that overlay the southern end of the burial. The basesherds tended to occur on the eastern side of the passage and the rimsherds in the centre and on the western side.

When fitted together the sherds formed an almost complete undecorated Bell-Beaker (3772, Fig. 117b). The ware is fine and both the external and internal surfaces are smooth. The pot was evenly fired, the inner and outer surfaces are brown and the core dark. The walls average 5mm in thickness and the vessel is 147mm high. The external mouth diameter is 128mm, the base 85mm. The rim is rounded and the foot unexpanded.

Pl. 80–Reconstructed Beaker vessel (3772) from burial in passage of passage tomb (Site 15).

The presence of sherds with the cremation indicates that they were associated. It is likely that the vessel was placed beside the burial but got broken, probably when the tomb was wrecked. This destruction also appears to have disturbed the upper part of the silt layer.

VESSEL IN PASSAGE TOMB, SITE 6 (3773, Fig. 118; Pl. 81)

Only part of this vessel survives. The ware is coarse and dark but the external surface is brown in places. The base is flat and 20cm in external diameter. As far as can be established the walls widened gradually outwards to reach an external diameter of approximately 31cm at the mouth. The rim tends to be flat-topped. Just below it, on the inside, are two broad horizontal channels. The outer surface of the body is decorated with incised lines but it is not possible to determine the overall pattern. On the upper portion were two bands of grouped oblique lines. Between these was a band of six horizontal, roughly parallel lines. On one sherd the oblique lines are in the opposite direction to those on the other sherds suggesting that there may have been a chevron pattern. A surviving part of the wall from near the base was decorated with concentric arcs (Eogan 1974, 30; 1976, 264).

These sherds were found in the north-eastern recess of Site 6 (p. 43). Most were around the edge of the cremation deposit but some were partially sunk into its surface. It is not certain how they got there. Concentration B was nearby but its pottery is of much finer ware. So, this incomplete coarse vessel appears to be an isolated find. It could have accompanied or contained a secondary cremation burial placed in the tomb on top of the primary passage grave cremation and merged with it, cf. the cremation burial found in a coarse Beaker vessel at Monknewtown (Sweetman 1976, 32, Burial 8). However, with the sherds from Site 6 it cannot be established if a complete vessel was deposited although sherds could have disintegrated at the time of the destruction of the site.

FINDS IN PASSAGE TOMB, SITE 18

Overlying the flag in the left-hand recess was a mixed deposit of pottery sherds, flints, charcoal, animal bones and part of a human skull. Although the overlying material is soft dark earth of historic date, nevertheless the deposit appeared to have been homogeneous and probably of Beaker date. Ms Dowling reports that the animal bones consisted of the top molar of a pig, two bits of scapula (possibly sheep), three bits of vertebrae (some possibly sheep), three leg bone shafts and a large piece, probably part of a pelvic girdle (cow or pig).

The pottery sherds (3774, Fig. 116) were part of a flat-based vessel, *c.* 21cm in diameter. From the base the walls project outwards and the simple rim was rounded. On the interior is a line, probably incised. It is not possible to determine the shape or height of the vessel. The ware is hard and compact, externally mottled brown but dark internally. The average width is 7mm. In ware, to some extent in colour, and in the internal rim decoration, this vessel closely resembles 3773 and rimsherd 3727 from Concentration D. These vessels stand apart from the main range of pottery of the four assemblages. Ms Brindley (pers. comm.) has compared 3773 to 'Grooved Ware'. Nos 3727 and 3773 can also be compared to pots found at Newgrange, apparently of Beaker date (O'Kelly *et. al.* 1978, 311–13).

There were twenty pieces of flint (Fig. 116; Nos 3775–94), only one an artifact (3775). This is a rounded scraper made from a flake knocked off the outer portion of a pebble. No. 3776 is a triangular piece, probably the tip of a blade, with some working along the long edges; 3777–81 are crude blades or flakes with evidence of slight working along the edges; 3782 is the remains of a core; the remaining twelve pieces (3783–94) are irregularly shaped waste flakes, one of which had been burnt.

The cultural and chronological status of the deposit overlying the flag and the isolated finds of flints is difficult to establish. If the objects over the flag form a deposit then they may have been part of a domestic assemblage of Beaker date. However it is not possible to prove this. Despite the presence of charcoal there was no evidence of a fire, but in view of the damage that took place all around the flag, the remains of a fire could have vanished. On this theory one would have to imagine a much-damaged tomb with Beaker people using what was originally intended as a basin of sorts by the passage-grave people. On the other hand, perhaps the material was deliberately deposited during Beaker times. There was, for instance, considerable secondary filling in the chambers and passage of the West Kennet (Wiltshire) transepted tomb (Piggott 1962, 26–30, 68–71).

DISCUSSION

The Beaker finds at Knowth consist of material from four separate concentrations and a burial, together with scattered sherds from other parts of the site. The concentrations were widely separated; the nearest to each other, B and C, were 40m apart. The nature of the activity as represented by the concentrations presents a puzzle but they can best be explained as the remains of domestic activity. None of the areas produced evidence for houses so it is possible that the concentrations are middens and that there were houses some distance away (cf. Bradley 1970, 333). However, hearths and pits at A, and the hearth, postholes and scoops at D indicate a living area and not a refuse dump. Perhaps tents, or other forms of impermanent structures were used. Scraps of flint from all four concentrations show that flint-knapping was practised, and lumps of kneaded clay from Concentrations B and D suggest pottery manufacture. This evidence, together with the artifacts and the large quantities of broken pottery, shows that considerable activity took place. All four concentrations were characterised by a dark layer directly over the old ground surface. This must have resulted from accumulated domestic refuse but in marked contrast to the Beaker settlement at Newgrange (van Wijngaarden-Bakker 1974) animal bones were absent, probably due to poor preservation because of the soil conditions. Overlying most of Concentrations A, C and D was a layer of yellowish or brownish material which appears to have been a deliberate deposit and not natural accumulation. It is the sort of material that could have been derived by demolishing and spreading the mounds of the smaller passage tombs but this has not been established. The spread over D might be throw-out from the digging of the basal ditch around the large mound (p. 7). Most of Concentration B was overlain by a structure possibly of Early Christian date (publication pending) so it cannot be established if this concentration was also overlain by a brownish layer. At Newgrange the yellow clay bank overlay the lower levels of the Beaker settlement (van Wijngaarden-Bakker 1974, 329).

The question whether the settlements were temporary or permanent has not been answered. The apparent absence of houses and the presence of postholes and pits in some areas suggest that impermanent structures were used, so perhaps Knowth was only resorted to during the summer season, the permanent settlements being the low-lying embanked enclosures or circles, such as Monknewtown. Indeed, the Rockbarton hearths and associated finds

Fig. 118–Suggested reconstruction of vessel (3773) in Passage Tomb 6.

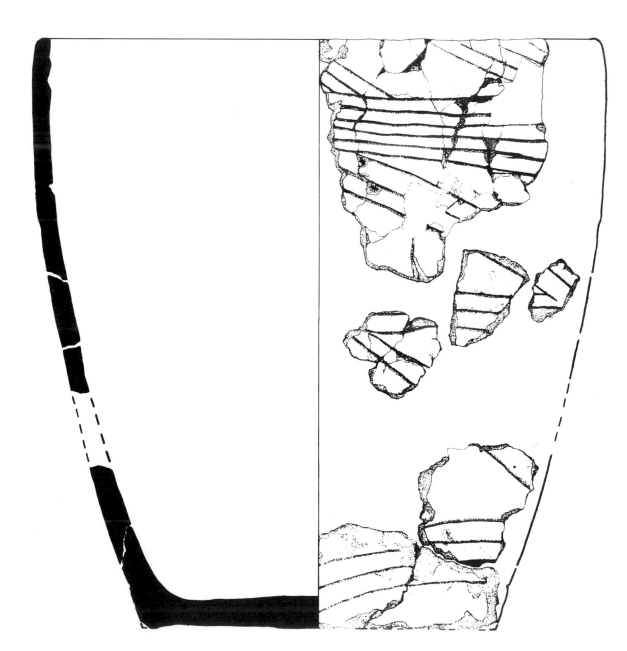

Pl. 81–Sherds (3773) from vessel in passage
tomb Site 6, and sherd (3727) from
Concentration D.

have been interpreted as seasonal camps (Mitchell and Ó Ríordáin 1942). But the amount of evidence for flint knapping and pottery usage and the layers of darker earth indicate a great deal of activity for seasonal occupation. However, the Knowth activity contrasts with that at the other excavated settlements at Brugh na Bóinne. Monknewtown was a large embanked circular enclosure about 80m in external diameter, used for both habitation and burial (Sweetman 1976). At Newgrange the settlement was unprotected but the structural remains included rectangular and circular huts and houses, postholes and hearths. Flint was knapped on the site (M. J. O'Kelly 1966, 98; 1973, 144). Simpson (1971, 135) has argued for two oval timber Beaker houses at Site D, Knockadoon, Lough Gur, Co. Limerick. Although a considerable quantity of Beaker pottery turned up at Dalkey Island, Co. Dublin, the only evidence for settlement was a small shell midden (Liversage 1968, 61). At the Beaker settlement at Ballynagilly, Co. Tyrone, there were three distinct settlement sites, with hearths, pits and stakeholes but no complete house plans (*Excavations* 1970, 20, ed. T. Delaney). Perhaps it is the nature of the abodes of the Beaker people in Ireland that eludes us, and lack of evidence for formal houses may not mean that there was no year-round settlement. Beaker houses are also rare outside Ireland. At the large English settlement of Belle Tout, Sussex, for instance, evidence for houses was limited (Bradley 1970).

Assuming that the concentrations represent domestic activity *in situ* the problems of duration and of simultaneous occupation still remain. The occupants of Concentration A at least differed from the others in their pottery which was predominantly coarse. The finds from Concentrations B, C and D are fairly alike. As pointed out below, the ware from these assemblages appears to belong in the main to Bell-Beakers with smooth profiles, generally fine, well-fired fabric with fairly thin walls. When there is decoration it is predominantly horizontal. There are minor differences in the pottery between the B, C and D concentrations; for instance, the ware in Concentration B has a smoother outer surface and more orange-coloured sherds than the wares in C and D which include many buff-coloured sherds. Perhaps the concentrations are the result of a settlement shift at Knowth itself, which might have had any of a number of causes, such as vermin or disease (Clarke 1970, 57).

Flint was worked on the site and glacial-drift flint was the predominant raw material. The percentage of artifacts relative to waste varied slightly from one concentration to another but averaged ten per cent. Scrapers, principally rounded, predominated at each concentration. Side and end scrapers occurred in small numbers. There were some blades, but only one barbed and tanged arrowhead was found. The thirty-five rounded scrapers were measured for length, breadth and thickness and the results are presented in Table C. These show that there was a general preference for smaller scrapers. None is more than 30mm long, only 9% are 30mm broad or more, and only 14% are more than 7mm thick. 45% are 20mm long or less, 51% are 20mm broad or less and 34% are only 5mm thick or less.

These figures compare very closely with those from the Neolithic occupation at Knowth (see p. 241; Table B) and rounded scrapers also predominated amongst the artifacts from the Neolithic settlement (p. 240). At Monknewtown rounded scrapers were also the main artifact type (Sweetman 1976, 58, 66–9) and a large variety of scrapers came from the Beaker horizon at Newgrange (M. J. O'Kelly 1973, 144). Scrapers were the commonest artifacts in the Grange enclosure at Lough Gur (Ó Ríordáin 1951, 49) and at Ballynagilly small convex scrapers predominated (ApSimon 1976, 22, 27). The flint evidence suggests a similar technological stage and basis of manufacture at all four concentrations at Knowth.

Table C—Comparative sizes of scrapers from Beaker Concentrations A, B, C and D at Knowth

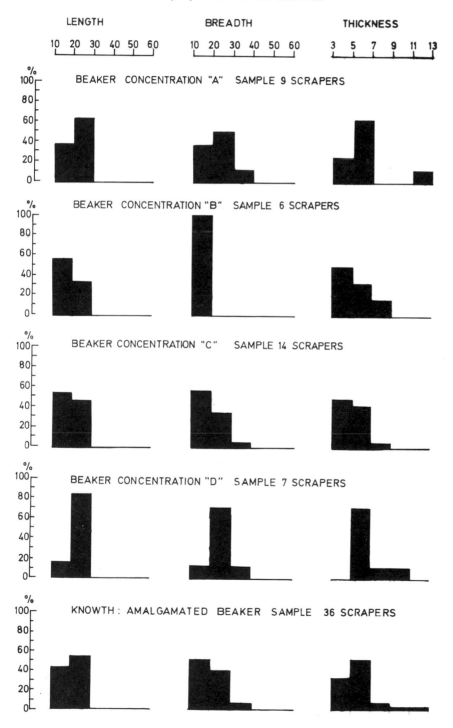

On the pottery evidence Concentration A stands apart from the other three. The Western Neolithic pottery, which occurred on the old ground surface, is likely to have been there from before the Beaker settlement and, therefore, need not be evidence of overlap. At this concentration coarse ware predominated. It is thick, gritty ware and it also differs from the fine Beaker wares in the shape of the vessels: they have curved sides. However, there was at least one shouldered vessel. The decoration is also different. Corrugations and cordons, but also incised lines and impressions of shells, fingernail and cord, were the main techniques used. There are many pitfalls in comparative studies of coarse wares; it is risky to assign such pottery to a phase unless it is found in a sealed context with datable material. However, there appears to be resemblance, both in ware and shape, between some of the Concentration A vessels – those with curved sides in particular – and coarse ware from Lough Gur, termed Class II by Ó Ríordáin (1954, esp. 333–40). Indeed, Site C at Knockadoon with its small amount of fine Beaker ware and large amount of coarse ware represents a rather similar assemblage, though on a larger scale, to Concentration A. Site C at Lough Gur also had a fair amount of Class I pottery. The houses at Lough Gur were circular. Site G (Lough Gur) was exclusively a Class II settlement, as no other type of pottery was found (Ó Ríordáin 1954, 426–28). The structure consisted of a semi-circular wall abutting onto a rock face which formed a natural wall. Ó Ríordáin described the structure as a 'hut roughly built to provide a shelter'. Bones of oxen predominated but there was limited evidence for sheep and pigs. At Site H (Lough Gur) there was a small amount of Class I pottery, about an eighth of the total, and a couple of Beaker sherds. Class II was the predominant ware. Traces of a wooden structure of uncertain shape but tending to be elongated were uncovered (Ó Ríordáin 1954, 429–35).

Coarse ware is now an established feature of Beaker assemblages in Ireland. As well as Knockadoon one can, for instance, cite Grange (Ó Ríordáin 1951, 55), Rockbarton (Mitchell and Ó Ríordáin 1942) and Monknewtown (Sweetman 1976, 39, 46, 57). In England such pottery was also found in Beaker contexts as at Risby Warren, Lincolnshire (Riley 1957, 52–4) and Plantation Farm, Cambridgeshire (Clark 1933). Coarse ware, of the form of Class II vessels, is also a feature of Rinyo-Clacton assemblages such as Rinyo itself in the Orkneys (Childe and Grant 1938–9, 24, Figs 4–5; see also Durrington Walls, Wiltshire, Wainwright and Longworth 1971, 78, p. 27, Fig. 32). Similar ware has a fairly wide distribution in Late Neolithic-Chalcolithic Europe such as the Horgan ware in Switzerland (Childe 1957, 295–7), from the collective tombs in the basins of the Seine-Oise-Marne in France (Bailloud 1974, 200–05) and in the Breton *allées couvertes* (L'Helgouach 1965, 292).

Ó Ríordáin argued that Class II ware was present at Knockadoon from the start of what to him was a Neolithic settlement and that gradually Class II supplemented Class I (the round-bottomed shouldered bowl). Ó Ríordáin visualised 'a picture of changing fashion in equipment revealed most advantageously by the pottery' at Knockadoon (1954, 431). But the depth of accumulation is so thin that stratification cannot be much relied on. Even if Class II ware was present from the beginning at some sites, e.g. Site C, Knockadoon, this in itself is not evidence for an early date. In fact, settlement at

Lough Gur need not have commenced earlier than the time when new elements, such as single graves (Herity and Eogan 1977, 107) were appearing in Ireland. At Lyles Hill, Co. Antrim, coarse ware did not come into use until after the cairn was built (Evans 1953, 45). Class II or its equivalent has been found in court tombs (Case 1961, 200) but it is difficult to prove that it was in a primary context. A couple of sherds of a coarsish pottery with a cordon have been found in the Knowth Neolithic settlement (p. 231, 942–4) but this ware is entirely different and there was no evidence for flat bases.

Apart from a sherd from Concentration C (2168), coarse ware is not known from any of the other three concentrations. However, each contains a small number of sherds of what is being called coarsish ware, B: 1644–48; C: 2168 and possibly 2193; D: 3710–26. This type of ware also occurs on other Beaker sites, e.g. Monknewtown (Sweetman 1976, 46, Fig. 12) and can also be compared to some of Ó Ríordáin's 'miscellaneous wares' (cf. Ó Ríordáin and de Valera 1952, 76–77).

Fine ware, present to a limited extent at Concentration A, is almost the only ware from B, C and D. Within this broad group there are variations. Some sherds (e.g. 1649) come from thin well-fired and well-finished vessels of smooth paste. What may be described as medium fine ware is the commonest variety. Professor Brindley (Appendix III) has shown that the grits are local, which indicates manufacture in the area, possibly at Knowth itself, a suggestion that the presence of the clay lumps reinforces (No. 1511). In addition to crushed grits (chiefly dolerite, sandstone and quartz) grog was used and there is evidence for coil-building. The surfaces were smoothed but there is conclusive evidence for burnishing from only two sherds (1621, 1640) and a couple of further sherds had slip (1662, 3247). There is some evidence for bowls (e.g. 3283) but it appears that the majority of vessels were Bell-Beakers with unaccentuated profiles. All-over-cord and Maritime Beakers do not occur. Many vessels were plain but others were decorated. Cord impressions are rare and usually confined to interior of the rim. Externally such vessels were decorated with other motifs such as incised lines or dots. Quite a few sherds have comb impressions but dots, shell and fingernail or -tip impressions also occur. Incision was the commonest technique. Basically the motifs were horizontally placed. The most frequent scheme was horizontal lines usually in bands with intervening blank areas rather like the beaker from Site C, Knockadoon (Ó Ríordáin 1954, Pl. 36). Horizontal lines in combination with other motifs such as bands, or fringes, of short vertical lines or fingernail impressions, and criss-cross patterns are found on a limited number of sherds from Concentrations B, C and D and on one sherd (1328) from Concentration A. These motifs can be paralleled at other Beaker settlement sites in Ireland, such as Monknewtown, Dalkey Island and the Lough Gur neighbourhood, especially site D (Ó Ríordáin 1954, 394–9) and the wedge-tomb (Ó Ríordáin and Ó h-Iceadha 1955, 38–44).

While similar sources for grit were used in the pottery nevertheless there are differences between the Knowth assemblages and those for Monknewtown and Newgrange. At Monknewtown the decoration tends to be haphazard and there is no interior decoration. At Newgrange there are polypod bowls and 'transverse arrowheads' (knives). Perhaps culturally related groups were living in different parts of Brugh na Bóinne.

Finds from wedge-tombs (de Valera and Ó Nualláin 1972, 114) indicate that Beakers were used as funerary vessels but evidence for positive Beaker burials other than in wedge-tombs is almost non-existent in Ireland, the Knowth cremation burial with its fine vessel is the only one of its kind from this country. Monknewtown had cremation burials. There, Burial II was in a Carrowkeel pot and Burial VIII was in a flower-pot shaped vessel of coarse ware (Sweetman 1976, 28, 32). At Lyles Hill, Co. Antrim, pockets of cremation were accompanied by sherds of coarse ware or Class II (Evans 1953, 45). A communal burial of fourteen individuals in a natural rock crevice at Caherguillamore, Co. Limerick, was accompanied by sherds of a coarsish vessel of Beaker variety and a 'Goodland' bowl, stone and bone beads and bone pins including one with a mushroom-shaped head (Hunt 1967). Ring-barrows at Rathjordan, Co. Limerick, produced Beaker sherds (Ó Ríordáin 1948). Beaker sherds have also been recorded from cists such as that in the small cairn at Gortcorbies, Co. Derry (May 1947, 15–17) or Grave 6 at Poulawack, Co. Clare (Hencken 1935, 204).

In the Boyne Valley there is now considerable evidence for settlement by people using Beaker pottery so Knowth is not an isolated occurrence. Further afield, but still in the east, are the Dalkey Island settlement and the wedge-tomb at Ballyedmonduff, where Beaker was primary, a few miles inland (Ó Ríordáin and de Valera 1952). At three places where excavation has taken place within the Brugh na Bóinne cemetery, evidence for large-scale Beaker activity has been found. Monknewtown is especially important as the Beaker people constructed a large earthwork there. Within the cemetery there is evidence for three further similar enclosures, two near Newgrange and the other at Dowth (C. O'Kelly 1978, Sites A, P and Q). In the Fourknocks region there are two (Hartnett 1957, 264–5, Nos 8–9), possibly three, banked enclosures. There are other scattered examples in the Meath area (information from Mr Leo Swan and Ms Geraldine Thornton, see Ó Ríordáin and de Valera 1979, 158–60). If further research establishes that these sites were erected by people who used Beaker pottery it would seem that there was intensive settlement in Meath, especially in the passage tomb heartlands. The question then arises whether this can be attributed to local spontaneous development or to cultural replacement. As yet we do not know enough about passage-tomb builders in their late phase. The Townleyhall evidence indicates that Sandhill ware was adopted there but on C14 dating this was in the first half of the third millennium B.C. (4680 ± 150 B.P.; *c.* 2730 b.c.; B.M.170). Subsequently a passage tomb was constructed on the site. Because these are no other passage-tomb elements, the Carrowkeel bowl from Burial II at Monknewtown can best be interpreted as a survival.

Fine Beaker ware is an international style and, as there is no evidence that this originated in Ireland, it must have been introduced or based on external prototypes. Indeed, it seems to derive immediately from Britain. There are comparisons between Knowth and the 'Northern' British Beakers as defined by Clark (1970, 108–29, 153–75, also 19–20, 425). However, the Beaker pottery may have parallels closer to home. For instance, there was settlement by Beaker people in Anglesey, north Wales (Lynch 1970, 84–108). The coastal sites, including a possible settlement at Newborough Warren, had sherds with cardium shell impressions, for instance, which can be compared to some of the Knowth sherds (2142–45). Anglesey and neighbouring Carnarvonshire have henges; Houlder (1968) excavated two at Llandegai. There the single entrance henge had a circle of pits containing cremations. The double entrance henge had a multiple cremation burial outside the southern entrance. There was another cremation burial in the centre. In the south-west of this site were three beakers in pits but no evidence for associated burial (Houlder 1968). Wales also has other types of enclosures – stone circles and what Grimes (1963) has termed 'embanked stone circles' and 'embanked earth circles'. These two groups usually have no ditch and at Meini-gwyr, Carmarthenshire, excavation has established that the material used in the bank was scraped up from the surface (Grimes 1963, No. 30). Unfortunately knowledge of the chronology or material content of these embanked monuments is limited but morphologically they offer comparisons for the Meath enclosures, or plain embanked circles, and the Grange (Lough Gur) embanked stone circle. At least it is relevant to note the presence of various types of enclosure on the eastern side of the Irish Sea, some of which have cremation burials and also Beaker pottery. Anglesey is of further interest, for at Bryn Celli Ddu there is evidence for contact between passage-tomb builders and enclosure or circle (henge) builders (Hemp 1930; Lynch 1970, 68; C. O'Kelly 1969). The passage tomb was built on top of a henge which in the words of Frances Lynch 'was deliberately destroyed by adherents of the older tomb-building religion'. This event was probably not only a clash of creeds but a clash of cultures as well, in effect a forceful re-assertion by the older passage-tomb builders over the newer circle (henge) builders. However, the triumph was temporary and Bryn Celli Ddu became the swan song of the passage-tomb builders. At Brugh na Bóinne at least one embanked circle forms part of the Beaker complex. Therefore, one can speculate that a complex was introduced from Britain.

In Orkney off northern Scotland enclosures (henges) concentrated close to the prominent passage-tomb of Maes Howe. The ditch encircling that site (Childe 1954–55; Renfrew 1979, 31–8) could be part of a subsequent henge although Renfrew suggests that both tomb and ditch were contemporary and there are important henges nearby at Bookan, Brodigar and Stennis (Ritchie 1975–6, Fig. 1; Renfrew 1979, esp. pp 39–43). The remarkable alignments with stone enclosures at the end at Carnac (Giot 1960, 122) and the stone circles at Er Lannic (Burl 1976, 130–6, Figs 19–21) in Brittany suggest that something similar happened there.

Stratigraphical evidence shows that Concentrations A and D postdate passage tombs 15 and 1 respectively. Charcoal from the dark layer of Concentration A has a C14 determination 3118 ± 48 B.P. (*c.* 1168 b.c.; B.M. 1077). A spread of charcoal between kerbstones 16 and 17 of Site 2 in which two sherds of Beaker pottery were lying (3744, 3759) gave a date of 3185 ± 255 B.P. (*c.* 1235 b.c.; B.M. 786). Both samples must have been contaminated as it is unlikely that Beaker was flourishing into the second half of the second millennium B.C. However, clay moulds, late second to early first millennium B.C.

were found at Sites D and F, Knockadoon. Ó Ríordáin (1954, 420) considered that there was a 'tendency for Class II pottery to occur with the moulds' at Site F. But the pottery was confined to or close to the house, whereas the moulds were scattered. At Site D the moulds were found grouped together at a high level. The evidence does not appear to be sufficient to say unequivocally that Class II was associated with the moulds.

At Monknewtown several C14 determinations have been procured from Beaker material but these vary considerably; 3810 ± 45 B.P. = 1860 b.c.; 2445 ± 40 b.c.; 2495 ± 70 =545 b.c.; 1130 ± 70 = a.d. 820; 4750 ± 65 = 2800 b.c.; 2440 ± 65 = 490 b.c.; 3465 ± 80 = 1515 b.c. (U.B. 728–734); (Smith, Pearson and Pilcher 1974, 269–76).

For Newgrange there are three dates: 3885 ± 35 B.P., 1935 b.c. (Gr.N.-6342); 3990 ± 40 B.P., *c.*2040 b.c. (GrN.-6343) and 4050 ± 40 B.P., *c.*2100 b.c. (Gr.N.-6344) (O'Kelly 1972). At Ballynagilly, Co. Tyrone, there are dates from three separate sites within the area of the Beaker settlement. These are 3905 ± 120 B.P., *c.*1955 b.c. (U.B. 200); 3850 ± 55 B.P. *c.*1900 b.c. (U.B. 309); 3960 ± 75 B.P., *c.*2010 b.c. (U.B. 316) and $3905 + 75$ B.P., 1955 b.c. (U.B. 356) (Smith *et al* 1971, 105–8).

The Newgrange and Ballynagilly dates and some from Monknewtown centre around 2000 b.c. It was probably also about then that Beaker people were living at Knowth.

The Knowth settlements are part of the Beaker complex of the Boyne valley whose establishment marks a new phase in Irish prehistory. The external background appears to be provided by the circle and enclosure builders of Britain. The Boyne Valley Beaker settlements were in an area that had been cleared and cultivated by passage-tomb builders over many centuries. In some regions Beaker people were incipient metal-workers (Case 1966) and copper ores occur a few miles up the Boyne valley at Beaupark and Brownstown (Clark 1952, 188). But all the earthwork evidence hints that the main areas of occupation were within the area of passage-tomb cemeteries at Brugh na Bóinne and at Fourknocks. This suggests that the passage tombs were the focus. These, of course, were important religious centres but they also reflect a rich and prolific society. The state of this society in immediate pre-Beaker times is hard to gauge. At both Knowth and Newgrange slip had come down from the large mounds but slip is not necessarily evidence for abandonment. The virtual absence of mixed assemblages, such as a fair number of tomb artifacts on the Beaker sites, could mean that the passage-tomb culture had ceased to exist but it is also possible that the absence is due to a rapid replacement of the passage-tomb culture. The Beaker settlements were in a known area of wealth. Cattle rearing was a vital part of their economy; at some sites they lived in fairly substantial structures while the building of the huge embanked circles indicates labour-intensive operations. Its duration is not known but there is evidence for bowl Food Vessel people in the Meath area, for instance, at the Mound of the Hostages, Tara (unpublished), and Keenoge (unpublished, see Raftery 1951, Pl. 10; cf. Ó Ríordáin 1968). These, and the later Urn people, may have been the successors of the Beaker complex.

Appendix one

MISCELLANEOUS FEATURES

Fireplace and pebbling (Fig. 119 bottom; Pl. 79b)

This lies 1m south of kerbstones 56 and 57 of Site 1. The pebbling consists of small stones, 2cm–4cm in diameter, packed into the old ground surface which is boulder clay. It appears originally to have covered an area approximately 5.8m by 4m. Only a few isolated patches remain. The fire-reddened base of the fireplace is 1.2m south-west of the centre of the pebbling. This measures 76cm by 44cm. It lies on the same level as the surviving pebbling, directly on the old ground surface. The pebbling was covered with a layer of natural sod. This was not recorded over the nearby Beaker Concentration B therefore the pebbling would appear to predate it.

No finds were associated with either the pebbling or the fireplace.

Curved trench (Fig. 119 top)

This has a U-shaped cross-section, it averages 35cm in width at the mouth and is cut into the natural earth. It is shallower at the northern end, *c.*15cm deep, but its depth increases to 23cm at the southern end. The shallowness towards the northern end is probably due to subsequent cultivation. The arc is 12m long; there is no evidence that it is part of a circle. However, there are later drains along the eastern side and in addition some of the original surface of the soil may have been removed.

At one point there was a spread of dark sticky earth perhaps due to domestic activity, 3.35m by 2.6m lying directly on the old ground surface. It contained five sherds of Beaker pottery and five flints. As these finds were not certainly associated with the structure, the pottery is described under isolated finds of Beaker pottery (p. 305, Nos 3739–3743, Fig. 116). The flints will be described with other isolated finds of flints in a subsequent volume.

Clear-cut evidence for the date and use of this feature is not available. It resembles the trench of the sub-rectangular structure (p. 211). The sticky dark layer cannot be associated with, or indeed disassociated from, the trench. The pottery sherds are not well preserved but seem to belong to the family of Beaker wares rather than to the Neolithic. They might represent a scatter from the nearby Concentration C area of Beaker activity (p. 270).

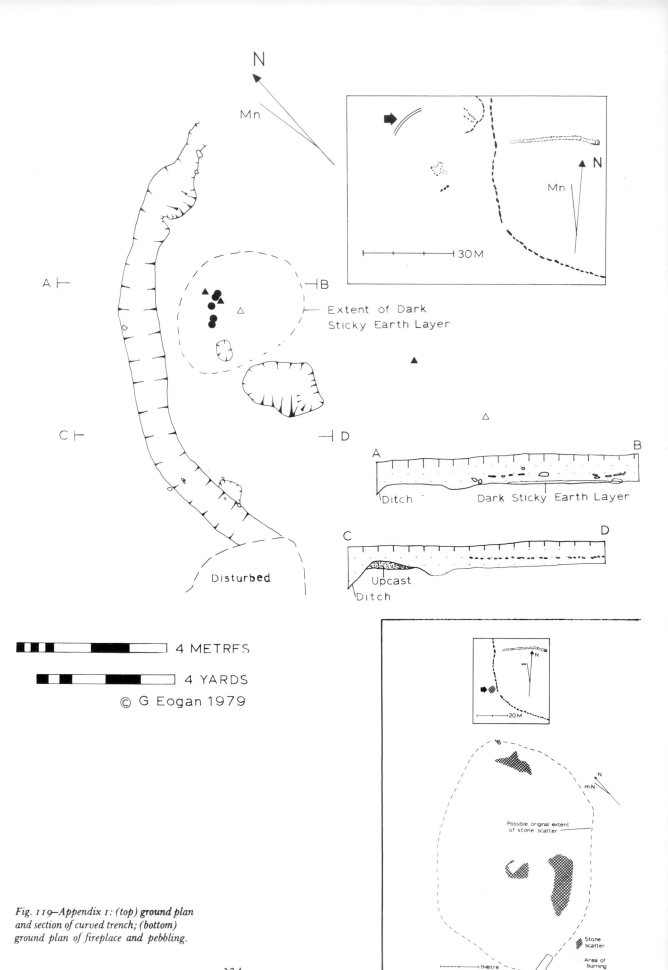

N

Mn

N

Mn

30 M

A ⊢

⊣ B

Extent of Dark
Sticky Earth Layer

C ⊢

⊣ D

A   B

Ditch   Dark Sticky Earth Layer

C   D

Upcast
Ditch

Disturbed

4 METRES

4 YARDS

© G Eogan 1979

N

MN

20 M

N

mN

Possible original extent
of stone scatter

Stone
scatter

Area of
burning

1 Metre

Fig. 119–Appendix 1: (top) **ground plan**
and section of curved trench; (bottom)
ground plan of fireplace **and** *pebbling.*

324

POLLEN AND SEED ANALYSES

W. Groenman-van Waateringe
Albert Egges van Giffen Instituut voor Prae- en Protohistorie (IPP),
University of Amsterdam[1]

During the excavation campaign at Knowth Dr Eogan and I took soil samples for pollen and seed analyses whenever it seemed necessary and promising. The results were rather meagre, largely because of the corrosion of much of the pollen. The samples therefore give only a rough picture of the vegetation and the impact of man on it. The results were as follows:

L 1965–51
Site 1. Sample taken from possibly natural sod layer from section in cutting/extension of Sites 13 and 14.
Pollen analysis demonstrated the presence of the following:
Pinus (pine) 2; *Betula* (birch) 5; *Ulmus* (elm) 2; *Quercus* (oak) 9; *Alnus* (alder) 31; *Corylus* (hazel) 15; *Gramineae* (grass family) 81; *Cerealia* (cereals) 1; *Cyperaceae* (sedge family) 2; *Plantago lanceolata* (ribwort plantain) 1; *Plantago maior/media* (great or hoary plantain) type 1; *Compositae liguliflorae* 5; *Compositae tubuliflorae* 1; *Ranunculaceae* 2; *Labiatae* (mint family) 2; *Caryophyllaceae*, 7; *Umbelliferae*, (parsley family) 1; *Campanulaceae* 1; *Polypodium* 4. (Total number of pollen grains in sample — 173.)

P 1970–11
Site 1. Sample taken from possibly natural sod layer from section between cuttings 29 and 30.
Pollen analysis demonstrated the presence of the following:
Pinus (pine) 2; *Ulmus* (elm) 1; *Quercus* (oak) 1; *Alnus* (alder) 9; *Corylus* (hazel) 15; *Gramineae* (grass family) 6; *Plantago lanceolata* (ribwort plantain) 4; *Compositae liguliflorae* 1; *Compositae tubuliflorae* 1; *Ericaceae* (heath family) 1; *Dryopteris* (shield fern) 2; *Polypodium* 1. (Total number of pollen grains in sample — 44).

P 1970–12
Site 1. Sample taken from possibly natural sod layer from section between cuttings 29 and 30.
Pollen analysis demonstrated the presence of the following:
Alnus (alder) 2; *Corylus* (hazel) 2; *Gramineae* (grass family) 20; *Plantago lanceolata* (ribwort plantain) 1; *Compositae liguliflorae* 2; *Dryopteris* (shield fern) 1; *Polypodium* 2. (Total number of pollen grains in sample — 30.)

[1] Pollen samples were prepared by J. Hilhorst, then of IPP. Seed samples were prepared and sorted by E. van Hoorn-van Benkel and seed identification by J. P. Pals, both of IPP

N 1966–30, 31

Site 1. Old ground surface and natural sod samples taken from the north face of cutting 13.

Too few pollen grains could be counted to permit a reliable interpretation.

In view of the presence of *Plantago maior/media* (great or hoary plantain) type, *Cerealia* (cereals) (not quite certain) and rather high values for *Poaceae,* influence by man is possible.

Z 1973–157

Site 3. Sample taken from mound material. Seed analysis showed the presence of *Ranunculus repens* (creeping buttercup).

L 1965–55

Site 14. Sample from old ground surface, cutting/extension of Site 14.

Pollen analysis demonstrated the presence of the following:
Pinus (pine) 3; *Betula* (birch) 4; *Ulmus* (elm) 5; *Quercus* (oak) 40; *Alnus* (alder) 37; *Corylus* (hazel) 59; *Hedera* (ivy) 1; *Gramineae* (grass family) 173; *Cyperaceae* (sedge family) 5; *Chenopodiaceae* (beet family) 1; *Rumex-a* (sorrel) type 4; *Plantago lanceolata* (ribwort plantain) 6; *Plantago maior/media* (great or hoary plantain) type 3; *Compositae liguliflorae* 3; *Compositae tubuliflorae* 3; *Pteridium* (bracken) 3; *Ranunculaceae* (crowfoot family) 6; *Labiatae* (mint family) 1; *Caryophyllaceae* 11; *Cruciferae* 2; *Papilionaceae* 3; *Umbelliferae* (parsley family) 2; *Galium* (bedstraw) type 1; *Dryopteris* (shield fern) 5; *Polypodium* 2. (Total number of pollen grains in sample — 383.)

P 1974–101

Site 15. Sample taken from area 7, square 44, from an area centred on a point 2.00m from north edge of square and 3.50m from the west edge, at a depth of 0.95m. This sample, *possibly natural sod,* was taken from a layer of similar material that overlies the boulder clay. The layer from which the sample was taken was in turn overlain by the mound of Site 15. Grass roots and earth worms had penetrated to the layer from which the sample was taken.

Pollen analysis demonstrated the presence of the following:
Betula (birch) 1; *Quercus* (oak) 4; *Alnus* (alder) 10; *Corylus* (hazel) 10; *Hedera* (ivy) 1; *Gramineae* (grass family) 35; *Plantago lanceolota* (ribwort plantain) 5; *Compositae liguliflorae* 5; *Compositae tubuliflorae* 4; *Pteridium* (bracken) 1; *Caryophyllaceae* 1; *Ericaceae* (heath family) 1; *Galium* (bedstraw) 1; *Lythrum* 1; *Dryopteris* (shield fern) 1; *Polypodium* 2. (Total number of pollen grains in sample — 83.)

P 1973–162.   Z 1973–162

Site 15. Sample taken from the mound material of Site 15.

Pollen analysis demonstrated the presence of the following:
Pinus (pine) 3; *Betula* (birch) 1; *Quercus* (oak) 6; *Alnus* (alder) 2; *Corylus* (hazel) 12; *Hedera* (ivy) 1; *Gramineae* (grass family) 44; *Cerealia* (cereals) 3; *Triticum* (wheat) type 1; *Cyperaceae* (sedge family) 3; *Chenopodiaceae* (beet family) 1; *Rumex-a* (sorrel) type 1; *Plantago lanceolata* (ribwort plantain) 10; *Plantago maior/media* (great or hoary plantain) type 1; *Compositae liguliflorae* 15; *Compositae tubuliflorae* 5; *Pteridium* (bracken)

7; *Ranunculaceae,* (buttercup family) 2; *Labiatae,* (mint family) 2; *Caryophyllaceae* 2; *Cruciferae* 2; *Umbelliferae* (parsley family) 1; *Ericaceae* (heath family) 1; *Lythrum* 2; *Dryopteris* (shield fern) 1; *Polypodium* 4. (Total number of pollen grains in sample — 133.)

Seed analysis showed the following to be present:
Rubus (bramble) 2; *Anagallis arvensis* (scarlet pimpernel) 1; *Cenococcus geophilum* (a fungus) 1.

Z 1973–159.

Site 17. Sample collected from the dark layer below the mound material of Site 17.

Seed analysis showed 2 *Cerealia* (cereals) of indeterminate type to be present.

Z 1973–160

Site 17. Sample collected from the dark layer below the mound material of Site 17, area 4, square 50.

Seed analysis showed 4 fragments of *Cerealia* (cereals), one of which is probably a *Triticum aestivum* (bread wheat).

Pollen analysis of the samples from the Beaker habitation layers gave no results whatsoever. However, seed analysis of the samples gave the following results:

Z 1973–163

Beaker Concentration A. Sample taken from area 4, square 22 from an area centred on a point 00m from the north edge of the square (i.e. junction with square 23) and 2m from the west edge at a depth of 1.10m. It was collected from the layer of soft dark earth with charcoal flecks and small stones which contained Beaker pottery. *Vicia* (vetch) spec. 2; *Rumex* (dock) spec. 2; *Cerealia* (cereals) indet. 1; 2 fragments of *Prunus spinosa* (sloe) and one fresh indeterminate seed, a recent intrusion?

Z 1973–164

Beaker Concentration A. Sample taken from area 4, square 23 from an area centred on a point 4m from north edge of square (i.e. junction with square 24) and 3m from the west edge, at a depth of 1.15m. Collected from the layer of soft dark earth with charcoal flecks and small stones which contained Beaker pottery. *Rumex* (dock) spec. 1; *Hordeum nudum* (naked barley) 1.

Z 1973–165

Beaker Concentration A. From area 4, square 15. Sample collected from the same layer as above (Z 1973–164) at a depth of 1.20m. *Corylus avellana* (hazel) 1.

Z 1974–107

Beaker Concentration A, area 4, square 36. Sample collected from an area centred on a point 3.60m from the north edge of the square and 0.30m from the west edge. From layer of soft dark earth with charcoal flecks and small stones which contained Beaker pottery. *Cerealia* (cereals) 5 fragments; *Chenopodium* (goosefoot) spec. 1; *Poa annua* 1 fresh example, a recent intrusion?

A sample of the yellow layer sealing the Beaker Concentration A was also examined:

P 1974–105   Z 1974–105

Area 4, square 36. Sample collected from an area centred on a point 3.80m from the north edge of the square and 3m from the west edge, at a depth of 0.95m. The sample was taken from an extensive layer of yellow clay which seals the layer of soft dark earth with charcoal flecks and small stones containing Beaker pottery. It may be redeposited mound material from Site 15.

Pollen analysis demonstrated the presence of the following:
Pinus (pine) 1; *Betula* (birch) 3; *Ulmus* (elm) 1; *Quercus* (oak) 19; *Alnus* (alder) 14; *Corylus* (hazel) 22; *Gramineae* (grass family) 103; *Cerealia* (cereals) 1; *Triticum* (wheat) type 3; *Artemisia* (mugwort) 2; *Chenopodiaceae* (beet family) 6; *Plantago lanceolata* (ribwort plantain) 26; *Plantago maior/media* (great or hoary plantain) type 1; *Compositae liguliflorae* 39; *Compositae tubuliflorae* 7; *Pteridium* (bracken) 3; *Ranunculaceae* (crowfoot family) 2; *Labiatae* (mint family) 3; *Caryophyllaceae* 7; *Cruciferae* 4; *Umbelliferae* (parsley family) 1; *Rosaceae* 1; *Lycopodium* (clubmoss) 1; *Dryopteris* (shield fern) 4; *Polypodium* 3; *Sphagnum* 1. (Total number of pollen grains in sample — 278.)

Seed analysis showed the following to be present:
Rumex (dock) spec. 4; *Chenopodium* (goosefoot) spec. 2; *Cerealia* (cereals) 18 badly preserved, probably *Hordeum* (barley).

The landscape must have been opened up considerably by man at the time that the sites from which the samples were taken were constructed. This is indicated by the large variety and high numbers of herbs. What remains of the former woods must have been composed mainly of *Quercus* (oak) and *Ulmus* (elm) on higher ground, flanked by *Corylus* (hazel) and *Betula* (birch) with *Alnus* (alder) in the river valley. Possibly the only real forest vegetation was to be found in the river valley.

There does not appear to be much change in vegetation composition from the Neolithic onwards. The amount of arboreal pollen is too small to be reliable so a slight change in the forest vegetation would not show here. With the presence of both *Cerealia* (cereals) pollen and seeds local corn growing has been firmly established at Knowth from the Neolithic onwards. The other results from the seed analysis are too meagre to give any idea of the kind of vegetation we are dealing with. The few seeds found do fit into the general picture we have about the vegetation, as they belong either to arable or to pasture land. It is understandable that when in Neolithic times most of the forest was cut down and replaced by tillage and pasture there would be no appreciable change in the overall picture.

Sample Nos	Site 1			Site 14		Site 15	
	L1965–51	P1970–11	P1970–12	L1965–55	P1974–101	P1973–162	P1974–105
Pinus	2	2	—	3	—	3	1
Betula	5	—	—	4	1	1	3
Ulmus	2	1	—	5	—	—	1
Quercus	9	1	—	40	4	6	19
Alnus	31	9	2	37	10	2	14
Corylus	15	15	2	59	10	12	22
Hedera	—	—	—	1	1	1	—
Gramineae	81	6	20	173	35	44	103
Cerealia 40mu	1	—	—	—	—	3	1
Triticum type	—	—	—	—	—	1	1
Cyperaceae	2	—	—	5	—	3	—
Artemisia	—	—	—	—	—	—	2
Chenopodiaceae	—	—	—	1	—	1	6
Rumex-a type	—	—	—	4	—	1	—
Plantago lanc.	1	4	1	6	5	10	26
Plantago maior/ media type	1	—	—	3	—	1	1
Compositae lig.	5	1	2	3	5	15	39
Compositae tub.	1	1	—	3	4	5	7
Pteridium	—	—	—	3	1	7	3
Ranunculaceae	2	—	—	6	—	2	2
Labiatae	2	—	—	1	—	2	3
Caryophyllaceae	7	—	—	11	1	2	7
Cruciferae	—	—	—	2	—	2	4
Papilionaceae	—	—	—	3	—	—	—
Umbelliferae	1	—	—	2	—	1	1
Campanulaceae	1	—	—	—	—	—	—
Rosaceae	—	—	—	—	—	—	1
Ericaceae	—	1	—	—	1	1	—
Galium type	—	—	—	1	1	—	—
Lythrum	—	—	—	—	1	2	—
Lycopodium	—	—	—	—	—	—	1
Dryopteris	—	2	1	5	1	1	4
Polypodium	4	1	2	2	2	4	3
Sphagnum	—	—	—	—	—	—	1

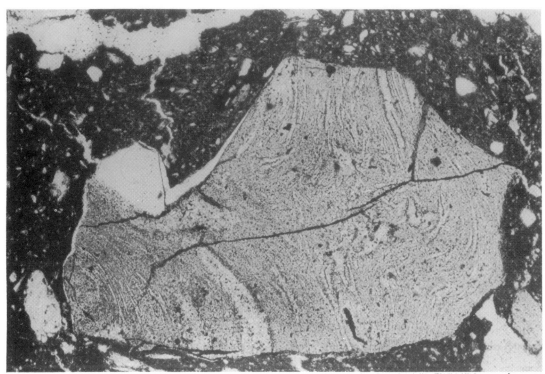

Pl. 82a–Sherd E70:1598, Knowth: large irregular fragment of porphyritic quartz felsite, attributed to south part of Slieve Gullion Ring Dyke. Flow banding and, at upper left margin, a quartz phenocryst are clearly seen. (O.L.)

Pl. 82b–Sherd E70:1356, Knowth: large grit fragments composed of coarse-grained, sutured quartz (vein quartz), slightly strained, with sharply angular small fragments of the same material. (X.Pol.)

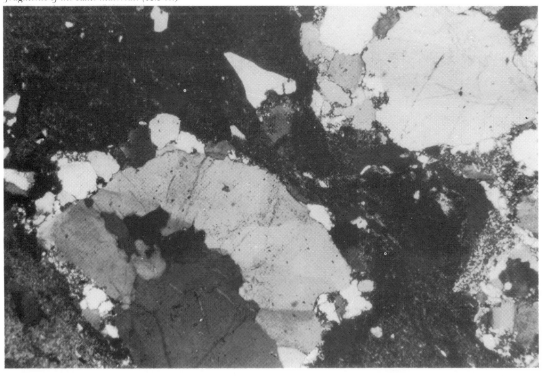

PETROLOGICAL EXAMINATION OF BEAKER POTTERY FROM THE BOYNE VALLEY SITES

J. C. Brindley
Department of Geology, University College, Dublin.

Introduction

In connection with a study of Irish Beaker Pottery undertaken by Ms Anna Brindley (1977) thin sections of thirty-six Beaker-type sherds from the excavations at Knowth, Newgrange and Monknewtown were examined petrographically. Such study provides evidence concerning the nature of the clay used as raw material and particularly of the detritus which was usually added to it, in terms of its lithological character and origin. It also yields information on the techniques involved in producing the pottery but this, though of considerable interest, is strictly within the field of ceramics study and is not discussed here. For comparative purposes Beaker material from Dalkey Island, Co. Dublin, and from several Lough Gur sites in Co. Limerick was also sectioned.

Some technical aspects

Beaker pottery is hand formed, by coiling, and the individual whorls of clay from which the pot was built up are often recognisable in sherds. None of the thin sections described here shows this feature, perhaps because in most cases the sections were cut parallel to the maximum curvature of the sherd and would thus lie in line with the base of the pot.

Air-bubbles are generally present (Pl. 86a), having been introduced into the clay during kneading. They appear as open cavities, often of irregular form and sometimes not easily distinguishable from holes left by rock fragments which have fallen out of the section, but usually they have become distorted by kneading and take on elongate forms, generally parallel to one another, and in line with the general fabric of the clay. This tends to be parallel to the surfaces of the sherd, but may wind around large pieces of grit or grog.

A *fabric* or aligned texture is invariably present in the fired clay. It results in part from the flattening of aligned air bubbles and in part from the parallel orientation of inequidimensional grains — mineral or rock fragments — in the clay. During firing, too, there is a general development of tiny scales of micaceous minerals through the mass of the clay. These minute crystals lie parallel to the textures produced by kneading the material, and produce a fabric which can be distinguished under polarised light. It is significant in distinguishing grog particles from the similar matrix in which they are embedded (Pl. 83a).

Appendix three

Petrographical examination

Thin sections were produced in the normal way from well-fired sherds, though it was found necessary to impregnate the more friable material, before cutting, with Lakeside 70. Sherds without additives, or to which grog alone had been added, showed a tendency to warp and much difficulty was encountered during grinding. It was not, in fact, found possible to produce good quality sections of such materials.

Extraneous material is usually added to the pottery clay to give it body and also to reduce the degree of plasticity and shrinkage on drying. In the coarse ware the largest fragments range up to almost 1cm in maximum dimension. This added material is either grog or rock detritus. In the fine ware, smaller particles of the additive are commonly single mineral grains, and rock fragments are few and confined to fine-grained types.

Pl. 83a–Sherd E 70:2558, Knowth: large fragments of grog in matrix with angular particles of clear quartz. (O.L.)

Grog consists of broken-up pottery fragments, and, since they are often identical with the enclosing matrix, they may be quite inconspicuous. However, since the fabric in each grog particle is clearly at variance with its surroundings (Pl. 83a) they are distinctly recognisable under polarised light. *Grit* is present either as coarse rock fragments or as mineral particles of fine sand grade. It is composed entirely of crushed fragments with sharply angular outlines which have suffered no subsequent abrasions (Pl. 86a). The only exceptions to this are some elastic grains from sandstones which have disintegrated so as to retain their primary character (e.g. the frequent millet-seed grains). In many cases the crushed grit aggregate particles show a seriate relationship so that fragments of all sizes throughout the range are present. Also, the material is often of a single rock type (e.g. Tertiary olivine-dolerite) of quite distinctive origin. Less commonly, the coarse and fine grits are of different character, and imply a mixture in the additives. Grog and fine mineral grit occur together in some sherds. Instances of grits of polymict composition are few. In almost all cases a single type of additive was crushed and added to the clay. Extraneous materials are in such limited quantities that, where present, it may be felt that they became incorporated in the clay accidentally. Since no worn sand grains were observed in the clay it is likely that the primary material of the pottery was a pure water-laid deposit.

Lithology of the grits

A few rock types dominate. *Ophitic olivine-dolerite* is the most distinctive rock type (Pls 87a and b). It occurs in sherds from all three localities, solely and mixed with other rock material. The material is beautifully fresh and in sharply angular grains. It is constant in composition, but with slight textural variations from medium to coarse dolerite and from ophitic to sub-ophitic in texture (Pls 85a and 87b). The rock is undoubtedly Tertiary olivine-dolerite, and the textural variations might occur in material from a single locality, though this is unlikely. It is a very widespread type in minor igneous intrusions throughout the northern half of Ireland, and is generally without particular traits associated with the individual occurrences. While it occurs in very small bodies as far south as Ardcath and Slane, the main bulk of these intrusions is in north-east Ireland. South of County Armagh it is most commonly found as glacially travelled, erratic boulders such as have contributed to the megalithic structures of Knowth.

Pl. 83b–Sherd E70:1412, Knowth: large fragment of recrystalised orthoquartzite with many fresh microcline grains. Matrix forms lower part of field. (X.Pol.)

Appendix three

Poryphyritic quartz-felsite is another most distinctive Tertiary igneous rock type which dominates the coarse aggregate in sherd E 70/1598 from Knowth (Pl. 82a). The porphyritic character and elaborate flow-banding are characteristic of the material which fills the south part of the Slieve Gullion Ring-dyke in the district around Forkhill, Co. Louth. It is not present in any other sections examined, though a variety of fine-grained acid igneous rocks are represented by small numbers of fragments among the grits of sandstone composition. Grains of a comparable nature have also been recognised in some of the sandstone fragments, and most likely they are Palaeozoic or older types. A distinctive fragment is the spherulitic felsite (Pl. 84b) from the stray sherd from Monknewtown.

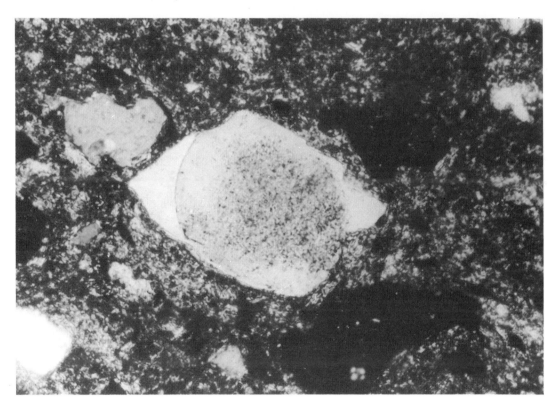

Pl. 84a–Sherd E90/65, Monknewtown: millet seed quartz grain, with quartz outgrowth. Grog is the coarse additive in this sherd. (X.Pol.)

Various quartz-sandstones (technically orthoquartzites) are strongly represented and are considered to derive from the *New Red Sandstone* of northern Ireland. This formation is confined to limited areas around the Antrim Plateau, to the Lagan valley and to the Kingscourt district. Its origin as a desert sand is manifest in the distinctive 'millet-seed' grains, which often have characteristic quartz outgrowths, and such isolated round grains, occasionally preserving traces of outgrowth (Pl. 85a), are recognisable in many of the sherds. The sandstone fragments are of various types — ferruginous sands with red iron oxides forming a matrix, sandstones with some clay material as matrix, and re-crystallised matrix-free, quartzitic sandstones. All of these show a variable degree of sorting according to grain size, and presence of fresh felspar among the sand grains (Pl. 83b) and the occasional presence of millet-seed grains. Consequently, it is believed that all of them correspond to sandstones from the New Red of northern Ireland.

Silurian greywacke is an impure quartzose sandstone with considerable quantities of clay matrix now largely sericite and chlorite. This composition gives it a character resembling the fired clay of the sherds, or pieces of grog, but the common presence of a well-marked cleavage structure distinguishes the fragments of this rock (Pl. 85b). It forms the uplands terrain of the Cavan-Down region extending to the Boyne Valley at Slane and most of the orthostats identified at Knowth are of this rock. Surprisingly, then, greywacke fragments are few and uncommon in the sherds to the extent that their occurrence may be regarded as accidental and a selective control was very clearly involved in the choice of grit materials.

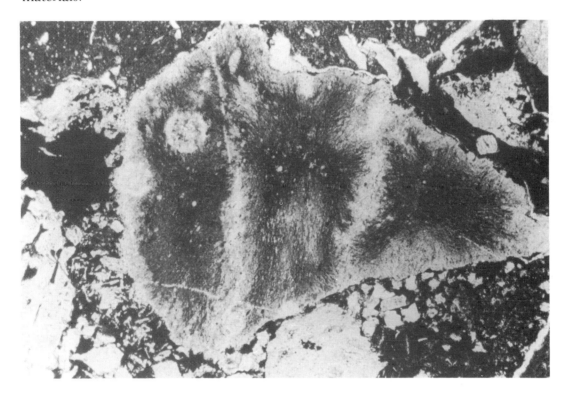

Calcareous sandstone types and calcite or limestone are referable to the Carboniferous Limestone, the rock formation on which the Boyne Valley megaliths are sited. Glacial boulders of these rocks constitute some of the Knowth orthostats, and it is perhaps from such material that the grits come, since sand limestones, though common in erratics from the north or from the Irish Sea area, do not occur in the Boyne Valley. The types are recognised in only two sherds (Pl. 88a), each from Newgrange, in neither of which they dominate.

Coarse *vein quartz,* in sutured very large-grained aggregates, is quite distinctive from other quartzose material in the coarse grits. The material shows various strain characters (Pl. 82b) and is associated with lesser amounts of fresh felspars and muscovite. Quartz veins or pegmatite veins, occurring in granitic or metamorphic terrain, are evidently the sources. While the material is not geographically distinctive the Newry Granite (Down-Armagh),

Pl. 84b–Sherd E 90/461A, Monknewtown: large fragment of spherulitic felsite as coarse grit particles. (O.L.)

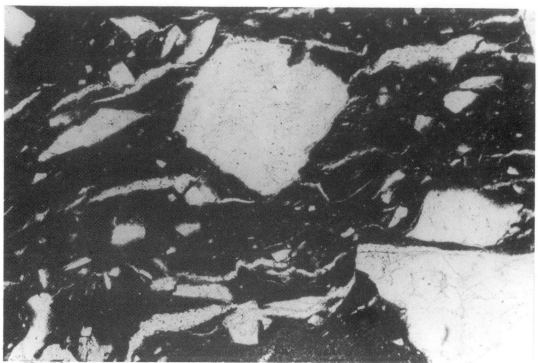

Pl. 85a–Sherd 111, Monknewtown: part of large fragment of ophitic olivine dolerite in upper part of field; angular grit including crushed quartz in matrix at lower part. (O.L.)

Pl. 85b–Stray sherd, Monknewtown: dark clay matrix with elongate air bubbles and small angular quartz grit; large fragment of cleaved greywacke (Silurian) at right of field. Grog fragments also present. (O.L.)

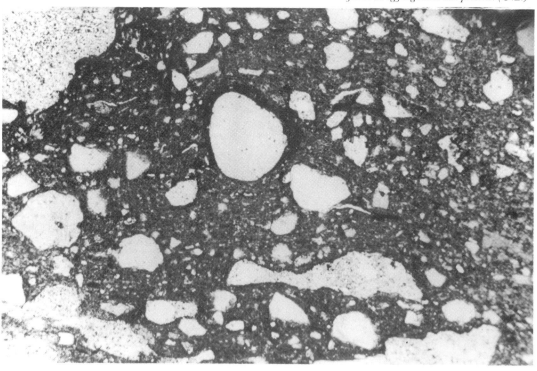

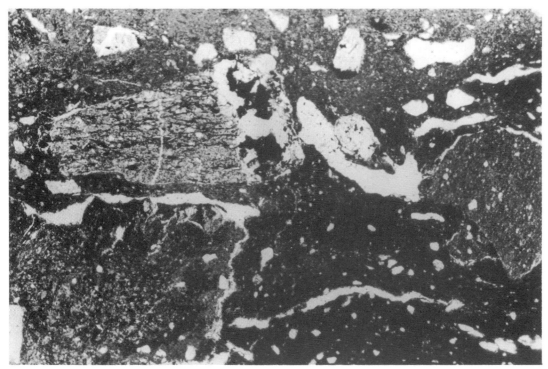

Pl. 86a–Sherd E 90/461A, Monknewtown:
seriate aggregate of crushed vein quartz
fragments, some splinter-like. Long
flattened air bubbles also contribute to
clearly defined alignment. (O.L.)

Pl. 86b–Sherd E 90/67, Monknewtown:
fine grit from a crushed sandstone; millet
seed grain near to centre of field; some air
bubbles. (O.L.)

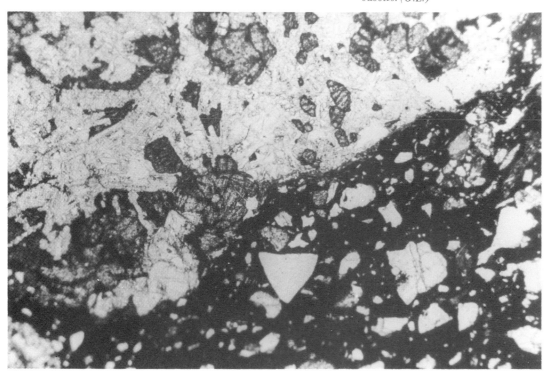

the Mournes, or perhaps the granites of south Tyrone are possible areas of origin, as, indeed, is the Leinster Granite.

Diorite, granite, acid and basic lavas, and metamorphic quartzite were recognised in rare grains as very minor constituents of the grits. They are clearly of little significance and in any case it is not possible to allocate them to specific areas.

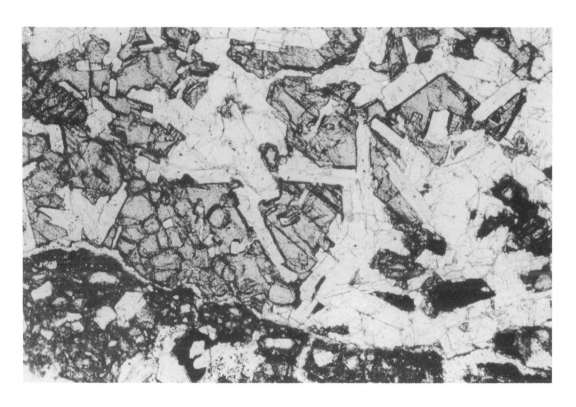

Pl. 87a–Sherd E 56/170, Newgrange: large fragment of ophitic olivine-dolerite occupies most of field; clay with small fragments of dolerite minerals in matrix at lower part. (O.L.)

The Knowth grits

Among the nineteen sections examined eight (see Tables 1 and 2) are dominated by grog and two others contain it in minor amounts. The latter carry in addition a fine grit of sandstone particles and quartz grains both of which probably derive from the same rock source. Two sections (K 76/216 and K 76/703) have some detritus of olivine-dolerite in addition. The second section shows the crushed quartz and dolerite fully intermixed as well as a few greywacke fragments which are probably accidental incorporations.

Four slides have Tertiary olivine dolerite as dominant grit, though two of these have coarse sandstone fragments in addition. Sherd E 70/1598 is distinctive in that the grit contains appreciable amounts of Slieve Gullion porphyritic felsite, associated with the common (?New Red) sandstone, and sherd E 70/1356 has this sandstone, and quartz derived from it, as the chief additive. Three sherds have distinctive vein quartz grit associated with felspar and muscovite.

Grits from Newgrange.

Five of the nine sections examined (see Table 3) are dominated by Tertiary olivine-dolerite. The grit ranges from coarse to fine in seriate manner and evidently represents simply crushed dolerite.

Occasional quartz grains and rarer greywacke fragments in three sherds have fine grit dominated by quartz grains, among which millet-seed shapes may be identified, and two (E 56/625and E 56/632) have sandy limestone and calcite in the grit which clearly emanated from the Lower Carboniferous, perhaps from glacial boulders.

Monknewtown grits.

Among the eight slides examined (Tables 4 and 5) there is only one (111) with grit dominantly of olivine-dolerite. Two (E 90/65 and E 90/339) have grog as the coarse additive with quartz sand showing millet-seed grains as a fine grit; the first sherd however, is essentially clay, with very little added rock material. Three sherds have sandstone grits — of types attributed to New Red Sandstone — with quartz grains derived from them as the fine material. The stray sherd is peculiar because clearly a very mixed aggregate of grog. Silurian greywacke, quartzite and diorite was added to the clay. Perhaps in this case the potter incorporated a local gravel of mixed composition, since no one source would explain the diversity.

Pl. 87b–Sherd E 126/97A, Newgrange: large sub-ophitic olivine dolerite grains in dense clay with elongate air bubbles and smaller dolerite fragments. (O.L.)

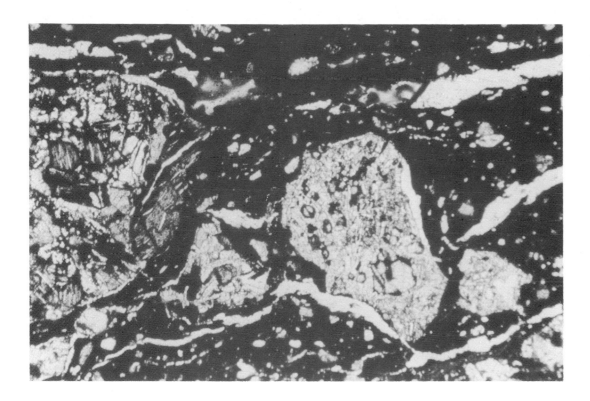

Other Beaker pottery.

Six sections of Beaker ware from the Dalkey Island site and eleven from the four Lough Gur sites — Grange Stone Circle, Megalith and sites C and D – were cut to obtain a picture of the composition of Beaker sherds from other parts of Ireland. In each case the materials were dominated by local rock types — Leinster Granite varieties at Dalkey, and Lower Carboniferous volcanics at Lough Gur — and no grits of exotic character were recognised. Fuller descriptions are not needed here.

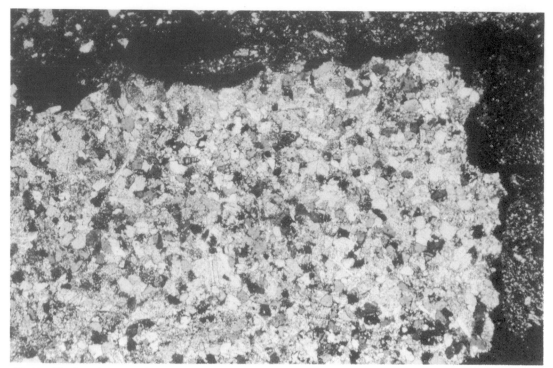

Pl. 88a–Sherd E 56/625, Newgrange:
large grit fragment of calcareous sandstone
(Lower Carboniferous?) in clay. (X.Pol.)

Pl. 88b–Sherd E 70/2121, Knowth: large
fragment of grog with well marked internal
alignment of grit particles and matrix, in
clay with many grit fragments showing
different orientation. (O.L.)

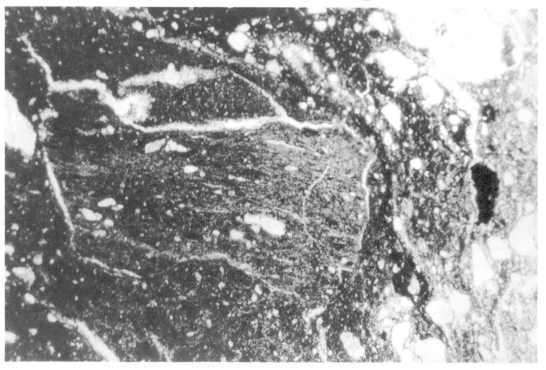

Discussion and conclusions

The basis of the Boyne area Beaker pottery was a uniform fine-grained clay without, it seems, any essential amount of sand grade or coarser material. Sherd E 56/153 from Newgrange is the sole example studied which is made of this material alone and sherds E 70/1611, E 70/1612, E 70/2790, E 90/65 and E 90/339 have no more than a slight admixture of fine grit. Apart from the different additives the pottery is remarkably uniform, though heavy coarse and lighter fine wares may be distinguished. Grog, or a natural grit, were commonly added in large amounts to modify the natural characters of the clay. This additive — existing pottery, rock, or perhaps gravel pebbles (the stray sherd from Monknewtown only) — was freshly crushed. Very large particles up to almost 1cm in maximum dimension constitute the coarse grit which is plentiful in the heavy, thick sherds. In light thin ware only fine grit of sand grade is present and this commonly comprises single mineral grains rather than rock particles.

Sometimes coarse and fine grits grade to one another in seriate fashion and the material is of one rock type only: in these cases a crushed rock was simply added to the clay. In other sherds grog fragments are present together with a fine quartz grit and the interpretation is that they were added independently. Examples are E 70/1611 and E 70/1612 from Knowth. In yet other cases coarse grits of one rock type are associated with fine grits of another: here the two fractions must again have been added separately.

The sherds are classified in five groups according to the composition of the additive, as follows:

Group 1, with grog as a coarse additive, occurs at all three sites, in eleven out of thirty-six sections.

Group 2, with Tertiary olivine-dolerite as grit, comprises ten sherds from the three sites.

Group 3, with the Slieve Gullion felsite, has only one representative from Knowth.

Group 4 grits are dominated by the various orthoquartzite sandstones attributed to the New Red Sandstone. Seven sherds in this group are spread over the three sites with only one from Knowth.

Group 5 has grits produced by crushing vein quartz and is the chief grit in three slides from Knowth.

Now, all of these grits are attributed to a northern source, either positively or with some degree of plausibility, but they would come, for the most part, from separate districts. Several of the sherds contain mixed grits as a result of which linkages occur among all the different groups. Groups 2 and 4 are associated in E 70/2757 which has some dolerite debris in the grit, most of which, however, is sandstone. Groups 1 and 4 are most commonly intermixed at all the sites since the grog usually has fine sand mixed with it. Groups 3 and 4 are clearly mixed in the sherd with felsite, and sherd E 70/1356 has some dolerite along with the vein quartz, thus uniting groups 2 and 5. The stray sherd from Monknewtown includes material from both groups 4 and 5. With this information it must be concluded that the pottery was manufactured at a site, or sites, where various of the rock types used were available together. The conclusion is also inevitable that the grit was not derived from rock outcrop but rather from a mixed drift or transported material, either littoral, fluviatile or glacial. The fact that such large quantities of rock were required would suggest that large glacial erratic boulders were used.

Unfortunately, knowledge of drift compositions is negligible. There is outline information on the lithology of the orthostats in several of the Knowth megalithic structures but none from Newgrange, and Monknewtown is not of stone construction. On this information it is possible that material from the Knowth orthostats, and perhaps those of Newgrange also, could have supplied the grits; but no more can be said.

Acknowledgements

Dr John Preston of the Queen's University Belfast was kind enough to confirm the identity of the northern Irish rocks. Mr Patrick O'Donoghue of the Geology Department, University College, Dublin carried out the photography.

Sincere thanks are also due to the late Professor M. J. O'Kelly and to Mr David Sweetman and the authorities of the National Museum of Ireland for making available for study material from Newgrange and Monknewtown and for agreeing to the publication of data in this Appendix.

References

BRINDLEY, ANNA 1977 A comparison of the finds from the Beaker levels at Knowth and Monknewtown. University College, Dublin. Unpublished thesis.

EOGAN, G. 1968 Excavations at Knowth, Co. Meath, 1962–1965. *Proc. R. Ir. Acad.* **66** C, 299–400.

EOGAN, G. 1974 Report on the excavations of some passage graves, unprotected inhumation burials, and a settlement site at Knowth, Co. Meath. *Proc. R. Ir. Acad.* **74** C, 11–112.

HODGES, H. W. M. 1963 The examination of ceramic materials in thin section. In Edward Pyddoke (ed.) *The scientist and archaeology*. London. Dent and Sons.

HULTHEN, B. 1975 *Technical investigations for evidence of continuity or discontinuity of ancient ceramic traditions*. Ghent.

SHEPARD, A. 1968 *Ceramics for the archaeologist*. Washington. Carnegie Institute.

Key to plates and tables

Plates are either ordinary light (O.L.) or with crossed polarisers (X.Pol.).

All magnifications are 50 times, except Pl. 84a which is magnified 250 times.

**Abundant, *common to occasional.

K — potash felspar	Palaeo — Palaeozoic
Pl — plagioclase felspar	Calc. sst. — Calcareous sandstone
Musc — muscovite	int. — intermediate
Qtzite — quartzite	C — coarse grit
Ferr — ferruginous	F — fine grit

Table 1—Additives (Knowth)

Sherd No.	Coarse grit	Fine grit	Grog
Concentration B			
E 70/1558	** seriate	**	
E 70/1611		*	**
E 70/1597		little	**
E 70/1598	**	**	
E 70/1612		*	**
Concentration C			
K 76/31		*	**
E 70/2757	some	*	**
E 70/2121	** seriate	*	*
E 70/2046		*	**
E 70/2153		**	*
E 70/2577	*	*	**
E 70/2790		*	**
E 70/1880		**	
Concentration A			
E 70/1309	** seriate	**	
E 70/1452	** seriate	**	
E 70/1356	**	**	
E 70/1412	**	*	
E 70/1383	**	*	
E 70/1458	** seriate	*	

Table 2—Lithology of the grits (Knowth)

Sherd No.		Dolerite	Felsite	Millet-seed grain	Sandstones	Other igneous	Minerals	Vein quartz, etc.
Concentration B								
E 70/1558	C	*						
	F	* *						
E 70/1611	C							
	F				*			*
E 70/1597	C							
	F							rare
E 70/1598	C		* *					* *
	F		*Sl. Gullion	*	*(millet)			
E 70/1612	C						*Pl	*
	F			*				
Concentration C								
K 76/31	C				*Qtzitic &			
	F			?	*Ferr			* *
E 70/2757	C	some						
	F			*	*Qtzitic		*Pl	*
E 70/2121	C							* *
	F		?				*Musc	* *
E 70/2046	C							
	F				*			*
E 70/2153	C				*Greywacke			
	F	*		*			*Pl	*
E 70/2517	C							* *
	F							* *
E 70/2790	C							
	F		rare Palaeo		*			*
E 70/1880	C							
	F		*Palaeo				*Pl *Musc	* *
Concentration A								
E 70/1309	C				* *			
	F				*		*Musc	* *
E 70/1452	C	* *			* rare			
	F	* *			*			
E 70/1356	C		rare		*			*
	F	*	Palaeo		*		Pl Musc	* *
E 70/1412	C	* *			Arkosic &			
	F				millet			*
E 70/1383	C				*		*Pl	*
	F							*
E 70/1458	C	* *						
	F	* *						

Table 3—Lithology of the grits (Newgrange)

Sherd No.		Dolerite	Felsite	Millet-seed grain	Sandstones	Other igneous	Minerals	Vein quartz, etc.
E 56/157	C		*Palaeo		*Greywacke			*
	F			?			*Pl	**
E 126/97A	C	**						
	F	**						*rare
E 126/97B	C	**						
	F	**						
E 56/170	C	**						
	F	**						*
E 56/172	C	**			*Greywacke			
	F	**						
E 56/153	C			Clay only — no additives				
	F							
E 56/625	C				*Qtzite —			*
	F				Calc.sst.			**
E 56/191	C	**			*Greywacke			
	F	**			?			
E 56/632	C							
	F		*Palaeo		*Qtzite		*Calcite	**

Table 4—Additives (Monknewtown)

Sherd No.	Coarse grit	Fine grit	Grog
E 90/67	** seriate	**	
E 90/65		*	**
111	**	*	
E 90/339	little	little	**
E 90/66	*	**	
E 90/360	** seriate	**	
E 90/461A	** seriate	**	
Stray sherd	*	*	*

Table 5—Lithology of the grits (Monknewtown)

Sherd No.		Dolerite	Felsite	Millet-seed grain	Sandstones	Other igneous	Minerals	Vein quartz, etc.
E 90/67	C				**			
	F	?		*	**			
E 90/65	C							
	F	?		*	*		*K *Pl	**
111	C	**						
	F	**		?				*
E 90/339	C							
	F		*Palaeo	*				*
E 90/66	C				*Ferr			
	F			*				**
E 90/360	C				*Qtzite			
	F			*				**
E 90/461A	C		*					**
	F							**
Stray Sherd	C		*Palaeo		*Qtzite & *greywacke	*Diorite, tuff & int. lava	*K	*
	F							*

BIBLIOGRAPHY

Abbreviations

Ant.	*Antiquity*
Ant.J.	*Antiquaries Journal*
Arch.	*Archaeologia*
JCHAS	*Journal of the Cork Historical and Archaeological Society*
JRSAI	*Journal of the Royal Society of Antiquaries of Ireland*
PPS	*Proceedings of the Prehistoric Society*
PRIA	*Proceedings of the Royal Irish Academy*
PSAS	*Proceedings of the Society of Antiquaries of Scotland*
TRIA	*Transactions of the Royal Irish Academy*
UJA	*Ulster Journal of Archaeology*

ALMAGRO GORBEA, MARIA JOSEFA 1973a *Los Idolos del Bronce I Hispano.* Madrid.

ALMAGRO GORBEA, MARIA JOSEFA 1973b *El Poblado y la Necropólis de El Barranquete (Almería)* (Acta Arqueologica Hispanica 6). Madrid.

ALMAGRO, M. and ARRIBAS, A. 1963 *El Poblado y la Necropólis Megalíticos de Los Millares.* Madrid.

ANDERSEN, N. H. 1975 Die Neolithische Befestigungsanlage im Sarup auf Fünen (Dänemark). *Archäologisches Korrespondenzblatt* **5,** 11–14.

ApSIMON, A. M. 1969 An Early Neolithic House in Co. Tyrone. *JRSAI* **99,** 165–8.

————— 1976 Ballynagilly and the beginning and end of the Irish Neolithic. In Sigfried J. de Laet (ed.) *Acculturation and continuity in Atlantic Europe mainly during the Neolithic period and Bronze Age* (Dissertationes Archaeologicae Gandenses). Brugge.

BAILLOUD, G. 1974 *Le Néolithique dans le bassin Parisien.* 2nd ed. Paris.

BORLASE, W. C. 1897 *Dolmens of Ireland* (3 vols). London.

BRADLEY, R. 1970 The excavation of a beaker settlement at Belle Tout, East Sussex. *PPS* **36** 312–79.

————— 1978 *The prehistoric settlement of Britain.* London.

BURL, A. 1976 *The stone circles of the British Isles.* London.

BURNEZ, C. 1976 *Le Néolithique et le Chalcolithique dans le centre-ouest de la France.* Mémoires de la Société Préhistorique Française, Tome 12. Paris.

CASE, H. J. 1961 Irish Neolithic pottery: distribution and sequence. *PPS* **27,** 174–233.

————— 1966 Were the Beaker–people the first metallurgists in Ireland? *Palaeohistoria* **12,** 141–77.

CHILDE, V. G. 1954–55 Maes Howe. *PSAS* **78,** 155–72

————— 1957 *The dawn of European civilization.* 6th ed. London.

CHILDE, V. G. and GRANT, W. G. 1938–39 A Stone Age settlement at the Braes of Rinyo, Ronsay, Orkney (First Report). *PSAS* **73,** 6–31.

CLARK, J. G. D.   1933   Report on an Early Bronze Age site in the south-eastern fens. *Ant. J.* **13**, 266–96.

———— 1952   *Prehistoric Europe: the economic basis.* London.

CLARKE, D. L.   1970   *Beaker pottery of Great Britain and Ireland* (2 vols). Cambridge.

COFFEY, G.   1892   On the tumuli and inscribed stones at Newgrange, Dowth and Knowth. *TRIA* **30** (1892–96), 1–96.

COFFEY, G.   1912   *New Grange and other incised tumuli in Ireland.* Dublin.

COLLINS, A.E.P. and WATERMAN, D. M.   1955   *Millin Bay* (Archaeological Research Publication No. 4). Belfast Stationery Office.

COLLINS, A. E. P. and WILSON, B. C. S.   1963   The Slieve Gullion cairns. *UJA* 3rd ser. **26**, 19–40.

CONWELL, E. A.   1873   *Discovery of the Tomb of Ollamh Fodhla.* Dublin.

CRAWFORD, O. G. S.   1955   The technique of the Boyne carvings. *PPS* **21**, 156–9.

DANIEL, G. E.   1950   *The prehistoric Chamber Tombs of England and Wales.* Cambridge.

DE VALERA, R.   1960   The Court Cairns of Ireland. *PRIA* **60**C, 9–140.

DE VALERA, R. and Ó NUALLÁIN, S.   1972   *Survey of the Megalithic Tombs of Ireland,* vol. 3. Dublin.

EOGAN, G.   1963   A Neolithic habitation–site and Megalithic Tomb in Townleyhall Townland, Co. Louth. *JRSAI* **93**, 37–81.

———— 1967   Knowth (Co. Meath) excavations. *Ant.* **41**, 302–4.

———— 1968   Excavations at Knowth, Co. Meath. *PRIA* **66**C, 299–382.

———— 1969   Excavations at Knowth, Co. Meath, 1968. *Ant.* **43**, 8–14.

———— 1974   Report on the excavations of some Passage Graves, unprotected inhumation burials and a settlement site at Knowth, Co. Meath. *PRIA* **74**C, 11–112.

———— 1976   Beaker material from Knowth. In C. Burgess and R. Miket (ed.) *Settlement and economy in the third and second millennia B.C.* (British Archaeological Reports 33), 251–66.

———— 1977   Two decorated stones from Knowth. *Ant.* **51**, 48–9.

EVANS, E. E.   1953   *Lyles Hill: A Late Neolithic site in County Antrim* (Archaeological Research Publications No. 2). Belfast. Stationery Office.

FLANAGAN, L. N. W.   1966   An unpublished flint hoard from the Braid Valley, Co. Antrim. *UJA* 3rd ser. **29**, 82–90.

FRAZER, W.   1893   Incised sculpturings on stones in the cairns of Sliabh-na-Caillighe, near Loughcrew, County Meath. *PSAS* **27** (1892–93), 294–340.

GIOT, P. R.   1960   *Brittany.* London.

———— 1971   The impact of radiocarbon dating on the establishment of the prehistoric chronology of Brittany. *PPS* **37**, II, 208–17.

GRIMES, W. F.   1963   The stone circles and related monuments of Wales. In I.Ll. Foster and L. Alcock (eds) *Culture and environment.* London. 93–152.

HARTNETT, P. J. 1954 Newgrange Passage Grave, Co. Meath. *JRSAI* **84,** 181–2.

———— 1957 Excavation of a Passage Grave at Fourknocks, Co. Meath. *PRIA* **58** C, 197–277.

———— 1971 The Excavation of two tumuli at Fourknocks (Sites II and III), Co. Meath. *PRIA* **71** C, 35–89.

HARTNETT, P. J. and EOGAN G. 1964 Feltrim Hill, Co. Dublin. *JRSAI* **94,** 1–37.

HAWKES, JACQUETTA 1941 Excavation of a Megalithic tomb at Harristown, Co. Waterford. *JRSAI* **71,** 130–47.

HEDGES, J. and BUCKLEY, D. 1978 Excavations at a Neolithic causewayed enclosure, Orset, Essex, 1975. *PPS* **44,** 219–308.

HEMP, W. J. 1930 The Chambered Cairn of Bryn Celli Ddu. *Arch.* **80,** 179–214.

HENCKEN, H. O'NEILL 1935 A Cairn at Poulawack, Co. Clare. *JRSAI* **65,** 191–222.

HENSHALL, AUDREY S. 1972 *The Chambered Tombs of Scotland,* vol. 2. Edinburgh.

HERITY, M. 1967 From Lhuyd to Coffey: new information from unpublished descriptions of the Boyne Valley tombs. *Studia Hibernica* **7,** 127–45.

———— 1974 *Irish Passage Graves.* Dublin.

HERITY, M. and EOGAN, G. 1977 *Ireland in Prehistory.* London.

HINGST, H. 1971 Ein befestigtes Dorf aus der Jungsteinzeit in Büdelsdorf (Holstein). *Archäologisches Korrespondenzblatt* **1,** 191–4.

HOULDER, C. 1968 The Henge monuments at Llandegai. *Ant.* **42,** 216–21.

HUNT, J. 1967 Prehistoric burials at Cahirguillamore, Co. Limerick. In Etienne Rynne (ed.) *North Munster Studies.* Limerick. 20–42.

JORGE, SUSANA OLIVEIRA 1978 O megalitismo no contexto neolítico peninsular. *Revista de Guimarães* **88,** 369–88.

LEISNER, G. and LEISNER, VERA 1943 *Die Megalithgräber der Iberischen Halbinsel: der Süden,* vol. 1. Berlin.

LEISNER, VERA 1965 *Die Megalithgräber der Iberischen Halbinsel: der Westen,* vol. 3. Berlin.

LEISNER, VERA and RIBEIRO, L. 1968 Die Dolmen von Carapito. *Madrider Mitteilungen* **9,** 11–62.

L'HELGOUACH, J. 1965 *Les Sépultures Mégalithiques en Armorique.* Rennes.

———— 1970 Le monument mégalithique du Goërem à Gâvres (Morbihan). *Gallia Préhistoire* **13,** 217–61.

L'HELGOUACH, J., BELLANCOURT, G., GALLAIS, C. and LECORNEC, J. 1970 Sculptures et gravures nouvellement découvertes sur des mégalithes de l'Armorique. *Bulletin Société Préhistorique Française* **67,** 513–21.

LIVERSAGE, G. D. 1968 Excavations at Dalkey Island, Co. Dublin. *PRIA* **66** C, 53–233.

LYNCH, FRANCES 1967 Barclodiad y Gawres — Comparative notes on the decorated stones. *Arch. Camb.* 116, 1–22.

———— 1970 *Prehistoric Anglesey.* Llangefni.

———— 1973. The use of the passage in certain Passage Graves as a means of communication rather than access. In Glyn Daniel and Paul Kjaerum (eds), *Megalithic graves and ritual.* Moesgård. Jutland Archaeological Society. 147–61.

MacADAM, R. J. 1861–62 Stone sepulchral urns. *UJA* 1st ser. **9,** 236–8.

MACALISTER, R. A. S. 1943 Preliminary report on the excavation of Knowth. *PRIA* **49**C, 131–66.

MACALISTER R. A. S., ARMSTRONG, E. C. R. and PRAEGER, R. Ll. 1912 Report on the exploration of Bronze-Age Carns on Carrowkeel Mountain, Co. Sligo. *PRIA* **29**C, 311–47.

McAULAY, I. R. and WATTS., W. A. 1961 Dublin radiocarbon dates I. *Radiocarbon* **3,** 26–38.

MÁRQUEZ, C. C., LEISNER G., and LEISNER, VERA 1952 *Los sepulcros megaliticos de Huelva* (Informes y Memorias, No. 26). Madrid.

MAY, A. McL. 1947 Burial Mound, Circles and Cairn, Gortcorbies, Co. Derry. *JRSAI* **77,** 5–22.

MITCHELL, G. F. and Ó RÍORDÁIN, S. P. 1942 Early Bronze Age Pottery from Rockbarton Bog, Co. Limerick. *PRIA* **48**C, 255–72.

MOGEY, J. M. 1941 The 'Druid Stone', Ballintoy, Co. Antrim. *UJA* 3rd ser. **4,** 49–56.

MOHEN, J. P. 1978 *Les tumulus de Bougon* (Extrait du *Bulletin de la Société historique et scientifique des Deux-Sèvres* 1977).

MOLYNEUX, T. 1725 *A natural history of Ireland in three parts, by several hands III.* London.

O'KELLY, CLAIRE 1969 Bryn Celli Ddu, Anglesey. *Arch. Camb.* **118,** 17–48.

———— 1973 Passage-grave art in the Boyne Valley. *PPS* **39,** 354–82.

———— 1978 *Illustrated guide to Newgrange.* Cork. 3rd edn.

O'KELLY, M. J. 1966 New discoveries at the Newgrange Passage-grave in Ireland. *Sborník Národního Muzea v Praze* **20,** 95–8.

———— 1969 Radiocarbon dates for the Newgrange Passage Grave, Co. Meath. *Ant.* **43,** 140.

———— 1972 Further radiocarbon dates from Newgrange, Co. Meath. *Ant.* **46,** 226–7.

———— 1973 Current excavations at Newgrange, Ireland. In Glyn Daniel and Poul Kjaerum (eds) *Megalithic graves and ritual.* Jutland Archaeological Society.

O'KELLY, M. J., LYNCH, FRANCES and O'KELLY, CLAIRE 1978 Three Passage Graves at Newgrange, Co. Meath. *PRIA* **78**C, 249–352.

Ó NUALLÁIN, S. 1968 A ruined Megalithic cemetery in Co. Donegal and its context in the Irish Passage Grave series. *JRSAI* **98,** 1–29.

———— 1972 A Neolithic house at Ballyglass near Ballycastle, Co. Mayo. *JRSAI* **102,** 49–57.

Ó RÍORDÁIN, A. B. 1968 Food vessels in Irish Passage Graves. *JRSAI* **98,** 163–9.

Ó RÍORDÁIN, S. P. 1948 Further barrows at Rathjordan, Co. Limerick. *JCHAS* **53,** 19–31.

———— 1951 Lough Gur excavations: the great stone circle (B) in Grange Townland. *PRIA* **54**C, 37–74.

———— 1954 Lough Gur excavations: Neolithic and Bronze Age houses on Knockadoon. *PRIA* **56**C, 297–459.

Ó Ríordáin, S. P. and Daniel, G. E. 1964 *Newgrange and the Bend of the Boyne*. London.

Ó Ríordáin, S. P. and de Valera, R. 1952 Excavation of a Megalithic Tomb at Ballyedmonduff, Co. Dublin. *PRIA* **55**C, 61–81.

———— 1979 *Antiquities of the Irish countryside*. Revised by R. de Valera. 5th ed. London.

Ó Ríordáin, S. P. and Ó h-Iceadha, G. 1955 Lough Gur excavations: the Megalithic Tomb. *JRSAI* **85**, 34–50.

Péquart, M., Péquart, St. J. and Le Rouzic, Z. 1927 *Corpus des signes gravés*. Paris.

Piggott, S. 1954 *The Neolithic cultures of the British Isles*. Cambridge.

———— 1962. *The West Kennet Long Barrow*. London.

Powell, T. G. E. 1941a Excavation of a Megalithic Tomb at Carriglong, Co. Waterford. *JCHAS* **46**, 55–62.

———— 1941b A New Passage Grave group in south-Eastern Ireland. *PPS* **7**, 142–3.

Pryor, F. 1974 *Excavation at Fengate, Peterborough, England: the first report*. Archaeology Monograph 3. Toronto. Royal Ontario Museum.

Raftery, J. 1951 *Prehistoric Ireland*, London.

Renfrew, Colin 1979 *Investigations in Orkney*. (Research Report XXXIII, Society of Antiquaries of London.)

Riley, D. N. 1957 Neolithic and Bronze Age pottery from Risby Warren and other occupation sites in North Lincolnshire. *PPS* **23**, 40–56.

Ritchie, J. N. Graham 1975–76 The stones of Stenness, Orkney. *PSAS* **107**, 1–60.

Schuldt, E. 1972 *Die mecklenburgischen Megalithgräber*. Berlin.

Shee, Elizabeth 1973 Techniques of Irish Passage Grave art. In Glyn Daniel and Poul Kjaerum (eds) *Megalithic graves and ritual*. Moesgård. Jutland Archaeological Society. 163–72.

———— (n.d.) L'art mégalithique de l'Europe Occidentale. *Prehistoria e Historia Antigua I*. Santiago.

Simpson, D. D. A. 1971 Beaker houses and settlements in Britain. In D.D.A. Simpson (ed.) *Economy and settlement in Neolithic and Early Bronze Age Britain and Europe*. Leicester. 131–52.

Smith, A. G., Pearson, G. W. and Pilcher, J. 1971 Belfast radiocarbon dates III. *Radiocarbon* **13**, 103–25.

———— 1974 Belfast radiocarbon dates VII. *Radiocarbon* **16**, 269–76.

Smith, I. F. 1965 *Windmill Hill and Avebury: excavations by Alexander Keiller, 1925–39*. Oxford.

Sweetman, P. D. 1976 An earthen enclosure at Monknewtown, Slane, Co. Meath. *PRIA* **76**C, 25–73.

Wainwright, G. J. 1979 *Mount Pleasant, Dorset* (Reports of the Research Committee of the Society of Antiquaries of London. No. XXXVII). London.

Wainwright, G. J. and Longworth, I. H. 1971 *Durrington Walls* (Reports of the Research Committee of the Society of Antiquaries of London No. XXIX). London.

Wakeman, W. F. 1848 *A handbook of Irish antiquities*. Dublin.

———— 1894 *Catalogue of antiquities belonging to the Royal Irish Academy now in the Science and Art Museum, Dublin*. Dublin.

Walshe, P. T. 1941 The excavation of a burial cairn on Baltinglass Hill, Co. Wicklow. *PRIA* **46**C, 221–36.

Waterman, D. M. 1963 A Neolithic and Dark Age site at Langford Lodge, Co. Antrim. *UJA* 3rd ser. **26**, 43–54.

Whittle, Alasdair 1977 Earlier Neolithic enclosures in North-west Europe. *PPS* **43**, 329–48.

Wijngaarden–Bakker, L. H. van 1974 The animal remains from the Beaker settlement at Newgrange, Co. Meath. *PRIA* **74**C, 313–83.

Wilde, W. R. 1849 *The beauties of the Boyne and its tributary the Blackwater*. Dublin.

———— 1857, 1861, 1862. *A descriptive catalogue of the antiquities of stone, earthen and vegetable materials (1857), animal materials and bronze (1861) and gold (1862), in the Museum of the Royal Irish Academy*. Dublin.

Wood–Martin, W. G. 1895 *Pagan Ireland*. London.

Woodman, P. C. 1967 A flint hoard from Killybeg. *UJA* 3rd ser. **30**, 8–14.

INDEX

Subheadings, when not in alphabetical order, follow the order of the text: passage tombs (including individual sites); Neolithic occupation; Beaker occupation; isolated examples or finds. Subheadings under Site 2, Site 3 etc. are in the order: tomb; mound; orthostats; kerbs; burials; finds.